Quest

Wai H. Tsang

14 / 11 / 19

Contents

1. Early Years   5

2. The Dark Forest   26

3. The Lotus Eaters   36

4. The Odyssey   53

5. Apocalyptic Expectations   71

6. The Wilderness   84

7. The Return   102

8. Working in a Church   116

9. The Future of Religion   127

10. The Fractal Brain Theory   149

11. Science and Religion   171

12. The Problems of the World   189

13. Revolutionary Movements   210

14. Political Philosophy   229

15. Deus Ex Machina   260

Chapter 1

Early Years

I was born in Hong Kong on the 16th of October 1969. Around the age of two, my family emigrated to the United Kingdom where my parents had been migrant workers, on and off, for a number of years prior to my birth. When I was conceived my parents were working in the UK but my mother decided it would be better if I were born closer to home. So from the outset my life would involve an intersection between East and West.

My earliest memories are as a small child living in Clacton-on-Sea, on the south eastern coast of England. I lived there for a year or so with my mother and father, paternal-grandmother and two older brothers. We all shared the downstairs section of a normal semi-detached house so things were a bit cramped but life was happy enough. My family didn't have very much money and my father worked as a waiter in a restaurant owned by a relative. Most of what my father earned was saved in order to open up a fast food outlet in the future. These were the main aspirations of my parents at the time, a business of their own and a better life for their children. Life in Clacton was good and I was a happy infant. When I was about four years old we moved again to a town some 30 miles or so away called Ipswich. It was here that I would be staying until leaving home.

Some details about my ethnicity. I belong to a certain sub-grouping of the people collectively known as the Chinese. My particular ethnic group and dialect is referred to as 'Hakka', which means guest people. We make up around one percent of the total of all Chinese people and in China we are mainly found in the South, though we are also widely scattered around about the globe. It seems the 'Hakka' are seasoned migrants. It is believed that we originally came from Northern China and steadily moved South many hundreds of years ago hence the label 'guest people'. I've also learned from several sources that the exact nature of our origins are quite mysterious. Through my research I discovered a possible reason why this should be so.

The reason why my ancestral origins should be mysterious is related to the fact that for some reason a disproportionate number of China's top reformers and revolutionaries over the past few hundred years of Chinese history have come from my particular ethnic group. In my research I have discovered that many of the 'Hakka' people from the areas in the New Territories in Hong Kong where my family are from, are most likely descended from the families of the remnants of the Taiping Rebellion which overran much of China during the 19th Century and which consisted mainly of 'Hakka' people. Incidentally the Taiping Rebellion was essentially an Apocalyptic movement led by the charismatic religious figure of Hong Xuiquan who claimed to be the Brother of Jesus after having mystical experiences and visions.

It seems very probable that some of my ancestors were rebels who fled to one of the Southern most parts of China, i.e. Hong Kong, in order to escape the avenging authorities and forces of the then dominant Manchu dynasty, who were themselves nomadic invaders from the frozen wastes of what is now North Eastern China and formerly Manchuria. This is because under China's laws of this period, the crime of treason or rebellion committed by one person was punishable by death upon the clan of that person up to nine generations, so there was a good reason why my ancestors may have had to keep their identities secret. I have come to learn that this is why some of the 'Hakka' came to be known by locals in the areas where they settled simply as the 'Guest people'. Because it was too dangerous for them to tell their neighbours who they really were or where they were from. So probably in order to escape a certain death sentence my ancestors would have fled to one of the remotest areas of Southern China.

When as a young adult I lived for a while in my father's village in the New Territories of Hong Kong I thought to myself that it seemed to be located in what would have been, before the land reclamation projects, a very inaccessible place. The village existed at the base of some not easily accessible mountains and facing a body of water, in what would have already been the remotest of places. It dawned on me years later and seems very sensible to me now that perhaps this was exactly the sort of place people might come to hide from vengeful authorities.

By a random chance of history, this distant far flung corner of Imperial

China now called Hong Kong would become a base used by the Imperial British to sell Opium, or 19th century style Heroin, to China. The opium addicts in China had no objections to this arrangement. However the Chinese authorities didn't like the idea very much and so you had the Opium wars. Indirectly through this detail of World history I would find myself living in the United Kingdom. The descendents of the original inhabitants of Hong Kong who were living there when the British came were given the opportunity to live, work and settle in the UK after the Second World War. And as a result my family and I came to be in England.

The language that the 'Hakka' speak is actually archaic Chinese and would have been spoken in the main cultural and power centres of China around a thousand years ago and before. This is during, what some historians consider, the golden age of Chinese civilization, around the time of the Tang dynasty. It comes to mind that my mother and father referred to Chinese people using an expression that translates as 'Tang people'. Apparently poetry written in China a thousand years ago only rhymes in the Hakka dialect that I speak and not in any of the modern dialects such as Cantonese or Mandarin.

Another relevant detail about the 'Hakka' or guest people, is that they are known for a love of books and learning. This is in a part of the World, i.e. the Far East where, partly due to the Confucian influence, all people generally already have a high regard for all things scholarly. I have been told that the 'Hakka' people do well in the higher education system in China. There is one theory that the Guest people originally descended from imperial courtesans and perhaps the sort of people who would have got to where they were by being good at learning things and passing Imperial exams. This may explain the book loving aspect of the Guest people. I would later on in my life face my own Imperial exams.

Another theory which seeks to explain the bookish element to the 'Hakka' is that it is thought because the guest people were migrants into areas which were already settled and farmed, therefore they had to settle in the less fertile areas of land. As a result the Hakka were never able to get very prosperous from farming and so there was a strong tendency in my ethnic group to enter public service or the military. And to be able to enter into and get ahead in these areas the Hakka paid a lot of attention to their education. This emphasis on learning and education whenever possible and as much as possible, was certainly the case in my family and with all my close relatives.

It seems the Hakka have for a long time had something of an association with revolution and reform. A recent Hakka revolutionary and reformer is Deng Xiaoping who put into the motion the economic reforms that are still underway in China today. Others include Sun Yat Sen the leader of the Republic of China after the fall of the Last Emperor and Lee Kuan Yew the political figure behind the transformation of Singapore. During the beginning of Deng Xiaoping's economic reforms, 5 members of the 9 members of the Chinese

Communist party's all powerful Standing Committee were declared Hakka. It has been said that during the Communist revolution the fabled 'Long March' was really a march through the Hakka territories of China's Hunan province, where Mao was able to gain much needed supplies and also new recruits from the very sympathetic Hakka villages located en route. Mao's ancestry is debated but he seems to have had Hakka roots. Nonetheless there seems to be a strong relationship between the Hakka of China and its revolutionary and reform movements that persisted even after the Taiping Rebellion.

During my childhood all this kind of information about my background was completely unknown to me. If my ancestors lived in some remarkable or exciting past then none of this had any relation to my life or that of my family. Back in Hong Kong my relatives were like poor hill-billies growing their own food and finding work when and where they could. In the UK my family were immigrants trying to become established and settled in a foreign land far from home. Anyway, back to my story, so around the age of four my family moved from the small town of Clacton-on-Sea to the slightly larger town called Ipswich.

Ipswich is a small quiet town which is famous for nothing except for the fact that the town's football team won a major tournament in 1978 called the FA cup. The only other two things worth mentioning is that the 80s pop star Nick Kershaw came from there and also the musician and legendary producer Brian Eno almost came from Ipswich, that is he came from an even smaller town just a few miles away called Woodbridge.

Soon after arriving in Ipswich my family opened up a Chinese fast food restaurant and initially we lived in the apartments above the shop. Life was much better now. We had more money coming in and much more living space. The rest of my preschool years was a happy time of play and discovery of my immediate surroundings.

The start of my time in primary school was generally happy, but early on I had a handicap which was that I couldn't speak English. However this problem seemed to be overcome very quickly. After I could converse with the people around me I remember I would talk a lot and very loudly, often being sent out of the class by the teacher. But I could also flip to the other extreme to become reflective and much less talkative. This was a trait I would retain into my adult life. As I progressed through infant school I had a very easy time of things. I was good at most topics and learned things quickly. I was a popular child with the other children and also with the teachers as well despite my misbehaviour.

I remember at a very early age, around the age of 4 or 5, my mother instilled in me a love of books and writing. She did this during our regular shopping trips together before I started going to school when she would take me to the childrens books section of the Woolworths department store in Ipswich and allow me to choose a book. This was followed by a load of encouraging words and perhaps other expressions of positive feedback. This was before I could even read, so of course I picked the books with the most interesting pictures, i.e. books with graphic depictions of monsters, space ships and fabulous settings. I think now about the pleasure I get from purchasing a book from one of the many bookshops in London, or when an order from Amazon.com arrives in the post. The pleasure I experience and sense of excitement. I realized one day and now fully believe that these responses were conditioned into me during those trips to Woolworths all those years ago.

Furthermore, around the same time, my mother also managed to condition me to love writing. Even before I could write, during these same shopping trips, I would regularly be taken to the stationery section in Woolworths. Writing pads or writing utensils, pens and pencils etc. of my choosing would be purchased for me. I did a lot of drawing before going to school and also remember often copying little snippets of writing from books my brothers were reading. Later on in my adult life, I would always keep a notebook with me and write in it my thoughts and ideas. I would also often copy, word for word, into these notebooks, passages from books or magazines that particularly resonated with me or else that I thought would be useful for me to have a copy of. I keep thinking that the scribblings I was encouraged to do so early on in life, primed me to become such a scribbler in adulthood.

Other than my mother the other two biggest influences on my life at this formative stage were my two brothers, who were eight years and four years older than me. I mention this because the age difference between me and them meant that at an early age I absorbed a lot of information and culture that was more appropriate for someone of greater maturity. I believe this gave me an accelerated development. I watched the same TV programs that they did, listened to the same music as them and also read their books and comics. This also meant I was exposed to material not entirely suitable for a junior. I remember watching 70s TV documentaries about the ills of the world and recall the chilling and fearful effect that they had on me.

So as a result of this exposure to adult media my eyes were opened very early on to the dark side of life. In retrospect this hasn't necessarily been a bad thing. I remember seeing the pictures in a book about a Nazi concentration camp and also the 70s TV mini series Holocaust. This together with documentaries about War, famine, racism and other social problems, the nuclear stand off at the time and illnesses like rabies and cancer; were probably instrumental in developing a mind set that somehow the purpose of my life was to make the world a better and more secure place. I was, at quite an early age, aware and concerned about a lot of the problems of this world. Sometimes I would ruminate at length about some disturbing fact about the world that I learned in some documentary or news program.

The angst today that I feel as an adult when I think about what's happening in the world is the same angst I felt back then as a child. This early awareness of human suffering and evil certainly influenced my early development and would again be a feature of my later life. From a very early age I remember I had a strong desire to right the wrongs of this World and to be able to do something about human suffering.

Something worth mentioning about my early childhood which is very relevant to my later life is that I was very religious in a quite peculiar way. My family were not really religious in any real sense except that we had ornamental Buddhas in the house though this was more through custom than any sense of religious obligation. I guess a little toy religion spontaneously formed within me, involving my own rituals and invented notions of God. I read in the UK science magazine New Scientist, that this phenomenon of young children inventing their own religions is not totally uncommon. Apparently it is a feature of the childhoods of many people. An Atheist would probably see in this an argument that religion derives from an immature frame of mind. I believe that as children we start out with something precious and life reaffirming. A sense of wonder, an affinity for the transcendent and an openness for the mystery. As we progress through infancy and into our teens then we seem to lose our default state of sensitivity and perceptiveness for the sacred.

Generally speaking my religion was a synthesis of bits and pieces from all over the place, i.e. ideas from sci-fi, world religion particularly Christianity and Buddhism, TV shows and Films and there was also a strong nature component. The festivals in my religion were borrowed in adapted form from the real world. For example, one of the most important dates of the year in my childhood religion, coincided with the Chinese Harvest Full Moon Festival, which traditionally consists of laying out a symbolic food offering to the Moon and the lighting of candles. Fire was involved in the ritual I created for this particular night, and it was the only time of the year I was allowed to play with matches. Fire always fascinated me as a child and I recall getting in trouble on several occasions for setting things alight. So on this night I made the most of it. This full moon night was to me an important time of meditation and prayer. The Moon and also the Sun generally played important roles in my religion and were imbued with secret meanings. Other festivals that became incorporated into my religion were Christmas and the Chinese new year.

My God was called 'Future' for the simple reason that the future was in its control. I felt a special connection with my God, though at this early stage 'God' or 'Future' was very much something outside of me and completely differentiated from who I was. In my religious system I was an agent of God and God was my helper. My inherent religiosity gave me a great source of strength and comfort. Looking back on things, it seems to me how similar my outlook then is to mainstream religion as I understand it now. This was partly due to the religious influences I absorbed but also probably due to the basic human yearnings with give rise to some of the aspects of mainstream religion.

In other words, aspects of mainstream religion and also a lot of my made up religion derived from the same source, the need to make sense of the world, the desire to deal with our fears and anxieties. Perhaps also a need to gain a sense of empowerment and a feeling of mastery or control over things which seemed chaotic, challenging or threatening. I believe that in a sense I recapitulated in my childhood the same processes by which certain features of the worlds religions also came into being.

My early exposure to real world religion would have come from school which would have consisted of sitting through a lot of Judeo-Christian Bible stories. But a wider view of religion was obtained from television. I remember that back in the 70s there seemed to be many more TV programs that covered religious subjects. I remember there was a weekly BBC religious documentary programme called 'Everyman'. I remember watching it avidly as long as there was nothing better on the other channels. All the religious sights and sounds I found very interesting and relevant to me. The things I saw and learnt would stimulate a lot of thought.

I remember around the age of 9 or 10, seeing a TV show about Islam and learning that pork and dogs were considered things to avoid within that religion. This led me to think that the reason for this was that pork would give people tape worm and that dogs may infect people with rabies. It doesn't matter whether or not these two conclusions were correct or not, these examples are only meant to illustrate the way I thought about religion even from quite an early age.

I particularly remember seeing a documentary about the Gnostics in or around 1980 when I was 10 years old. The programme explained that the Gnostics 'knew in God' as opposed to people of other religions who have 'faith in God'. Though I was still a junior, I quickly decided that this was what I was and I remember explaining this belief I had of myself, that I was a Gnostic, to my best friend who was called Adam. He was from a Christian family and went to church every Sunday, so we occasionally found ourselves having little discussion about religion even at this early age. It seems uncanny to me now, as this minor and brief childhood musing about Gnosticism seems now like a mysterious foretelling of events and circumstances that would affect me in powerful ways, decades later in my adult life. I would truly become in adulthood the Gnostic that I whimsically believed myself to be as a child.

In late 1977 and early 1978 when I was aged 8, something came along which really caught my imagination and had a massive influence on my early life. This was the film Star Wars. The story line, the characters, the setting and the action in the film, so excited me. It really made a huge impression. I couldn't get enough of it. I remember getting the toys, the sound track and the comic books. Everything and anything to do with the film was, for my young mind, attached with a special significance and meaning. The effect that the film had on me was tremendous. Not only did it excite my imagination, it seemed to awaken in me a whole new way of looking at myself and my world. Much of childhood was already imbued with a sense of the magical and spiritual. It is as if my life also became touched with a sense of things epic and things mythological.

However I do understand better, later on now in life, why the movie Star Wars had such an effect on me and it has to do with the power of mythology. Here was a modern re-telling of an ancient and indeed timeless story about the battle between the forces of Good and Evil, and the journey of the hero from a state of innocence and powerlessness to one of mastery and accomplishment. It had a very powerful effect on me. My early life in my preteens can be meaningful divided into two stages. The first stage is my early life, before the coming of Star Wars and the second stage involves my early life after I had seen the film and became so entranced by it. I believe the film influenced my early development in subtle and deep ways. Even though I didn't know it at the time, the film was helping to nurture my sense of the sacred and transcendent. As an adult I would come to more fully understand the meaning behind it.

I had actually had my first taste of mythology a few years earlier when I was 5 or 6, when at school they made us watch a serialized adaptation of the Greek classic Odysseus made for children's television and shown at schools. The format of this series was very simple reflecting the state of much of children's TV in the UK back in the 1970s. The story was read out by an actor and what was shown on the TV screen was a slow succession of artwork which illustrated the narrative. Even so, I remember I was totally captivated by the things I heard and the pictures that I saw.

The story was about the sea voyage of Odysseus and his men as they try to make their way, back from the Trojan war, to their homes. During this arduous trip they visit various islands along the way. On each island they would come across some strange mythological character, creature or creatures and some sort of challenge would be posed by each of these encounters. The tale of Odysseus is so well known that many of the characters featured in the story are a part of the common vernacular, for instance the one eyed Cyclops, the Sirens and the Lotus Eaters. In the unfolding of the myth, as Odysseus and his sailors overcome each challenge they meet on the various islands, they get slowly closer to their homeward destination. However along the way Odysseus' travelling companions are gradually either lost or killed until finally only Odysseus is left. He eventually arrives back at his own house, there is one final battle at the end with rivals who would take for themselves what is rightfully his. Then at last he is reunited with his wife and the story ends. I still remember this children's adaptation of the Odysseus story vividly, but it was nothing more than an entertaining bit of infant school TV. It certainly didn't have the same kind of effect that Star Wars would have on me a few years later. Nonetheless in retrospect I can see that in my adult life, many of the hidden meanings of the myth Odysseus would become manifested in my own personal real life journey.

Early Years

So my early childhood was fairly normal. As I progressed through primary school I did well. I was considered by the other kids at school and the teachers to be able and talented. Funnily, I remember one time in Primary School when I was 10, in 1979 during the time of the General Election of that year and when unemployment was a major issue, I was voted by my class as the child most likely to get a job when he grew up. This was so ironic when constrasted to the colourful, eccentric and slightly deviant existence that would become my life in adulthood.

So I had made a good start early on, despite my language difficulties, and found school work easy. I often sensed that my fellow pupils struggled more than I did. So I developed the attitude that I didn't have to do as much work as everyone else and still get better results. This attitude made me lazy and held back my development during my teens. At the same time these early experiences probably helped to give me confidence in my academic abilities and intellectual powers later on in life. Also being popular as a child would help to insulate me from the loneliness and isolation that I would experience during various periods in my adulthood.

At around the age of eleven after entering high school my development accelerated. I did well in most subjects at school even though I didn't do very much work. I mostly didn't hand in homework and was constantly late in the morning, but probably because I did well in class and in exams, I seemed to get away with a certain amount of indiscipline. I also tended to avoid school quite a lot and enjoyed the extra free time to do what I wanted.

Around about this time, a TV show would have a great impact on my life. It was called Cosmos, and was a 13 part series of documentaries presented by the astronomer and great popularizer of science, Carl Sagan. It presented the big view of science, covering everything from the birth of the Universe, the stars and galaxies, to the evolution of life and the emergence of humanity and civilization. I was probably already predisposed with an interest in things technical, mechanical and scientific, but it was probably the TV series Cosmos that really ignited my interest in science.

So I remember as a teenager I would play around with chemistry sets at home. I had a telescope and took up Astronomy for a while and was a keen birdwatcher for several years. I also took a more general interest in nature and liked to study about plants and animals. I would spend lot of time in the surrounding countryside outside of Ipswich. The natural world has always been something very close to my heart.

Later on in my teenage years I became swept up in the home computer craze of the early 80s. One of my older brothers bought a computer in 1983 when I was 13 years old and this would change my life forever. I really became quite obsessed with computers and computer programming. I devoted a lot time teaching myself how to program. I would spend hours and hours totally engrossed in the process of designing and coding little computer games and science simulations. I absolutely loved it. I also spent a lot of time playing computer games as well.

During my teens as I became more and more engrossed in science and anything to do with computers, I can see now that my little mystical and spiritual world retreated. My mini toy religion that I'd created as an infant no longer seemed as meaningful or as relevant to me when my head existed in these technical realms. However there were certain times when this feeling of the sacred, that I had much more in my early childhood, would return. This would be triggered sometimes by nature and natural events, perhaps a full moon, a stunning sunset or perhaps a walk in some peaceful woodland. Nature would be my temple and this is something I retained all through my life. Other times I would regain my sense of the mystical through a process of reflection. I remember that all through my childhood I was interested in philosophical matters. This interest would intensify in my early teenage years. I would spend a lot of time thinking about the purpose of life, who I was and what was the nature of reality. It was at around this time that I developed an increasing tendency towards solitude and mental reflection. During these times of contemplation I would occasionally regain my feeling for the sacred that I had most of the time as a small child.

From a very early age I enjoyed avoiding school. By the time I was around 15, I avoided school a lot. Perhaps when I was 16 or 17 the days I attended school became fewer than those when I stayed away. The irony here was that I valued knowledge, loved to learn new things and thrived on intellectual challenges. The problem was I saw school as an impediment to my learning and intellectual development. A lot of the things we learned at school I thought irrelevant and the pace of learning was far too slow. Also some of the teachers didn't know how to keep control of the classroom and which sometimes meant only very little teaching actually went on. This problem was compounded by the often low quality of the instruction. So I had decided from a quite early age that going to the lessons at school was a waste of time and avoided school as much as I could.

I would spend this free time, that I created for myself, writing computer programs and learning all about computers. But most of all I loved to think and read. I also enjoyed cycling all around the countryside surrounding Ipswich. Sometimes instead of cycling to school I would take a massive detour and cycle to a seaside town called Felixstowe which was about 10 miles, or so, away. I did this because it was nice to walk along the sea front and it was a great context for thinking about the larger questions of life. But more importantly there were a lot of video arcades there with all the latest computer games. It felt great to be doing my own thing.

However this apparent lack of interest in education and avoidance of school created a lot of tension between me and my parents especially because, there was and is a strong emphasis on the importance of learning among members of my ethnic group. In fact, for me to gain a good education and formal qual-ifications would have been a main and critical criteria by which they would have judged their own success and effectiveness as parents. Like a lot of Chinese and especially Hakka parents the idea is to get their children educated to at least a university degree level So my truancy and free spirited approach to things was a major problem for them. It led to a lot of conflict and argument. But I was willful and stubborn as a teenager and full of rebellious energy. At the end of the day there wasn't much that they could have done to alter my be-haviour. My recalcitrance was compounded by a sense that I knew better what was good for me. Also in my immaturity and naivety, during my teens I didn't really give my mother and father due respect. In my mind at that stage of my life I thought they were a pair of under achieving low ability individuals, but how wrong I was. I had no idea that in their youth they had undergone a sort of mythic quest of their own and had embarked on a perilous adventure. They had actually achieved a lot more than I gave them credit for.

They had started from a context of upheaval and poverty which is what Southern China and Hong Kong would have been just before, during and im-mediately after the Second World War period. My mother was born during the war Period which was characterized by suffering and famine. There was a terrible pain that my mother carried with her all her life. As a baby her own mother had left her to die alone out in the countryside somewhere. This wasn't because she was a girl baby but because the Japanese were invading and my mother's mother was fleeing to her home village which was more in the hin-terland. Her husband my grandfather was away in the army fighting. People were being killed and women were being raped by the advancing Japanese army so there was a stampede of people trying to escape. Apparently proba-bly due to a combination of stress and malnutrition, my grandmother wasn't producing breast milk and had generally lost all hope, therefore abandoning her baby my mother.

But by some miracle the grandmother, my own great grandmother found my mother alive, days later, after she'd heard what had happened. She took her in and raised her till early infancy. This was a time of great chaos and there wasn't enough to eat but somehow they all got through it and managed to sur-vive the war. A lot of people died violently and prematurely during this time.

After the war was over my mother was returned to her own family and was raised by them till she left home. This early childhood trauma of my mother's would sometimes surface in my own childhood, when she was in a particularly depressed mood or when I seriously misbehaved and upset her enough. I sup-pose when you hear the same thing enough times then the emotional impact becomes gradually lost over time. It was only after my mid-teens that I came to understand better the seriousness and full gravity of what had happened.

After the War and in the changes brought about by the Communist Revo-lution, my mother's family had their land and properties confiscated, so were reduced from a state of relative affluence. Her father didn't fit in well with the new regime and towards the end of his life and during the Cultural Revolution that occurred from 1966 up to the death of Chairman Mao in 1976; like many people living in China at the time, my grandfather found himself in prison for no real or good reason other than dissent. He was released from prison pretty immediately following Mao's death with the change in regime and end to the cultural revolution, but died himself shortly afterwards. It is one of those powerful memories of my own childhood. I was actually watching my mother as she was reading the thin blue airmail letter from China. I knew they meant a lot to my her because they brought news about loved ones living far away. But this particular letter told my mother that her father had died.

At some point during my mother's childhood, my grandfather had pointed his daughter towards Hong Kong and told her that's where her future should lie. While growing up she did well in school and was expected to get a place in a top university which would have allowed her to perhaps climb the ranks of the communist party. But she chose a different path, so that as a young woman my mother made the perilous escape across the border from China to Hong Kong, dodging border guards and the sound of their barking dogs, trekking across dangerous mountain paths and swimming across bodies of water. After a spell as a factory worker she married my father.

My Father had grown up in Hong Kong and would have been in his early or preteens during the War years. He remembers vividly the Japanese invasion when he was a boy and was forced to labour in their building of fortifications and defences. He never had the chance of an education so was illiterate. But I would more than make up for all the books he never read. As a young man he recalls doing paid work for the British colonials as a manual labourer, shipped off for certain periods of time to other nearby outposts of the, by then fading, British Empire. Though he doesn't actually know exactly where he'd worked, perhaps Burma or some such place.

Later taking advantage of the opportunity to work and settle in the United Kingdom, he made the long boat journey to England. This was something of an adventure for him seeing all sorts of new sights and strange people that he would have never before encountered. The boat would have stopped at various stages to pick up more passengers. He recalls how the ship made a port of call in India and picked up a rich diversity of passengers there. It was a real journey into the unknown.

Once arrived in the UK he worked long hours as a waiter in some of the first Chinese restaurants which were springing up at the time and lived the classic immigrant story, sending money home and eventually bringing the family over too. Though it was the case that before the entire family came over, my mother had started working in the UK too with my grandmother on my father's side, staying in Hong Kong to look after my two older brothers. After my mother became pregnant with me, she returned to Hong Kong and stayed there until the entire family came to the UK when I was about 2 years old.

The story of the early lives of my mother and father is one of hardship, adversity and struggle. The hardship of life during wartime, the upheavals of the Communist revolution and the poverty of the period following the War. Then there was all the adversity and struggle they faced in trying to make it in this world. Working their way up from nothing, the adventures involved in coming from China to Hong Kong and the coming from Hong Kong to the United Kingdom. Then there was the struggle of trying to become established in a far away country, strangers in a strange land, not speaking the local language and encountering the basest forms of racism and discrimination.

They worked hard and were sustained mainly by the hope and desire of a better life for their offspring. Their courage and determination was inspired by the dreams of an easier and happier future for them. So they did their toil, labour and sacrifice basically in order that I could enjoy the potential of a comfortable middle class existence in a reasonably prosperous industrialised country. This was the adventure and undertaking of my parents that had occurred in their lives and which had created the circumstances that I found myself in during my childhood and teens, and of which I was mostly unaware while I was growing up.

I remember there was a generally feeling of restlessness in my teens. Ipswich was a small quiet town and felt far from all that was happening in the rest of the World. It was the kind of place where once you get to a certain age then you'd start to think more and more about leaving. Often I would day dream about escaping from this uneventful back water of a town and embark on a life of adventure and exploration. I would imagine myself as Luke Skywalker, one of the main characters in the modern myth Star Wars and saw my situation as similar to his at the start of the film. I was a bored youth living in a nondescript small rural based town far far away from where all the action was going on in the World. But I wanted to be part of it, to be part of the action. While cycling to school I would see the American A10 Tank buster planes flying overhead on their training flights always flying in paired formation. The Cold War between the NATO Alliance and the Warsaw Pact was still going on at the time. I imagined I was like Luke Skywalker gazing up in the sky looking at space ships belonging to a far flung galactic empire. In my case, these particular vessels were emissaries of the United States Empire and Ipswich, Suffolk was like a distant outpost of it.

A significant feature of my life as a teenager was that I wrote songs and formed a little three piece rock band with two friends, one playing drums, the other bass guitar and myself singing and playing rhythm guitar. This activity came about through a general passion I've always had for music but at this time also a teenage love affair I had with the American new wave band Talking Heads. However my interest in this musical sideline steadily diminished as my interest in technical and philosophical matters increased during my late teens.

I can now see with the benefit of hindsight that the band was important for my development in that it gave me training in the process of standing in front of a crowd of people and giving some kind of performance. We performed live in various Ipswich pubs around half a dozen times. The response from the audience, which consisted mainly of other kids from school, was generally bad. My band mates played well but my performances usually ranged from bad to embarrassing. I did have my moments where things sounded reasonable but overall I didn't do very well.

However in the wider scheme of things, I can see now that these early unremarkable forays into live performance would help to prepare me for later on in my life. The negative feedback and ridicule I had to endure would serve to toughen me up psychologically and make it easier for me start public speaking in my adulthood. This teenage baptism of fire would especially help prepare me for communicating very controversial ideas that can elicit hostile reactions from some people.

Something happened at around the age of 16 which helped to set the course of my life. I rented the science fiction film Bladerunner from the local video shop and watching it seemed to crystallise a fascination that has seemed to be a part of my life from very early on. This fascination involved the idea of human-like robots and Artificial Intelligence. These were the stuff of 70s and 80s Sci-Fi films, TV series and also the Science Fiction comic books, all of which I can see in retrospect formed a significant part of my childhood. It was this coupled with my near obsession with computers, that gave me a firm and vivid idea of what I was going to do with my life.

There was character in the film named, Dr Eldon Tyrell, who had designed the artificially intelligent brains of the human-like robots called replicants, who were the focus of the movie. I was thoroughly inspired by the film. So much so that I became gripped by the thought that the purpose of my life was to discover how the brain worked and unlock the mysteries of the mind. I also imagined that as a natural result of these efforts I would give to the world artificial intelligence, become rich, famous and all the other things that over ambitious teenagers dream about. My mind was made up, I now had to realise my chosen path. There's a strange continuity behind all this in that I learned much later on that the guy who made the film Bladerunner, was inspired to do so after he'd himself watched the film Star Wars mentioned earlier.

And so I had my ultimate goal in life. I would be the person to figure out how the brain worked and from that become the creator of artificial intelligence. The rest of my time before leaving home would never be the same after this and a definite course had been set up for the rest of my adolescence and my adult life. I started to study really hard, on my own initiative, all the books and material relating to the mind and brain sciences that I could get my hands on. As a result of this concentrated study, I thought for the first time what a good idea it would be to go to University in order to help take things further.

Also at around this point in my life I was getting really restless and greatly desired to leave home and move away from this small town called Ipswich. So my attendance at school improved slightly, particularly after I was offered a place at University and so had to put in some work in order to make the grade. And so my mind seemed to come alive some more. The rest of my time as an adolescent living with my parents; was spent preparing for my ultimate goal and also working fairly hard to obtain a place at the University of my choice which luckily, I managed to do by scraping together just enough credits in order to get in. This I did in 1988 and London was the place I went for my studies.

Leaving home was quite a dramatic experience. I found myself transported from a small quiet town into the heart of busy London. I went to Imperial College of Science and Technology, part of London University, a major research centre and as the name would suggest a place full of scientists and technologists. The sort of place I thought I needed to be. I initially lived in the halls of residence. So my first entry point into my new life away from home was in the very affluent South Kensington and Knightsbridge area. Quite a contrast from my hometown. I remember feeling a bit overwhelmed with London at first but the sense of freedom from being away from home was exciting.

I quickly became disillusioned with the course I was doing which was computing science with a high content of artificial intelligence subjects. I discovered that what was known in academia about artificial intelligence and the best theories about how the brain worked, were at best primitive or else plain wrong. This caused me to become a bit of a renegade student. I embarked on a course of self study and decided for myself what I would need to know in order to figure out how the brain worked. Though I didn't have much time for the course I was enrolled on or much affinity with a lot of the other students, still I enjoyed the stimulating conversations with some of the very intelligent people you'd meet randomly on campus. Also I loved the access to the libraries and the amazing selection of books and materials that they contained.

During my first year in university while living in university halls of residence I had an almost nightly ritual of walking to some shops nearby that opened 24hrs a day. When I first discovered them it was a revelation to me, the idea that I could go off to buy snacks and drinks in the early hours of the morning. Being quite nocturnal as a student I was a constant visitor to these places typically doing my shopping at 1 or 2am in the morning. On my way back I would often sit in the cemetery of a church which was on the way there and very close to where I was living. I loved to sit in this church yard while eating snacks I'd just purchased. I remember spending a lot of time sitting in that church yard in the middle of the night, it was great place to have a long undisturbed think.

During my three years at university I hardly ever attended, mainly showing up for exams, to photocopy handout notes and also to chase up course work from some of my fellow students. On quite a few occasions I was summoned to the senior tutor's office and several times threatened with expulsion, but by some miracle I always managed to pass the year and get through to the next. Though it was always very close, and so I would spend the Summer holidays back in Ipswich, not quite sure whether they would take me back or not for the next academic year.

At the end of my time at University I even ended up with a degree, though only a pass ranking. Technically I thought I'd failed because I hadn't handed in enough course work. I only discovered otherwise when I went to the administrator's office to collect the deposit on my locker keys. I looked on the results list pinned up to a notice board because I just wanted to see how some of my friends had done in the exams. I was very pleasantly surprised to discover that the university decided to give me a degree anyway. It certainly made my mother very happy.

The funny irony is that during my time enrolled at university, but not attending much, I studied a lot! Though I spent hardly any time studying my course material, except during the Spring and that was in order to pass the exams. I read far and wide but where my time was mainly focused on, was the study of the brain and related fields such as psychology, cognitive science and artificial intelligence. I was extremely focused and my thirst for knowledge was immense. I seemed to read constantly and when I wasn't reading I was thinking. The only other activity which took up significant amounts of my time during this period was playing my electric guitar. I had only a few friends at University who were on a similar wavelength to me and with whom I could discuss matters of mutual interest. Mostly my time was spent alone and completely obsessed with anything to do with the mind and brain.

After University I stayed in London for a few months during the Summer and Autumn. I continued to live in the same lodgings in Cricklewood, North London, that I'd found to accommodate myself during my final year in college. During this time I was in an in-between state wondering what my next move would be. I did use this time productively studying and learning new skills. I went through an intense Philip K. Dick period during this time and read 1 or 2 of his sci-fi novels every week, they had a strange resonance with me. Also I continued my studies of all things relating to the brain, behaviour, computers and artificial intelligence. I devoured books and spent many hours a day reading or thinking about what I'd read.

In the Autumn of 1991 I decided to move to Hong Kong and live there for a while. In the back of my mind I had this idea that somehow I'd be able to make a lot of money quickly, and then not have to work and be able to finance myself and my studies. And so in November of 1991 I sold off most of my possessions, packed my bags and got myself a one way ticket to Hong Kong.

Early Years

Hong Kong was the place of my birth, but I knew nothing about the place, as my family had emigrated to the United Kingdom when I was only two years old. And I had never returned until making this expedition in my young adulthood. It was something of an odyssey and journey of self discovery, a chance to visit my roots and perhaps learn something about who I was.

At first things went well, and I was very excited to be in an exotic part of the world. It really seemed like an adventure at first. I was filled with the optimism and boundless energy of youth. However I was also quite naive about various aspects of life and things quickly deteriorated. I didn't speak the most commonly used local dialect so had to get by on just using English. Also the money I brought over from the UK started to run out. I found it difficult to get a job and was increasingly frustrated by my language barrier.

Once the novelty of being in a different part of the world had worn off I then started to become more aware of the negative side to my circumstances. Also I was constantly being stopped by the police and asked for identification. This would typically happen when I was walking down the street or shopping somewhere. Why this kept happening was due to two reasons. Firstly the time in question was before the 1997 hand over of Hong Kong, by the United Kingdom, back to China. So back then the local Hong Kong police had a big problem with illegal immigration by Chinese nationals seeking financial opportunities. So carrying ID was mandatory and all illegals were detained and subsequently deported. The second reason why I was constantly being stopped by the police is that my physical appearance was subtly but distinctly different from the locals. This is partly because I belong to a particular minority cultural/ethnic group, as described earlier, and some of us display unusual physical characteristics which distinguish us from most Chinese people. I stood out a bit even when walking down the street so the police would pick up on this.

So here I was in Hong Kong, broke, unable to communicate and feeling harassed by the police. I was feeling a little lost and despairing. I didn't know what to do but an advertisement in a newspaper would seem to set my life on a new course for a while.

I was reading the main English language newspaper of Hong Kong, the South China Morning post when I chanced upon an advert from Cathay Pacific airlines. The advertisement was calling for trainee pilots, no experience required. They'd train you up from scratch and then put you into the control deck of a jumbo jet. The advert caught my eye because it was an unusual job to see advertised and also because it took up most of the page. But at first it didn't really interest me. Being a pilot just wasn't one of those things that excited me very much. However I saw the salary offered, thought about the opportunities for travel and then I thought about my current situation. There was only one sensible thing to do under my present circumstances. I sent off for an application form.

Soon I found myself spending a lot of time going to and from Hong Kong airport where Cathay Pacific airlines had their headquarters. There I had to go through a lot of mental tests, medical examinations and interviews. Just about everything was examined, ones eyes, physical fitness, mental agility and reflexes etc. It was a lot of time consuming hassle but I managed to pass.

I got onto the initial stage of the training program and was sent off to do basic flying training. At first I was really quite indifferent about whether I succeeded in completing the training program or not. But as I got deeper into it, I started to really get into the idea of being an airline pilot. It really started to seem like a useful way out of my present predicament in life. I can remember getting quite excited by it all, it seemed that a host of new possibilities were opening up. I can also recall that, in my naivety, I seriously thought that once my training was complete, I could pursue my on going studies into the brain and mind while working full time as an airline pilot. I got the idea in my head that I'd be able to read my neuroscience books while the auto-pilot looked after the plane. I also pictured myself studying scientific papers about the brain and artificial intelligence, in fancy hotels all around the world, in between all the long distance flights. In retrospect, it all seems really ill thought out now, but I was young back then and eager to have it all. So it was with this mind set that I set off for Perth, Australia.

So I found myself living on the grounds of an aerodrome located in a place called Janderkot, which is like a suburb of Perth, Australia. We lived in some prefabricated dwellings, a dozen of which were clustered together to house all the cadets who used the aerodrome's planes and airfields. The daily routine would consist of a couple of flights supervised by an instructor. There was an early morning session and then another one in the afternoon. Also there were classes where we sat in lecture theatres and were taught relevant facts. At first I quite enjoyed it and liked the views from the plane while in the air. It was quite exciting. After the days training was over we would all relax and take it easy. Sometimes we would drive to Perth city centre and look around the place. I recall that we had a barbeque just about everyday and the food was very cheap to buy.

Something happened which caused my interest in becoming a pilot to start to waver a bit. I can recollect the events which triggered this subtle change of mind set. It was due to my coming across some old magazines which quite inspired me and re-awakened a side of me that had been dormant for a while. It happened like this. One day my fellow cadets and I all drove together to Fremantle which is a nearby town. My impression of the place was that it seemed rather new age and hippy. We went to the town market and I stumbled across a pile of magazines from the late 70s called 'Omni'. I was an avid reader of Omni in my childhood even though it was quite an adult magazine and a mature read. My older brother used to buy it while he was at college and would pass them on to me. The magazine was a mix of technology, science, science fiction, psychology, ecology, arts and spirituality. It used to so inspire me in my preteens and used to fill my head with all sorts of weird and wonderful ideas. It definitely had a powerful influence on me during my childhood. I bought a dozen or so copies and read through them over the next few days in my spare time. This had the effect of making me introspective and really stimulated the intellectual side of me. It seemed to give a massive boost to my passion for learning and in particular my interest in brain science and artificial intelligence.

Over the past few months, while I was struggling after moving to Hong Kong, my studies into the brain and mind really got sidelined a bit. But now I once again felt an intense motivation to learn about the brain and think about artificial intelligence. I found myself spending more and more time on my own, away from the other cadets. My brain seemed to really come alive with interesting thoughts. When not flying or in the lecture room, I would spend all my spare time reading and thinking about other things. I remember going for long walks in the middle of the night in the countryside around the airfields. The sky always seemed to be clear and the stars looked so bright. My immediate surroundings were really conducive to having focused concentration and so I had a lot of good ideas around this time. This routine continued for a while but then something happened which would change the course of my life once again.

I was on a training flight and coming towards the end of the session. So I was manoeuvring the plane, positioning it in order to make the final approach for landing. Everything was going fine but as we approached the runway I got a message from the control tower requesting that I use another runway because the wind had suddenly changed direction. The aerodrome had three different runways, all facing different directions. This was so pilots could avoid landing against strong cross winds, which could make things difficult. So I did a lot more manoeuvring and got the plane on course to land on one of the other runways. But then again it happened. We got another message from air traffic control telling us the wind direction had changed yet again! So we were advised to use the third runway. All this was a bit disorientating. For the second time I had to manoeuvre and re-position the plane for a third attempt at landing. While I was doing this a strange thing happened. Very suddenly everything went white and the loud noise of the plane's engine seemed to fade away into inaudibility.

This may not be widely known but sitting in the cockpit of a small single engine aircraft is a very noisy experience. During all flights, headphones are worn. This is for two reasons. Firstly to protect the ears and hearing of the pilot. Also in order to allow communication between the occupants of the plane using the intercom system built into the headphones. It would be very difficult to communicate otherwise. But even with the headphones firmly in place, the sound of the engine is still pretty loud. So for things to suddenly go quiet was a pretty dramatic change of perception.

Outside it was a grey and cloudy day but up in the air things still seemed pretty bright. However, along with my hearing going quiet on me, suddenly seeing only white light everywhere was very shocking indeed. I still had a sense of my body and who I was but it was as if I had been transported to some other place. At least it felt that way. It was as if I was no longer in the plane. This state persisted for what felt like several minutes. All the while I could still think. I recall that I was in quite an anxious state. The best way to describe my situation is that what was happening to me was a lot like one of those times when one wakes up in dream, realising that one is dreaming but is unable to wake up in reality.

A brief while later I started to feel completely different. I felt calmer and in less of a panic. After this I felt a strong presence of someone or something and it was communicating with me. It was not talking to me in ordinary language, with words that I could repeat. It seemed to be communicating with me in pure thought. It was as if I was given thoughts to think that were not my own. Somehow these thoughts came from outside of me but were then projected directly into my mind. The message that I received if put into words would be something like 'Wai, this is not your purpose in life', 'Your destiny lies elsewhere' and 'You're needed to carry out a certain role in this World and this isn't it'. This seemed to go on for quite a while.

Then all of a sudden I snapped out of it. Suddenly the loud noise of the aircraft returned and I could see the sky all around me. Through my headphones I could hear the flight instructor saying to me 'Wakey! Wakey!'. I realized too, that I was hyper-ventilating and also knew immediately that this heavy breathing would be clearly audible to the instructor through the microphone on my headset. God I thought, I've really screwed up. Very quickly I snapped back into action and got to grips with controlling the plane again.

I must have seemed passed out or having a seizure of some sort. But judging from where the plane was I couldn't have been gone for that long. Certainly not more that 10 seconds or so. However it felt as if I had been away from the plane for many minutes, perhaps half an hour but this was impossible. I proceeded to land the plane, it was a rough landing as I still wasn't totally together. After taxiing the plane back to the hanger I went back to my lodgings. I was quite shook up and many thoughts were going through my head. I knew that flight was a disaster and would look very bad on my record. I started to become resigned to the fact that perhaps I didn't have the 'right stuff' after all. My hopes of becoming an airline pilot quickly unravelled. I felt despondent and uncertain about my future.

The time came when our performance as cadet pilots was assessed by the airline in consultation with the flight instructors. Sure enough as I expected, I was failed and expelled from the training program. I felt devastated by the decision. It was the first major failure in my life. Even though I never wanted to become an airline pilot until I saw the newspaper advertisement, as I went through the selection process I found myself desiring the position more and more. By the time I arrived at the aerodrome I seriously wanted to fly aeroplanes for a living. But that opportunity was no longer open to me, my ticket to a secure and stable life vanished into thin air. Now in retrospect I can look back on things philosophically, but back then it really felt like a major disaster.

I returned to Hong Kong and feeling a bit of a failure, concentrated totally on my studies into the brain and mind. It was the only thing that could give me real satisfaction and take my mind off things. Immediately on my return I was in a state of melancholy for a bit. I recovered but then when Spring came, the weather turned very miserable. It didn't stop raining and it started to get very hot and humid. This together with the stresses I was going through already put me into something of a borderline state. I just managed to keep a grip on things sufficiently to get by on a day to day basis, but sometimes my behaviour would get a little peculiar.

In the middle of the night I would sometimes wander about in the country side around the New Territories in Hong Kong and think about how the brain worked. Sometimes I would sleep out in the open air, and sometimes I just wandered about all night without sleeping as my head would be filled with thoughts that kept me awake. My mind started working in ways that were completely new to me. I really had a lot of interesting and creative thoughts that my mind would quite spontaneously generate.

During this time and also long after as well, I recall that I would think about the message I received in the sky. However it could give me little help in my predicament but it perhaps did give me a sense that somehow my life had a higher purpose and meaning to it. The strange experience that I had in the airplane back in Australia, probably gave me an awareness of a feeling of destiny. With the benefit of hindsight, I can see now that this almost certainly helped to provide me with the necessary hope which enabled me to go on pursuing my long term aims. However my situation in Hong Kong became very unhappy and it was going nowhere so I decided to return to the UK.

Chapter 2

The Dark Forest

After an eventful trip to the Far East following finishing university, I came back to London. My state of mind wasn't very good towards the end of my six months away from the UK. Pretty much immediately on my return my head and mood was much better. I tried to look for work but the employment situation at that time was very dire. It was 1992 and right in the middle of the trough of one of the worst economic recessions in years. So I drifted into a routine of living off state welfare payments. Out of poverty and a lack of options I found myself living in the cheaper and less glamorous areas of London. I always seemed to find myself living with drop-outs, prostitutes, petty criminals, and those generally on the margins of society.

It was the Spring of 1992 when I returned to London. Initially I lived in Peckham, South East London for a short while and really disliked it. The area was run down and all around I thought I could sense an unhappy and aggressive vibe. I remember on the day I moved out of Peckham I saw a telephone box cordoned off with police tape and beside it was a quite large pool of congealed blood. The whole area depressed me, so I moved to Turnpike Lane in North London. I found this particular area slightly more agreeable.

Here I lived in rented accommodation in a house that was shared with what most people would call undesirables. People who had fallen in life. The bloke who lived in the room next door was a professional burglar but I didn't have anything worth stealing so I didn't have too many complications with my neighbour. I learned that he and his gang had burgled the house next door. I would often see him walking down the street, say hello and notice him carrying some piece of consumer electrical item in a sports bag and always a different object each time. I didn't ask any questions, it wasn't necessary. Also just about everybody else in the house was also involved in some sort of petty crime.

My days were spent studying and thinking mainly. I was very focused on learning about the brain and trying to work out how it worked. For pleasure I would play my electric guitar a lot. My life was stable for a bit, I had quite a productive Summer in that house. My life hadn't turned out as a I had planned at this point but I still felt a part of mainstream society. My life hadn't really deviated too far from the norm.

However, that would soon change. The house was raided by the police in the Autumn. This was because a few days prior to the raid, the police had spotted a large cannabis plant growing in the garden. This was when they came looking for the bail jumping brother of my burglar neighbour. Everybody in the house was taken to Tottenham police station. It was a new experience for me to see the inside of a police van. I remember being questioned and telling the police woman who interviewed me, that I thought that a cannabis plant i.e. grass, was like 'grass' as in an unmowed lawn. Both police officers in the interview room found that quite amusing. I was 21, had lived quite a sheltered existence and was probably somewhat naive.

I was given a lift back to the house by a friendly police constable. I was the only member of the house given a lift, the others had to make their own way back. We chatted in the car. It would have become pretty clear to him that I was just some fairly well behaved, generally law abiding young guy who had just come out of college and had found himself in the wrong place at the wrong time. Arriving at our destination he gave me some kindly advice and told me in no uncertain terms to get myself out of that house and also out of this particular part of town. I shortly after heeded the first part of his advice but didn't quite follow through on the second part about moving away from the area.

After the raid, the atmosphere in the house became a bit unpleasant. Several of the people were charged and things became rather unfriendly. There was a lot of paranoia and a couple of fights. The place got a little crazy with broken furniture, a broken bathroom sink and smashed windows. At around the same time, I was offered a room in a nearby squat which is a disused house, often in a state of disrepair, that had been taken over by people of no abode. Through a loop hole in UK law, which existed at that time and due to the great number of empty properties in 1990s London, this was a not uncommon practice. This squat was about 10 minutes walking distance, still in Turnpike Lane North London, so moving to my new lodgings was a very straight forward process. It so happened that the brother of a school friend of mine, who was the drummer in the band I'd formed in my teens, was already living there and I paid him a visit. A room was going free and I told him about my current situation so he invited me to move in.

In retrospect, now I can see that this was a move into a darker and seedier dimension of modern life. A dimension even lower than the strata of society I was at that time already occupying. And it was probably the most appropriate place for me to have been at that time. It was as if my state of mind had fallen and now correspondingly my life had also fallen. My physical surroundings would come to reflect my inner reality. The Dark Forest can describe a physical context and it can also describe a state of mind. Sometimes the Dark Forest is both.

Now I really was in the Dark Forest, if there was any doubt in the matter previously. This assessment was now completely appropriate. I was low life, living with low life. The squat was in quite a bad state. It was dirty, there were dogs everywhere and it smelled doggy. My room was small, and had bare floor boards with nails sticking out of it that once held down carpeting. The last tenant was a heroin addict who used the room while he was 'cold turkey-ing' or in the process of trying to break his heroin habit. There was a slight lingering smell of vomit in the background which I could never quite clear. Anyway on the plus side the roof was in good order and the electricity was free, so at least I was never cold while I lived there.

After moving into the squat in the Autumn of 1992, I seemed to enter a whole other reality of deviance, subversion and counter culture sentiments. I would meet and get to know people that most people would never come across. True deviants, anarchists and subversive types. Now I was living with beggars, hard core druggies, assorted musician types and various extreme drop outs.

Some of the crowd in the circles I was hanging out in, were called crusties. This was because they never washed and rarely changed their clothing. As a result the dirt would become encrusted onto their clothes, hair and skin. Invariably, the crusties were very heavy heroin users and this was the main cause of their condition. In fact their lives revolved around the use of this substance. They were more often than not beggars, though some of them were also involved in petty crime.

There was a young lady living downstairs who was a full time beggar. She owned a very overweight doberman dog called Tina and her father was in prison for armed robbery. Being too young to sign on and claim government benefit payments she derived all her income from begging in tube stations with her dog. She made quite a lot of money, a pretty looking young girl in very shabby looking clothes sitting in London tube stations with her begging cup in hand and over weight doberman dog curled up next to her.

By way of past times her favourite hobbies were injecting amphetamine sulphate, smoking cannabis and looking after her dog. In a way she acted as my guide and teacher in a world about which I was totally naive. Effectively she took me under her wing. Here I was someone who had such grand plans and goals for my life being looked after and tutored, concerning the facts of life, by a teenage runaway. She ran away from home because she had been sexually abused by an uncle. As for me, I was a fish out of water but now in hindsight the things I learned and saw, have been invaluable in broadening my world view and in advancing my understanding of human nature.

As I got to know the people I was living with and those in the associated scene, I discovered that a very high proportion of them had been physically and/or sexually abused as children, or else had suffered a major trauma in their early development. This was a lesson that I would never forget and it taught me that there are reasons why a lot of people end up as social outcasts. Looking back on things, I see now, that the problems I faced were little or nothing compared to those of some of the people I knew back then.

So here I was, a year out of University where everybody had high expectations, but now in my present context living a very unaccomplished life. As I got to know better this land of the fallen, it became clear to me that I had ended up in the outer fringes of society. I was totally out of my normal context and the sort of clothes I wore really made me stick out a lot. I had really bad dress sense and looked really square. But at the same time I was generally accepted by the people around me. In a sense, everybody in this environment was an outcast and a reject. Most of the people had ended up living in this counter-culture and deviant underground world as a result of some trauma and pain that had been inflicted upon them but which could not be cured, only temporarily numbed through the use of mind altering substances.

Underlying the scene was a lot of sorrow and angst. Perhaps partly as a result of this there was also a definite sense of camaraderie. There was a lot of sharing, and more often than not, people looked out for one another. The world would seem hostile to many of the people I knew at this time, so partly as a result of this everybody stuck together. And because of the way that these people looked and behaved, they would certainly elicit a hostile reaction from a lot of mainstream people. There was a lot of deviance, criminality and bad behaviour but also I found in some of the people I met here selflessness, loyalty and honour. I learned for myself that you can't always judge people from appearances.

One thing which helped me to be accepted by some of the people in the squat scene, even though I was so obviously un-hip and straight looking was that I could play Jimi Hendrix tunes on the guitar. Even though my playing ability wasn't even close to that of fabled guitar wizard Hendrix, nonetheless to a lot of people and the untrained ear there would not have been too much of a perceptible difference. So like some sort of magic talisman my electric guitar helped me to gain the trust and friendship of some of the people I found myself meeting. After a short time I became known and introduced as the guy who could play Jimi Hendrix numbers on the electric guitar. People would ask me to play for them and it allowed me to quite instantly gain peoples liking and respect. Which was fortuitous, for there was nothing about me which otherwise would have been of any value in this underworld.

I wasn't useful in a fight, I didn't have a great reputation or inclination for criminality (which was respected in the present context) and wasn't very street smart at all. All the things about me which might have been valued in a different situation, i.e. being well informed and well read, computer related skills and a pleasant manner were irrelevant in this squat underworld.

However the ability to play guitar to a certain level of proficiency was a valued and respected skill. My electric guitar was like a key, for it opened doors for me. It allowed me to gain access and win a level of familiarity with some deviant and anarchic people who otherwise wouldn't have had any interest or time for me.

I remember sometimes it would seem as if we lived like feral animals. I remember going off on scavenging missions to the back of supermarkets in the middle of the night. This was in order to collect the food that had gone past its sell by date, which had been thrown away in the rubbish skips. I didn't have much money and would spend a lot of what I had on books and magazines, so doing this really helped me to stay alive. I could never get myself to go begging, and anyway I was too well dressed so probably wouldn't have made any money anyway, but a lot of the people I was hanging out with did.

It was a simplified and humble existence but there was an incredible sense of freedom and incomplicatedness. Looking back on things now saddled down with the responsibilities, obligations and various complexities of life, there is definitely a side of me which can still really appreciate aspects of the life that I lived all those years ago. But it wasn't such an ideal existence.

For I should mention that I witnessed a fair deal of violence in this lawless sub-culture. Life really was quite cheap and sometimes a little brutal. People really did live fast, burn their candles at both ends and also sometimes died young.

I remember going to a large crowded squat party in Stoke Newington and saw quite an amazing spectacle. There was a large garden, it was dark, and there were many bonfires. There were all kinds of colourful people everywhere, bikers, punks, skin heads, crusties and ravers. I could see that everybody gathered together with their own kind in big groups all sat around the fires. It was as if everybody gathered together with their tribe. Bikers with bikers, punks with punks etc. The analogy was obvious to me. I thought that this was like the world and the different nations all with their separate identities and territories. All the nations and all tribes had gathered together that night to come to the same party but they all sat separate from each other.

Mostly it was good natured, however there was an incident involving one of the lady beggars I knew who was from Wales and had a very thick Welsh accent. Possibly due to this fact, she got into a fight with one of the English skin head girls and had some of her fingers bitten rather badly. Her face was also quite seriously scratched. This wasn't the sort of glamorised violence you'd see in Hollywood movies, but the really nasty brutish kind. It was a horrible sight. I would witness things like this with some regularity. In retrospect it all seems rather depressing, but I remember at the time it could also be quite stimulating in a strange kind of way.

Actually I remember there was a whole gang of Welsh squatters who lived in various places quite nearby and who all came from a Welsh town called Armonford. One of them was the previous occupant of my room in the squat. I remember I gained their trust and spent quite a lot of time hanging out with them. I also remember they would be constantly getting into fights. Come to think of it now, the brawl mentioned a little earlier between the young Welsh woman and Skinhead girl was just the tip of the iceberg. It seems now that often when I'd go some place, club or party with any of them, there would be some violence.

The scariest incident was at a party in a smallish night club in Brixton, South London, where there was a large gang of youths in their late teens, who had been acting anti-socially all through the night. One of the youths provoked one of my Welsh friends, a tall, peaceful and even docile looking man but with a very violent temper, by pulling his long dreadlocked hair and making fun of him. As a result of which there was a fight, with my companion punching the lout hard in the face several times I believe. I didn't see the actual incident but only the aftermath. There was blood everywhere, the face of the provoker seemed mashed, his nose was surely broken. The party was stopped, the loud music silenced and the bouncers (security) broke up the fight, herding the gang out of the club but thankfully allowing my friend to stay inside with an angry gang of youths waiting outside to exact revenge. There was only three of us, my violent friend, his girlfriend and myself, so it was quite a tense situation. We were effectively stuck in the Night Club. Luckily the club owner sympathised with our situation and allowed us to use a back exit with a taxi cab waiting to take us away. As the was car pulling away into the main street we could see the gang waiting for us outside the club.

So this is the context in which I found myself. This whole squat scene really was like the underworld or the dark forest and in it I saw a lot of strange and weird things. It was a realm of darkness, badness and sadness. Punctuated with quite a lot of physical violence which I'd witness first hand. This had a lot to do with the sort of people I was associating with. I'd witness human nature too often expressed without moral constraint, reflection or any thought of consequences. It was a pretty wild scene. I was learning about the wilder sides of human nature but I was also learning about myself. Sometimes I felt like an ethologist in a field study, fascinated and curious, always eager to learn and sometimes asking too many questions. This would get me into trouble a little later in our story.

Quite early on during my time living in the squat I became addicted to cigarettes. Just a year or so previously the whole idea of smoking would have been completely anathema to me. It was just something that I thought I'd never ever want to be getting into. I remember there were two young women who worked in a dentists surgery nearby at the end of the street. One of them was from Germany, the other was from Italy and was doing a degree in psychology, working part-time at the surgery to help pay her expenses. They used to come over and hang out in the squat. They seemed to have a fascination for the sleaze and low life scene of the squat. Anyway they both smoked and would generously hand out cigarettes during their visits and I would smoke with them every now and then.

During this time I was reading an unusual book called 'The Mesolimbic Dopamine System', it was all about the chemical pathway in the brain that is involved in motivation and also in mediating the effects of all addictive drugs and substances. By sheer and incredible coincidence one of the editors of the book also happened to be one of the lecturers of the young Italian psychology student who would come visit. I thought it was so amazing to know somebody who was also interested in the brain and behaviour. I used to really enjoy chatting to her, unfortunately the pleasure of her company was always accompanied by cigarette smoking.

And so I was lying on the scruffy sofa one evening, reading the book on the physiology of addiction and contemplating what it is to be addicted. There was a packet of cigarettes lying around and I lit up and smoked, all the while thinking about the brain chemical dopamine and the process of addiction. Thoughts relating to my lovely psychology student friend would also pop into my mind. Up to that point I didn't consider myself addicted to cigarettes. I only ever smoked them when offered and that was only sometimes and with some people. I wondered about the process of addiction and what it would feel like. I lit up perhaps one or two more cigarettes that evening all the while carefully introspecting what sort of effect they were having on me. My experiment on myself and subjective study done I thought nothing of it.

I think the next day or perhaps the day after I went out and purchased a packet of cigarettes. A short while after that I carried out the same transaction down at the local newsagent again.. and again.. and again. My life for the next two years would partly be characterised by a quite heavy smoking habit. And so, I remember the process by which I became a nicotine addict. i.e. through reading a neuroscience book about addiction edited by a scientist who was a teacher of the young woman who would keep offering me cigarettes. This was a shame, because I really didn't have much money to live on and this new addiction was definitely a burdensome strain on my already limited financial resources. I was often broke. I recall there were times I didn't think twice about picking up a half smoked cigarette off the pavement and lighting it up.

There again nicotine and cigarette smoking was probably the most innocuous form of substance abuse indulged in the present circumstances under discussion. The whole scene I was living in was saturated with drugs. And so my first exposure to hard drugs happened while I was living in the squat in Turnpike Lane, North London. Though in this scene the most common substances of abuse were Heroin, Amphetamine, Cannabis and Special Brew (A cheap high alcohol content beverage popular at the time). The one substance which really interested me the most was the drug LSD.

My first experience with LSD happened in October 1992, it was an utterly strange and powerful experience but hardly spiritual or transcendent. I recall now that the drug was used quite recreationally. It was something to do when you were broke and bored which was quite often the case. The colours would become brighter, there were severe alterations of visual and auditory perception. Also ones sense of humour was magnified tremendously and I remember times when I would laugh so hard, vigorously and at length with such merriment, that the next day the bones in my chest literally hurt. But again none of these experiences were really mystical or 'transcendent' at all. Looking back on this time, I realise now, with the benefit of experience and better knowledge, that the quality and dosages of the psychedelic substances I was getting and ingesting in the squat scene, was rather low. At a guess, I would have only been using a small fraction of the dose required to produce any sort of transcendent experience.

Even before my time spent in the squat I already had a certain fascination for the drug culture. This probably derived from certain books I'd read such as the novel ' Scanner Darkly' by Philip.K.Dick; certain TV programmes I'd watched in my teens such as a documentary on LSD that was shown by the BBC in the late 80s; And certain kinds of psychedelic music from the 60s that I loved, produced by bands such as the Beatles, Jefferson Airplane and Jimi Hendrix. Also my keen interest in the brain and neuroscience definitely helped to predispose me to becoming curious about psychoactive drugs. It's impossible to spend so much time reading about neurochemistry and brain receptors, without ever wondering what would be the affect of manipulating their normal action. And this I did.

I remember that while living in the squat I was reading a book about the brain neurotransmitter serotonin and all the different kinds of serotonin receptors, their actions and how they were distributed in the brain. I would also during this period ingest substances such as LSD which would activate my own serotonin receptors and cause radical changes in my perception and states of consciousness. In my enthusiasm for learning things I was a keen scholar and in the recklessness of my youth I was my own guinea pig. Much of my life in the squat revolved around reading big hefty specialised neuroscience books about the brain and taking various psycho active substances while contemplating the effect they were having on my own brain and consciousness.

Initially when I first moved into the squat my working routine continued during the daytime. Most days I would work in the local public library, reading and thinking mainly about the mind and brain. I would find escape in my books, notes and thoughts. But the surroundings weren't very inspiring at all. The whole area seemed a little dreary to me and I felt very far from the centre of things. At the same time I did have my dreams, and they sort of acted as my refuge. However my aspirations and ambitions seemed distant indeed, I was nowhere in this life and in this world. As time passed, my situation seemed more and more hopeless. I had set ambitious goals for my life, but here I was living with beggars and eating food out of rubbish bins.

I stayed on in the squat for the rest of the Winter and some of the early Spring but moved out shortly after. This was due to my circumstances getting a bit dangerous. One of the people in the scene became obsessed with the idea and developed a paranoid delusion that I was an undercover policeman or police informant. It's true I did ask an awful lot of questions, but this was more out of a childlike curiosity rather than a desire to gather police intelligence. Also the clothes I wore were a little square. This was because I had very bad dress sense and as a result I did stick out of the crowd a bit. In spite of this, I was accepted by most of the people around me. And those in my immediate circle thought that the idea of me as a police man or police informant, completely ridiculous and stuck by me.

There was an incident one night at the house I was staying, where while having a talk with my paranoid associate, I was attacked and got into a scuffle with this person who was spreading the rumours that I was connected to the police. It was a horrible scene in a small downstairs kitchen with large kitchen knives lying around everywhere and two large dogs barking away hysterically which belonged to my adversary. The dogs were familiar with me because during more amicable times with their owner, normally a more or less generally decent bloke, I would play with them from time to time and even take one of them out for walks. It was for this reason that they didn't attack me otherwise I believe I would probably have been badly mauled. Still the mad barking added greatly to the general atmosphere of menace and danger. Pretty quickly, one of my Welsh friends, intervened who knew us both and who didn't believe I had anything to do with the Police. He grabbed my assailant bundled him into the corridor, pulled out a knife and threatened to stab him if he didn't back off, which he did.

Fortunately I wasn't harmed. Even so it was a stressful and frightening experience. My attacker was in a state that a psychiatrist would probably label 'amphetamine psychosis', being a keen injecter of the drug and who had been doing a lot of it in the days and weeks leading to the incident. So there was plenty of scope for mishappenstance and serious accident that evening. However due to pure luck and a little help from my friends I came away relatively unscathed, though more than a little shaken. I remember how, immediately after the incident, my heart was pounding wildly and how I chain smoked that night, rather unusually .

Anyway, it was no longer safe for me to be living in this scene so for my own personal safety I decided to move on. It was time to make a strategic exit, there was no point in trying to work things out. I was living in a very deviant and rather violent scene that was partly characterised by a total disrespect for authority and also a festering hatred of the police and anything to do with the law. Having rumours circulating about me being a police informer or under-cover policeman, though completely false, wasn't good for my health mental or otherwise. It wasn't good to be living in fear of physical attack.

Funnily enough, quite by coincidence during this time I was reading a neuroscience book all about the amygdala, which is a part of the brain playing a central role in the expression and elicitation of the fear response in animals and humans. So I was studying about the neurobiology of fear while my life was lived during this time, in a state of paranoia and fearfulness.

I moved out of the squat in Early May 1993 and immediately after secured lodgings in a bed and breakfast in the North London area called Archway. I was still very much in the dark forest and would remain there for a number of years. The period in the squat was probably the darkest patch of the woods. My life as a lost and lonely soul would go on for a while. A social reject and failure in my own mind, low status and low self esteem, I would struggle on in the dark forest.

Chapter 3

The Lotus Eaters

I found myself drifting in this world, unemployed, lost and lonely. To recap, after finishing university I went to the Far East for a bit and came back to London after a troubled period while over there. On returning to the UK I found myself living in the seedier areas of London and exploring modern society's darker underbelly. I lived for a while in a squatted house with a very deviant crowd. After an interesting, turbulent and rather dangerous time I left this scene because it got too risky for me to stay there.

In the Spring of 1993, I moved to Archway North London and lived in a bed and breakfast owned by a lovely Irish landlady. This was a much needed halcyon period of reflection and getting myself together. I started going out with my first girlfriend and had sex for the very first time. Her name was Sara and she was the same psychology student who would visit me back in the squat. The fact that she was studying psychology and was interested in neuroscientific things was probably one of the things that attracted me the most about her. Someone I could talk about the brain and mind with, whilst we were together. She was quite a grounding influence on me, a regular, well adjusted and straight young lady. From time to time, she would pester me to go find a job and become more integrated into society. I found this a little tedious. Anyway, there weren't many job vacancies available in the UK at this time, especially not for those without work experience. Nonetheless I really enjoyed being with her, she was my only connection at the time to the world of normality and correctness.

If my girlfriend was a respectable influence on me then another friend of mine would steer my life toward back to wild and deviant side of life. Kian was someone I had met back in the squat scene who was the brother of the girlfriend of the brother of one of the people I was living with in the squat and whom I had know from my home town Ipswich. He came over to visit from time to time. After seeing my book collection and being something of a book lover himself, he noticed my Philip K. Dick novels and my extensive collection of books about the brain; we struck up an intense and stimulating conversation and quickly developed a bond. Kian was a seasoned denizen of the alternative and counter culture underworld having been given an early start by his father; who as a product of the 60s Woodstock generation and was also something of a free radical himself. Kian was attracted to the wildness and deviance that he encountered in the squat and associated scene. Later on, my friend would act as a sort of guide and teacher to me on all things counter culture or alternative. We kept in touch and he would visit me in my new lodgings to hang out and chat.

It was in early Summer soon after I moved out of the squat, that Kian introduced me to a friend of his called Fraser Clark who was an old hippy who edited a counter culture magazine and organized underground parties. He took me to his flat in West Hampstead which was very messy and filled with very large house plants that made the place look a bit like a conservatory with a big desk in it. There was a funny scruffy looking dog that trotted about all over the place adding to the relaxed and laid back atmosphere.

I didn't know it then but I was entering into the land of the Lotus Eaters and Fraser was the local de facto king and sage of this domain. He was just about to start up a regular weekly club night which was to be called Megatripolis and during my visit he was talking about it a lot. It promised to be something different.

Fraser started a magazine in the 80s called Encyclopedia Psychedelica which was dedicated to the promotion of aspects of the counter culture and later another journal called Evolution which concentrated on rave culture. It was largely through the connections that he made through his magazines that he launched himself and his crew into the world of party organization and promotions. Most of the London psychedelic partying scene from the early 90s onwards, emerged either directly or indirectly from the three events that he'd organized over the years which were called in chronological order, Megatripolis, the Parallel University and the Warp Experience. The offshoots including club nights such as Return the Source, Club Alien, Escape from Samsara and Synergy.

 In effect he was a sort of Johnny Apple seed of the psychedelic counter culture. This interesting, colourful and charismatic character acted as the Timothy Leary or Ken Casey of London's psychedelic crowd. Leary and Casey were two famous, or infamous depending on how you look at it, 60s promoters of psychedelia and 'mind expansion' through the use of psychoactive substances.

So at this point in time back in 1993, the Megatripolis event was to be his next venture and it was going to be held in London's famous Marquee club on the equally well known Charing Cross Road, best known as a music venue and a place I sometimes used to go to as a student to see the live rock bands. This Megatripolis event would be something quite different however. Not only would there be music, dancing and socialising. There would also be talks given by underground writers and academics with interesting things to say. A place where new ideas and trends would be given an airing. It was billed as a festival in a club. Out of loneliness and an interest for exploring other aspects of life I found myself going to the early Megatripolis parties with some regularity.

At Megatripolis I seemed to be meeting a lot of people with the same interests and outlook as myself and made some friends. There were a lot of people involved in the arts, media and also technology. There would always be a significant contingent of old hippies from the sixties or early seventies. The kind of people who told stories about dropping acid at Pink floyd and Jimi Hendrix concerts. I met many New Age types and many people who were either current or ex members of the Osho sect renowned for their hedonistic ways. Many of the people there were the children of the children of Woodstock. Young adults the same age as I was, whose mothers and fathers were involved in the 60s and early 70s counter culture. Also of course a lot of more ordinary people such as curious students or kids from the suburbs would show up. It was a pretty eclectic mix of people.

I distinctly remember at this point coming across the phenomenon of people who thought that they were God or had experienced 'one with the Universe' states of mind. I was meeting quite a few people who quite openly expressed that they were God or else admitted that they believed they were God only after you got to know them a bit better. I also met quite a few people who seriously thought that they were either the Messiah, the second coming of Christ, the return of King Arthur or something else along those lines. It was all a bit bewildering at first but a lot of my life afterwards would be spent making sense of this kind of thing.

I hung around this scene for several months and would dabble with a little drug experimentation here and there but at this point the pull of the psychedelic crowd wasn't that great. Mainly I would experiment with the drug LSD.

I would then do other things for about a year or so without very much involvement in the land of psychedelia. My attention shifted completely to the main passion of my life up to that point. My interest in computers, brain science and artificial intelligence returned. At this time my life was more of a technological and scientific odyssey rather than a mystical or spiritual one. I dreamed that one day I would gain recognition for my ideas and theories about how the brain worked. It was also always in the back of my mind to commercialise my ideas. I had grand plans to one day go to silicon valley and start a software company. Around this time I would avidly read books about how the microcomputer revolution happened. Also from books and magazines I loved to learn about the work going on in hi-tech research institutes around the world. It made me feel closer to a world I yearned to be a part of but was very distant from, in my circumstances at that time. I also read the biographies of people like Steve Jobs or Bill Gates and found them inspiring and instructive.

For the rest of 1993 from the Autumn onwards and throughout 1994 my involvement with the psychedelic scene would on a fairly sporadic on and off basis, be much more off than on. I really got heavily back into my life goal of figuring out how the brain worked and the creation of artificial intelligence. So I spent a lot of time reading, computer programming and thinking. My life was back on its default track and I enjoyed a productive halcyon period. I got a lot done, my skills and ideas evolved a lot.

After a few fateful twists and turns in my life, I found myself gravitating back to the land of psychedelia. I would come to call this crowd the worldwide psychedelic trance scene, the modern day 'lotus eaters'. Alternatively they might also be called the present times Soma drinkers or perhaps the new age manna munchers.

So who are the Lotus eaters? The Lotus Eaters are characters from the classical ancient greek myth called Odysseus, also known as Ulysses which we've already mentioned in an earlier chapter but we'll recap a little again here. Probably the best known myth in the Western world, it describes the sea journey of the hero Odysseus and his crew, on his return from the Trojan war back to Greece. Along the way he and his crew stop off at various lands in the process encountering all sorts of strange beasts and various scenarios. Some of the better known adversaries that Odysseus encounters will be familiar to a lot of readers, for instance the Cyclops and the Sirens.

Perhaps a slightly less well known chapter in the myth of Odysseus is the visit to the island of the Lotus Eaters. This is the first stopping off point of the voyage after leaving Troy. On arriving at the island Odysseus sends some of his sailors to investigate the place. They find a land where the inhabitants are fond of ingesting a plant called the Lotus. The result of eating this strange plant is that the Lotus Eaters are put into a kind of sleepy stupor. When Odysseus's sailors eat the Lotus then they too succumb to the plants power and fall into a deep sleep. Unable to awaken themselves, they are trapped on the island until Odysseus comes to their rescue. And so free from the hold of the lotus plant, they all set sail for the next destination and leave the Lotus Eaters behind in their terminal slumbers.

What does this all mean? The puzzle is clarified when we understand mythology as spiritual allegory. That is, myths far from being fantastical nonsense stories for children, are rather the symbolic representation of the distilled spiritual and mystical wisdom of various peoples and entire civilizations. Seen in this light, the story of the Lotus Eaters becomes a reference to a recurring phenomenon found in early and primitive religion. That is, the use of certain plants and substances have often found their way into the religious rituals and ceremonies of the world's religions early on in their initial development and evolution.

For instance we have Soma described in the Bhaghavad Gita and other ancient Indian holy texts. 'Soma', literally means, 'to press out and extract', and there exist ancient Sanskrit texts which refer to the Lotus plant as Soma. In pre-Zoroastrian Persia we find the Huoma, which was some sort of psychedelic beverage. In Bible we find the enigmatic Manna, the food that fell from heaven.

Staying in antiquity we have the mysterious Kykeon, which was ingested in the sacred rituals of the Greek Eleusinian mysteries to enable the initiates to gain states of union with the deity within. Also in Ancient Greece the Oracles of Delphi are believed to have entered into their mystic states through the inhalation of certain hydrocarbon gases mixed with the smoke from laurel leaves. Something similar is also believed about the Sybil of Rome and how she gained her prophetic powers.

Then we have the blue lotus or lily of the Nile which was used by ancient Egyptian high priests. Incidentally, this blue lotus may have been identical with or closely related to the lotus that is referenced in the story of the Lotus Eaters. The greek mysteries are believed to have originated in Egypt and brought to Greece by the mystic sage Pythagoras.

In Buddhism we have references to the White Lotus plant, which in chemical constitution if not color, is identical with the Blue Lotus. The mystical and revolutionary White Lotus movements of late medieval China, get their name from this psychedelic plant.

Most modern scholars believe that Taoism, which is the mystical and spiritual tradition of China, originated from Siberian Shamanism, which is known to make use of the psychedelic Fly Agaric mushroom. The word 'shamen' actually comes from this area. It is a Jurchen word, they being the ancestors of the Manchurians, and lived in Southern Siberian and the frozen wastes of what is today the North East outskirts of modern China. Zen Buddhism is the Japanese version of a synthesis of Taoism and Buddhism called 'chuan', that emerged in ancient China.

Finally in one of the earliest myths and also the oldest recorded story known to man, that is the tale of Gilgamesh, we find the 'Plant of immortality', most plausibly also a reference to some psychedelic plant.

What we're seeing here is the description of, or allusion to the ingestion of plant extracts, fungaloid preparations and other substances, in order to facilitate mystical states and holy communion with God. But back now to the story.

It was in early 1995 that I started to get more involved with the London psychedelic scene. This came about indirectly out of loneliness and the desire to meet girls. Around this time I used to go to psychedelic parties with a friend called Joe, I'd met quite randomly at a house gathering in Brixton.

Joe and I had a shared interest in all things technological. My friend would a little later on be working as a journalist, writing reports for the technological section of the UK newspaper the Guardian and also Wired magazine UK. We used to talk a lot about all the future technological possibilities. I used to tell Joe about my dreams and aim of working out how the brain worked and creating Artificial Intelligence. I felt he respected what I was up to and kept an open mind about things. This was not the reaction I got from a lot people who learned about my ambitions. The common response was derision and incredulity.

It was Joe who first introduced me to the burgeoning World Wide Web and growing online scene. Joe's dad was a New Age writer and helped to coordinate an organization called Alternatives which organized public speaking events and was based in a central London church near Piccadilly Circus called St James. We would go along from time to time to hear the speakers who talked about various spiritual and ecological issues. It was my first introduction to the New Age at a time when I thought 'New Age' was what happened at around the time of a person's birthday. I didn't know it at the time but years later I would gain a lot more familiarity with St James and the various events that took place there, when I would be working there full time for a while.

Apart from a mutual interest in technology another thing Joe and I had in common was that we were both single young men who wanted to meet young women. So during this particular period of my life, with some regularity I would be venturing out, together with my friend Joe, to various Psychedelic parties.

In February of 1995 I used the drug MDMA, better known as Ecstasy, for the first time in a monthly party event that gave itself the quite mystical sounding name of 'Return to the Source'. Together with the kind of repetitive, pulsating and quite hypnotic dance music played in these sorts of events and the quite spontaneous dancing that the drug elicited; this added up to produce a state of incredible euphoria, excitement and bliss that lasted for an hour or so. The drug also produced a wonderful sense of empathy together with feelings of love and kindness for all the people around you. These feelings would slowly subside over the course of the night but even the day after there would be a sort of after glow of the feelings and sentiments of the previous night.

In this way, the drug was powerfully reinforcing. In a sense it was addictive but not in the same way as say nicotine and cigarette smoking. The main difference is that with cigarettes there was a two fold process of addiction.

This would involve on the one hand the rewarding carrot and on the other a sort of punishment stick. The carrot was the initial rush, stimulation and feeling of satisfaction derived from smoking. The stick was the feeling of unease and state of dissatisfaction that would arise when a person addicted to nicotine hasn't had his or her fix for a while. The situation with Ecstasy was rather different. The stick or negative reinforcement effect was much weaker and wouldn't produce the tread wheel style addiction of nicotine. Though there was a come down or drop in mood associated with Ecstasy which would occur several days after, the thought of taking more ecstasy to cure the negative feelings associated with this phase would never occur to most people. Not in the same way that every smoker knows how to cure the effects of not having had a cigarette in a while simply by lighting up another one. However there was a positive reinforcement or rewarding carrot effect produced by Ecstasy and this was very powerful indeed. Once you had experienced the effects of the drug in a friendly social setting together with the correct kind of dance music, you just wanted to do it again. And again. And again.

Inexorably and irresistibly I was drawn back towards the land of the lotus eaters. If psychedelic trance music was the siren song that drew me close then it was the drug ecstasy which acted as the bait and hook, which would bind and keep me in this druggy scene.

1995 had begun productively, my head was in gear and I was getting a lot of productive things done, reading, thinking and computer programming. However as the year progressed and my time spent in hedonistic pursuits increased then inevitably my discipline and level of gainful activity diminished getting to the point where most of my time was spent going to clubs, taking drugs and spending time with the people that I would meet in London's psychedelic club land. As this happened I saw less and less of my friend Joe. As my life was becoming more degenerate, Joe was devoting himself to his career in Journalism.

So a little later on I progressed from being a casual party goer, to a more regular patron and then becoming more involved and helping to organize and promote the parties. Something which definitely encouraged this transition was that in the Spring of 1995 I moved to the Farringdon area in London which is just a little West from the City of London's financial and business district so quite centrally located. My new home was very conveniently located next to all the most useful transport links.

My new base positioned me perfectly for going to any and every psychedelic event in London. And this I did a lot of. I lived in this place from May 1995 right up to the January of 1997. Many of my memories of this time are associated with drug experimentation, recovering from these activities and hanging out with people who were obsessed with psychedelic drugs. This was a time in my life when I really neglected my studies and I didn't really do all that much reading, thinking or writing in my notes.

The Lotus Eaters

In the Summer of 1995, a few months after my move to Farringdon, a new club called the Parallel Youniversity opened in a large warehouse style club called Bagleys in Kings Cross, which was a short walk from where I lived. Living so close I went every week. It was partly as a result of this that I became totally immersed in the world of psychedelia. Initially I volunteered to help with the setting up of the club event, mainly in order to get in for free. So I would show up a little early a do a little work. This was quite enjoyable and was a good way to meet the people involved.

I progressed over the Winter of 1995 and 1996, to taking control of the booking of DJs and selection of music for the club. This put me in a good position to meet a lot of people and this I did with much interest and enthusiasm. During this time I was able to get to know much better the strange and non conformist denizens of this druggy counter culture. Also I happened to be in the perfect context and social milieu for the systematic exploration of psychedelic drugs. And this I did for a couple of years, on and off, mostly on.

My life around this time was very strange. I would go out to psychedelic night clubs and parties, Thursday, Friday and Saturday every week, for months on end and sometimes also going out on Sundays as well. It was a very social time and I got to meet a lot of interesting people. I would typically go to bed at around 7 or 8am in the morning, sometimes later, and then wake up in the late afternoon or early evening. At one point in the Winter of 95/96 I was jolted by the realisation that I saw some daylight, having not experienced it for weeks. It was a completely aberrant lifestyle. I existed completely outside of the mainstream of society. The only people who I spent my time with were the loose collection of odd balls, strays and drop outs that would congregate regularly in psychedelic night clubs.

Also I would start to encounter a lot of people in this scene who were very interested in Indian culture and going off to visit India as often as they could. This was at the time when a certain kind of psychedelic music call Goa Trance was making headlines in various fashion magazines and getting some TV attention too. Through getting to know and talking to such people I was given introductions, though superficial, to elements of Eastern philosophy and religion which would have been new to me at the time. It was enough however to arouse my curiosity and some of what I heard seemed to resonate with thoughts about God and reality I was already having. I remember that I would spend a lot of time thinking about philosophical questions relating to things like the nature of reality and also the nature of consciousness.

My interest in computers and science was very neglected during this time. However I did maintain a keen interest in brain chemistry. Indeed I did spend a lot of the time thinking about my own brain chemistry for my life was completely centred around acquiring, taking and recovering from taking psychedelic drugs. The sort of substances I used were drugs like LSD, DMT, 2CB, Ketamine and Ecstasy. Also there would be occasional use of various types of psychedelic mushroom and cactus. Mostly the experiences I had during this period were neither mystical nor mind expanding, but rather more mind numbing and purely hedonistic. I recall at this time getting into a lot of discussions about drugs with the people I knew and exchanging notes on their effects, it was all part of the culture.

Still I had the chance at this time to systematically explore the mystical properties of some of these psychedelic substances and gain various insights. Through these experiments with psychedelic drugs I did obtain several full scale mystical experiences and these probably numbered around a dozen or so. Many of these experiences were of a vivid but fragmentary nature and some were extremely powerful and totally out of this world. On a few occasions I even managed what may be described as 'At one with the Universe' or 'Union with God' experiences, completely stepping out of space and time and transcending the confines of 'normal' consciousness.

However there was a problem with this method of obtaining mystical states. Due to the short cut way in which they were brought about, i.e. through the ingestion of psychedelic drugs and also due to the lack a spiritual framework or discipline through which these experiences could be interpreted; there was an inability to successfully integrate these mystical experiences usefully or meaningfully into my wider existence, i.e. my life outside of the world of psychedelic drugs. Therefore though I experienced these interesting and extreme states of being, there was a separation between, on the one hand, this exciting laboratory of consciousness and on the other, my day to day existence. There was an almost complete separation between the two worlds. Apart from the use of these substances producing a massive come down after their effects wore off, which involved a state of extreme tiredness, impaired memory and concentration, which lasted perhaps a few days; when not under the influence my normal perception of things wasn't radically altered at all. This highlights one of the limitations of using psychedelic drugs in order to gain mystical insights. It's the difference between finding the Holy Grail on the one hand, versus on the other hand obtaining the prize but also bringing it back to Camelot where it is able to make a difference in normal everyday affairs. Psychedelic spirituality is analogous to Heroin happiness, it wears off when the drug wears off.

One of a my closest associates at this time of my life was a like minded soul called Patrick who was a few years older than me and came from Manchester in the North of England. We met in London's psychedelic rave scene in late 1995. Someone who might have been seen by some as a bad lad, Patrick had explored some of the illegal avenues in life and had been in prison once or twice. Though when I knew him he was trying to reform his life. Apparently he had something of a turn around a few years earlier after he was hospitalised as a result of excessive drug use, when he had a close call with death. Though he survived he had unfortunately suffered permanent liver and kidney damage from this episode.

Patrick was a keen fan of the US band The Grateful Dead and would even fly over to America specially to see the band play live. Perhaps the heavy druggie LSD sub-culture associated with this band, inspired in Patrick a major interest in psychedelic drugs or perhaps he already had an affinity for psychedelia and gravitated towards that particular scene as a result, I'm not sure now. Anyway this interest in Psychedelic drugs was one of things that we had in common.

Also Patrick, as a part of his efforts to get back on the straight and narrow, had taken on a degree course in Philosophy with a special interest in metaphysics and the Philosophy of Religion. We used to have endless discussions on these matters and talk a lot about life in general. It is relevant to mention, that in particular and on numerous occasions we discussed the 'everyone is God', and 'we are all one consciousness' idea.

On top of this we would go to night clubs and parties together and experiment together with various exotic psychedelic drugs. Patrick was a real adventurer and explorer of life going to places and situations I wouldn't risk entering into myself. I learned a lot from my friend and he probably influenced my behaviour pulling me more towards modes of being that I might have otherwise avoided. In retrospect he was an important influence at that stage in my life and gave me another angle on things. Our association probably contributed to my degeneration. Though I see now that this was a necessary stage I had to go through in order to arrive at better things.

A particularly destructive pattern of drug abuse started in the beginning of the Summer around late July which lasted right through to the end of the year. In the Summer of 1996 I started to use the drug ecstasy with careless regularity and reckless quantity. Anyway, the upshot of this is that I had some pretty good times, however as the Autumn of 1996 wore on my life steadily fell into increasing states of decadence and degeneration. By the time December rolled by, my head was definitely in an altered state. The chemicals that I had been indulging in over the preceding 3 to 4 months, left me in a state of significant dysfunction. My life was a complete mess, my values and life goals seemed to be erased and I sort of became a different person for a while.

In retrospect now it is clear to me that I went through a process of self destruction which was brought about partly through excessive drug use but also through the neglecting of my personal health. I was not eating or sleeping properly during this time which added to the weakening of my body and mind. My powers of concentration were much diminished, my moods and energy levels were much lower than normal. It wasn't a good place to be and I knew that things had to change. By the time of the Winter Solstice coming to the end of the year I was starting to get a little sick of my degenerate existence. I was just beginning at this stage to start having thoughts about cleaning up my act and getting my head together. My life seemed to be slowly shifting away from my existing patterns of behaviour.

While this process of self annihilation was very detrimental to my being and my purpose, at the same time this road of excess did in a very real sense lead to a palace of wisdom. Even though I wouldn't have planned out this course that my life had taken, I can see now that there was a prize at the end which I definitely consider to have been worth the cost.

So what was this prize? It was this. After I had undergone my period of self destruction, for several months afterwards, I existed continuously in what may best be described as a continuous borderline mystical state. The run of reckless behaviour I had engaged in eventually culminated in a state of mind which enabled me to see some things I hadn't been able to perceive previously. I went through a process of dramatic mental alteration brought about by a pattern of repeated drug abuse and bodily self neglect. And in this state new ways of seeing became accessible to me that were previously beyond my perception and imagination.

Starting from just before the Christmas of 1996, a door in my mind seemed to open, and out of that door came thoughts, ideas and visions that I believe came from transcendent realms. I could see and think clearly about matters that previous to this time seemed rather untransparent. For instance I had my first encounter with the experience of being in union with God in the Summer of 1993 but I had no way subsequently to integrate what I had experienced into the rest of my life. It was something which I knew was the truth, known through direct experience but also back then it was a truth which I had absolutely no way to think about, so it was really pushed into the back of my mind. But now, all the mystical experiences that I had prior to that time, became suddenly accessible and comprehensible to my rational mind. It seemed as if the idea that everyone was God, which was something of a suppressed thought, now became something I couldn't stop thinking about.

That which before, I had considered unreality i.e. the mystical, now became the more authentic and true reality; and what I had previously assumed to be normal everyday reality, I began to more clearly recognise as illusory. Before this time, I had allusions to this being the true state of affairs several times in my life up to this point. But now if I had any doubts concerning the unreality of the material world, then by this time these had all but vanished. So this was the state I found myself in towards the end of 1996, which would continue for a while. During this time a series of spiritual insights came to me and I first began to see dimly aspects of mystical truths which would become more fully transparent and comprehensible to my mind later on in my life. The mystical insights and visions came rather freely and vividly. The veil between the temporal and the transcendent became very thin indeed. What had been a trickle became a steady flow and the things I saw, the wisdom I gained, would make reality never seem the same again. Because of this I started to become inordinately interested in religion, mysticism and various philosophical matters.

It was this state of mind and with these thoughts that in the beginning of 1997 I left my flat in Farringdon to go and stay with friends for an indefinite amount of time. I spent the last month or so of my time living in Farringdon, relatively drug free although I had taken up smoking cigarettes for the first time since quitting about 2 years previously. This would have been in the December of 1996 going onto January 1997. While existing in this borderline mystical state naturally I spent a lot time thinking about philosophical, meta-physical and religious issues; and would dwell on these sorts of matters incessantly. Also for a period of 2 weeks or so in January 1997 my mind would also be quite preoccupied with morbid and hypochondriacal thoughts.

I moved my possessions into storage, this included my books, my computer and bits of furniture that I had acquired; and so effectively I was now living out of a large back pack. I did however take my electric guitar with me on this new phase in my life. This change of scene was very motivated by my desire to escape my old way of life. So I moved out of my flat in Farringdon where I had become so immersed in the world of drugs and the counter culture and moved in to stay with friends living in a flat in the North of London Muswell Hill area. I didn't know it at the time but this turned out to be the perfect context for my philosophical and religious explorations.

I found myself moving in to a large spacious flat, rented by two friends I had met when I was involved in London's psychedelic party scene. They were a couple from Texas, in the United states, who had been in a relationship but were now best of friends. They really helped me out at a time when I really needed some place to escape and get my head together again. I was living out of a camping backpack and sleeping on the floor in the corner of their living room. I can't believe now how I could have lived like that but will always be eternally grateful to my friends for providing me with a place to live when I really had nowhere to go.

My life was in a pretty pathetic state. My hedonism, decadence and excessive behaviour had left me almost totally dysfunctional for a while. At the same time because of my state of mind, I tended to pay not much attention to my material circumstances. So at that time in my life my surroundings didn't really matter to me much at all. My head was completely focused on the metaphysical, mystical and religious.

The flat itself was full of religious and mystical images and artefacts and thus provided a stimulating backdrop for the thoughts that were going on in my head. From waking up in the morning right up to falling asleep in the night time I thought incessantly. Sometimes visions would appear in my head which were so vivid that I would become totally distracted from some of my daily activities. Sometimes I would find myself in a shop or something like that and then become gripped by the thoughts and visualizations that were going on in my mind to the exclusion of everything that was going on around me, for many minutes at a time.

My day would typically involve waking up and going straight into my thoughts. Then I would eat and leave the house to go wandering, thinking all the while during the walks and visiting public libraries to sit, read, think and write in my notes. I read a lot of books about religion, mysticism, philosophy and the relationship between science and spirituality. I would walk a lot, and often walk from Muswell Hill into the centre of London, a journey on foot that would take a couple of hours. So my days were spent walking, stopping off at a public library, walking some more, visiting another library and so on. I really got a lot of thinking and reading done and in retrospect I can see that this period was an important formative phase for my ideas and philosophy.

After getting back to the flat where I was staying, I would typically find my American friends smoking cigarettes and watching the television. It was not uncommon that I would find myself ranting about my latest thoughts and ideas to my hosts and I remember that they were supportive, patient and quite encouraging. If they sometimes found me tiresome then I was too engrossed in my little mystical universe to really notice. I really was in another world. In this world but not of this world, as the expression goes.

This state of affairs carried on until the early Spring 1997, when the change in the weather seemed to awaken my worldly mind a little and I started to consider earthly matters once again. Around this time my head was returning to normal again but I was still spending quite a lot of time with my mind focused on religious thoughts. As my mental state was slowly reverting back to something more like how it was before my road of excess, so it seemed that the mystic door which had opened up months before, now slowly seemed to close again. The spiritual insights and mystical visions became much less frequent as my brain became more regularly functional again. In retrospect I can see now that this time of my life was a valuable one in terms of providing me with new ways of seeing and new ways of understanding.

As already mentioned, at the beginning of the year and slightly before, I had already started to feel that I had really taken enough drugs. Now I was becoming increasingly wary of their detrimental effects. My desire to put a stop to my drug use altogether would not be immediate. One of my flatmates was working in the scene as DJ and I was still heavily tied in socially with it and so would still go to psychedelic parties but only about a couple of times a month, a big change from my previous pattern of 2 or 3 times a week. The hedonistic dimension of the drug culture started to have less and less of a pull on me. Also I was probably getting diminishing returns in terms of new experiences and insights derived from the scene. As my drug taking diminished so my mental fitness and powers of concentration started to return. But then something happened in the Spring of 1997. In early May of that year a major upset would bring my now minor pattern of drug taking to an abrupt end. And which would cause me to try to put the whole world of drugs and substance abuse completely behind me.

Around the month of May 1997, I learned that my close friend and drug experimentation companion Patrick had died, at the age of 29, from an overdose of a cocktail of various intoxicants. I was utterly devastated by the news and it really shook me to the core. We had spent a lot of time together going to clubs and generally hanging out. We also talked a lot together about life in general and about religious and philosophical matters, so his demise and the circumstances around his death came as a real blow. It also forced me to think hard about my own situation and all this put me into a profoundly depressed state. It certainly made it clear to me how reckless my way of life had been.

I thought what a waste it all was, someone dying at such a young age with so much of his life ahead of him and someone with potential. The fact that he had a small daughter aged about three or four added to the tragedy. Patrick and his daughter's mother had separated but he was quite dutiful when it came to taking his offspring for days out. I met up with the two of them together on a few occasions when he was looking after his daughter, usually in some cafe or restaurant in central London. She would have been just old enough to have some brief memories of her father, but who would never get the chance to know him. It was all very sad.

Also some of the circumstances surrounding my friends death made the feeling of grief more intense and also prevented a sense of closure. Towards the end, my friend had lapsed back to a previous mode of existence and employment which involved the movements of and trade in the drug cocaine; making deliveries to media, music and advertising companies and also banks so helping to stimulate London's commercial and creative operations. He had been arrested months before his death in possession of a large quantity of some illegal substance and was facing a court case and, what he thought, a certain long jail sentence. I remember this hung on his mind a lot and depressed him immensely. At some point he decided to jump bail and during the last months of his life existed as a fugitive on the run from the law. Partly as a result of this and also partly due to the fact that my life was starting to move away from the world of substance abuse, I lost contact with my friend.

I knew he was living in a house owned by a criminal associate somewhere in London, this is where he was found dead. I didn't know this person or the location of the place where my friend was in hiding and also I had moved house recently as well so we lost touch with each other. As a result I never got to see my friend Patrick during this desperate and final period of his life. After his death there was this horrible feeling of guilt and regret, a feeling of 'What if?', 'What if I was there to help, perhaps to advise or merely console?', 'What if this?, or what if that?, then perhaps my friend wouldn't be dead etc.

On top of this sense of loss and grief things were further complicated by other circumstances surrounding Patrick's death. Due to a variety of reasons, my friend had a few antagonisms with various people associated with London's Psychedelic party scene and made some enemies. After his death some of these people choose to openly criticise my dead pal, unfairly and inappropriately I thought, which encouraged in me a definite hatred for these persons. These sentiments helped me to develop more of a distancing between myself the world of psychedelic drugs. If I already had less of an affinity for this scene, then some of the feelings floating around in my head at this time, caused in me an outright rejection of some of the attitudes and outlook of the people with whom I had been hanging out. There developed in me a strong desire to abandon my previous mode of existence. To engage in more wholesome pursuits and strive for better things.

This was definitely one of the most wrenching times of my life, exacerbated by the fact that my mental state at that time was still quite delicate from the chronic pattern of drug abuse I had been indulging in. The sense of grief and anger was probably made more intense by the fact that my brain was still in a recovering stage and emotionally weak. During a turbulent few weeks, I really reorientated my life and set a new course. I now wanted to re-enter the 'normal' world and I had the first inklings that the purpose of my life was to somehow communicate the basic mystical insights that I had to the world at large and mainstream society.

It was this process of pain that helped me to wake up from the slumber that I had been in, the sleep of the Lotus Eaters. Also it was this mental and emotional turbulence which gave me the escape velocity to take charge of my life and leave the island of the Lotus Eaters. It was at around the Summer Solstice, a month or so after learning about my friend's death, that in my mind, I finally made the break. My entire outlook and mental state seemed to change rather dramatically. It was a powerful point of transition, my life was being steered towards a totally different course. Somehow and in some way I first started to believe and see clearly that the purpose of my life was to communicate to the world the idea that everybody is God.

I didn't really have a clue as to how I might go about this task of explaining to the world the visions I had seen and the mystical ideas that I had, but I knew that to accomplish my objectives I had to learn a phenomenal amount of knowledge from all the various areas of human learning. So all through the Summer right through to the end of 1997, I read voraciously finishing at least two or three decent sized books a week. I would typically spend 7 to 8 hours a day reading, day in day out. It got to the point that I became temporarily short sighted during this time as a result of all the time I spent staring into books. I would find it difficult to focus at a distant object, even though normally I had good eye sight. Mainly I read books on Philosophy, Science, Religion, Spirituality, History, Psychology and Neuroscience, but also I read a wide variety of periodicals as well. I was getting myself ready for the purpose of my life. Aside from studying, the rest of my time was spent jogging, meditating and playing my electric guitar.

I should also mention that during this time, I experienced a reawakening of my interest and long held dream of working out how the brain worked and creating Artificial Intelligence. My notes from this time reflect this and I remember that 1997 was a productive year where I gained many new insights into how the human mind worked. However, although at this point in my life I saw some connections between the brain and mind on the one hand and mystical/spiritual truths on the other; they were at the same time still areas of learning that existed in separate compartments within my head. The full integration of the neuroscientific and the spiritual would come a couple of years later, when it became clear to me that the processes of the brain are totally correspondent with the processes of human history, the evolution of life and also the overall process of the Universe. It was later on that I would become better able to articulate the idea that the mystery of consciousness and the mystery of God are one and the same. Also after much study I would later in my life be successfully communicating to the world my radical theories concerning how the brain worked.

I remember getting a lot done at this time. It was a relative halcyon period of my life but at the same time there was a sense of unease. At the back of my mind there was always the troubling thought that I had jeopardized my long term aims through the senseless way that I had lived over the past few years. There was a feeling that I had wasted valuable time and that it was necessary for me to play catch up. This definitely acted as a kind of spur, as I really got down to work in the latter part of 1997.

Also on my mind through out this time of intense study were thoughts about my recently deceased friend Patrick. Death generally, was a thought that occupied my mind quite a lot during this time, coupled with related reflections on the transience of life and eternity. Probably partly due to the process of mourning my dead friend and also as a result of the kind of things I was reading and thinking about, I felt a closeness with death. This focus and meditation on death gave me more of an eternal and wider outlook on things. In the contemplation of the transience and fragility of life I was able to get a better orientation towards the permanent and transcendent.

This time from the Summer Solstice of 1997 onwards I can, with the benefit of hindsight, now understand as a process of recovery and restoration and perhaps even initiation. This time of healing following on from the self destruction I brought about upon myself through personal neglect and the extensive consumption of various types of psychoactive drugs. In retrospect I can see that this was a very necessary thing for me to have gone through to get to the stage that I am at now. Sometimes we have to go through some extreme situations in life in order to experience profound personal transitions. This process of reconstruction, healing and recovery would be much enhanced when through a series of chance encounters I was given the opportunity to engage in some confidence building and strengthening activities. Slightly later on I would suddenly start doing some work as a musician playing guitar in front of quite large audiences in various parts of the world. This would help me to regain my confidence and strength.

My life was now completely drug free and I no longer had very much in common with most of the people that I had spent the past few years hanging out with. My life went through a total re-orientation and I was living a very different existence from my previous one in the land of the Lotus Eaters. I would continue to get my head and body together. I would continue to prepare myself for what I had to do in life.

The moral to this particular stage of my story is this. In the same way that Odysseus' sailors became trapped on the Island of the lotus eaters, once they had partaken of its fruits, so it is that the spiritual aspirant or mystical quester may find his or her journey halted by the use of psychedelic drugs. In fact the continued and repeated use of these powerful substances may, in a manner similar to the effects of the mythical Lotus, cause the adventurer to fall into a chronic stupor and even cause some people to totally lose their minds. With a bit of bad luck and without Odysseus to rescue you, then experimentation with psychedelic drugs can mean it's game over and the end of the odyssey. I guess I was lucky. Various things happened which helped to give me the impetus to leave the Island of the Lotus Eaters and carry on my journey.

Chapter 4

The Odyssey

After a period of self destruction and self neglect, also shaken by the death of a close friend, I decide to clean up my act and get serious about life once again. At the start of 1998 an opportunity manifested itself which would pull my life course off on a strange trajectory for a while. I spent a while in the role of musician, playing electric guitar in a psychedelic trance dance act, touring all over the world. It was a musical interlude that became part of the wider mystical odyssey. During and around this time I had three powerful mystical experiences which would reveal to me the nature of God and provide for me answers to questions that I had been on my mind a while.

Starting in the beginning of 1998 I rather suddenly found myself working as a live musician and playing guitar in shows around various parts of the world. I was asked to accompany the electronic dance act Cosmosis on a world tour to help promote their new album. In retrospect the whole thing was a perfect setup and I believe it was all set up in order that I may have several key mystical experiences. I got the job, because the guy behind the act Cosmosis saw me playing my guitar at a party and thought it would be good to have me on stage with him. Prior to all this I would quite often take my electric guitar to play solo at various social gatherings and party events. I did this because I was asked but also because it meant I could get into places for free also it was a great way to meet people. Quite by chance I happened to be playing in the right place at the right time.

This rather sudden detour on my path was certainly something a little different from my existence at the time. Having experienced something of a quite introverted period in life, I then found myself having to play a very extroverted role. Performing in live shows, travelling and meeting people really brought me back into the world. It helped to build up my confidence as people were always keen to talk to you and the feedback from the audience was always positive.

As a result of this new trajectory I was given the opportunity to talk to a lot of different kinds of people about my mystic and spiritual insights. The reaction to my philosophical rantings wasn't always positive but I didn't really care, I was obsessed. My head was rather filled with mystical and philosophical thoughts, so whenever I had a conversation with anybody the subject matter would very inevitably turn to my obsession. Some of the people whom I spoke to during my travels were very receptive and encouraging, this helped to motivate me even further. I had recovered a lot from my period of self destruction and started to feel my strength and confidence returning.

Playing guitar with the psychedelic trance outfit Cosmosis was initially very exciting and satisfying. It gave me a chance to travel and meet lots of people. Although on reflection most of what I saw was airports, hotel bedrooms, guest rooms and psychedelic trance parties. All of these are pretty much the same where ever you go. Also most of the people I met were total drug heads, and it was a scene and mind set that I'd already left behind. However all the same I did have a good time and I did enjoy all the social interaction. Also the repeated experience of stepping onto a stage in front of lots of people and performing would give me a head start when I would take up public speaking a few years later.

It was an interesting coincidence to me, that I would meet up with the two other members of the Band that I formed as a teenager, whilst on tour with Cosmosis in two widely separated places in the world. One ex band member who played drums in my band was then working for a human rights organization in Moscow, Russia. The other who played Bass guitar was working as a journalist in Sydney, Australia. They both came to the respective concerts I played at these places as well. It seemed very synchronous and fateful at the time. My band I'd formed as a teenager was a failure. Somehow seeing my old friends provided a sense of continuity but also one of closure. It closed that long phase in my life, when in the back of my mind I associated the idea of performing in front of a load people with rejection and ridicule. This was one of several fruitful happenings and revelations that occurred during my musical odyssey. Later that year I had two powerful mystical experiences which in retrospect seem like the reason why the hand of providence had led me along this musical detour.

The first one occurred in Byron Bay, Australia and the second in Zurich, Switzerland. In the first experience I was given a radical view of the nature of time and saw powerful images of distant ancestors and previous lives. In the second experience I was given a vision of the cosmic tree. I saw all existence and also myself as a part of a single all encompassing Cosmic tree. I'll give a more detailed account of these two episodes together with the events and circumstances surrounding them a little later.

I'd like to mention at this point that all through this period in my life, the idea that everyone is God and the notion that this is my own ultimate and real identity, was something that was constantly on my mind. About a year previously, in early 1997, I had found myself in an extended borderline mystical state which lasted several months. During that period the notion of ones inherent divinity was something close at hand and invaded my day to day existence, even if at the time I couldn't fully understand it. During the rest of that previous year I had spent every spare moment of time studying anything that I thought might help me to understand this divine mystery; that while I was a person and mortal human-being somehow simultaneously, in my eternal and infinite self, I was also God.

So I spent a lot of my time reading up on the mystical and religious literature, but also studying ideas from science and philosophy that might help me to better grasp this sacred truth with my rational mind and also in order that I may one day clearly articulate it. This pattern of behaviour had molded and shaped my personality and mind set greatly. I really thought about these sorts of things practically all the time to the exclusion of much else.

So the upshot of this was that even though I was doing a lot of work as a musician playing guitar all over the place and leading a social and extroverted lifestyle, at the same time my head was far off some place else. I did play and practice my guitar a lot at this time but my focus was really on other things, my real devotion was to the sacred and the transcendent. Everything was really a backdrop for the real action which was going on in my mind. I was getting myself ready to somehow explain to the world at large this most amazing, astounding and fabulous of all truths, that a persons real identity is God.

In the course of my travels I found myself in Melbourne Australia. The act Cosmosis was scheduled to do a performance at a party to be held miles out in a national park which really did seem like the middle of nowhere. It was in the middle of an endless expanse of eucalyptus forest and I remember that the drive there was long and twisty. It seemed far away from civilization. A psychedelic trance party was organized at this location and the band I was touring with would play there as the main attraction.

During the party familiar faces seemed to pop out from nowhere and all over the place. I encountered many people from the very international psychedelic trance scene that I had met at trance parties in the UK. It was great to see them again. This particular gig in Melbourne was attended by many familiar faces.

For the first time I got a real sense that this small but internationally scattered sub-culture, called psychedelic trance, was really like some kind of family or secret society. A society bonded together by a shared interest in a certain type of music, a passion for travelling, a certain constellation of shared beliefs and also a fondness for taking powerful psychedelic drugs.

I had first encountered this scene back in London during a particularly decadent and hedonistic phase that lasted a couple of years. Back then I would often go out clubbing and hang out at psychedelic trance parties. This lifestyle of frequently going to clubs exposed me to the kind of people I was encountering a lot during my time in Australia, whilst playing my guitar at psychedelic trance parties or 'doof parties' as they're known out there.

Collectively the people in question may be called the International Psychedelic Traveller Community. They came from many countries and from all backgrounds, although people from the more industrialized countries and also the middle classes were disproportionately represented. Their lives were characterized by a tendency to travel a lot, often to back packer destinations and in particular to places like India and Thailand.

The kind of music produced by Cosmosis was for a time, in the mid nineties, labelled Goa Trance after the former Portuguese colony in India. This was because during about this time and before, the place Goa was an important centre for the world psychedelic scene and attracted many free spirited people from all over. Just the kind of people who would gravitate towards taking psychedelic drugs and going to trance parties. Also a lot of psychedelic trance dance music was produced by people with a strong affinity for Goa, so during the mid 90s the expressions Goa Trance and psychedelic trance were interchangeable.

In recent history there has always been a connection between psychedelia and India. The late 60s and early 70s witnessed an explosion of interest in Eastern mysticism which was to a very large degree precipitated by the relatively large scale use of the drug LSD. So many people in the West started to explore Hinduism, the religion of India. During that period India became a premiere hippy mecca and many young people from the industrialised countries made their way there on journeys of self discovery or else merely in order to take more drugs.

It seemed like there was a resurgence of interest in India during the mid 90s when I was exploring the psychedelic counter culture in London. As a result of this I would often meet a lot of Western people with a great affinity for India while I was going through my druggy clubbing phase. This probably helped to form in me an initial interest in Indian philosophy and religion. It certainly exposed me to ideas which helped to shape my outlook and encourage certain mystical tendencies that I already had.

In a not so subtle way my life had become entangled with the international psychedelic trance scene and I can see now that this relationship has been a factor in my personal evolution. I'm still in the process of understanding what is the role of this unique and global sub-culture in the wider scheme of things. This strange family and secret society may, I speculate, have some role to play in the proper unfolding of world events leading towards the fulfilment of the prophecies contained in the world's religions. And maybe not. Another feature of the scene apart from the decadence is the dysfunctionality and unrealized potential of the people who spent too much time involved with psychedelic drugs.

I was quite fascinated by the fact of the popularity of the psychedelic trance among Israeli youth. I would encounter many young Israelis in my travels and hear their tales. It seemed a common rite of passage for young Israelis to do their national service, then afterwards go to India, take loads of psychedelic drugs and then return home somewhat transformed and given new ideas. I keep imagining the psychedelic trance scene in Israel as being a recapitulation of the Manna cult, a resurgent Kabbalah and just maybe some sort of spiritual vanguard. Then again this may all just be wishful thinking.

Anyway, it was during this period of my life in the role of travelling guitar man that I got the chance to see and get to know better this world psychedelic scene. It was a funny position to be in as I was, in a sense, totally on the inside of the scene, but at the same time I was also something of an outsider. Though I had and still have a lot of liking and affinity with a lot of the people who are a part of the world psychedelic community, I can also see the inherent limitations of using psychedelic drugs as a means to facilitate mystic states.

It was a funny time of my life and a strange irony. A year previously this would have seemed an ideal situation. I was totally immersed in the land of psychedelia and had the opportunity through my work as a musician to go to psychedelic parties all over the world. However in my mind I had already left the land of the Lotus Eaters. Throughout all this period it really felt as if I was only really passing through. However this strange interlude provided the perfect backdrop for my continuing mystical and philosophical ruminations, that would occupy my mind a lot of the time. Also during time I would experience several powerful mystical experiences the first of which occurred a few weeks after my brief time spent in Melbourne. We continued our tour of Australia and ended up in a place called Byron bay.

Just before coming to Byron Bay I had contracted a strange lung infection which caused me to cough a lot and drained my energy. Also the strains of being on the road had caused my relationship with my travelling companions to deteriorate. These were the circumstances that I found myself in as we made the drive from Sydney to Byron Bay.

As we were nearing the town our driver and guide was telling us something about the place. I discovered that Byron Bay was the most Easterly point on the land mass of Australia. Also I found out that whales would converge upon the waters around the town during their breeding season. Our driver also mentioned strange energies associated with the place thought to be able to affect peoples states of mind and even cause them to go a bit insane. He said that certain sensitive types couldn't stand this energy and had to live in the hills a few miles away from this energetic epicentre. I remember thinking to myself what a load of nonsense, but I would think otherwise later on.

Byron Bay is an extremely beautiful part of the world with some great countryside and many stunning beaches. The town itself is rather small and is characterized by the strong new age and hippy presence. It was quite a paradise but at the same time a little dull. I soon became quite bored of my surroundings and settled into a routine of going off by myself in order to read and think.

The time came when I had to do the performance with the band. The gig was held in the most unusual of places. We were to play at a psychedelic trance party that was to be held in a warehouse that used to be a whaling processing station. That is a place where the bodies of large whales were turned into heating oil, whale meat and various other industrial raw materials. I remember that the party wasn't very well attended with perhaps no more than a few hundred people. The crowd were mainly young with a lot of teenagers but I distinctly remember that a lot of the people present didn't seem all that happy. I also remember that the whole place smelled strange and I couldn't help thinking about all those slaughtered whales. At some point that evening I made the connection. I realized that if the whales came from all around the world's oceans to the waters just off Byron Bay to breed then this would have been a convenient place for the whaling industry to have set up a base. It was a horrible thought the idea of whales coming from all over the world in order procreate only to be slaughtered for their monetary value. It did bring me down a bit.

So in this unhappy context we did our performance. It wasn't very inspiring at all and I didn't get the same high that I'd normally get while playing music in front of an audience. Also the virus or infection that I had contracted in Sydney our previous port of call, was still affecting me adversely. Looking back and reflecting on that night, it all seems a bit surreal to me now. A psychedelic party full of unhappy people held in a place where whales got chopped up and processed. It isn't the kind of place I'd associate with a good time.

After the show, in the days following, my mood dipped noticeably. We would be staying in Byron Bay for another week and I remember that I got very bored. My health seemed to deteriorate. My lung infection got worse and my immune system didn't seem to be able to shake it off. But what was also getting worse was my mental state. I felt agitated, restless and my head would fill with intrusive and strange thoughts. The words of our driver seemed prophetic. Was my head being affected by these strange energies that he talked about.

I remember one day, I was sitting in the back garden of the house where we were all staying. All around were the famous cane toads. They would stop in their tracks when they walked into an obstacle and would remain motionless for hours. I knew about their potent psychedelic properties and was aware of the practice of licking the toad's glands in order to obtain a dose of their psychoactive agent. However I abstained. I thought that in my present state it would not be a good idea to indulge in anything like that. I was quite concerned that I was losing it a bit and didn't want to exacerbate the situation. I really was only just managing to hold it all together. Also it was slightly less than a year previously that a close friend had died from drug abuse. This shocked and saddened me greatly and made me quite wary of drugs and mind altering substances for quite a while. Sitting surrounded by all these psycho active cane toads would have been an irresistible indulgence for me a couple of years previously. But now here I was adamantly not wishing to alter my consciousness but rather wishing that my head would go back to 'normal' again.

In this general state I remained for several days. I found myself at the house a lot avoiding company, reading and playing guitar a lot. I recall at this time I was reading a translation of the Bhagavad Gita I had purchased in Sydney and also a book I had recently bought in Byron Bay called 'The Power of Myth'. This book contains the transcripts of an American TV series of the same name which consisted of the renowned expert on world mythology, Joseph Campbell being interviewed. It was these activities which probably helped me to keep some sort of a grip on things. Something would then occur which interrupted this stable but unagreeable state of affairs I found myself in. I decided to go to a party in a house located deep in the woods surrounding the town. Certain things I did at this gathering would help to trigger a mystical experience, a series of visions and some vivid metaphysical insights later on.

I found myself at a smallish hippy psychedelic traveller gathering in somebody's house which was in the middle of dense woodland. It was quite an idyllic spot, there were bright stars in the sky and it made me think of Endor, the forest planet in the movie Revenge of the Jedi. The crowd gathered were hardcore psychedelic types, friendly and laid back. I recognized some more people that I had met back in the UK at trance parties and it was fun to learn more about them.

At some point an attractive young hippy chick handed me a biscuit from a tray containing several of them. I didn't think anything of it, so naturally I accepted one and happily bit into it. It didn't taste very good and then it dawned on me that the biscuit was probably laced with psychedelic plant extracts or perhaps some strange fungaloid. I had already swallowed a bite and was feeling a little concerned about possible adverse effects it might have on me, particularly in my current weakened and slightly unstable state of mind. Hard drugs were something that I had carefully avoided for almost a year since the death of my close friend, so I had a feeling that I had broken a strict taboo I had imposed on myself. I wrapped the rest of the mostly uneaten biscuit in a disposable handkerchief and would end up flushing it down the toilet before the party was over. I stayed on a while chatting and drinking red wine. Then it was time to go, the small crowd I had come with all drove back to the house.

Feeling rather tired I wanted to go straight to bed. I went to my room, lay on my back a while, had a think about the nights events and then decided to go wash, brush my teeth and turn in for the night. But the bathroom which was next door to my bedroom was occupied. I laid down on the floor and waited for the person in the bathroom to leave.

As I was waiting I could feel a warm sensation come all over my body. I lay there with my eyes closed but as if behind my eyelids I could see pulsating colors and small lights that jiggled about. I was quite drawn into the spectacle at first but then felt a gentle anxiety that all was not right. I remember visualizing quite vividly, that the virus from my lung infection had invaded my brain en mass, and I lay there thinking that it was this which was causing me to see these things. Looking back on it now, it was probably a combination of the illness, the exhaustion, the unpalatable biscuit and the few cups of red wine I had, which was causing the experience. And perhaps also the strange new age 'energies' which are thought to be particularly concentrated in and around Byron bay.

As I lay there motionless witnessing and contemplating weird things, the nature of the things I could see with my eyes closed changed. The simple patterns and lights gave way to more complex images. I saw people, animals, trees and a lot more besides. At first these images were disjointed and seemed to come in and out of view, mixing randomly then disappearing. Gradually things became more coherent and I slipped into what may best be described as a very vivid lucid dream. Everything seemed as real as 'normal' reality. It became so real so as to be no longer dream like. It was as if I had been transported to another place. What I saw was this.

There was snow everywhere, it was very bright with the Sun low in the sky. There were trees here and there and I seemed to be located on the edge of some woodland. All around me were people, perhaps a few dozen. Everyone was dressed in clothing made from furs and animal skins. There was a fire or the remains of one and I could detect the strong smell of burning wood. There were the beating of drums or perhaps just the rhythmic sound of primitive and improvised percussive instruments. It was a kind of ritual, some of the people were moving about in a strange stylized way, others were seated and looking on. I also noticed that those around me were a mixture of oriental looking and also nordic looking people. Some of them had blonde hair and fair skin and some of the others had black hair and a darker complexion.

The Odyssey

Then I suddenly shifted back to 'normal' reality. I was back in Byron Bay laying on my back. Now I felt I was being given a message. I seemed to be thinking thoughts which were not my own. It was being impressed upon me that somehow the events I saw in the vision were somehow intimately related to my present situation.

A little later I drifted back into another set of images and visions. This time I experienced myself as a small child with my mother. It was before the time I started school, I must have been about 4 years old. I remember I used to wait for my mother to wake up, while playing in an upstairs room that was the living room of the house. Then my mother would carry me down the stairs, and make me something to eat. After this time spent together my mother would get down to work preparing food to sell for the family business which was downstairs from the upstairs apartments where my family lived. I would go off into the yard and play by myself. But here I was almost a quarter of a century later transported back to my early childhood not merely recalling these memories but actually reliving these experiences and seeing through my own eyes as a 4 year old. It was as real as real can be! It was as if I had been transported back in time, everything was so incredibly vivid and clear. The sights, smells and sounds some of them long forgotten came back to me with a shocking familiarity.

Then things shifted again and I was back in the present, back in this small Byron Bay room lying on my back. I was fully aware and thought to myself that I was having a mystical experience. I also thought that I was losing my mind, perhaps never to return. There was a feeling of excitement but also one of apprehension. I could feel my body pulsating now, I imagined that my body was glowing like a hot charcoal. Then I crossed over a little to the infinite but not completely. I was straddled on the borderline between the mundane and the mystical, the temporal and eternal and between micro-cosmic and cosmic. I was not myself yet I was not 'one the Universe' and in a state of union with God. It was as if the Universe was about to enter me but was stuck in the process and here I was at the half way point.

In this state I had a powerful mystical vision and insight that was a great metaphysical truth being communicated to me. I saw in a series of abstract images that the future was caused by the past, which is what we normally understand; but also that the past was being caused by the future. I saw clearly that past and future were totally immeshed with one another. Everything that would be considered the past was necessary for future events to happen, just as everything that was in the future was necessary in order to construct the past. There was perfect symmetry, the future and past fashioned one another in a perfect and harmonious entanglement.

My mind was directed to think about the two vivid visions that I had slightly earlier. It was revealed to me that the events I had witnessed in the snowy, wooded landscape with the peoples dressed in skins and furs, was something that had happened in the distant past. It was also revealed to me with a powerful impression that somehow those events were somehow an important and decisive point in the history of the human race. I saw vividly that all that has happened in human history had somehow emanated from that strange mystical gathering that happened so very long ago. Then I saw that the situation and circumstances of the world today, were directly related to what I had seen. The present age and those events that probably happened in prehistoric times were inseparably bonded together. That little mystical gathering in the snow was necessary for and set off the process which led to the construction of the present world. At the same time the existence of the state of the present world had brought those prehistory events into being.

After that I went through the same process with the vision that I had of myself as a child. This time I was seeing the nature of the past and the future in relation to my life. I was shown what we would think is obvious, that my present situation were caused and set up by all those defining events in my childhood. But then I was shown that my eventual destiny and the ultimate purpose of my life had caused all those events of my childhood to happen in the first place. The future was setting up the conditions of the past necessary for its own realization! The future was causing the past, just as the past was seemingly causing the future. It was a shocking and stunning metaphysical truth that was being intentionally and forcefully projected into my mind. I was being shown an important aspect of the nature of space, time and existence. Even to this day, this insight feels as though it had been seared into my mind. I was in a state of awe and wonder. I contemplated what I had seen and what had been communicated to me.

Gradually I came back to a more normal state of mind. I went to the bathroom next door. Everyone in the house was asleep by now, it was late and I must have been away for some hours. I brushed my teeth and did the necessary final acts for the day and finally went to sleep.

After the mystical encounter that night we would stay on a few more days in Byron Bay. I didn't feel much better and still a little borderline and slightly agitated. Although my mood would also enter into clearer periods. Finally it was time to leave Byron Bay and also Australia. We flew over to Japan. While on the plane I remember my mood and state of mind changed noticeably. I suddenly felt clearer, focused and more peaceful, exactly the opposite to what I had been experiencing for the past couple of weeks, especially during the stay in Byron Bay. By the time we got to Tokyo's Narita airport I felt completely transformed and back to my normal self.

A short time later after returning to the UK, I discovered that I no longer had a place to stay. My friend from Texas who had given me a place to stay for the past year or so had been deported. He had apparently not obtained the proper visas for staying in the UK so was staying illegally. One night while driving his girlfriend's car around town badly he was stopped by the police and given a one way ticket to the United States. Anyway as a result my circumstances changed and so for a while I slept on friend's sofas, on various living room floors or sometimes in peoples spare bedrooms.

I remember I was reading the Bhagavad Gita a lot at this time and had 3 different translations in my holdall travel bag. I effectively lived out of my holdall and guitar case. In my semi-homeless state I still found the opportunity to meditate a lot, mainly using my breath as the focus. Around this time during the Spring of 1998 sometime in May I would have another powerful spiritual experience.

This mystical experience was certainly precipitated by circumstances and events that occurred in the few days leading up to it. I happened to be in Brighton, on the South Coast of England, staying with my friend Kian, whom I've already mentioned in an earlier chapter. It was a Friday night and there was a party in the house where I was staying. There were several interesting people at the party whose company I found stimulating. I drank a couple of beers but avoided the cannabis that was going round. I didn't get very much sleep that night because I turned in really late and also because I had to wake up early in the morning, around 6am'ish. I had to make an early start because I had a concert to play on the next day which was a Saturday. This gig was to be at a psychedelic trance party in Zurich, Switzerland, so there was a lot of travelling to do that day.

The long journey to Switzerland started with a bus journey to Brighton train station. Then I took a train to London Victoria, followed by getting the tube to Pinner in periphery of North west London where the musician I would be travelling with lived. A short break and then a taxi to Heathrow airport. From there a plane to Zurich. As the plane approached Zurich there was a lot of turbulence and also lightning. Finally there was a car ride from the airport to the house where we would be staying before and after the gig.

On arriving at the house, I felt that my body and mind were really exhausted but the excitement of being in a foreign country and the enthusiastic hospitality of our hosts, made it hard to relax. After some food there was time for a few hours sleep but I recall my mind was racing, so I only managed to have a bit of a lie down.

Around close to midnight we were driven to the open air site where the party was now in full swing. We were in a large stone quarry located in the hills surrounding Zurich. It was quite surreal as these kind of events can often be. All around things looked like an alien landscape, complete with rocks and boulders everywhere. Also of course there were masses of people, many hundreds, perhaps more than a thousand even. There were fluorescent decorations strewn about everywhere and ultra violet lighting which gave everything a strange luminance. As we set up the music and sound equipment on the small stage where we would be performing, I remember it started to rain just a tiny bit and also there was some lightning. It was a very dramatic and exciting scene. I thought that all the expensive audio equipment was going to get rained on but we continued to press on and finished setting up all the gear. Luckily the rain didn't really get going very much. So after a short wait it was time to get on the stage and the performance began.

The shows were usually a pleasure to do and the feeling of excitement and adrenaline I felt during them could be intense. I would have a beer before going on, but during the show I would also drink a lot of caffeinated beverages. This psycho-active input combined with the general circumstances and physical exertion from dancing around on stage meant that during these performances I often got really high. This would have been clearly visible in my expression and movements. There is something distinctly spiritual about losing yourself in front of an audience while dancing to rapid and repetitive beats. I would often feel a sort of merging with the audience, and could get into these what might be called borderline mystical states quite easily. This is how I felt that night but it was only after the show that the real full blown mystical experience happened.

After coming off the raised platform that served as the stage I felt very very good. People came up to express their appreciation for the show and this reinforced my feeling of well being for a short while. I was drenched in sweat and my shirt stuck to my body. I sat down for a bit and it was then that the exertions of the past few days and the just finished live performance were now catching up with me. I started to feel very tired. Then my mood dipped rather noticeably, from a feeling of exaltation to one of uneasiness. People would still be approaching me saying things in German or Italian, but I didn't understand what they were saying. I suddenly felt very agoraphobic and a little agitated. So I got up and wandered off.

I wanted to be alone but there was no chance of getting back to the house until one of the people I came over from the UK with, had finished doing his DJ slot which was quite a few hours later. So I walked along a steep path going up one of the tall hills. Walking a while I put some distance between myself and the crowd below. It felt like something of a relief to be away from the party but then I realized how cold my body had become. My clothes were still damp and this worsened the situation. Not just feeling cold, my body also felt as if every molecule of glucose and all reserves of energy had been used up. I started to shiver and wondered what I was going to do next. It was almost pitch black, however I could see the lights from the party down below which provided the only light. At this point a state of panic set in.

Now I really felt totally exhausted. I sat down cross legged and at this point my body was shivering quite violently, almost convulsing. I recall thinking to myself what a disaster this all was. There was a real sense of danger and jeopardy. There was no shouting for help as I had wandered away far from the crowd and there was nobody about in my immediate vicinity. I remember thinking how an air ambulance might have to be called and how embarrassing it would all be. The thought crossed my mind that I might even end up dead. I was in a terrible state, sitting there in my damp clothes and shivering like mad. This went on for a short while, with all sorts of worries going through my head but then things changed. A state of calmness descended upon me and my body became at rest. I seemed to lose sensation of my body and my mind strangely became indifferent to what was happening to me. In retrospect, what happened to me was that I was going into a trance. This was strangely appropriate, as I was at a trance party.

So I sat there, half way up the top of a tall hill, motionless and in a trance. I no longer felt cold but I do remember that insects were crawling all over my skin and body. I was totally unconcerned and didn't react to these intrusions. I distinctly recall that I thought about a picture in one of the Bhagavad Gitas, I was reading around this time. It depicted a meditating Indian yogi whose meditation was so protracted and intense that the plants around him over time grew all over his body. He seemed to merge with nature. I remember thinking that I was like that yogi.

A little later my thoughts ceased and the visions began. First of all there was a cascade of geometric forms and Islamic'esque patterns. They swirled, danced and pulsated. Gradually these patterns receded more into the background and then I saw an awesome vision of a tree. This tree was so immense it was the size of the Universe. It was intricate and vast. It would also change its appearance in a mysterious way. One moment it would seem like an organic tree like the ones we normally see and then it would seem crystal like and semi transparent.

Then I apprehended that this tree was the Universe and that everything within the Universe was a branch of this cosmic tree. It was given to me to see, that I too was a branch of this cosmic tree. I apprehended also that the tree branched into the core of my being and that I too was like a miniature tree. I was a branch of the cosmic tree but I was also a tree on my own. I was a microcosmic tree that was a branch of this all encompassing cosmic tree. Then I saw the things of the Universe, atoms, people, animals, nations, planets and even galaxies and I apprehended that they too were all like trees. And all these things and everything else also branched off and radiated from the cosmic tree, that was also the Universe.

The vision came to a peak when I saw that not only was I a smaller tree and a branch of the cosmic tree but also that at the same time the cosmic tree was also me! I contained within me the entire cosmic tree and I was the Universe! After this I entered into what might be described as a state of mystical union with the Universe and the Cosmic Tree. I became God...

...After an eternity I returned. It was dawn and the Sun was shining directly onto me. I slowly came to and remembered where I was and the events of the night before. My whole body ached and I felt very stiff all over. I was covered in ants so I had to pick them out and brush them off; they had gotten everywhere even in my ears! I tried to stand but my legs were completely dead. I looked down and could see that the trance party had died down and most of the people had gone home. At this point I could see my travelling companions from the UK walking up the hill towards me. They had been wondering where I had got to. I felt weak and my legs felt very wobbly, we made our way down the hill together. After a short wait we were all driven back to the house. I went straight to bed and had a very deep sleep. We returned to the UK later the same day. I recall on the flight home I couldn't stop thinking about the vision and was very introspective.

The two mystical experiences that had occurred in April and May of 1998, the visions I had experienced in Byron Bay, Australia and the visions of the Cosmic Tree I saw in Zurich, Switzerland had a powerful effect on me. I wanted to tell everyone what I had seen, but was frustrated at my inability to articulate in a coherent and meaningful way, the awesome visions that I had experienced. As was something of a habit by now I would rant and be quite forceful in getting those around me to listen to my insights. This alienated a lot of people and I became a bit of a social outcast. I started to find the interests that most people had, utterly mundane and totally uninteresting. In a very short space of time, my life shifted from being somewhere in the vibrant social centre, to somewhere else on the lonely outer fringes.

I was involved in the world of psychedelic trance music until the Summer of 1998 when my association with the band Cosmosis came to a naturally conclusion. Towards the end of my stint as a musician I got a little bored with the process of performing on stage with my guitar. I remember on several occasions coming off stage after a performance and feeling rather empty inside. There was always a little rush at the start coming on stage and facing a live audience but the novelty factor and stimulation level had progressively diminished over time. The highs and satisfaction I derived from playing music became less and less. I knew my destiny was some place elsewhere.

My life re-oriented itself back toward my higher purpose and long term goal to communicate the truth about God to the world at large and main stream society. Also around this time I once again returned to my long time obsession with working out how the brain and human mind worked. By now this interest in things neuroscientific and psychological had started to become integrated with my deep interest in the religious and philosophical. I started to see a lot of meaningful connections between on the one hand, the structure and physiology of the brain and on the other, certain ideas from the world of mysticism and religion. Though I wasn't quite sure exactly what it was and couldn't articulate it very well, even to myself; I had a strong intuition that there were very deep relationships between mind, brain, consciousness, cosmology and God.

There followed the start of a period of solitude, study and reflection which would come to last several years. I became something of a loner. I started to feel a growing sense of mission, and decided that I would dedicate an indefinite amount of time to prepare myself for what I had to do. This period of my life was a sort of incubation period. It was a remaking of myself that lasted around four years. It straddled my late 20s and early 30s. I threw myself totally into my explorations into things mystical and spiritual together with my studies into the brain and mind. So in the final months of 1998 after finishing with the band Cosmosis and playing guitar a whole load I embarked on this new and quite different phase in life.

The early part of this period was lived as something of a total outsider. I didn't speak to people very much and my days were spent reading and thinking. This was a pattern of behaviour that was already a feature of my life on and off but never to this extent or intensity. I would read in public libraries a lot and also bookshops, mostly located in central London. Most of my time each day would be spent staring at a book or else writing in my notes.

I walked everywhere, perhaps spending around 4 hours each day, walking from place to place. Often during my walks I would be thinking up ways to express to other people the ideas in my mind. Sometimes while walking I would chant meditation mantras in my head or else just listen to my portable music player. It was a very simplified and idealistic existence. I was totally driven by my goals and mostly I felt a certain satisfaction with life because I had a strong sense that I was pursuing my true purpose. However, sometimes I felt intolerably lonely and something of a loser. I didn't have a job or much money and I didn't have a girlfriend or many other friends either.

It was during one of these periods of melancholy that I experienced one of the most powerful mystical encounters of my life. It was on the Winter Solstice of 1998. During the days leading up to this point my head was in a terrible state. I was feeling very depressed, my mind seemed disorganised and I was having trouble concentrating. I couldn't think properly and my life seemed to grind to a halt. My thoughts and my dreams became inaccessible to me which deprived me of my only real source of pleasure and meaning in life at that time. My mood spiralled uncontrollably downwards and into oblivion.

I felt as if my life had been a total waste. I felt somehow cheated by fate, as if the Universe had played a cruel trick on me. It seemed the cosmic intelligence had systemically led me towards a certain course in my life, only for me to discover that the path led nowhere. What was this obsession I was gripped by that caused my life to deviate so far from the norm and lead me to such a sorry state?

It was in this state of mind that I decided to demand a sign from the Universe. It was as if I was saying to the Cosmos, 'show me some proof of the validity of the crazy life I'm leading or else I won't play your game anymore'. I felt on the point of giving up. I recall during this time my mood would get so bleak that I would get some sort of a fleeting sense of relief by imagining that I was going through the process of suicide and hanging from a rope by my neck. I guess that's how the process of self annihilation works. You imagine doing yourself in, get a feeling of imagined satisfaction from it and then go on to do it for real. However this would never have been anything I would have actually considered seriously. I could imagine it as I can imagine a lot of things but to actually do it would never have be an option for me. Firstly it would be a complete waste but most importantly I would never be able to put my mother and father through the ordeal. They having scrapped, toiled and struggled for all the benefits in life that I enjoyed, it would have been so utterly wrong for me to have voluntarily thrown my life away even if I personally didn't place any value on my life; which can be the prevailing sentiment during times of deep depression.

So I went about one day with the aim of looking for a sign from the Cosmic Intelligence the appearance of which would give me justification for my existence and reassurance that my life path was valid. Setting off from my house, on the morning of the Winter Solstice of 1998, I went for a very long walk hoping to receive a message of some sort. I walked hours and hours all over London looking for a sign. I looked in the sky, at the people on the streets, all over. Perhaps I'd see a massive shooting star, meet some mysterious mystical person with a message for me, or see some other extraordinary sight. But nothing happened. I walked everywhere all over London only stopping for fast-food and cups of coffee and still nothing. In all I walked 9 hours and after this time no sign had appeared, no message had been received. So at around 8pm, in a state of total disillusionment, I went to sit in Marylebone public library. I really needed to rest my tired legs which were feeling a little numb by now. I felt immensely weary but at the same time quite stimulated by all the coffee that I had drunk. I suppose my head was probably already in a somewhat altered state from all the walking and concentration on looking for this sign from the Universe that didn't appear.

On entering the library I felt cold, tired and empty. I sat down at one of the desks in the upstairs reference section of Marylebone library and stared into space for a while. Then I saw an opened book on the desk next to mine. Looking closer I saw my name in big bold capital letters beneath a very strange picture. I couldn't believe my eyes and felt sure I was hallucinating, after all I was in a very shakey state. But I looked again and there it was. The book was an encyclopedia of mysticism and the book was open on a page with a picture of an early Gnostic Christian symbol for God which I later discovered was called Abraxas. It was a mans torso with a rooster's head, carrying a whip and a shield, and two snakes for legs. Below this depiction was my name WAI. And a sentence printed beneath read *'Gnostic adherents believe that religious belief should be based on experiential self knowledge and not on inherited dogma'.*

On seeing this I was filled with an immense and intense internal laughter. It was as if my entire life had been some sort of huge joke and I'd just been supplied with the punch line. This feeling grew into a intense feeling of happiness and warmth. Also it felt powerfully sexual in a strange and magnified kind of way. Then I felt being turned inside out, I lost my sense of the world and my body. Words cannot describe where I was or what I was at this stage. I was something totally outside the realm of space, time and matter. I was infinity and also eternity. Within my being was the totality of all things that are, all things that have been and all things that will ever be. I became God...

...Eventually and after an eternity I started to gradually re-enter physical reality and regain the sense of my body. My sense of time and space returned. Then I started to see a vision. I saw a huge chain of beads on a thread. The thread was endless and the beads seemed infinite. It was an awesome sight writhing and swirling like a dancing snake, but making movements and transforming itself like no physical animal could. This was against a backdrop of intricate geometric patterns. Multicoloured and pulsating, living and breathing somehow. It was like the geometric forms that decorate the inside of Muslim mosques, but the colors were much more intense and with a metallic quality. After a while something was happening to the beads. Each was breaking up and disintegrating.

I could see that each bead was hollow and the surface was like a thin membrane. The surface of each bead was unravelling into a spiral like the rind of a perfectly pealed orange or apple. Inside the unravelling rind were myriad fragments that were contained within each of the beads. Each of these fragments was in turn a bead but much tinier than the original that enclosed it. I saw that all these smaller beads were in turn strung together by the same thread that joined up the larger beads. In this way the larger beads and the smaller beads contained within the them were all joined up by a single continuous thread. The process repeated itself again and again. Each of the multitude of beads could unravel to show that they in turn contained another galaxy of tinier beads also linked together like a necklace, and so on.

Eventually something different happened. This time my focus was drawn to a single bead as it started to disintegrate and its skin started to unravel into a rind. I could see that the unravelling was very ordered and produced a long thin strip like an unravelled bandage made of some flexible material with a metallic sheen. I was drawn toward one end of this thin strip and then I could see images. I could hear sounds and I could feel sensations. I saw images of a baby, then images of a small child. I watched and then realized the baby and child was myself at different points in my life. I saw myself as a teenager, witnessed things that happened to me that I can remember today. There were happy moments, stressful moments and also traumatic ones. I literally saw my life flash by before me in a chronological sequence. As I saw myself progressing through my life and getting older, I realized what was happening. As this replay of my life was heading towards my current point in life, I felt an intense yearning to see beyond and know what was going to happen to me in the future. I witnessed some events associated with the time I spent working as a musician earlier that year and then things zoomed ahead towards my present situation. I felt a strong sense of excitement, I thought to myself 'Please let me see!, please let me see!'. But then the curtain was drawn shut and a veil was lowered. I regained my senses and was back in reality again.

It felt like those occasions when sometimes we experience a lucid dream and become fully conscious of ourselves while still dreaming. Usually when I start to lucid dream, I get so excited by what is happening to me and by all the things that I would like to do within the lucid dream that this causes me to wake up. And once I awaken from the dream it is impossible to return.

Once again I was sitting in a public library in London, and one of the librarians was walking around telling everybody that the library was about to close. I slowly got up and made my way to the exit. As I walked out of the building into Marylebone road, everything seemed to have a glowing aura around it. The buildings, the cars, the people. Life felt epic and awesome. Everything felt special and significant. Life was mythological and magic. A little earlier I was feeling exhausted and empty, now I felt invigorated and life became filled with meaning. As I walked home I remember I just couldn't stop smiling. I couldn't help thinking about the strange vision and the mysterious looking picture that contained my name in bold capital letters.

Later on I was able to figure out that what I saw was a vision giving me an insight into the nature of God and the relationship that individuals, including human beings, have in relation to God. I was shown the passage of the transmigration of the indivisible and undivided soul of the one ultimate God weaving through all the life forms of the Universe, sequentially one life at a time, one day at a time and one moment at a time. The beads in the vision were all the various life forms that have lived or will ever live in the Universe. And the single thread which passed through all the beads was the life journey of the one God spanning the lifetimes of all the creatures existing within one Cosmic Cycle containing the beginning and end of a Universe. The one God that was me, everybody and everything else. The initial string of beads that I saw in the vision were the life times of whole Universes strung out in a row, each bead corresponding to an entire Universe from beginning to end, all of them linked together in a never ending cycle of creation, destruction and rebirth.

This vision and experience so invigorated me, it seemed I had been given a vital piece of a large jig saw puzzle which made the other pieces that I already had fall into place. A lot of things which were opaque to me now made sense. Earlier that day I was feeling utterly alone, but now I felt that the entire Universe was with me. I was feeling that my life had totally lost its meaning but now my sense of mission had been restored. The days following this experience were filled with a wonderful afterglow. The grotesque image of the roosters head with the man's torso with snakes for legs would keep popping back into my mind.

Chapter 5

Apocalyptic Expectations

The year 1999 was a time when I was heavily influenced by the prophecies contained in the major religions of the World. During this period I existed a lot of the time in a state of fervent expectation. I thought something dramatic would happen that year which would profoundly change the World and alter the course of history. I fully expected this great happening to be somehow fully relevant to my own path.

The previous year 1998 was an eventful one. I had been working as a musician playing my electric guitar in various diverse and far flung places. During this time and also afterwards as well, I had several powerful mystical experiences accompanied by a series of vivid visions which I believe revealed to me something about the nature of God and the Universe. The most significant of these mystical experiences occurred towards the end of that year on the day of the Winter Solstice of 1998. This experience had been precipitated by a chance discovery of an ancient mystical symbol depicted in a book that contained my name 'WAI' in big bold letters. I felt the hand of providence guiding me and making things happen around me in order to lead me to my destiny. Just previously I had doubts about my life and my path but after this experience I felt a strong sense of certainty in the correctness of what I was doing with my life.

So I started out in the beginning of the year 1999 with a strong sense of mission and in a highly motivated state. I was making a lot of plans, my head was filled with thoughts about how I was going to communicate to the World the idea that everyone is God. I was very focused on my goals and kept myself very busy working steadily throughout January and February. Then in late February something unplanned happened. Quite by chance in a cafe I met a young French woman. We had a brief and intense relationship, we seemed to have so much in common. It felt great, and gradually by stages as I got to know her better, I was falling in love with her. I don't know if I was yearning for a partner or a mother substitute but it didn't really matter. It soon dawned on me that I really wanted her. But then she dumped me.

I'm still not sure what happened. I think perhaps my strong sense of purpose and the strength of my convictions, gave me an attractive presence; but my lack of a job, money or status in society worked against me. I really don't know. There were aspects to my character and physical appearance which would have been attractive to members of the opposite sex. However as people got to know me and discovered what I was really about, learned about my goals and beliefs then generally people I met would become horrified. The details of what my life was about, probably gave most people the strong impression that I was totally insane.

So I spent most of 1999 feeling broken hearted. It felt quite bad and I had never experienced it so severely before. Despite this troubling pain or perhaps as a direct result of it, I managed to have probably one of the most creative periods of my life. I remember suffering from an intense depression in the Spring of 1999 but then rebounding from it into a very motivated and productive mind set. My head wasn't in a very happy state and I felt agitated and discontent a lot of the time. Yet out of this state of angst I was able to get a lot done.

My mind seemed to produce an unending stream of interesting and useful ideas concerning the brain and functioning of the human mind. Increasingly I was seeing deep and close relationships between the workings of the brain and the workings of the Universe. In trying to understand the mind of man, I realized I was at the same time getting a glimpse into the mind of God. And also, while I was studying mystical concepts and ideas relating to God; I would constantly be finding correspondences between that and what I knew about the brain and mind.

Over the years I had formulated many ideas and concepts in order to understand and explain how the brain and mind worked. Now over the course of the Summer, all these ideas started to fully connect with the mystical visions that I had seen. Two separate worlds in my mind, the mystical and spiritual versus the scientific world of Brain Science and Artificial Intelligence, started to converge and join seamlessly with each other. It was an awesome feeling to experience what seemed like a cosmic revelation unfolding in my mind. I had a tremendous feeling of destiny. It felt as if my life had been a process of integrating the myriad fractured pieces of some vast puzzle. I had been assembling the smaller pieces to make larger pieces, and then in turn assembling those pieces to make even larger ones and so on. Now it seemed that two very large and integrated pieces of the puzzle that I had pieced together over the years were coming together and interlocking perfectly. I believed I was seeing truths that had never before been apprehended. It felt good and so it was for several months.

A lot of interesting ideas concerning the brain that had been floating around in my head for years, were really coming together. If before I was only really seeing the trees, now I was starting to see the whole forest. I made a lot of progress at this time in my long term project of understanding how the brain and mind worked. So a lot of my time at this point in my life was therefore taken up by intellectual pursuits.

Apart from that, 1999 was the year that Millennial fever gripped me. I was already somebody with a keen interest in the prophecies for the end times contained in the world's major religions. So I was expecting something dramatic to perhaps happen sometime this year or early in the next. This state of expectation was further heightened when I saw a series of documentaries about the prophet Nostradamus shown on Channel 4. Previously I was rather skeptical about the writings of Nostradamus, in the same way I don't pay much attention to Horoscopes. I only considered prophesies contained in the scriptures of the worlds religions to be valid. However, as I watched and learned more about the life and predictions of Nostradamus, my mind changed. I recall, I was quite impressed by what seemed to me to be clear prevision of the place and circumstance of the assassinations of the Pope and also of J.F. Kennedy. As a result of this, when I learned about the famous or perhaps notorious Nostradamus prophecy for some great awakening in month seven of 1999, I believed something would happen in July of that year, something significant, life changing and perhaps even a little apocalyptic.

I remember how on the last day of July in 1999, after nothing had yet happened that month, I devoted that whole day in search of a sign from the Universe. I did something similar the previous year during the Winter Solstice and something extraordinary did happen; so that taken together with the Nostradamus prediction put me into a keen state of expectation and hope. But all that day, absolutely nothing happened, nothing mystically significant and certainly nothing worth mentioning. I was definitely disappointed. So the exact date i.e. Month Seven of 1999 mentioned in the Nostradamus prophecy came and went without incident.

I returned my focus to my work, but my millennial fever returned a month or so later when there was a full Solar Eclipse in the August of that year. Again, I thought that this would be the trigger for some major event of far reaching effect on my life and the fate of the planet. But again, nothing happened. I saw the eclipse, but then life went on as usual, without any sort of noticeable spiritual transition in society at large or any sort of change at all. So I continued with my work.

September came and things slowed down a little. I had a very productive Summer but now my creative run was coming to an end. The ideas no longer flowed as my mental fluidity and energy levels became lower, however at this time, rather thankfully the troubling pain that I had carried with me all throughout that year, in the back of my mind, as a result of my failure in love, eased. In retrospect I suspect now that perhaps this background angst that I carried with me all Summer, actually helped to fuel my work and creativity. So I took things a little more easier at this point and relaxed my pace a little. This state of relative tranquility was disturbed by a series of uncanny coincidences or what might be called synchronicities which led up to a strange mystical experience in an Evangelical Church.

One day I was walking along to the house of a friend I had known from school in Ipswich and who was, like myself, now living in London. We'd kept in contact and would see each other from time to time, on this occasion we were going to have some food together and catch up with each others news. When I came to the beginning of his street I noticed a large poster advertising something called the 'Alpha Course'. According to the information on the poster it had something to do with Philosophy and Christianity. I must have taken note of the poster without really thinking much about it.

As I chatted with my friend over dinner We caught up on things and the conversation meandered towards discussing what various mutual acquaintances of ours were doing. At some point my friend mentioned that his brother had moved to London and was now working in a church in London. He said he had become involved in something called the Alpha Course. I mentioned the poster I had seen on the end of his street. My friend then told me that the church where his brother was working was the headquarters of this Alpha Course. As we talked on, he went on to describe where this church was located, in the Kensington/Knightsbridge area of London. It occurred to me that I knew this church well.

Quite by chance it happened to be the church that was located almost next door to where I first lived when I came to London. It was less than a minutes walking distance from the University Halls of Residence where I lived during my first year in college. The church was the Holy Trinity Brompton in Knightsbridge. I had a nightly routine of visiting some nearby shops that opened 24 hours a day, in the early hours of the morning. On the return journey, weather permitting, I would sit in the churchyard located around the church, which was between where I lived and the shops. As I sat I would proceed to eat the snacks that I'd recently purchased and think about life and whatever was on my mind at the time.

All these connected coincidences, the large poster advertising the Alpha Course, then my friend's brother happening to be involved with it and then also the headquarters of this Christian movement located in the church I used to live next door to. I sensed a strong feeling that through these synchronicities I was being given a message by the Universe. So I had to find out what these coincidences meant. Soon after, my friend and I both enrolled on the 'Alpha Course' to see what it was all about.

A few weeks later, I found myself queuing with my friend outside the church where we were about to find out what this Alpha Course was all about. It was a pleasant Autumn evening in late September. The queue was very long, this Alpha Course had obviously attracted some interest. I found the surroundings very familiar, just how I remembered it all those years ago. We were near the end of the queue and it moved quite slowly. It was a relief when one of the stewards allowed us to jump the queue and go right to the front. This was probably due to my friend's brother working at the church. It added to the sense that I had been directed here by the Hand of Providence. I felt excited it seemed to me like a little adventure.

Inside, the church was large and quite modern looking. We were provided with some dinner from the serving area and sat down to eat and chatted with some of the other attendees. I noticed that most of the people present were young adults in roughly the same age group as myself or perhaps slightly older. On talking to a few people I also got the impression that there were a disproportionate number of people from the commonwealth countries i.e. Australia, New Zealand, Canada and South Africa. I had already read somewhere that the process of secularisation was a generation behind in the former colonies, so this made perfect sense to me. The people were very nice, decent, respectable and clean. Definitely the sort of people your mother would like you to be friends with. All the while I was feeling a growing excitement and there was a strong sense that something important was going to happen. I also had this expectation in the back of my mind in the days leading up to this moment.

After the food everyone sat down in rows in front of a stage area in preparation to hear the sermon. There was some singing of hymns, which I found difficulty in joining in with. The music accompanying the hymns was quite catchy in a funny sort of way but the words to the music sounded cheesy and uncool, they were all about praising Jesus. I couldn't relate to it at all. Then a strange feeling came over me, a sort of nausea combined with a sense of heightened attention. My heart was beating fast. I thought at the time perhaps it was the food not agreeing with my constitution. I started to sweat. It was warm and I could feel surges of adrenaline going through my body. When the singing stopped and the sermon started I started to relax a bit but still felt strange.

As the sermon progressed and I started to digest what the preacher was saying I started to feel agitated. I was a little incredulous at the things I heard, some of which to me were very obviously false. Here I heard with my own

75

ears what I already knew some Christians believed, that is the idea that all of the Bible was literally true. The Bible was being presented as the infallible word of God. Up until then, I'd always had the idea that this version of Christianity was only really believed by simple Hill Billy people living in the more remote parts of America. But here I was seeing and hearing an obviously highly educated and well spoken person, talking the grossest nonsense about religion and Christianity. Also I got a strong sense of the intolerant nature of this Alpha Course when the speaker talked about the invalidity of other religions. I distinctly recall the speaker saying word directly to the effect that a good Alpha Course student should of course be tolerant of other peoples religious beliefs while at the same time recognising that they're wrong. So I switched off a little and went into my own thoughts. I reflected on the whole situation and realized that even though I felt a liking for the people around me, at the same time I also felt a sense of detachment.

The sermon ended and there was more singing. By now I really felt an aversion to the substance of the sermon and what the Alpha Course was all about. As the music and mass of singing voices flowed and swirled around me I could feel my perception and state of mind change markedly. I slipped into an altered state of consciousness and everything around me became subtly but distinctly transformed.

Things started to look strangely cartoony and the people around me seemed to take on something of a slightly doll like appearance. Time seemed to slow down and the singing became unintelligible as if everyone was now singing in some exotic foreign European language. I felt a terrific surge of adrenaline and my heart was beating fast. I felt a bit dizzy and disorientated but tried not to let it show. But soon a relative calmness set in and I could think more clearly.

Then I went further into this altered state of consciousness and had a vision where my whole perception of the church and my immediate surroundings changed. The church became like an ark or some ship coursing through the ocean deep. I no longer felt that I was in Knightsbridge, London, where the church was located.

Then I felt a strong presence of evil outside this church or ark where I now was. It was as if all the troubles, suffering and evils of this Universe were located immediately outside the church but were being restrained and kept out by the walls of this sanctuary. I imagined all the demonic, destructive and life harming forces of the world lurking immediately outside this protective bubble called the church, seeking to demolish and devour. I could totally sense the presence of what I imagined. I gazed at the people around me and outwardly they seemed happy and quite contented. But then I saw everybody around me in a completely new light. I saw deep inside them and felt their inner pain, their sadness and their fear. I felt affinity and compassion for them even a sense of love.

These feelings of empathy were not very common place during that point of my life, which was lived almost completely detached from the life and the world of most people. But in this instance I felt a connection with the people around me. We were all together in this ocean of darkness trying to reach some place of light and security. We were all in this ship trying to find its way to the safe shores but I also knew in my mind that this particular ship had lost its course. It protected people from evil and promised salvation but had no idea about what salvation was. It didn't know how to steer towards the light. It was hopelessly lost at sea, all the while believing that it knew the true path.

Then I thought how ironic it all was. The lost sheep were convinced that they knew the way home and also that, only they knew and nobody else. After a while I came to and things seemed more normal again. However I remained in a highly charged state and this might have made me seem a bit distant to some of the people I later interacted with. My head was racing with thoughts and images.

The evening came to a close and I proceed to walk a while with my friend. Together we cut across Hyde Park which was close by. I said goodbye to my friend at Marble Arch tube station and then feeling energetic I decided to walk the mile or so to Primrose hill in order to have a think. My head was buzzing with thoughts about religion.

While I gazed out over London on the top of Primrose Hill I reflected on the events of that evening. I felt I had got new insights into the meaning and importance of religion. I felt a certain distaste for the variety of religion I had just encountered earlier. It seemed very different from religion as I understood it. I didn't have a label for it at the time but after a little further investigation, I discovered that what the Alpha Course represented is religious fundamentalism. It was the anti-thesis of what I was about and what I represented. This religious fundamentalism was the religion of intolerance and small minded bigotry. The religion of rules & regulations; fantasies, fairy tales and fables taken as literal and absolute truth.

Then I reflected on my life and came to some realizations. I realized that at some point in the future, my ideas would come into conflict with those of the religious fundamentalists of this world. The same kind that I had encountered earlier who insisted that every word of the Bible was absolutely true and that it should be taken quite literally. I felt a sense of trembling when I considered what I was up against. I felt my life being steered towards the world of main-stream religion. So I first started to see that my purpose was ultimately bound up with the world of established religion. This was something new to me.

Up till then, even though I already had it in my mind that the purpose of my life was to communicate my ideas about the divine and the mystical revela-tions I had experienced. However up to that point I had it in mind that I would be talking about these things to people much like myself. I had imagined that my future audience would be the young and open minded, Neo Pagans , New Age types, the Psychedelic crowd and assorted open minded and progressive liberal intelligentsia. The kind of people who were interested in questions concerning God, existence, mind, consciousness and the meaning of life.

Now I felt I was being directed by the Universe to prepare myself to communicate my message to the mainstream and the sort of people who would get involved in Organized Religion and Cults. I didn't feel up to the task. This world of Organized Religion, Sects and Cults was a scene that I had long considered corrupted and spiritually bankrupt. There seemed to me a total incompatibility between what I was doing and what existing religion was all about. How can you possibly communicate to a Fundamentalist Christian or Muslim say, that he or she is God? I felt it was an impossible goal. I felt a certain level of fear and trepidation.

Then I thought about the meaning of the strange coincidence relating to the location of the church from where I had just come. It seemed to me a little uncanny that this church should be located right next door to the university where I studied and which was my first home in London. It felt highly significant because the university where I studied also happened to be one of the densest concentrations of Scientific and Technological research in the UK. This physical juxtaposition between on the one hand, a World respected centre of Scientific research and on the other the central headquarters of what might be called the Fundamentalist led Christian revival in the United Kingdom made me think about the relationship between science and religion. This juxtaposition between science and religion would mysteriously keep recurring in my life.

I thought about the kind of people I met at Imperial College, it was full of Atheist Scientists and Technologists. What would these sorts of people think about what I was doing and what I believed. They would have certainly considered me totally insane or perhaps merely a bit deluded. How would you go about explaining to these sorts of people that their real identity is God and that we are all one consciousness? Wouldn't it be just a hopeless as trying to do the same with a Religious Fundamentalist?

Then a strange sensation came over me, a sort of afterglow of my earlier state of mind. I was standing at the top of Primrose rose hill looking over London. The city now seemed to have a sort of aura around it which wasn't there a little earlier. My visual perception was slightly altered again but not to the extent or the way it was earlier in the evening. Then my mind became very lucid and in an instant it all became clear to me. I saw what a perfect set up reality was. The scales fell from my eyes and I saw how everything that had happened in my life had already been perfectly set up by something outside of myself. I had a strong sense that the things that were happening to me in my life were carefully scripted by a reasoning yet inscrutable Cosmic Intelligence.

I thought about the synchronicity trail that had led me to this current moment stood on top of Primrose Hill and the events earlier that day. I thought about the visit to the church, the funny coincidence that it was practically next door to where I used to live and where I studied. I thought about the friend's brother who happened to find himself working there and the poster advertising the activities of the church that I saw at the end of the street where my friend lived. Then I reflected on the events of the previous year, all the circumstances that lead to the powerful mystical experiences that I had culminating in the seemingly chance discovery of the ancient mystical symbol that had my name written on it in big bold letters.

Then I thought about all the events and experiences over my entire life leading up to my current circumstances, the kind of person I was and the unusual goals I had set myself in life. I reflected on my obsession with the idea of working out how the brain worked and creating Artificial Intelligence that had mostly characterized my life from my late teens onward. I traced back the events and circumstances of my childhood that had led to my fascination with computers and so onto my obsession with the brain and Artificial Intelligence.

It seemed very clear to me that everything that had ever happened in my life had been totally preordained. It seemed as if everything was just too perfect to be down to chance or contingency. I directly apprehended how every little step and everything that had ever happened to me, all the minute details of my life had been meticulously planned and intricately put together in order to bring me exactly to what I was doing with my life.

My thoughts then wandered back further and I thought about my ancestral past and close associations that my ethnic group had with the process of revolution and reform in Chinese history. But then wasn't this what I hoped to ultimately achieve, that is, a revolution in the realm of ideas and a reformation of peoples beliefs. I considered the way that I had come to be living in the UK. How my ancestors had fled to one of the Southern most points in China i.e. Hong Kong, most probably to escape from the Chinese Imperial Authorities. Which then just happened to be the place chosen by the 19th century British Imperials for their base for selling Opium to China. And then how this detail of history, would many years later in the following century, lead to my family emigrating to the United Kingdom. Which then put me in a position to be living in London and speaking English, which for what I was doing was the perfect place to be and the perfect language to be working in. What an absolutely perfect set up I thought to myself.

I then further extended this line of thinking to everything that had happened on the planet even in the distant past and then right back to the beginning of time and the birth of the Universe. Then again, I comprehended just how intricately the cosmic plan was contrived. Everything was planned, everything that has ever happened or will happen in the Universe right down to the last detail. Right down to the last detail of the position of every single atom. Sometimes Providence reveals herself in an obvious way perhaps in the form of uncanny coincidences or synchronicities, but it went much further than that. Absolutely everything that occurs, has occurred or will occur does so through the hand of Providence. In my day to day life I had the normal assumption that I was the doer of my actions and the thinker of my thoughts. But I apprehended in a very powerful and direct way, that I am not the thinker, it is the Universe that thinks through me and that I am not the mover, but rather it was the Universe that was moving.

I was in something of a mystical state accompanied by an awesome feeling of destiny and an immense sense of fate. My life will be devoted to communicating to the whole World the ultimate truth that a person's real identity is God and that we are all one consciousness. I saw clearly that my purpose and my mission was to make this idea of the 'Oneness' and total inter-connectedness of all things, understandable and perhaps even acceptable to everybody, Scientist and Spiritualist, Atheist and Agnostic, Secular Humanist and Religious Fundamentalist, Young and Old, Wise and Simple, everybody.

I saw a gigantic task ahead of me, a seemingly impossible mission ahead. But who was I to take this on? Who was I to believe that I could possibly succeed in this incredibly ambitious aim of taking the most inaccessible of truths and communicating it to the World. I was nowhere in this life, a poor isolated stranger and complete nobody. Someone with very little resources and few friends or connections. All I had in this world were my ideas and my dreams. All I owned were my notes, my books and my electric guitar. Surely I was deluding myself. Once again I felt discouraged and full of self doubt. I didn't feel up to the task.

I further reflected on my situation in life and the circumstances earlier in the year surrounding how I got this point. I thought about the meaning of my life long obsession with trying to work out how the brain worked. That Summer I had a most creative period where my ideas had evolved rapidly and I had gained many new insights into how the brain worked. I started to see the big picture and had a strong feeling that I was on the right track. At the very least, I believed that I was far ahead of anything that was happening in academia and the big research institutions. What I would read about the latest brain theories being talked about in science magazines and academic research papers, I found primitive and limited. Though my own theory was incomplete it was starting to become very encompassing and powerful. Also to me it seemed I had an amazingly elegant and beautiful way of describing a lot of data about the brain in a unifying way, and far more advanced than anything else out there.

Relating my thoughts about my brain theory to the earlier thoughts about the perfect set up that reality was, I then saw clearly that likewise my work on the brain was similarly guided by providence. Then I extrapolated into the future and felt sure that my theory would turn out to be correct. This was because my entire interest in the brain and all the work and study I had put in to working out how it all worked, had also all been part of the Cosmic setup that had lead me towards and made it my purpose to communicate to the World that 'Everyone is God'. For it was my neuroscientific and technological quest that led me in a roundabout way to the discovery of my true nature.

It seemed utterly clear to me that I could hope and even expect to achieve my ultimate aims. Like in the Star Wars movie I strongly felt that 'The Force' was with me. Providence will be my guide and my helper, for it seemed so obvious to me now that she had always been.

All the pieces of my life were coming together. Everything that had happened in my life had lead me up to this point and also prepared me all along, for me to do what I had to do and what I had to do was this. I would continue my work on the brain theory and inevitably I will complete it and produce something compelling, even definitive. Then in the future this would give me the necessary platform and sanction in order to communicate the truth that 'Everyone is God'.

Why should it be any other way. I had already arrived at the conclusion that the mystery of God and the mystery of Consciousness were one and the same. Therefore who else will have more authority to tell the World what is the nature of Consciousness than the person who also explains to the World how the brain works. So therefore in so doing I'll also be explaining the nature of God. Once again it seemed so perfect. So set up.

Then I felt a surge of energy flowing through me and I became gripped by a feeling of determination and resolve. My life had seemed like a random muddle. My teenage ambition of trying to work out how the brain worked had taken my life on a strange trajectory. I had led an extremely turbulent and chaotic life which led me to becoming some sort of crazy modern day mystic. But now things no longer seemed so random but rather completely ordered. Things had been completely set up to create somebody whose aim it was to try to explain the notion that a person's real identity is God. I also saw very clearly that the theory of the brain that I had spent the better part of my life working on was also part of this set up. My scientific and technological aims in life regarding the brain theory and the creation of artificial intelligence, would be the stepping stone which would enable me to complete the bigger goal of explaining to the World that Everyone is God.

My perspective had completely shifted. What had seemed an impossible and futile task, now seemed completely achievable, indeed inevitable. I thought now that the current atheistic and materialistic ideas associated with science were mere passing fads. A temporary aberration from the true state of being. The nonsensical beliefs of the Religious Fundamentalist were mere comfort mechanisms, opium for the people as it were, or else a vehicle for tribal and nationalistic instincts. All of this nonsense would surely be replaced by something far better. Something that is also the original truth at the heart of religion and something that is completely compatible with science and reason; and as I discovered later on in my journey, something that gave rise to science and the age of reason in the first place.

A little earlier on I was considering how futile it would be to try to communicate the truth that 'Everyone is God' to most normal people and in particular very religious people or those who were very scientistically minded. But now it seemed to me that what I was wanting to convey was exactly what they needed to know.

Once again I was standing on Primrose Hill London gazing out over the city. Only now my wider outlook had completely changed. The separate pieces of the jigsaw puzzle that made up who I was had come together. It felt that I had become awakened to what I had to do in the world and with this life. I had fully woken up to my purpose and who I was.

The rest of that year after the mystical episode at the top of Primrose Hill was quite inspired by all the plans and thoughts that were in my head. My work progressed steadily. There was now a definite sense of mission if before there were a cluster of partially defined and loosely connected goals. Now all the separate strands of my life had merged. The time I spent studying the brain and thinking about how it worked became directly relevant to the spiritual side of things. And the time I spent reading religious texts, meditating and contemplating the sacred became bound up with the scientific and technological side of my life.

Earlier that year I had been gripped by Millennial fever. Because of the year i.e. 1999, I strongly entertained for a while the possibility that something earth shattering was going to happen. So at various stages in that year I would find myself in a state of anticipation and expectation. But nothing happened. The famous Nostradamus prediction didn't come to pass and the solar eclipse of that year was pretty unremarkable. After this, my attitude towards the prophecies changed. The prophecies were not something to wait for and passively witness the unfolding of.

Instead if I truly believed that I was God, which to me was the only certainty that a person could ever have, then surely I should take a more proactive view of things. In the same way that God was not something that was to be found outside of myself then by the same token, the prophecies were not something that would unfold purely through some outside supernatural agency. I started to develop the viewpoint that humans becoming agents actively involved in the unfolding of the prophecies and helping to bring them about went hand in hand with the idea that Everyone is God. That as God we indeed create our own realities and should therefore take it upon ourselves to change the World. Later on I would learn that this proactive perspective on things is known as 'Providentialism', whereby humans are the agency that realizes the prophecies. It would become an important part of the message.

As a manifestation of the one God in a human body with a finite life span and limited physical powers, I knew I couldn't influence the motions of the planets or alter the positions of the stars. However if Providence allowed and fate intended, or put another way, if the Force was with me; then I should certainly be able to figure out how the brain worked, create artificial intelligence and explain to the world the mystery of consciousness which is also the nature of God. So these were my relatively modest aims at this point in the story. The goals and scope of the mission would expand greatly later on in my life.

By the time it came to the end of the year I had no prophetic expectations for anything to happen on the last day of the year when 1999 would become the year 2000. Having a background in computer science I did think that perhaps there may be some sort of catastrophic technological software failure as some commentators had predicted. The so called Y2K bug that was supposed to bring down a lot of computing infrastructure at the stroke of midnight in the first moments of 2000. But even that didn't happen. Nothing apocalyptic happened, but why should it have?

The outcome and unfolding of the prophecies is something that we create, not something that just happens. I still firmly believed that the prophecies are now. That is, the prophecies of the worlds major religions are talking about presents times and the current state of the world. I felt incredibly fortunate to be living at such a critical and momentous juncture in world history and the destiny of the human race. As the year 1999 unfolded I gained for myself a much better understanding of what my exact role was in this World. All I wanted in life was to be a part of the process whereby the proper unfolding of the prophecies and a happy outcome to the problems of this world, would be realized. I was so very happy to be living in 'interesting times'.

Chapter 6

The Wilderness

After the year 1999, which was a time filled, on and off, with apocalyptic expectation; there followed an extended period of reflection and exploration. I would spend a fair bit of time checking out the religions and various cults found in London. It was a time of incubation and an important formative period. I knew what I had to do with my life, the problem now was figuring out exactly how to do it. It was a time when I started to see much more clearly what the mystical path involved. I also had to come to terms with and direct towards constructive purposes strong messianic impulses which were entering my mind at this time.

The year is 2000, I was 30 years old and almost my entire adult life had been spent in a state of separation and alienation from normal society, the world of careers, child rearing, mortgages and paying taxes. I now had it in my mind to come back into the world and share the things that I had learned. I was now on a mission to try to explain to the wider world this idea that a person's true identity was really God and also that the prophecies found in the World's religions were manifesting in present times. All of these aims in turn merged with the original goal I had set myself during my teens, that of figuring out how the human brain worked and the creation of artificial intelligence. I was very fired up with zeal and enthusiasm for all the goals that I wanted to accomplish, but at the same time my years of dysfunctional living, had left me inadequate with respect to the aims that I had set myself.

For years, to the neglect of most other things, what had mainly occupied my time was reading, writing, thinking, meditating and guitar playing. These activities mostly defined my life from the time of leaving home to go to university right up to the time currently under discussion. So as a result of this I was quite unworldly and quite lacking in some of the basic skills required for modern living, such as waking up at a decent hour, being able to hold down a job and keeping appointments with people. There followed a period of preparation and training, where I identified the skills I needed and then set about to acquire them.

The first thing I needed to acquaint myself with was the world of religion. If the purpose of my life was to communicate the truth about God then it was necessary for me to know what people thought about God and also what the World's religions had to say on the matter. So from around the year 2000 onwards and also slightly before, I set about going all over London to join in with religious activities and also to talk with religious and culty people in order to discuss their beliefs and get to know what sort of people believed in what. In other words to get into the mind of the religious believer and see things from their perspective.

I would visit churches, temples, mosques and the headquarters of various sects and cults or any religious festival that I knew was going on in town. This field study was much augmented by book learning and the things I would read at any one moment would have correspondence with the places and religions that I was visiting during that time. So for instance, If I happened to be visiting a lot of Buddhist temples and meeting a lot of Buddhists then I would spend a lot of time reading Buddhist scriptures and also learn about the history of Buddhism from various sources. The religion or cult that I was investigating at any one time would focus my studies around relevant material and really helped to integrate all the facts in my head in a meaningful way. So these visits to religious and culty places allowed me to meet and discuss with the appropriate people, the things that I had read and which would be on my mind.

I had a definite idea of what the truth was i.e. that Everyone was God, and this was often not the same view that other religious people had. So these meetings would often degenerate into a debate when I would express my own religious views as reasonably and persuasively as I could, but of course my views were usually seen as quite heretical and aberrant. However these discussions and meetings really aided my study of religion and gave me practice in talking about and presenting my viewpoint.

Another beneficial side effect of all these visits to the cults and religions based in London was that these sorts of places could be a great opportunity to get a free meal. It seemed to be a standard culty recruitment technique, i.e. feed them, befriend them, then indoctrinate them. Often because this was the underlying intent, the food could actually be quite good. So my genuine interest in religion had the positive consequence of improving my diet as well augmenting my spiritual perspectives on life. I actually worked out that with detailed knowledge of the times during which free food was served by the various cults and religious organizations based in London, and a willingness to travel around a bit; then you could satisfy most of your nutritional requirements while at the same time hang out with religious or culty people. These were exactly the sort of people who were most interesting to me at this point in my life.

Years ago I was living with beggars, degenerates and social outcasts, sometimes feeling like David Attenborough or some ethologist doing a field study. I seemed to be repeating the same process in the land of cults and organized religion, studying the people I found in this quite different context.

It was during this period of investigating into the nature of religion that I learned that the idea that everyone is God can be found at the heart of all the World's great faith traditions. This came about partly as a result of the fact that around this time I was trying to convince religious people of various faiths that their true identity was God. So in order to do this I had to learn about their faiths in order to communicate with them in a way that they could appreciate. This led me to systematically read up on the history and development of the World's religions, which led to the following great discovery.

Almost without exception, a pattern was repeated in the evolution of all the world's religions. Time and time again, the idea that a person's true identity is God was the seed and catalyst that would kick start and stimulate the formation of a religion in the first place. A prophet would experience being one with God and it was this which was key to the initial formulation of religion. Then over the course of time this truth would be obscured, censored and suppressed so that later on this central idea behind all World religion would become forgotten and lost. Often the truth would be maintained by esoteric sects or unorthodox sub-groupings of the World's religions. Ironically these esoteric sects which held the original truths that the founders of religion believed themselves, would be considered by their co-religionists as heretics or even apostates. So for example we find the Gnosticism, Rosicrucianism & Freemasonry existing withing Christianity; the Sufis of Islam and the Kabbalah mystics of Judaism, the Tantrikas and Advaita Vedanta of Hinduism etc. Anyway, back to my story...

So I was preparing myself for what I had to do with my life which was to communicate to the world the idea that everyone is God and also that the prophesies of the World's religions were manifesting in present times. I decided that a key skill I needed to get to grips with was how to implement web sites and to learn how the internet and world wide web worked.

It was rather fortuitously and quite synchronous that in the fall of 2000, I was put on a government run training program which taught unemployed outcasts like myself how to write HTML (which is an acronym for Hyper Text Mark-up Language), which is the script in which internet websites are written. Later after the course finished, I stayed on with the organization which ran the web design course working as a trainer. This enabled me to sharpen my web design skills. It also gave me a 9 to 5 routine of having to wake up at a decent hour and going to an office like environment five days a week. This helped my reassimilation into normal mainstream society. I think the process of trying to teach people how to create their own websites and explaining to them various aspects of how computers and the Internet worked was actually a useful activity in gearing me up to later explain to people that they were God.

This routine lasted about half a year into the Spring of 2001. During this time I also kept up my religious studies and also taught myself a lot about information technology, including things which I considered useful for my mission. This included new developments in IT that had occurred since I finished my degree in computing science some 10 years previous to this time. And so in this way I equipped myself with technological skills useful for communicating my religious and mystical ideas.

At this point in my life there existed in me a terrific tension. There was a massive gulf between my world changing aspirations on the one hand, and my day to day reality on the other. In many respects and in the eyes of most people I was something of a complete failure. So much had been expected of me by my peers and people who knew me as I was growing up. But I hadn't achieved anything much at all that was visible. I had not really accumulated anything much tangible with my life. No assets, nor gained any status or any sort of recognition within wider society. I felt like a sort of loser, an underdog. Often during the day and early evening, my head would be filled with awesome thoughts, my mind would soar majestically in the realm of ideas and visions. But then this would often be punctuated by a crashing fall when I came back down to earth to the reality of my physical circumstances and the life I was leading.

I recall that at around this time in my life I would sometimes entertain intense Messianic thoughts. For instance sometimes I would think about mystical things, contemplate at length my true nature as God and this might lead me into thinking of doing Messianic things. Or lead me to thinking that I was the chosen one and had a special unique role to play in the proper unfolding of the World drama. At the same time I was keenly aware that I was absolutely nowhere in this World, a sort of under achieving drop out and lonely clown. I recalled that during my time spent in the psychedelic underworld, from time to time I would come across people who had Messianic aspirations. How I enjoyed making fun of them and thinking how ridiculousness they were. Now here I was the most ridiculous one of them all.

This Messianic undercurrent had already been a background feature of my life and make up. A year or so earlier in 1999, I had in the back of my mind anticipated that the Nostradamus prophecy which predicted some happening in the July of that year, the awakening of the *'King of the Mongols'*, might involve something either directly or indirectly happening to me personally. However nothing transpired, yet still the belief clung to me that somehow in my life I would be playing some sort of instrumental role in the unfolding of the prophecies. Also in the Winter Solstice of late 1998 I experienced a strange synchronicity, accompanied by a powerful mystical experience of being one with God, when I stumbled across a depiction of the Gnostic God Abraxas and which had my name written underneath it in big bold letters. This had encouraged me to believe that I was destined for something unusual and dramatic.

I suppose this messianic outlook would have mainly come about through these mystical experiences of being God that affected me so much in the previous few years. Also this attitude would probably also have been due to the fact that even before my life had taken something of a religious turn, I was already embarked on an undertaking which I believed would have World changing consequences, i.e. working out how the brain worked and creating artificial intelligence. My intention and long term goal had always been to do something significant with my life. After the discovery that my real identity is God and my life taking on a decidedly mystical and religious orientation, then how I saw my role and purpose in this World, started to border on the messianic with the occasional complete crossing over.

Three things would conspire around 2000 to 2001 to make me think hard about messianic matters. They were in chronological order, firstly watching the Matrix movie in the Spring of 2000, secondly a computer game called 'Deus Ex' which captured my attention in the Summer of 2000 and thirdly watching the TV adaptation of the Dune Trilogy books in early 2001. All three of these media influences had a very high messianic content. The sci-fi Movie and modern myth, The Matrix was about a prophesied chosen one who would save a world and release an enslaved people. The computer game Deus Ex involved a character who as the game progressed would hold the fate of the World in his hands and determine the future of the planet. Finally the Dune TV series based on the books by Frank Herbert was a modern Myth set on another World, also involving mystical experiences and a prophesied messianic character who would revitalize a troubled world and bring about a better new order. I see in retrospect how these modern myths, two in the form of video media and the other communicated as a computer game, influenced me and inspired in me some wild messianic thoughts.

The story lines behind the Matrix movie and Dune are quite well known and follow the classic mythic as well as apocalyptic archetypes. They are inspiring modern myths along the same lines as the Star Wars movie or the Lord of the Rings books and films. Whereas the game Deus Ex and the story line behind it is not so well know and actually quite obscure so we'll provide a quick summary here. I should note also that this game has been said in various places to be one of the best of all time.

The game is set in the future with a look and feel that was influenced by the Matrix film. The undercurrent of the game was one of conspiracy theories and a number of different groups vying for power and world domination. In this context the main character who was controlled by the player of the game had to work his way through this game world, learning about all the plots and sub plots, all the while gaining skills and abilities, as well as weaponry. Eventually through the twist and turns of the game's story line the main character, i.e. the player, would find himself at the centre of all the intrigues, at the heart of the world conspiracy and be in a position to determine the future outcome of history choosing one of several endings, one where he effectively becomes like a Messiah figure, another involving plunging the world into a state of chaos and the other is where he helps a secret society to maintain their control of world events. All the endings are world changing.

It has been said that the interactive nature of computer games may have the effect of influencing people's behaviour in real life. This may or may not be the case, but this particular computer game Deus Ex certainly served to accentuate certain attitudes and beliefs that I already had and would definitely have encouraged certain sorts of behaviours and thoughts of the Messianic variety. In particular I remember how one piece of dialogue in the game Deus Ex grabbed my attention and stimulated a lot of thinking. At one point in the game one of the central characters was talking about some of the central motives and beliefs behind world politics and world history. He described how the adherents and members of the secret societies believed that, *'The most enlightened or intelligent man will eventually seize the Eye in the Pyramid and remake the World for everyone else.'* I remember how this one piece of dialogue really caught my imagination. This will perhaps seem laughable to a lot people, the fact that I thought I was receiving deep and meaningful messages from a computer game. Nonetheless I believed it gave me an insight into what the unfolding of the prophecies and a Messianic role might involve.

The Eye in the Pyramid is a recurring theme in the conspiracy theory literature. It is widely seen to represent one vast world encompassing dominance hierarchy with the top of the pyramid, i.e. the Eye, being the overall point of power and apex of control. A symbol found on every US one dollar bill, it is often associated with Freemasonry and the mysterious, perhaps completely fictitious, 'Illuminati'; who are widely believed by conspiracy theorists to be a continuation of the more historic Bavarian Illuminati allegedly controlled by the Rothchilds banking interests of Europe from a few hundred years ago, to present times. The pyramid is also associated with the Masonic 'Great work of the ages', which some conspiracy theorists interpret as the building of a Tyrannical One World Order. So in one sense the building of the great pyramid is still a work in progress or the 'Great Work' in progress. A crown for the jewel and a seat in which the eye may sit.

Reflecting on the state of the world, I saw a hierarchy of nested pyramids, each one a organizational hierarchy and all the pyramids of various sizes and scattered all over the planet. These pyramids were essentially formalized status hierarchies. So for instance each country and its respective social and political structures would form a pyramid. In turn each of these societal pyramids would be made up of smaller constituents pyramids which might be various legal or political institutions and also perhaps corporations, conglomerates or other sorts of commercial entities. I also saw how these smaller constituent pyramids would become merged together into larger pyramids and also become encompassed within larger pyramids which had a wider scope.

So Companies and Corporations would merge, and Countries would come together into trading blocks and other political confederations. Then I saw how this process would inevitably lead to the formation of a single all encompassing pyramid that spanned the entire world.

I saw how the various forms that this pyramid might take and the various events which might lead up to its creation. For instance the final world pyramid might come about through a process of World War and the dynamics of dominance and submission. Alternatively a clandestine world conspiracy might bring about the world pyramid through some secret, sinister and cunning process. Also we may have a situation whereby through a process of co-operation, symbiosis and the progressive entering into relationships of mutual benefit, on ever larger and increasing scales then perhaps in this way the world would become as one. Else the world pyramid might gradually come about through processes deriving from feelings of mutual love and friendship that might somehow come to permeate the world and its people. I came to understand that all these various sorts of processes would be happening at the same time and most of which were already happening.

But later on I came to see that there was one critical factor which might really catalyse this process of bringing together humanity and also neutralize those aspects of the world which were causing all the conflicts, divisions, disharmony and strife. This had to do with solving the ideological and doctrinal problems of this world. i.e. all those problems relating to beliefs, ideas, world views, narratives and how people perceived themselves and reality. I would come to see that at the heart of the worlds problems was a problem of a lack of vision and understanding. I would later come up with an understanding of things and a vision which I saw as the necessary key to unifying the world and bringing together humanity as one.

Due to this sort of reasoning and frame of mind, I saw the emergence of the World Pyramid as something natural and inevitable. It was the exact nature of this global social, economic and political entity which was uncertain. Whether it would be a dystopian One World Tyranny or a utopian Global Village, a world without borders and one of justice, equality, liberty, compassion and love. I saw the formation of this World Pyramid as being something intrinsic to what the prophecies were all about and in my wild and unfettered mystical messianic imagination I supposed that I might one day play some sort of role in determining the outcome of the world situation and the Great Work, the World Pyramid.

I settled on the idea that it was role of the Messiah or Mahdi to somehow climb to the top of the World Pyramid as it was forming and as the last bricks were being put into place. Then to get himself or herself into a position whereby he or she could determine the final make up of the Pyramid and the nature of it. In a sense he or she would for a time seize the Eye, in a sense be the Eye, and be in a position to remake the world, rewrite religion and completely re-order the affairs of humanity. In effect determine the future course of history.

Also I saw that in the mind of the Messiah a battle would be taking place and it was really the outcome of this internal psychological Cosmic Battle which was critical in determining the future course of the planet. This was the battle between Good and Evil but happening within the psyche of the person who was the conclusion of history and embodiment of the Zeitgeist or Spirit of the Age. The person whom according to Hegel would be 'The Genius of the Age'. If this battle was lost then the world would become an evil place. An ecological and environmental waste land, devoid of spirituality where religion in the hands of an evil Messiah would become an instrument of total control, in a way that some of the Roman Emperors and Muslim Caliphs of Old, could only dream of. Also a technological dystopia where the best of human invention is used to suppress, control and oppress. A total and perpetual One World Tyranny ruled by the bloodline of the Messiah and his chosen ones.

I also saw that if this Cosmic Battle within the mind of the Messiah was won for the side of Good then a better and happier world would emerge and one that corresponded to what was described in the prophecies of the world's religions. The planet and world ecosystem and environment would be saved, there would be a spiritual revival and values such as selflessness, justice, meritocracy, freedom and truthfulness would be revived and institutionalized. In other words the human condition will have been redeemed and world history will have a happy ending after all.

So these sorts of thoughts were going round in my head at this point in my life. Unconstrained, unchallenged, ungrounded and at times utterly Messianic. So my head soared in these sorts of areas of consideration, but the reality of life was quite frankly pathetic. As already mentioned there was a huge chasm between where my thoughts and aspirations were concentrated at this point in my existence and my quite unremarkable, under-achieving life.

The thought processes that go on in the mind of a person gripped by this sort of Messianic mindset would be quite strange to most people. It is a state of possession, of being 'possessed'. A form of divine insanity and would be quite laughable and ridiculous to folks who have never gone through it. At the same time, this mind set is accompanied by an incredible sense of self belief and a confidence which can translate into inspired work and productive thoughts if properly channelled and accompanied with a certain degree of discipline. In these states of mind the impossible was completely doable and the very difficult became completely natural. I remember during this time my attempts at understanding how the Brain worked and working out how to create Artificial Intelligence was making steady progress, propelled in part by these sorts of Messianic energies.

In retrospect these states of mind can seem completely insane and an expression of a deranged mind. They could also be most exhilarating and would be accompanied by intense highs. A extreme state of mania better than most drug states and in some ways even better than sex. But they were also followed with states of despair and utter despondency. These more negative states would also be useful periods of critical reflection and a time to re-assess all the Messianic output in a different light.

A psychiatrist would undoubtedly diagnose bipolar disorder and infer some kind of chemical imbalance in the brain. To me these states of mind were a completely natural consequence deriving from the experience of being God or having been 'One with the Universe'. I also noticed that sunshine, chocolate and caffeine would help to propel the messianic upswings. Again, a psychiatrist would say mania and over active dopamine chemical systems in the brain. From the inside looking out, they were exalted states of mind bordering on the sublime and straddling the gates of Heaven; borderline mystical states in other words.

I suppose this Messianic insanity will sometimes be a natural consequence deriving from the experience of having been 'One with the Universe', or having become the Universe or God. A person experiences himself or herself as the ultimate and then has to reconcile this with normal reality. On returning from divine heights and coming back down from the Seventh Heaven there is a process of having to assimilate this experience into everyday life. Having already experienced God directly and having realized that this is the true nature of things and our real identity, a person may then in his or her efforts have to integrate this self knowledge or gnosis into the rest of their worldly existence, and go through periods where they wonder if they may be the Chosen and Expected One of world religion. I think this is probably a more common experience than most people realize even psychiatrists.

In a funny sort of way it is not so absurd for a person to think that they may be the purpose of human history and the central agent of the prophecies of world religion, if they have already come to believe and understand, rightly so, that their real nature is the central focus and reason for world religion in the first place, i.e. God.

As mentioned earlier I had actually encountered and met, mainly in the psychedelic counter culture, dozens of people who at some point in their lives thought that they were something along the lines of the Messiah, the return of king Arthur or Second Coming of Christ. Later on in my life this would become an increasingly common occurrence. Due to my path, my various activities and by sheer chance, I would meet and become contacted by Messiahs with some regularity. At some point it dawned on me that this was something that was part and parcel of the mystical path and not some kind of deviance in this context. Rather it was something that was often a quite inherent part of the mystical and spiritual odyssey.

Earlier on in my life it was something that I mocked and found incomprehensible and totally ridiculous. But now I was seeing things from the inside. If before I considered 'would be' Messiahs and Christs from the perspective of a neuroscientist or even perhaps a psychiatrist, here I was now the patient with more understanding and sympathy for the people I used to mock.

Though of course my new found sense of affinity did not extend to all Messiah wannabes. Often your typical Messiah candidate would generally be some bloke with a huge ego who spent too much time passively sitting around smoking cannabis and boasting of all the glorious things that they were going to do to Save the Planet and Change the World etc. I recognized there was something of this in my own make up, though without the sitting around and taking drugs aspect; not at this stage in my life anyway. I knew there had to be a better and more productive way that Messianic thoughts and motivations, mainly deriving from the experience of being God, could be channelled so that Messianic energies could become a force for good, instead of a path to ridicule and ostracism. So that people on the Messianic path, instead of alienating people and alienating themselves, could instead generate a more positive reaction from people; also going on to achieve tangible goals that could be appreciated by other people and be beneficial to wider society.

Furthermore there was another reason why I believed that a Messianic outlook, while being a social liability, was at the same time a very positive thing. This is because in the same way that the mystical experience of being God would sometimes naturally led to Messianic thoughts, as described earlier, there was also an interesting reverse relationship. This was a really interesting thing that I discovered and it was this.

By being in the Messianic frame of mind and in ones imagination taking on the role of World Saviour while actually doing things and thinking thoughts to manifest this identity; then on one level it could be the source of great motivational energy but also more importantly it could actually bring me closer to states of mystical connection with God. The process of taking on the role of the Messiah and trying to manifest the Messiah within oneself and in ones life was in itself a mystical practice which I found could produce borderline mystical states and also which in turn would feedback on and encourage the process of trying to manifest the Messiah in our lives.

A few years later I would learn about a mystical discipline, from India and indirectly via Tibet, called Deity Yoga which is a part of an esoteric tradition, preserved in these parts of the world, called Tantra. This involved taking on some of the attributes of God, such as compassion or wisdom, as personified by some divine figure or physical manifestation of God, perhaps a Shiva, Buddha or Christ, and then trying to live out these attributes in our real lives. In effect consciously trying to live life as a physical manifestation of God in order to become God.

So I had stumbled upon my own version of Deity Yoga, except in my case the physical divine persona I was trying to manifest was that of the Messiah, Mythic Hero or World Saviour. And the attributes of the focus of my self created Deity Yoga were those that I imagined of the Messiah and what it would take to become a key agent in the process of bringing about the outcome of the prophecies, i.e. a World of Justice, Peace and Unity; together with the overthrow of corrupt tyrannical powers and the rescue of the Environment and World Ecosystem.

Though my system was basic and imperfect it seemed to work for me, inspiring me, giving me hope, motivating productive actions and furthermore also making me feel closer to states of union with God. I came to understand the idea of the Messiah as being a Mythic Archetype that exists within everyone and that everybody could potentially tap into it and manifest it either partially or fully in their lives. I also had the idea that the notion of the Messiah can be fused with the traditional mystical discipline of Deity Yoga whereby the Messiah and its attributes would become the meditation focus and what the mystical practitioner would try to manifest for real in his or her life.

Furthermore and importantly, I also saw an essential unity between the Messiah figure and the meditation focus of Tantric Deity Yoga on the one hand and as previously discussed; but also on the other hand I saw this was really the same thing as the archetype of the Mythic Quest Hero. So that there was essentially not really a difference between the Messianic Saviour figure of world religion and the Quest Hero of mythology, they were the same idea told in a slightly different way and with a great deal of overlap between them.

Therefore I came to see that the myths of my childhood, i.e. Star Wars and the story of Odysseus, had really set me up to come to believe the messianic things that took a hold of my mind, i.e. the desire to change the world and shape the course of history. Also I came to see that both sub-consciously and sometimes consciously, these myths I had been taught early on in my life had a powerful effect in shaping the course that my life took. I came to believe they were a powerful factor behind how my life had deviated so far from the norm. They were a significant reason why I had come to form the sort of outlandish teenage dreams which had propelled my ambitions and which had led me to the eccentric existence I now led. I came to fully understand and believe that this was not only the power of myth, but also the purpose of myth!

Another mystical input to my life would increasingly become more of a feature of my mystical path and mission around this time. It related to the ancient symbol for divinity that I'd encounter a couple of years previously on the Winter Solstice of 1998 when a book lying open, I chanced upon in a public library showed a picture of a strange being with a rooster's head, a man's torso carrying a whip and sword and two snakes for legs. Underneath the picture was my name 'WAI' in big bold letters and some text relating the symbol to Gnosticism. This synchronous encounter triggered in me a powerful full blown mystical experience of Union with God. But what was particularly special about this mystical experience was that I returned from it with a powerful reminder of it that I brought back to normal reality and which I could use as a sort of talisman to help reconnect myself with the state of being God. The very image of the strange and rather monstrous ancient symbol for God that I had encountered had the effect of connecting me back to the experience of being God if I focused on it for a period of time. It became, I learned later on in my journey, what was referred to as a Yantra or visual meditation focus.

The day after I had the mystical experience triggered by the picture of the ancient symbol for God, I went back to the library and made a photocopy. It was funny that a mere picture could be filled with such meaning and relevance for me but I knew nothing about what was depicted except that it related to the Gnostics somehow. In the months and years that followed, largely through using some of the early Internet Search Engines that were popular at the time, through typing in some of the other unintelligible words that surrounded the strange image I was able to learn that the thing depicted had a name and that name was 'Abraxas'.

Once I had the name I would quite regularly trawl the Internet for anything and everything I could find out about Abraxas. I discovered that Abraxas was a name for God that was used by the Gnostics, particularly those based in and around Alexandria, Egypt in the earlier centuries AD. Apparently the name also had a more ancient lineage that could be traced back to early Judaism and even, some speculate, back to Ancient Egypt. I also learned that the concept of God as Abraxas, encompassed both the light and the dark. This integrated well with the understanding that I had already arrived at, around this point in my life. Already for me God wasn't a benevolent father figure, rather to me God was Good and Evil, Male and Female. It seemed perfect that a symbolic representation of a conception of God, i.e. Abraxas, should have awoken the God within me. The true God whom I now know was referred to by the Gnostics, whom I believe to be the original true Christians, as Abraxas.

As a part of my Internet research, I particular enjoyed collecting images of what are known as Abraxas Gems or Abraxas Stones, also sometimes coming in the form of amulets. All of which had on them variations of the same image that I saw in the book. These images had the same effect on me that the original image from the book elicited, they made me feel connected and kept me in a mystical state of mind.

In the course of my research I read about some of the interpretations concerning what the different aspects of the image of Abraxas meant. So I learned that the Shield stood for the protection of wisdom; the Whip represented driving power; The Rooster's head represented wakeful vigilance; and the snakes were associated with the Divine Feminine. Instinctively I felt that these were qualities which I had to develop in myself and some of which I was lacking. I don't know if it was a conscious decision that was made at any point, but without giving it much thought I came around to the idea that somehow my life involved the process of manifesting Abraxas in my person and in my actions, and by so doing I believed I would become a more complete manifestation of God. So I used the images of Abraxas as Yantra or meditation aids that I'd use in the process of becoming a host that would take on and physically embody the idea of Abraxas and therefore also of God.

Somewhere further down the line, this idea of trying to manifest Abraxas became merged with the idea, described earlier, of taking on the goals and imagined attributes of the Messiah or a World Saviour in order to achieve states of spiritual connectedness and borderline mystical experiences. So it was around this time that a basic pattern of systematic mystical practice started to be established and became an integral part of my life. I had converged upon the constellation of ideas that in order to achieve full God realization, the process would involve bringing Abraxas, i.e. God, fully into my make up and doing things in life towards messianic goals and helping towards the realization of the happy ending to the world's problems that the prophecies described.

In effect I had developed my own primitive yet effective version of Deity Yoga and Tantra. I had formulated my own system of spiritual practices and disciplines which worked for me. It seemed to have come from within myself quite spontaneously while also absorbing some of the experiences that I'd had and the things that I'd learned in the years leading up to this period, especially the Abraxas and Messianic aspects. Also I incorporated some of the existing practices that I had already been doing such as Mantra Meditation or the practice of mentally repeating a word or phrase either aloud or in ones head; in my case I would do this internally and in silence.

And of course there was the constant study of things Religious, Philosophical and Neuroscientific all of which would help me to feel more connected. I saw definitely that my mental life, the thoughts in my head and my powers of mind were intrinsic and essential parts of my mission and path. Study and thinking became to me a spiritual and mystical discipline. I was encouraged in this way of looking at things by what I'd read in the Bhagavad Gita about 'Jnana-marg' or the path of knowledge, also referred to as 'Sankhya' where analytical reasoning was seen as a yogic spiritual discipline which had the potential for manifesting God Consciousness. Also the ancient Greeks saw philosophical contemplation as one of the means of facilitating connection with the divine. This all made perfect sense to me and was also confirmed by my personal experience. I well knew that my thoughts could sometimes lead me to states of inspiration and spiritual ecstasy that reached the sublime. I had already experienced many instances where my extended contemplations of the divine would take to borderline mystical states of consciousness.

During this Wilderness period of my life spanning the year 2000 to the end of 2001 I was mostly living by myself in a small flat in an area of London appropriately called Gospel Oak. It was very near a large stretch of open land and green space in London called Hampstead Heath. In it was a lot of beautiful woodland. For a while this became my mystic grove and natural temple. If this was a time in my life when I needed to reflect and meditate then being so proximate to nature really helped me in that process.

I had a regular mystical exercise where I would spend hours walking around the heavy wooded areas in the dark late at night and contemplate mystical, prophetic and philosophical matters. I would meditate on the thought that I was God and the idea that Everyone else was too. I also contemplated what I needed to do and the road ahead. I would get into states of intense focus and borderline mystical connection, a subtle but distinct altered state of consciousness.

Then towards the end of this mystical exercise I would walk and stand on Parliament Hill, so named because it is believed that this was the spot where Guy Fawkes stood with his co-conspirators hoping to watch the Houses of Parliament blow up. So naturally you can get an amazing view of London from here. I would emerge from the isolated and lonely woodland with my mystic thoughts and in my mind return to the City. Gazing over the night time view of London I would then think about how I might communicate my mystical revelations to mainstream society. Sometimes this involved talking out loud to an imaginary audience in front of me but I was actually literally talking to the city in front of me. So for a while I was the voice who had just come from the wilderness of the woodland of Hampstead Heath, returning to civilization to communicate my message. This would go on for an hour or so, sometimes a bit longer. Then I would go home.

I should add for the sake of completeness that I also used nicotine in this little exercise. I would purchase a pack of 10 of the weakest strength cigarettes, and during the course of my ritual smoke around 5, discarding the rest in the same bin everytime, as I left the heath to avoid becoming addicted. In my head I imagined I was being as a Native North American using tobacco in a controlled and ritualistic manner. I considered myself a non-smoker at this point and didn't smoke outside of this ceremonial context. I see in retrospect that the use of nicotine as a stimulant probably made me perform this little ritual more times than I would have otherwise done if it didn't involve this slight chemical facilitation. And perhaps that wasn't a bad thing, I got a lot of thinking done during these excursions and the talking to an imaginary audience probably gave me some useful public speaking practice.

A strange altered state of consciousness happened to me around July of 2001 while I was having sex with the lady who lived in the apartment next door to mine. These encounters would happen quite unpredictably and never to any sort of plan or routine. From time to time she would quite unexpectedly knock on my door, usually late at night, and then we'd end up in bed together. On this particular occasion my neighbour caught me at home during a period of intense concentration and focus. I had spent all day thinking hard about philosophical and religious things. I remember the weather was hot and it was something like the middle of a heat wave. At the moment that she knocked on my door I was probably in a moment of philosophical contemplation.

I let her in, we chatted a little and then we were having sex. However my mind seemed to be locked in the sort of thoughts I was thinking about most of the day. I kept thinking about the Everyone is God thing. My body was fully into the sexual act but my head was some place completely different. I felt myself close to orgasm, but at the point of climax I didn't feel anything, instead I lost all sensation of my body and of time and space. It wasn't a full blown union with the Universe or God, sort of experience. Even so reality, my physical surroundings and my body seemed to disappear and for a while I was in a tranquil place of pure white light. It was as if I was still my normal self but taken out of my physical context for a while and seemingly transported to another dimension without forms or landmarks, just white light. I kept thinking to myself the thought, 'it's beautiful, it's beautiful...'. This lasted for what felt like 5 or 10 minutes. Then suddenly I was back in my room in bed. Physically I had orgasmed but what I had experienced subjectively was something quite different from normal.

Somehow the combination of sexual excitement, the summer heat and sunshine (also probably caffeine & chocolate I'd used earlier that day), the intense study of things philosophical and religious, together with the general otherworldly mind state I was in around this time; all came together to produce a radically altered state consciousness for a short while. It's perhaps relevant to also mention that I was intensely hyperventilating for a while around and after the point of climax, which probably was a factor in the production of this experience.

Quite by accident I had stumbled upon this ability that we possess to channel sexual and other sorts of emotional or motivational energies in order to transform it into something that could elicit altered states of consciousness. This sort of thing was integral to the mystical disciplines of Tantra mentioned earlier. Later on I came to learn more about this process, and came to understand that it wasn't just sexual energy which was fuel for this process of consciousness expansion and achieving altered states of mind, but rather all the energies of life were really part and parcel of the spiritual journey of mystical awakening. Around this time I would reflect on these sorts of ideas a fair deal.

Regarding how I came to terms with idea of the Messiah and Expected One I evolved a doctrine that I believed would make the idea of trying to manifest the Messiah archetype in ones life, less offensive and less the object of ridicule to other people. While it was unwise, pretentious and alienating for someone to claim to be the World Saviour nonetheless the truth of the idea that there was a planet to be saved was quite apparent.

There had to be a way of utilizing the Messiah that potentially exists within all of us towards beneficial effects. I decided that for anyone to claim to be the Chosen One or Messiah was firstly immodest but also an assertion that too often came from a place of ego, insecurity, need and ultimately selfishness. It was really for others to judge who or what we are and it was senseless for anyone to go into this sort of mindset unless their purpose was to become and stay a complete social outcast or else to form a cult that would likewise be separated from the rest of mainstream society.

I had learned in my study of cults that this was often the path by which they came into being. Someone would claim to be the Messiah, Maitreya, Mahdi or Second Coming and persuade some other people to believe their claim. Some of these cults could go on to become quite large new religious movements, but they would always be limited by the messianic claims upon which these organizations were founded. For if membership to these cults or new religious movements required potential adherents to believe that their respective founders in each case were the chosen ones, then if for any reason this was rejected by the prospective recruit, it would also mean the rejection of the cult or new religious movement.

The problem for all the cults and messianic sects that I learned about was that none of the self proclaimed messiahs had actually achieved anything messianic and most had not achieved anything even remotely world changing.

It boiled down to the fact that it was no good to just claim to be the Messiah or Chosen One; rather more importantly what a person had to do was to deliver the messianic goods and actually realize the goals and requirements that would qualify a person to be judged as the Messiah. With regard to someone trying to manifest the messiah archetype or persona in their lives, what this meant is that it is futile, a bit stupid and even dangerous to claim to be the Messiah. But rather it is in our actions and the effect we have upon the world that we manifest the messiah principle.

Even though the messianic mindset can serve as a powerful internal driving force, a sort of personal myth that can inspire a person to do great things, it would generally be sensible to keep this powerful energy and deity yoga focus as a private matter. To other people and the world at large it is through our actions and achievements that we are judged, so the meaning and purpose of the messiah archetype and our internal messianic energies or motivations, matters most in relation to what we are able to manifest in our lives and in the real world. The messiah archetype will have been corrupted if the only thing it produces in a person are idle claims and arrogant boasts.

So I decided that the Messiah was an archetype and divine persona that existed within all of us. The Messiah would be an idea that was the embodiment in a person of all the hopes and yearnings that humans have for a better and more just world. But I also saw that we could take it upon ourselves to manifest this persona or archetype in our lives so that in our physical forms we realize and actually embody the Messiah. So that in our lives and in our actions we become, if not the Messiah, then at least a reflection of the messianic principle. Therefore we become as the Messiah and the agency that helps to bring about the realization of the prophecies and the creation of a better world. And even if we weren't the actual Messiah and Chosen One of the prophecies, supposing this as a future possibility, then at least we could be servants of the messianic principle and help set up the conditions for greater and better things to come.

It was as if the divine purpose was like a baton race where a long series of runners passed a baton or stick to each other, with each runner covering part of the total distance to the end of the race. This was a very long baton race and it potentially involved everyone who'd ever lived in human history including myself and everyone else. So even if I wasn't the runner who carried the baton to the finish line, it would still a privilege to have carried the baton some of the way and helping to set things up for later runners. I decided that I shouldn't fixate myself on narcissistic thoughts of being some sort of Messiah or Chosen One, but instead I could derive real benefit for myself and for others, from seeking to embody the messianic principle in my life and perhaps helping to contribute towards manifesting messianic achievements through my actions.

And so I came to reconcile my messianic thoughts and desires to change the world with my everyday existence. I realized that what mattered was what I was able to translate from my imagination into reality, or what I was able to make concrete and meaningful to others. Though I had nothing to show for my life I had the intention to make a significant contribution to human affairs.

My messianic tendencies and identification with the Gnostic God Abraxas which merged together, then went on to merge with my existing aims in life and my mission to communicate to people that 'Everyone is God' together with my long term goal to explain to the world how the brain worked and the creation of artificial intelligence. Also added to this mix was my equating the Messiah archetype with that of the Mythic Quest Hero archetype. Which went hand in hand with my coming to see the essential unity between the storyline of the prophecies of the world's religions on the one hand, and the elements of the recurring storyline of world mythology, on the other.

These separate strands of my life fused into a single whole and became my inner persona and driving force. I had reconstructed myself after my period of self destruction, by constructing a mythic mystical identity and trying to live this out in real life as best I could and as far as I dared.

The Wilderness

The things I did in my ordinary life to realize my extraordinary aims became my spiritual practice, so that the goals of my life together with the things I needed to do to achieve those objectives became my mystical path. The mission became my meditation and my work became my worship. I saw an outer journey involving doing things and realizing achievements in the real world and the reality I shared with other human beings, while at the same time there would unfold a corresponding inner journey where I sought to become one with God.

Chapter 7

The Return

My life had been something of a deviation. Most of my adult life since leaving home and finishing University had been lived on the margins and outer fringes of mainstream society. I had become involved in various deviant and counter culture scenes and had explored some of the more colourful aspects of life. After having experienced a series of mystical episodes I decided that the purpose of my life, together with working out how the brain worked and creating Artificial Intelligence; was to communicate certain sorts of Philosophical and Religious ideas to mainstream society.

It was in the year 2001 that it occurred to me that I needed to become a public speaker and a proficient one at that. At first I thought the best way to go about it was to first concentrate on the written word by producing literature outlining my ideas and somehow getting these distributed to my initial audience whoever they were, for at that time I didn't have any idea but I slowly realized that I had to get people's attention in the first place and the only way of doing that was to present my thoughts and ideas in public talks.

A significant factor which helped to get me 'out there' promoting my message was the events of September 11th 2001 when the World Trade Centre buildings were destroyed. Years ago in 1996 I'd gone to New York on a short visit, and was taken to the top of one of the towers and admired the amazing panoramic view. I remember also being impressed by the sheer scale of the buildings as my friend and I walked towards them looking up from street level near their entrance. The political events that followed the attack which I followed closely, along with most other people, motivated in me a desire which was already present for a while, to get out there and communicate my religious ideas, particularly those of a prophetic nature. Current affairs started to suddenly seem a lot more interesting and this also boosted my interest in relating the prophecies contained in the world's religions to these unfolding affairs. All throughout most of 2001 it was always on the back of my mind to get myself ready to start public speaking and this I did early in 2002.

My first public speaking appearance was on the 14th of February. It was to a crowd of 20 or so people at an intimate venue in Kings Cross, London and it was an evening that was hosted by a small underground esoteric organization called the 'Vision Network'. It was a strange collective of odd and unusual people who got together to host talks about various matters concerning mysteries, esoterica and spirituality.

Before I gave a talk for them I had already attended several sessions in the year or so leading up to that time. I remember that the quality of the speakers and the number of people in the audience would be extremely variable. Most of the people who attended the meetings were eccentric people and bohemians. Some of them were without a job and without family or many friends. There was a aspect to this scene as being something for outsiders. Though some pretty mainstream people would pass through, i.e. students, academics and regular seeming people with an interest in more esoteric or controversial matters. It was this eclectic crowd that gave me my first opportunity to give a live public presentation of my message. This context was entirely appropriate for my first public speaking appearance because I was myself a total outsider who didn't have very many friends and who still existed only on the outer most fringes of society. So it was these people who first showed an interest in the things I had to say. Even in these very early public speaking attempts I would make new friends and supporters.

This first talk I gave was an introduction to the idea that everyone is God presented from a mainly historic, philosophical and religious perspective. I also talked about the prophesies contained in the scriptures of the world's various great faith traditions in relation to current events. The talk went down very well and I discovered something that I'd already suspected, that I liked giving public talks to a room full of people.

So much so that immediately in the weeks following this first appearance I prepared and promoted myself for a further 4 more talks in order to say all the things I couldn't fit into the first talk. This was a lot of hard work as I had to now hire the use of the venue myself and it was down to me to get people to come and be members of the audience. I gave a talk a week and I remember that this was a very intense time. I had to prepare and memorise the material but then I also had to do all the promoting.

I would telephone just about everyone I knew to ask if they would like to come. Also I would ask anyone I met or came into contact with whether they were interested in learning that their real identity was God and that the prophesies were currently unfolding. In retrospect it all seems a little bit pathetic and desperate but at that time I was too fired up with zeal to notice. As a result of my enthusiastic efforts in promoting my series of talks I actually managed to get people to come which in retrospect was quite an achievement. Effectively I was able to arouse sufficient interest in people that they would want to come and hear my presentations about God, the Universe, the meaning of life and everything else too.

In those very early talks which I organized on my own, the attendance was modest averaging around 10 people or so but I never had an audience of less than eight people. I was so passionate about communicating my message that even if no people showed up I would have given the talk to the walls of the venue but luckily this never happened. After I had done these four talks which covered and elaborated upon the main themes of my message, I felt emboldened by the experience.

The public speaking had the beneficial effect of allowing me to suddenly meet a lot of people compared to my previous existence which was quite isolated. Also in presenting my ideas about the prophecies and current affairs, I would receive a lot of feedback, most of it positive and encouraging, some of it negative and a proportion of it rather hostile. In all cases this accelerated the development of my embryonic worldview, forcing me to define my ideas better, to read up around them and also to investigate opposing views, sometimes reinterpreting them and even assimilating them into my growing knowledge base.

I would so often be asked by a wide variety of people, 'What do you think about this?' or 'What do you think about that?'; so at the very least I had to be able to formulate replies to all the sorts of viewpoints I would be hearing about. So either way and in every way the process of public speaking was very beneficial to me in formulating my message and worldview, and accelerated my intellectual development that wouldn't have been the case if I'd merely spent the same amount of time only reading books and thinking to myself in isolation.

I met a lot of young people and students who were enrolled in one or another of London's big universities and educational establishments. They were in the process of formulating their own worldviews and so was I. Often it would be in conversations with the young that I found the most stimulation and insight. Unburdened by the years of accumulated indoctrination that older folks acquired and not yet saddled down with jobs, children and mortgages, they had the time, freedom and fresh outlook to see things in a way that was harder for older and more 'experienced' folks to achieve. So I learned a lot from the younger crowd, even if I didn't necessarily always agree with the views they held, they often gave me new ideas and new angles for communicating my message.

In the very early years of public speaking I'd also often meet and speak to a whole load of various new age people, psychedelic types, people who were involved in new religious movements and radical left wing politicos. I also came across a lot of people who might be called 'conspiracy theorists', though I don't necessarily use this term in the perjorative sense. Of course politics and people will be conspiratorial and some of these conspiracies will be pretty big and wide-ranging. What is considered to be conspiracy theory and widely ridiculed will sometimes turn out to be true becoming accepted and established fact. But also of course, people can be completely ungrounded in their speculations.

Still it was important to get an idea of all the viewpoints out there even if at the very least it might help to motivate the formation of a better interpretation of things for people. It was in this initial phase of getting my message out that I first started to become consciously aware that a definite and distinct worldview and political philosophy was starting to form in my head. Once this realization occurred then the process was accelerated further, as I came to explicitly interpret everything political, social, economic and historical, that later came my way in relation to my embryonic worldview and the political philosophy that was starting to become a growing and important part of it.

In the beginning my public talks were really about religion. But because a central part of the message related to what was the correct interpretation of the prophecies contained in the major religions then I inevitably found myself talking about historical and political issues. Because I was trying to present a rational and plausible view that the prophecies are now, i.e. directly relating to the world situation today, then this meant the early public talks also covered current affairs and what was being reported in the news. Of course the topics of politics and religion are usually controversial and contentious even when considered separately; and so much more so when considered together. So in the process of regularly doing public talks and communicating my political and religious views to members of the general public I was forced to sharpen my understanding and broaden my knowledge of things. This was so that I was better able to address the concerns of a wide variety of people and also to be a position to sensibly answer their varied questions and criticisms. In this crucible my worldview or weltanschauung started to evolve quite rapidly over a period of a decade or so and of course continues to evolve.

I should at this point explain the meaning of the German word 'weltanschauung' to those readers who are unfamiliar with the term. The expression translates literally as 'worldview' but in the German philosophical and political tradition, a sort of organic and holistic unity is implicit in the description.

So there's no word really quite like it in the English language.

A weltanschauung is really the sum total of all the ideas, scientific theories, attitudes, laws, morality, religion and aspects of culture that are shared by the members of the same social group or tribe. It can mean something relating to the whole of society but also something which is contained in the mind of the individual. The holistic dimension to the word weltanschauung means that there will exist a set of tight relationships and interdependencies between all the various ideas and ideals contained in the weltanschauung. So in my previous use of the expression 'worldview', I really mean it in this wider sense of 'weltanschauung', so from now on I'll use these terms interchangeably and in the same sense.

The 20th century American philosopher Willard Van Orman Quine came up with a similar idea which he called the 'knowledge web'. Another American academic, this time an Anthropologist called Anthony Wallace, came up with a notion which he termed the 'mazeway' which similarly was the complete cognitive map contained within an individual. So the expressions weltanschauung, 'knowledge web' and 'mazeway', really point towards the same thing.

I remember around this time becoming very influenced by Wallace's ideas, because he also elaborated upon how the 'mazeway' or weltanschauung of a society came into being and the circumstances in which it could be changed and replaced. He described the process of 'mazeway resynthesis' which would occur during a time of crisis and/or rapid change. In these times of transition then the ideas and worldview which had previously held a society together and allowed it to prosper, would then become dysfunctional, outdated and no longer serve a beneficial or productive purpose. So that in these circumstances the people might be destroyed for a lack of knowledge or perish for a lack of vision.

From his studies in anthropology, Wallace described how it was that in these times of crisis, the mazeway of a society would need to be radically evolved and altered. Furthermore he emphasized that the very survival of the society could depend on it. This idea of mazeway resynthesis would go hand in hand with the process which Wallace called 'cultural revitalization', whereby the new resynthesized mazeway which normally came into being in the mind of an inspired individual, would come to be adopted by the other members of the social group. This new and better mazeway, weltanschauung or knowledge web; would then regenerate a society and make it more functional, effective and increase its chances for survival and prosperity

Another way of describing mazeway resynthesis and cultural revitalization is to call the process a 'paradigm shift'. It was the philosopher of science, Thomas S. Khun who coined the expression to describe the process by which revolutions in thinking would occur in science. If we take paradigm to generally mean an interrelated constellation of ideas, and not necessarily scientific then we could also use the expression 'paradigm shift' in a wider sense. Here we would be talking about a master paradigm which encompassed all the other paradigms existing within a society, not just scientific but also artistic, legal, philosophical, religious, ethical and so on. Which would be exactly convergent with the ideas of Wallace and the notion of weltanschaunng or knowledge web.

Another useful idea in this context is expressed in the German compound word 'weltanschauungskrieg' which translates roughly as a battle between world views. In the context of present discussion it means that when a time of paradigm shift or cultural revitalization is occurring, then the emergence of the new paradigm will not necessarily be greeted with open arms. But rather the established powers that be, within the society in crisis, will seek to suppress and stamp out the new paradigm and its adherents. This will be because the new worldview will necessarily directly challenge the established dogmas, doctrines and ideologies upon which the existing institutions and power structures of a society are based; and from which the people at the top of those structures derive their authority.

Also it may be the case that during the time of paradigm shift or cultural revitalization, more than one new paradigm may emerge and they might not be mutually reconcilable with one another. In which case any new paradigm will face the prospect of competing with these rival new paradigms as well as the established one. So this is the weltanschauungskrieg or battle in the realm of ideas and competing worldviews.

All of this relates directly to popular notions relating to the power of ideas. Indeed the pen is mightier than the sword, and the sword will often fight on behalf of the pen. Or the idea that *'you can resist an invading army but you can't resist and idea whose time has come'*.

All through my life I'd been a keen follower of current affairs and always tried to keep up with the latest news. On top of this I read a lot of periodicals and books about politics, society and world history. I thought that I was quite knowledgeable and 'clever' when it came to understanding what was happening in the world and how it all worked. I'd assumed that the information supplied to me from the established periodicals that I read, the major television channels I watched while growing up, and the books from reputable publishers I'd devour; would all provide me with a complete and balanced view of the world and give me a comprehensive perspective on the whole spectrum of human understanding and intellectual pursuit. But as I went through my life journey, I discovered that often quite the opposite was the case. Through the mainstream media I learned that I was really seeing the world through a distorting lense and sometimes what was being presented didn't actually have much basis in fact or correspondence with actual circumstances.

I came to understand that many of the political, economic and historical 'facts' I'd accepted without much questioning were really merely a completely one sided interpretation of things. I learned that historical 'fact' was often made up, on the one hand, in order for people to feel good about themselves, give justification for social norms and reinforce existing power structures; also on the other hand, to paint other peoples in the worse possible light, justify prejudice and maintain exploitative relationships between peoples.

What I learned is that almost everything we see, hear and read in the mainstream media and a lot of the ideas which circulate around in academia and we read in books, is a representative of the existing dominant world view. So that politics, history, the news and almost all the information that we access through mainstream channels is interpreting through the lense of the dominant worldview. I also learned that sometimes this can be a distorting lense. It is even the case that new stories and even 'scientific' findings may be fabricated to support and bolster the dominant world view. Furthermore and most importantly I learned that the dominant worldview and the ideas and ideology contained within it, is controlled by those who are dominant in a society. Therefore the worldview of a society will be manipulated and at the same time protected by those in power, because a worldview is an important social construct for helping those who are already in power, keep it that way.

A lot of my education involved an unlearning of the quite narrow perspectives that were provided for me in school, by the mainstream media, the educational system and the established worldview. Looking back on things I didn't go to school as much as most people so perhaps I was slightly less conditioned and indoctrinated. But nonetheless I absorbed a lot of the dominant worldview and I took it for granted. And I didn't really question its truth and validity.

However in the course of my life I would leave the mainstream of society and go through a path that led to a host of diverse and sometimes wild experiences which would radically alter my perception of things and give me new ways of seeing things. I discovered that this new perspective made a lot more sense, had much more consistency , integratedness and broader scope, than my previous more conventional outlook.

I would come to completely dismantle into component pieces, my previous cognitive map and established worldview as it existed in my mind and which I'd previously absorbed from mainstream society. Discarding some of the pieces and rearranging the constituent pieces that were left. Into the new emerging composite I would add to it other less established ideas, views and notions that I had assimiliated during the course of my journey. And I would continue to do this throughout my life, continually augmenting, extending and evolving my new worldview.

So my mazeway became resynthesized and a new weltanschauung or worldview became incubated and formulated in my mind. From this new perspective and fresh pair of eyes, my political philosophy, views on society and economics would later develop; resting on firmer foundations and more fertile soil than that offered by the previous worldview which I'd discarded but was still dominant in the society in which I found myself. So I had to now go about the business of communicating my resynthesized mazeway to wider society and the world at large. The process of cultural revitalization, paradigm shift and weltanschauungskrieg would commence.

Even in my earliest beginnings in public speaking and in my first attempts at communicating my message and worldview, I had it in mind that these ideas may one day have some kind of larger effect on the world. These first attempts at public speaking were very rewarding and I was encouraged by the positive feedback I received. Also through public speaking I have discovered that many people have had similar experiences to myself and also shared my views. This was a very heartening experience which inspired and motivated my efforts even further. So I had discovered that I could give a longish public talk, hold peoples attention and cause people to become excited and enlivened as a result. People came, people stayed, people listened and even more encouragingly people also came back. So I decided to look for more public speaking challenges.

In the Spring of 2002 I purchased a mini step ladder from a hardware store and proceeded to spend my Sunday afternoons at London Speakers Corner, standing on my little platform giving condensed presentations of my message.

Speakers corner, which is in Hyde park, is a place where anybody may say whatever they like to whoever happened to be gathered there at any time, though most people present would know to congregate there on a Sunday, along with the tourists who came specially to see the spectacle. The place came about through an Act of Parliament in the 19th century which created this forum for free speech. Speaking there was something very different from the public speaking I had already done earlier in the year. For one it was in the open air with members of the general pubic and tourists wandering about from speaker to speaker. But the most noticeable difference was the amount and ferocity of the heckling. It was difficult to say a complete sentence without being interrupted and sometimes the barrage of heckling was incessant. This provided me with good public speaking practice even though most of the time was spent dealing with hecklers rather than delivering my message. I remember the first couple of times I was left rather shaken by the experience, but with perseverance I started to develop a thicker skin and the ability to deal more effectively with the hecklers.

I continued this routine of spending Sundays at speakers corner right through the Spring of 2001. During the Summer I didn't go as much and this was probably because I had arranged several talks which were held in rented indoor venues during this time. But I returned to speakers corner from the Autumn of 2001 right up to the time the weather started to become less hospitable around late November. Looking back on things I can see that this time spent at Speakers Corner provided invaluable public speaking experience, which made giving talks in more controlled and less chaotic environments seem much easier and more straight forward. It also gave me a chance to receive feedback from a diverse range of people who wouldn't otherwise have had the opportunity to hear my message at such an early stage in my development as a communicator. All in all Speakers Corner was and is a wild place and I felt literally like a voice in the wilderness (of London's Hyde Park).

During this time in my life when I started public speaking I would often go along to St James Church in Piccadilly, on Monday nights in order to hear the talks which were a regular feature there. About 7 years earlier a friend had introduced me to the Church and the Alternatives Organization which hosted the regular Monday night talks. My friend's father was one of the directors of Alternatives so we could get in for free and I would hang out there from time to time.

The talks which were mainly focused on New Age topics didn't really interest me massively at that point in my life. Fast forward to early 2002 and things were very different, I was very different. In the intervening 7 years I had transformed from a narrow minded Scientific Materialist into a more open minded Mystical Idealist who believed that a person's ultimate identity is God and that we are all one consciousness. Furthermore my goals in life were very different. Back in the mid 90's my overriding goal was to understand how the brain worked and to start a software company based on the things I discovered. In contrast, at the start of 2002 my life's immediate purpose was to communicate to the wider world this idea that Everyone is God and also the notion that the prophecies contained in the worlds religions are really about present times and the world in which we are living today. Also I had it in my mind to sharpen up my public speaking skills and I thought that by sitting through a lot of public talks, whether they were interesting to me or not, would help me to improve my public speaking technique.

It so happened that another friend of mine, who was sympathetic to what I was trying to do and who was also a volunteer at Alternatives, suggested that I come along to hear the talks and perhaps get some ideas. This I duly did and so from January 2002 up to April of 2003 I would spend most Monday evenings down at St James Church Piccadilly to help out with the Alternatives events and check out what the New Age had to say and how they were saying it.

Since my previous encounter with the Alternatives Organization in the mid 90s there was a change of management and the atmosphere was a little different, slightly less colourful and alternative seeming, but the basic format of the evenings was essentially the same. I would show up early and help out a bit perhaps helping to move and arrange a few chairs or other bits and pieces in order to not have to pay to get in. So it was basically a cheap night out for me where I could see people do public speaking. Over this time I managed to get a fair idea of some of the recurring themes and ideas that make up the diverse and disparate ideology of the New Age as presented by the Alternatives

Organization.

Most of the talks I heard during this period were quite dreary and dull though there were also one or two gems and several more quite memorable presentations. Certain ideas would come up again and again. Often a speaker would relate some unpleasant life experience that happened to them and then the punch line of the entire talk would be that bad things happen to us to help us to get into a better situation in life. Quite true but not very profound. Another idea I'd encounter with some regularity was the assertion that there is no Enlightenment or the idea that everybody was already Enlightened, which really amounts to the same thing. But the real focus was self development and life improvement. 'How do I find a soul mate?', 'How to get rich?', 'How to stop worrying?' and generally 'How to get all the things that you want!'.

I'll add that I would discover a recurring sentiment that was quite often expressed by the speakers I heard and also shared by more than a few of the Alternatives regulars. This was the notion that you help the world by working on yourself. Put another way, you make the planet a better place by making your own life better. This was often accompanied by the belief that through this process of working on oneself, a supernatural 'energy' would radiate from ones being and automatically improve the lives of those around you. But there was a corollary to this perspective which was to not get too involved in trying to change things in this world outside of ones own immediate and personal concerns. Besides this sort of thing, there were also talks that were more spiritual, mystical or prophetic but these were a small minority of what was on offer at Alternatives.

In retrospect I can see that I definitely benefitted from sitting through all these talks. I probably sat through around 50 during this period which lasted about 16 months. Even the bad talks where the speaker was awful and the ideas I found disagreeable, often actually helped me to formulate my own material in response to the things that I heard. It didn't matter whether a speaker was technically good or not because I would learn both from their mistakes and also from their example. All in all, this was a useful context for me to be in at that particular time when I was just starting public speaking. Also I made friends with some of the other volunteers and also with some of the people who would pay to come hear the talks so for a while it was time well spent.

This state of affairs ended in the Spring of 2003 when I decided to quit being a member of the Alternatives team. I started to see a corrupt and rather self centred side to the New Age as represented by the Alternatives organization. I started to find that the whole scene was too obsessed with money and overly concerned with selfish ends. Some of the things I witnessed whilst a member of the Alternatives team I found, quite frankly, a little disturbing. So ended my involvement with the Alternatives organization. I probably didn't get much out of the content of the talks, but nonetheless with the benefit of hindsight I can definitely see it was a good thing for me at that time of my life to have taken the time to see other people do public speaking in order that I may do my own public speaking better.

In the beginning of 2003, I started to regularly use a small venue called Watkins Esoteric Centre in order to host my own talks which I self promoted. It was actually an esoteric shop with a meeting space in the basement and located in the heart of London's West end just two doors away from Watkins bookshop, which is the oldest esoteric and best known spiritual bookstore in the UK. The Watkins Esoteric Centre, which was an extension of the book-shop, sold all sorts of Esoteric, New Age and Mystical items, i.e. ornaments, pray beads, tarot cards, crystals, incense etc. It had a great atmosphere. The manager of the shop was a very nice guy and trusted me with the keys to the place so I could lock up and leave whenever I wanted.

So taking advantage of this flexibility, some of the talks that I held there and the socializing that carried on afterwards would go on until round 3am in the morning with a 7pm start! I remember these events could be real marathon sessions and tests of endurance fuelled by chocolate and caffeine. The talks themselves, which including questions and answers could quite easily go on for almost 3 hours. The intense socializing following the talk, which gave me a chance to really get to know what people thought about various things, went on for some hours afterwards. I can see now in retrospect how these public speaking events that I organized provided for me an excellent training ground, allowing me to sharpen my speaking skills and to try out new material in front of a regular and receptive audience.

I would end up using the place 9 times over a period of around a year or so. During this time I saw my audience expand from around 10 people to well over 40 when the venue became too cramped to accommodate any further ex-pansion in the size of the crowd. It was great having a regular venue because it really allowed me to develop and fine tune my message. By putting myself on the treadmill of constantly having a public talk to prepare for and do, it kept the aim of developing my public speaking in mind, and it imposed on myself a useful level of self discipline.

I also started to acquire a small but loyal following of people who would consistently turn up at each and every talk. A side effect of this was that I had to produce new material for each talk so that I wouldn't have to keep saying the same things and repeating myself to the same people. This forced me to expand my knowledge of things relating to spirituality, prophecies and mys-teries, that I could speak confidently about. So this led to a lot of studying new topics and interests that I otherwise wouldn't have delved into so deeply. This had the effect of accelerating my learning and intellectual development. Also the fact that all the reading and studying was geared towards giving public talks and handling people's related questions, meant that I was in a highly motivated state. This helped me to cover more ground and to absorb more information than would have been the case otherwise. It was as if I committed myself to facing an oral examination in front of a room full of people every month or so. This prospect of having to satisfy a live audience was very stimulating and helped to focus my mind nicely.

Starting in 2003 I started getting invitations to do public talks as a guest speaker for other peoples events. So I would find myself speaking at vegan gatherings, student events and various types of social clubs. This gave me further experience of speaking to different kinds of people. However due to the nature of aspects of my message, i.e. that everyone is God and the prophesies are now, my talks in these contexts were not always well received. These occasions, even the ones where the audience reaction was quite negative, were usually places where I would still make new friends and expand my mailing list. You could please most of the people most of the time but some of the time you didn't end up pleasing very many people at all, and that was just the way it goes.

I can see now looking back on things how the process of organizing and presenting my message in various public speaking contexts, was very helpful towards the goal of getting myself back together again. Having to regularly face an audience and giving successful talks, does wonders for a person's confidence and sense of self esteem. Also the fact that I was presenting and promoting my own talks meant that I had to do things like finding and hiring venues. Then there was the significant task of getting people to come along to the talks, which involved contacting people, distributing fliers and generally selling myself. It is clear to me now that all these activities did a lot to make me more worldly and bring me back into the normal flow of society.

Most of my time from the start of 2002 right up to the Spring of 2004 was heavily concentrated on preparing myself for and promoting public talks about my message and related themes. But by the beginning of 2004 I was starting to look for new challenges and desired to expand my horizons, whilst continuing with my mission to explain to the world that a person's real identity is God and that the prophesies were unfolding in present times.

Then something would happen in April of 2004 which would cause my life to shift again in another direction. In one of those synchronous moments I was thinking about life and contemplating my next move when my mobile phone rang. It was a friend of mine calling me in order to tell me that the church where he worked was looking for someone to fill a vacancy. The church in question was St James Piccadilly and it was a place I knew well because of my involvement with the New Age Alternatives Organization with which I was involved for a while, up until a year previous to my receiving the offer of the job vacancy at the church. The post that needed filling was the position of Verger at the church, which is sort of like a priest's assistant and caretaker of the church and its grounds.

My friend who called me and who was working there was someone I knew from a completely separate context with no connection to the New Age, whom

I'd know for years and just happened to be working there. So it immediately seemed like the hand of fate at work again. I was immediately curious and interested in the job and a few days later I was interviewed and then accepted. Then a week or so later, something even more synchronous would happen literally hours before I was to start my new job in the early hours of the morning and on the same day as my period of employment would begin. The events leading up to this strange mystical encounter began the day before.

It was a Sunday in late April. I was due to give a talk in the evening at a Vegan Raw Food gathering, where I was invited as after dinner guest speaker. It was a busy day and I remember that I was preparing for the talk right up until the last minute. The vegan meeting where I was to give the talk, was held at a venue called the Green Angels, located in Borough just South of London Bridge. Around this period it was a well known counter culture hangout. A good place to meet people interested in alternative lifestyles and self experiment. Also it was the kind of place where you would meet a lot of people who were very spiritually interested or mystically inclined. Hence I was invited to speak there that day.

There was probably around 80 people in the room, some of whom I knew but mostly everyone was new to me. It was a sunny day and I was feeling good about things. As I arrived at the venue with the flip chart roll containing my diagrams and accessories in hand, I remember feeling confident and looking forward to giving the talk. For this reason and also because I had done a lot of preparation for the presentation the talk went well and the audience were very appreciative, I really enjoyed it. The subject matter of the talk was the idea that everyone can and perhaps should think of themselves as the world saviour. I also talked about the role of psychedelic substances in the history of religion and also in relation to the prophesies. I had an intuition that the kind of people I expected to be present in the audience would be receptive to these perhaps more controversial topics. As expected the feedback was very good.

After the event I hung around the venue chatting to people and answering peoples questions related to the talk more in depth. As it got later and most people had gone home, one of the organizers of the gathering offered to give me and a lady friend I was with, a lift home. So we waited right to the end which was some time after midnight.

We all got into the car and were driven back. But instead of going straight home I decided to go to the house of the friend I was with and have a cup of tea. To be honest I probably had it in the back of my mind and was hoping that the cup of tea would lead onto sex. So even though I knew that I was to start a new job the next day and had to wake up early, nonetheless I decide to make a massive detour on the way home. We were dropped off outside the Seven Eleven shop near Camden tube station. My friend wanted to get some biscuits to have with our tea. Anyway I quickly selected what I wanted, paid and waited for my friend. A short while past and my friend still hadn't decided what she wanted to buy. I grew a little impatient and frustrated. It was late and I was quite tired. I couldn't understand why it should take someone so long to decide which biscuits to buy, especially when there wasn't much of a choice on offer anyway. So I went to wait outside the shop.

As I walked out I could see a little old lady with a shaved head sitting beside a telephone box on the pavement and holding something in her hand. She was aged about 70, small and had a round boyish looking face. As I walked closer she said to me in a childlike sounding voice, 'Would you like to buy my book?'. I didn't particularly and I didn't really think about what she said so probably had the impression that she was begging. So I probably said something like, 'Sorry, I don't have any money'. Anyway, she persisted and continued to ask me whether I wanted her book. I looked at it and was stunned by what I saw. The title of the book was 'WAI WAI', which is my name repeated twice. I don't think I've ever been offered a book for sale on the street, apart from religious or culty promoters looking for recruits, and the one time this happens the book title just happens to also be my name. Funnily in China, when you say someone's name twice, it's a term of endearment.

I felt a jolt and suddenly became much more aware and fully awake. As I turned up to look at the old lady's' face she seemed strangely transfigured, slightly doll or cartoon like and her features became more defined. She seemed to emanate a power and energy that wasn't present on first seeing her and I felt gripped by her presence. I told her that my name was Wai and with the same spelling as that of the title of her book. So she asked me whether I'd like to have it. I said yes and she handed it to me.

At this point my friend came out of the shop and came up to where we were. She joined in our conversation and had a real rapport with the old lady. My friend shared with the old lady a child like quality in her manner and speech and so they really hit it off. They talked whilst I stood there examining the book. Reading the back of it I learned that it was about a tribe of indigenous people living in the Amazon rain forest called the 'Wai Wai'. Shortly after we said our goodbyes and started walking away. After walking some paces down the road, I turned around and looked at the old lady. I saw that she was looking straight at me and nodded her head at me a few times. I could feel the hairs on the back of my neck standing on end.

I reflected on the incident as I was walking with my friend to her flat. It seemed to me that not only was it strange and synchronous to have received the book from the little old lady. The timing made it especially curious, that is in the early hours of the night before I was start my strange new job, the next day.

Chapter 8

Working in a Church

In the Spring of 2004 I found myself starting work in a most unusual and controversial Christian Church located in the heart of
Central London. A place where traditional religion met with new
age spirituality and also the world of new religious movements.
A place where lords and aristocrats would come to use the same
space as beggars, outcasts and drug addicts; though usually not
at the same time. The complete spectrum of humanity seemed
to come to this place to pray, sit quietly, sleep, mourn, sightsee
or attend some service. I'd originally planned to work there for 6
months, I ended up spending 10 years there.

So I found myself employed as a verger working in perhaps one of the
most controversial and progressive churches in the country, St James of Piccadilly London. Even though over the years there has been a lot of effort put
into trying to reign in the controversies and make the place rather less radical.
It's unusual nature came about as a result of something of an experiment that
was indirectly put into motion by the then Bishop of London in the early 80s.
Back at that time the church was facing an uncertain future due to the steadily
diminishing congregation which would then have hovered at around a dozen
or so senior citizens.

Evidently Anglican Christianity had become less relevant to the locals of

Mayfair and Soho, two London districts which circled the church in its very central location literally seconds away from Piccadilly Circus and the famous Statue of Eros. It seemed the steady process of secularization, that has been particularly acute in European metropolitan centres, would force another church to close its doors. However the Bishop of London made a bold decision and gave an up and coming priest called Donald Reeves the mandate to do whatever he saw fit in order to revive the church and save it from closure. So began the experiment in progressive Christianity called St James Church Piccadilly.

Reverend Reeves, an energetic and quite charismatic character set about the task with an open mind and very innovative spirit. He transformed a conservative outpost of the Church of England into a place which embraced a variety of spiritual and political perspectives. As a result all sorts of non Christian beliefs would find a home, platform, meeting place or venue at the church. Anything from the various strands of the New Age, Sufism, Zen meditation and Gnostic Paganism to Freemason groups and Knights Hospitallers. A truly eclectic mix of a diverse variety of expressions of spirituality and religiousness. Also there was a strong Inter-Faith and Ecumenical emphasis at St James.

Apart from the spiritual openness of the place there was also a firm embrace of various ecological, environmental and left leaning political causes. It is perhaps for this reason that the Prime Minister of the UK at the time, Margaret Thatcher, variously called Donald Reeves, the 'Red Vicar' and 'a very dangerous man'. Also St James took up the cause of women and openly homosexual priests at a time when it was much less accepted than currently is the case. Reverend Reeves definitely put st James back on the map. Also in large part due to his charismatic preaching he managed to really boost the congregation and regular Sunday attendance from a hand full of elderly people to more varied crowds sometimes reaching the low hundreds; who would come from all over London to hear this quite radical preacher.

By the time I started working in the church the era of Donald Reeves was something of a golden age to some members of the congregation I would talk to and who would fondly recall memories of their 'Red Vicar'. He was certainly much loved if not always admired. After he finished his tenure in the late 90s and he moved on to do peace work in the former Yugoslavia, working towards reconciliation between Orthodox Serbs, Catholic Croats and Bosnian Muslims. A man who walked his talk.

The St James I came to be working in, though still quite radical, was far less eccentric than it had been in former times. A lot of the former extremes had become more contained and the regular attendance at the church had also somewhat diminished since its charismatic attractor had departed. Still it was a good place for me to be and where I felt quite at home.

We discussed earlier how I had been a semi regular at the Church, years before in the early 90s, when a friend of mine would take me there. My friend's father was a New Age writer and also a director of the New Age organization called Alternatives that used the church on Mondays to host talks. Years later in early 2002 around the time I was starting public speaking I would help out a bit with the New Age Alternatives organization on Monday nights in order to hear the public talks that were still a regular feature. This time round I severed my links to the Alternatives New Age organization after I started seeing a side to it that was rather self centred, crassly commercial and the anti-thesis of being anything spiritual. So I left in not exactly friendly terms. The funny thing is, I would find myself back at St James working there, but this time for the church itself, almost exactly a year to the day, after my having left the Alternatives organization. My employment at St James would later on give me further opportunity to study and learn more about the New Age. I had come back to work at St James quite randomly as I knew somebody who was already working there and whom I'd met in a completely different context, and who had telephoned me one day telling me about a vacancy and asking if I'd to like to come work at St James Church. I took up the offer.

The work at the church involves a great diversity of roles and tasks. The formal job name of Verger derives from one of the historical roles played by someone who did the equivalent job in the past. A Verger would in the past and also still in the present, lead various religious processions, i.e. a funeral procession or perhaps a wedding procession. The verger leading some such procession would hold in front of him a verging stick or rod. Apparently a verger is so named because in times past when crowds were less self organizing, the verger sometimes had to use his verging stick to beat people to the verges i.e. the sides of a path, in order that the religious procession may proceed. A verger may been seen as a jack of all trades working in a religious context and this is especially true in St James, where we basically did everything the priest didn't do, to keep the place going which was a lot.

So my work in St James church was varied. As one of a tight team of four Vergers at St James essentially we were the glue that kept the place running 7 days a week, from Morning to late Evening and often later into the night. On one level I performed caretaker duties, which included locking up, unlocking, basic maintenance on the place and also cleaning. This is one side of the job which I found humbling, in a positive way, but also character building. That of keeping the place in tidy working order, cleaning toilets, mopping up sick, also picking up hypodermic syringes and occasionally human excrement. All part of working in a busy West End church in the heart of London. Other miscellaneous duties would involve things like clerical and office work, handling money, going to the bank, putting up posters, answering the telephone and really everything and anything that needed doing. I was also in charge of room hire for a while, so that involved a lot of time, emailing people and making up invoices, etc. So the job involved a rich variety of roles.

Perhaps the central role of the church verger relates to all the ceremonial and liturgical stuff that goes on in a busy working church. I've already mentioned the more formal role of leading religious processions but relating to any religious event there is a lot of setting up and clearing away. This includes rearranging bits of furniture, lecterns, alters and the like. Also setting up and sound checking microphones and generally making sure everything runs smoothly. Then of course there was the main Sunday services and myriad details that need to be attended to in order to make everybody happy. Once religious events were underway then a significant part of the job involved hovering about in a black cassock, which is a long ankle length robe, and generally making the place look more formally religious by dressing up in this sort of garb. Apart from the main Sunday service, throughout the year there were a number of memorial services, weddings, baptisms and the occasional funeral.

I can see now in retrospect that by working in this sort of context and seeing these major currents of other people's lives, how this has given me a lot of opportunity for reflection and thinking about life. Perhaps giving me more of a sense of what life is all about for most people. I remember the numerous memorial services that I witnessed as part of the job and thinking about the people being remembered, the sort of people they were, judging by the recollections of the close friends and relatives read aloud. Also comparing what sort of people they were to the number of people who actually came to their memorial service and the quality of the crowd. You'd see a pattern that the people who pulled a good crowd for their memorials were generally generous, selfless, and with a good sense of humour. The sort of people who lived for others. Otherwise attendance wouldn't be as good. I would sometimes think about what would happen after I died and how people would remember me. Would anyone even bother to arrange a memorial for me and how many people if anybody would come to fondly reflect on my life and legacy. Indeed working full time in a busy church really provided a good context, as well as the stimulus for thinking about the larger questions in life and seeing ones own life from a larger perspective.

The job allowed a lot of autonomy and independence which I liked, also it required a lot of responsibility which it was useful for me to acquire a sense of. A good thing about the job was that a lot of the time involved doing quite menial tasks, so that my mind was not completely taken up by work related duties. This gave me a lot of space in my mind to think. I would often find myself thinking of ways to explain my ideas to people or writing book or website passages in my head, while standing about during some church ceremony say. Also because my mental faculties were not very taxed by the job, at the end of the working day I typically still had loads of energy left to work on the message and the mission.

Another useful aspect of the job was that it involved a lot of social interaction and this over the years really helped me to sharpen my human interaction skills, which in turn has been helpful in making me a more natural sounding public speaker I believe. A typical day would involve dealing with a diverse spectrum of people, anything from beggars, tourists and tradesmen to spiritual types, retirees and children.

Five days a week, in the front court yard of the church was an arts and crafts market selling all sorts of items from all around the world. The market traders were a hard working bunch, very multi-ethnic, working class and un-pretentious. The culture out there in the court yard was something of a contrast to that which existed inside the church and really added a pleasant and inter-esting dimension to the job. I found I could strongly relate to the traders, many of whom were like my parents and the sort of people I grew up with. I could relate to them easily and had sympathy for their concerns. Although there was a full time market manager, my job would often involve collecting the market rent which gave me the opportunity to become really familiar with the traders and their backgrounds.

A sometimes challenging and also character building part of the job was that apart from all the other tasks that we had to do, the vergers at St James also doubled up as security; having to deal with any troubles and misbehaviour that would with some regularity occur in the church grounds. This included dealing with the homeless who were allowed the freedom, within designated areas, to sleep in the church when nothing else is going on or if people didn't mind homeless people sleeping through their ceremony or event.

The homeless come in a wide variety and many are perfectly reasonable and friendly. There are the homeless mentally ill, homeless drug addicts and beggars along with transiently homeless who have perhaps just come out of prison or have been recently evicted from some hostel. In fact we were told by a social worker at a nearby homeless shelter that the people who we dealt with would often be those who were banned from all the other places and there-fore had nowhere else to go and this was usually because they got into fights. Some of the younger homeless were not so different from the sort of people I lived with and befriended in my early 20s just after finishing university when I found myself living for a while in a North London squat. Generally I could more often than not quite relate to the homeless, particularly the younger of them. They often had a colourful background and I would from time to time find myself interested in their lives and how they came to be homeless. I would sometimes think to myself that if fate had worked out slightly differently then perhaps I would have been one of them, sleeping on the same church pews.

I should also mention that in my dealings with the homeless the job would occasionally involve confrontational situations because one of my duties in-volves telling people, some of whom are difficult at the best of times, who were coming down from drugs and who you've just woken up; to vacate the church and go out into the cold and wet in order that some musical concert or ceremony may take place without their presence in the vicinity. With a friendly, firm and patient approach this part of the job was generally executed without aggravation or negative reaction. However I can recall numerous occasions when this lead to direct confrontations, having to face people down and watching homeless geezers ranting and raving with loud indignation at being evicted from the relative comfort of a warm but hard wooden church pew, to go out into the cold and even harder London streets.

Yes, I can recall a number of tense and stressful situations with various homeless gentlemen threatening to kill me, beat me up, break all my fingers etc. or else declaring how they were going to burn down the church and do other unspeakable things. It's true broken windows and other forms of vandalism were something of a regularity at various times. Though this was probably the most difficult part of the job at the same time I can see how over the years this aspect of the job toughened me up psychologically and even directly helped my public speaking by giving me a thicker skin. Of course this process was made less daunting by the fact that if things got too out of hand then the police could be called but this was a last resort.

Although I never personally experienced serious mishap in my dealings with the homeless I knew that in the past, sometime before I started working at the church, there was a serious incident where one of the vergers was assaulted by a drunken homeless guy and badly beaten around the head. I heard that after the incident he was never quite the same again. I was told about another incident where a few years previously a church verger working in another church had been stabbed to death by some deranged homeless guy while locking up. Also Slightly before I started work at St James, a previous employee, this time a female verger had been cornered by one of the homeless sleepers and threatened with a knife held up against her face. Apparently she never returned to her job after that. So my dealings with some of the homeless would involve a lot of due care and attention, and a wariness deriving from a recognition of the fact that I was regularly dealing with sometimes potentially dangerous people who were constantly in and out of prison for offences such as grevious bodily harm, which I knew for a fact.

Sometimes on reflecting about the homeless I would come to think that somehow the Universe or Cosmic Intelligence had set up this circumstance to be a part of my life for a reason. It seemed that there was a higher meaning behind my having to work and deal with people who might be considered at the very bottom of society, those who were completely on the margins and outside of the normal social order. Even though this sometimes presented difficulties for me in the form of confrontation situations or otherwise challenging tasks such as cleaning up their vomit or excrement; apart from making me psychologically stronger and more assertive there was also the effect of instilling in me a sense of compassion which wasn't really there before.

As I got to know some of the homeless then I couldn't help but be drawn into their lives and sympathizing with their troubles and predicament. I came to better understand their constant trips to prison and drug addiction. There was always the thought of the precariousness of their lives. At the end of the day, as you got to know some of the them, except for those who were obviously mentally ill, then ultimately there wasn't all that much difference between the deviants and 'normal' folks of the world. A few wrong twists of fate and a string of bad luck could mean that even the best of us, or perhaps our sons or daughters, may end up in a similar situation.

Sometimes I would learn about their deaths on the streets. One young woman I came to know was found dead in a doorway from a heroin overdose. From time to time you would hear on the homeless 'grape vine' about homeless people dying from drugs or violent incidents.

After years of dealing with the homeless sleepers at St James, you developed a tougher exterior and came to learn that firm and friendly, but not too friendly, manner which was most effective in dealing with people who could sometimes be problematic. After a while it became routine and predictable and nothing could seem to faze or upset. However there was one incident that occurred in the Summer of 2011 which definitely made the heart beat fast and the mouth dry.

I was locking up one evening when I noticed a homeless guy hidden away, sleeping in a corner of the church. I tried to wake him up but he wasn't budging. He was actually awake but pretended to be asleep. After a while of trying to get the guy to get up and leave I realized that he fitted the description of someone who had been causing a lot of trouble recently on the church grounds, being verbally abusive and physically threatening people. So I decided to walk away and call the police on my mobile phone.

But in my impatience I had made a big mistake of doing things within earshot of the homeless guy. He had got up and was coming towards me threatening to stab me with a hypodermic syringe if I carried on calling the police. Seeing the needle in his hand I described what was happening to the police operator on the phone. He told me to get out of there, I could hear the stress in his voice, and obviously I was gripped with a strong sense of danger and imminent peril. So I turned and ran, bolted up the short flight of 12 stairs leading to a locked door at the top which allowed access to the offices of the church.

I remember fumbling a while for the right key among my big bunch of 20 plus keys to open the security door. Time seemed to dramatically slow down, I thought in my head that the guy might be immediately behind me, and about to stab me in the buttocks with some aids and/or hepatitis infected hypodermic needle, so I nervously looked back quickly once or twice. Eventually I found the right key, got through the door, dashed into the office and without thinking, instinctively went around looking for weapons. I found a big heavy metal maglite torch and a long ceremonial vergers wooden rod. I paused a brief while but then decided to go back into the church.

I went back down the stairs, kicked open the big wooden door that lead from the office area into the main church area and went through the door.

Working in a Church

Glancing around the church I immediately noticed that the fire escape doors located at the far opposite side of the church were flung open. I realised that the guy with the syringe had fled. After checking things were in order I went out to the courtyard and chatted to some of the market traders who were still packing up their stalls after a days trading.

A little later the police came over and told me that they had intercepted the homeless guy as he was running down the street. The police on the streets must have got the emergency call and sprung into action within a few minutes or even less. This quickness of action and prioritizing on the part of the police was reassuring to me and I was most impressed. Later that evening at home I reflected on the matter and could detect that my stress levels were still elevated. It was a very unpleasant experience but yet something good came out of it and this occurred the very next day.

News had gotten around of what had happened and one of the homeless sleepers called Taffy with whom I was friendly came up to me in the church gardens and told me how terrible he thought the behaviour of the syringe guy, and gave me his support. In the course of our conversation we came to talk more about our personal backgrounds and he told me at some point that his real name was Justin. Then there came to me a flash of recognition. I said to him, 'You're from Armonford in Wales aren't you?'. Taffy or Justin was stunned, and said words to the effect of 'How can you have possibly known that?'. And so I came to learn that Taffy was one of the gang of Welsh squatters that I had befriended all those years ago living in the North London Turnpike Lane squat scene.

Though I hadn't really known him well, because he was always something of a lone operator and existed mainly separate from the rest of the Welsh gang, I had definitely seen him several times and we may even have been introduced at some point. His appearance now was very different from his quite baby faced features of 20 years ago. The chronic drug abuse had taken its toll and his features were prematurely aged. Also his skin color was a ghostly pale and his normal appearance now was of someone who wasn't quite well. So it was easy not to connect the Taffy who slept in the church from the Justin whom I vaguely knew so many years ago.

So I was right when I would sometimes think to myself that if fate had been different then it could easily have been the case that I might have been one of the homeless sleepers at St James instead of one of the vergers. If I had stayed in that squat scene and gotten into heroin then who knows, I might have ended up as Justin's druggy pal, begging in London's West End, sleeping in homeless shelters and on church pews.

I had a long chat with Justin and we discussed mutual acquaintances. It was a very heartening and happy conversation. I discovered that many of my old friends and acquaintances that I'd imagined may have died prematurely from drugs and dangerous living were actually alive and well. Justin was the then boyfriend of the Welsh squatter lady I pulled away from a fight with some English skin head girls. I learned that she was well and now had a few children. My other prone to violence Welsh friend whom I spent a fair bit of time with was also alive and well. This was a very pleasant surprise for me. Apparently he had tried to commit suicide after his girlfriend left him, by driving a car into a building at high speed, but the airbag had saved him.

I could in return relate to Justin that Wendy, who was the runaway teenage beggar girl we both knew, was likewise alive and well and now had a settled life and several children. She had a couple of years previously contacted me out of the blue after discovering my website through a friend. Over 20 years previously we were all young people who found themselves in a troubled, insecure and degenerate scene. So some of the people who had lived for the now and didn't hope much for the future managed to find for themselves later in life a measure of security, happiness and also hope for the future in their children. My conversation with Taffy gave me a great sense of closure but also continuity.

Now onto something very different, another and integral dimension of working at the church was music and this manifested itself in different ways. Firstly and most obviously a lot of hymn singing goes on in a church and I rediscovered the pleasure of singing during my time there. It was fun and satisfying to stand at the back of the church during some service or ceremony and join in with the hymns. And how amazing it was that I was being paid at the same time! I used to reflect on the importance of singing and how this positive and beneficial aspect of regular church attendance was being lost through the ongoing process of secularization. What a shame this was. But I supposed there was still karaoke and singing along to the radio or mp3 player. This rediscovery and development of my singing voice is definitely one of the positive things I took away from the church.

Due to the William Blake associations the church had, the hymn Jerusalem to which Blake contributed the lyrics; came up a lot for instance in the weddings or memorial services. After ten years working there I'd probably sung the hymn over a couple of hundred times. Then of course there were the many carol services during Christmas where all the golden oldies were rolled out. The words and poetry of the traditional hymns were quite pleasing to sing. It was a disaster when the church updated the lyrics of the hymns sung during the main Sunday service. The familiar words were replaced with new more politically correct and 'right on' phrases which some members of the congregation were tasked to produce. These new lyrics didn't quite sound right and jarred the ears. Why replace great words with amateurish and mediocre ones, I'd ask myself. What would they do next, replace Blake's words to Jerusalem for something more 21st century Britain?

Apart from the hymns, the church also functioned as a hired music performance venue. So there was a lot of classical music performed at the church most days of the week. A lot of top talent performed there and the musicians were generally a fun crowd to deal with. Perhaps half a dozen times a year, a big name rock or pop band would hire the church for some special exclusive performance. Bands and acts who came along included REM, Bryan Adams, Sean Lennon, Patti Smith, etc. For these events the place would undergo a dramatic transformation from an active worshipping church to something more like a mainstream music venue. The rock concerts were great fun to work on, including the lead up which involved small armies of roadies shipping in all the sound and stage gear.

One particularly memorable moment was seeing Yoko Ono who came to watch her son perform. It was like seeing a piece of 20th century history in my work place and what memories the area must have had for her I thought. She had met John Lennon at an art gallery which was literally a couple of minutes from the church, and which was in turn a few doors away from the club where Jimi Hendrix gave his first UK performance having almost literally just come off the plane. Also a few minutes walk away in Saville row was the recording studio where the Beatles recorded the album Let it Be on the roof top of which they gave their last ever concert. The spire of the church can be seen from the video footage of that famous last gig, beside shots of George Harrison. So the place and area were also rich in another sort of more contemporary history which strongly resonated with me.

On the 26th June 2008, I found myself quite astounded when the synchronicity trail of mysteriously linked happenstances continued to manifest. Another startling occurrence happened which would encourage me in my mission and reaffirm to me that I was on the right track.

On that particular day I was working in the church and there was to be a memorial service held in the afternoon for a very well connected lady who seemed to have a lot of upper class friends. I remember that in the days leading up to the service there was a sense of anticipation that this was going to be quite a major event and from the number of telephone inquiries received about it, I expected it to be well attended, which it was with several hundred people showing up. The Prince of Wales would be sending a personal representative so just from this I could tell it was going to be a posh affair.

The church by virtue of its location was a place where typically memorial services would happen with some regularity, at least several a month on average. So even though this memorial service in question was a little more of an event than usual, it was part and parcel of the normal routine of working in a busy West End church. So to me it was just another days work. I got into my long black vergers robes and got to work on the event, helping to make sure everything ran smoothly.

The crowd who had gathered filled the church and was generally made up of smartly dressed and well to do looking people with some middle class bohemian looking types. As things progressed I realised that this particular memorial would be something quite different from the norm. The lady whose recent passing away was being remembered by the occasion was a certain Shusha Guppy who was originally from Iran and who married a well off English man. Because of this background, the service was a mix of Islamic traditions incorporated into the Christian memorial service format and held in a church. So the service began with a sung recitation of passages from the Koran which was highly unusual and also at one point a sufi poem was read out.

During the address and talk about the lady's life, which happened to be presented by the right wing conservative philosopher Roger Scruton, there were many references to Sufism and the lady's quite mystical outlook in life was recounted. Apparently the lady's father back in Iran had been a theologian, philosopher and professor at Tehran University who had given his daughter a thorough background in esoteric Sufi teachings. This I found interesting given that the idea that 'everyone is God or Allah', which is the central Sufi tenet, also happens to be a belief I wholeheartedly shared. In fact a major part of my life was devoted to the communication and promotion of this notion. So this mystical aspect to the memorial service made it interesting and pleasing for me.

What took me by complete surprise was that when I was glancing through the order of service leaflet and reading about the lady, I learned that the lady's husband was an English explorer by the name of Nicholas Guppy. I realised that he was the same person who wrote the book 'Wai Wai' that the strange homeless lady had given to me over four years earlier. It might have seemed just an amazing coincidence if this was all there was to it. But the highly mystical references made during the service, which put me very much in a spiritually receptive frame of mind and the fact that I had received the strange 'Wai Wai' book on the same day, in the early hours of the morning, that I first started working in the same church, where this memorial service was being held; all of this struck me as quite mysterious and very synchronous. The Universe was giving me a sign, and I was fully receiving it. I felt a heightened sense of alertness and the hairs on the back of my neck were standing on end.

During the Summer Solstice which preceded the memorial service by a few days, I was in the process of making plans and charting the course for the immediate future that lay ahead. I was feeling a closeness to the mystic dimension of life and changes were happening within me that manifested as altered behaviour patterns and an up swing in my motivational levels. Through the occurrence of this uncanny synchronicity deriving from the location, matter and significant details of this memorial service, I felt that the Cosmic Intelligence had given me a nod and a wink. I believed that the hand of Providence had set things up for me to be exactly where I needed to be, in order to prepare me for what I would have to do in the future.

Chapter 9

The Future of Religion

An important reason why the hand of Providence had put me in the position of working in a church for 10 years, was to get a deeper understanding of religion and learn not just Christianity but also all the other major religions, the New Age and even the world of cults and sects. It would also give me the perfect context for evolving my own ideas relating to the future of religion.

Even though St James Church was a mainstream church of England establishment, it existed on its wild west fringe. This was for a variety of reasons which I discussed in the last chapter. All sorts of controversial, heterodox, heretical and sometimes suspect beliefs would find their home here as represented by the various groups and diversity of people whom I'd encounter at work, over the years. This was the perfect context for my religious studies. If earlier on in my life, I had to make the effort to go visit different places in London, to learn about the world of religion and religious people; then it was very beneficial to my evolving worldview and especially its spiritual aspects, that by working at the church, London's world of religion and religious people came to me.

Of especially great interest to me was that for a variety of reasons I discovered that there existed a quite heavy gnostic undercurrent to the place. Though the idea that everyone is God or that somehow we are all one consciousness, is certainly not standard Church of England teaching, nonetheless these sorts of beliefs found, for a while at least, a home at St James. One of the reasons why this was the case probably had to do with the history of the church and two important historical characters who were associated with the place. They were the English mystic, engraver and poet William Blake, the other was the renowned architect and Freemason Christopher Wren.

This historical dimension to St James Church made the context more appropriate to me and made it feel more right that this was where I was supposed to be. Christopher Wren actually drew up the plans for the building. Anecdotally St James is thought to be one of Wren's favourite designs. Significant to me was the fact that Wren was a mystical Freemason and also one of the founding members of the Invisible College which would evolve to become the Royal Society of Science and one of the leading scientific institutions of the world, that would do so much to promote the growth and spread of the scientific method. Due to this background it felt good to me, that I happened to be working in a building that Wren had designed. There were masonic symbols inscribed all over the place including places not accessible to members of the general public.

Then there was a heavy William Blake connection. He was Baptised at St James because his family lived nearby in his early years and apparently he played in the church grounds as a small child. However Blake in his adult life would come to reject the church and was buried at the Nonconformist cemetery Bunhill Fields in East London. Still the folks at St James celebrated the fact that he was baptised there and the baptismal font there, created by the famous English sculptor Grinlin Gibbons, would often be referred to foremost as the spot where Blake was baptised. It certainly attracted a lot of tourists, mainly Americans, who would come to pay homage.

Also the William Blake Society for a long time had a base at St James and once a year on Blake's birthday a memorial lecture, organized by the society, was held at the church in his honour. The secretary of the Blake Society was a regular visitor to the church who was naturally always very keen to talk about him and answer my questions. There is a corner of the church which is used by the Blake Society to promote events and publicise new related works such as books etc. Over the years, just by regularly perusing this area I would come to learn a lot about Blake.

Personally there was a reason why Blake had a special significance for me. In a book I read years before, I saw one of Blake's engravings which depicted a naked man sitting on a rock, with a roosters head, his head rested on his hand and seemingly in a state of contemplation. The figure depicted was called Albion but to me what I saw was Abraxas, which was a Gnostic idea of God that had great significance and meaning for me. It was also known to me that Blake was fully aware of Abraxas and matters relating to it.

I discovered after I'd started working at the church a small book of engravings by Blake titled 'All Religions are One'. This was a central part of the message I was communicating in my public talks, though I summed it up in a slightly different expression, i.e. 'All World Religion is One Religion'. Comprising only 10 pages, Blake's little book talked about what he called the 'poetic genius' which he equated with the source of prophecy. He described how he believed all religion and all the 'sects of philosophy' as coming from this one source. He also described the 'voice in the wilderness' and the 'true man' who would become the embodiment of the poetic genius and source of prophecy. I came later to equate the true man with Albion and therefore abraxas and gnosticism. I also came to believe that what I had been communicating and was planning to do later in my life, was really the same message that Blake was trying to communicate in his own unique way. Then there was the Apocalyptic dimension to Blake's worldview which also resonated strongly with my own ideas.

William Blake has been referred to as England's only prophet, his poetry considered by some as mystically inspired. We've already mentioned that he himself believed that the Poetic Muse and the Spirit of Prophecy were from the same source and of the same quality. His most famous poem Jerusalem, which was set to music by composer Sir Hubert Parry in 1916, is a popular hymn often sung at weddings and other ceremonial occasions. In it Blake describes Jerusalem as built in England's 'green and pleasant land'. But what is not widely known is that Blake didn't intend it as parable but rather in common with many others of his time, he saw Britain as the actual site of a New Jerusalem where the elect would gather to witness the Second Coming. Further describing his vision of the future he wrote, *'The fields from Islington to Marylebone, To Primrose Hill and Saint Johns Wood, Were builded over with pillars of gold, And there Jerusalem's pillars stood'*.

I had earlier in my own life come to see London as a place with special mystical and spiritual significance. I already saw London not just as Jerusalem but also Babylon, Meggido (commonly translated as Armageddon), Sodom and Gomorrah all rolled into one. London to me was Babylon due to its very cosmopolitan nature. It is truly a wonderful 'Babylon of races' as the expression goes. People from literally every place in the World had come to live, study and work in London. And London is Meggido because just as this city was located at the critical location in the ancient Northern Kingdom of Israel where trade routes from Asia, Europe and Africa intersected, so it is that London occupies this same position today. With it's special connections with the Americas, the Commonwealth Nations, the European Union and the former outposts of its former empire; so it is London that is the new Meggido. London is the new Sodom and Gomorrah due to its fantastic openness, diversity, tolerance and freedom. A place of colourful experimentation, creativity, culture and vice. A place that is very open to new ideas and accepting of alternative life styles. Finally London is Jerusalem which literally means 'City of

Peace' because it is the place with probably the best race relations in the world though there is much work to be done. In terms of relations between people of different nationalities, creeds and genes, though not perfect it's not too bad.

I also knew that London was the perfect place to start the spread of a world changing mystical, spiritual and scientific revelation that would include a definitive theory of the brain, and the creation of artificial intelligence. For in London there is to be found every sect, cult and religion; also as mentioned earlier people of every race and nationality. To be found in London are the sons and daughters of parents from all over the globe together with the many young people who came to London from the world all over, pulled to the city as if by some magical mystical strange attractor. I imagined that these would be the sorts of people who will be the first to receive and accept the message and new worldview, i.e. those who are young, mystically inclined, idealistic and also possessed of at least some familiarity with the English language.

English will be the initial language used for communicating the truth. It is fortuitous that English is the main language of commerce, pop culture, science, technology and also the Internet. Once the revelation is initially communicated in English from there it will be translated into all other languages by some of those who first receive it. So from London the message will be spread far and wide by people of all nationalities returning to their respective locales as representatives of the new worldview.

I came to see London as the eschatological epicentre and the point of mystical emanation and radiation. London would be ground zero and that the time of detonation would be 2012. Naturally due to my outlook and some of the ideas about the nature of London that had already formed in my head, William Blake's prophetic words certainly resonated with me. My affinity for Blake and some of his works, gave an extra layer of meaning to my being at st James Church on a day to day basis.

London was certainly a place where interesting people came from all over the world and working at St James and the Piccadilly area was a great place to meet a lot of these people. Slightly before I started working full time at the church, I had met there a striking looking young lady who was working and living in London, but was originally from Bosnia. She grew up mainly in Austria where her family had escaped as refugees from the conflicts in the Balkans. She was extremely blond and had the bluest eyes of anyone I'd ever met. Most unusually for a blond blued eye young woman, she was from a Muslim background and had a brother back in Austria called Muhammad. She once related to me her vivid recollections of the morning prayers in the cold unheated mosque back in her homeland as a child, and would on other occasions talk about other quite mundane memories of this sort which nonetheless fascinated me and I had an interest in.

On a slightly less mundane note, she once told me that her family were about to be killed by a group of Serb militia men who had discovered them all hiding in the cellar of their home during the time of the troubles in Balkans. But they were saved by the fact that the leader of the death squad had been taught mathematics by my friend's mother when he was a little boy. So he didn't have the heart to allow the family to be exterminated and ordered his men to move on. So they managed to escape with their lives, and I came to know for a while their extremely beautiful daughter now grown up.

She once told me that her ancestors came to Bosnia on white horses a long time ago from a distant land and also that she was descended from the Gnostic Bogomils who historically lived in the Balkans. The story seemed so fantastic and too romantic such that I probably thought it must have been some fanciful family myth handed down over the generations. A sort of Bosnian urban legend. It didn't completely register to me at the time that what she told me were historical facts and a completely accurate telling of things.

During my first year or so working at the church, there was an art exhibition held there which was related to the war in the former Yugoslavia and especially to the massacres that had occurred in Bosnia. I met a young lady volunteer who had the role of a steward, guarding the paintings and handing out information leaflets to people who came to view the exhibit. She told me her father was from Italy and that her mother was from Bosnia. Also she had blond hair which she said she had inherited from her mother. But most interestingly she told me that her ancestors had come to Bosnia on white horses in the distant past and also that she was descended from the Bogomils.

A short while after this meeting I read in a book that some of the Gnostic Cathars of Southern France who were mostly wiped out by the Catholic Church, managed to escape to the Balkans where they settled in what is now Bosnia. Zoom forward around 800 years, and I would for a while be spending some stimulating and very pleasant time with one of the future descendents of these Gnostic Cathars who had saved themselves from the fires of the inquisition and who herself was more recently fortunately saved from the fire of a Serbian death squad by the sentimental recollections of its commander.

The idea of London being some sort of mystic attractor may seem a little abstract but it was encounters of this sort which made things a lot more definite and concrete for me. It was personal stories such as these which gave me a very strong sense of the convergence of world history towards an eschatological conclusion which I felt was very close, and I increasingly came to believe was centred in and around London.

In a completely different manner another Gnostic connection, and indicator of the hand of providence at work, came my way a few years later in 2009 when my old childhood friend Adam, whom I'd known since we were both age 5, got in contact with me via Facebook and some mutual connections. We'd lost contact after high school because sometime in our teens we started to have different interests and were no longer so close by then. As children we were both very interested in nature and were keen ornithologists. Some of my happiest childhood memories were with my friend, bird watching in the parks in my hometown and the surrounding countryside. Later on my pal developed more of an interest in another kind of bird but I was a slower developer and gravitated towards a growing interest in home computers. So we didn't really spend much time together in our later teens.

Later on in our lives it seemed that there was some mysterious connection between us. While I was supposed to be studying at London University and enrolled on a degree course, I would visit a hostel near Imperial College called Lee Abbey and which was run by a Christian charity. I didn't have many friends and didn't go visiting very many places and this was perhaps the one I'd go to socialize occasionally. Some university classmates were staying there. Many years later I learned from another school friend that Adam had been working and living at Lee Abbey, at around exactly the same time that I would have been visiting the place. We may have passed each other in the corridor but not recognized each other out of context. It seemed like the strangest of coincidences. About 20 years later he would email me out of the blue after absolutely no contact at all, to tell me that he'd already seen my website and completely shared my mystical gnostic views!

Apparently he'd for a long while become a monk and taken all the vows, spending years doing charity work helping the poor in Bolivia. At some point he couldn't take the celibacy anymore, and so was now married and living in a Christian commune in Canada. I'd years ago in childhood, aged probably 10 or so, told Adam that I was a Gnostic because I saw a TV program about esoteric Christianity, and that instead of believing in God, I 'knew' in God. I had no idea then what this really meant then.

After a colourful and eccentric life, and a dozen or so full blown mystical experiences later, I came to understand that Gnosis meant to understand that our real nature was God or the Christ. It is an amazing synchronicity it seems to me, how our two lives seemed to have so many mysterious parallels and both leading to a commonality of belief. Two nature boys from the same small nowhere town would separately go on our unusual life journeys spanning the globe and arrive at the exact same conclusion relating to God and religion. The hand of providence was at work in both our lives. I'm fascinated to discover how this particular synchronicity trail will progress in the future.

Of particular interest to me was how often I'd meet people at the church who were totally sympathetic and fully believing in the idea that everyone is God and that we are all one consciousness. At one point this even included two prominent people at the church. This included one of the part-time priests at the church, who was fully into this more Gnostic side of Christianity. She once described to me a mystical experience of 'oneness' that she had which had turned her on to a more esoteric interpretation of Christian scripture. In many of her sermons she would often allude to mystical themes of oneness and the God within, with frequent quotations from the Gnostically oriented

Gospel of John in the Bible and also occasional references to the very mystical Gospel of Thomas and even the Vedic Upanishads.

One of her underlying aims, she told me, was to try and gently communicate these sorts of ideas to the wider Christian community and the world at large. Apart from her sermons and in large part towards this end she set up a discussion group that met once a month called 'Awakening to God'. She did this in collaboration with another Gnostically oriented member of the St James congregation, who at the time was also the Chair of the Parochial Church Council (PCC). So for a time there was a significant Gnostic and excellent heretical presence at St James, and with which I could totally relate.

I remember sitting in for a short while during one or two of these meetings, which consisted of about 20 or so people who were drawn mainly from the Sunday congregation with a handful of others who had come to know about the meetings from the posters which advertised them placed on the street billboards outside the church. They were always held on a Sunday shortly after the main service so always clashed with one of the busiest times for me. Anyway, when I briefly attended one of these meetings, I gained an insight into how a progressive Christian audience might react to the idea that everyone is God when the Gnostic Chair of the St James PCC and priestly collaborator narrated a short parable which came very close to saying directly, to the participants attending, the idea that 'Everyone is God'.

He told a story which he suggested at the outset, to the people gathered room, was an allegory for our relationship to God. The story in very brief outline went something like this. There was a land where there was a king and his subjects. The king died so another king came along. Then that king also died but this time round another king could not be found. There was a period of kinglessness. Then at last the problem was solved and everyone became their own king and all was right again in the kingdom.

After the story was told there seemed to be a brief moment of stunned silence. Looking around at the faces of most the people in the room I could see that the implication of the story wasn't easily digested. There was a sense of incomprehension and puzzlement. The narrator of the story seemed to sense the mood and fairly quickly moved the discussion on to a less challenging and less directly gnostic approach to things. From this episode I gained a insight into the difficulties that might be involved in communicating these sorts of ideas to even a very open minded and consciously progressive Christian crowd. Nonetheless there were quite a few members of the St James congregation who were quite comfortable with Gnostic ideas and related ideas such as reincarnation.

Other examples of people I met at the church who were fully believing in the idea that everyone is God included some of the traders who worked in the market. At one time or another there were several 'gnostic' traders who had stalls in the church court yard market. One of them was an Ismaili Muslim and follower of the Aga Khan who sold glass ornaments. I fondly remember the Gnostic discussions we used to have and how we used to lend each other Gnostic books. Some of the texts he gave me to read really gave me an insight into esoteric Shia Islam that I could never have easily gained otherwise. Some of these texts, which were extremely obscure, gave me a perspective on the life of Muhammad and early Islam that seemed so very real and also seemed to me more actual than the idealised accounts that I would be told by most Muslims especially Fundamentalists. This sort of thing I definitely considered one of the major perks of working at St James church. I probably wouldn't have met and made a connection with people like my Ismaili friend had I not been working there.

Also in the market I remember three sisters from India who for a while ran a stall selling imported Indian clothing and various arts and craft produce. They were all followers of the Indian Guru Mataji who is perhaps most well known in London for her regular appearances held at the Royal Albert Hall. Years earlier I had actually attended one of these gatherings after picking up a flier advertising the event. I wasn't all that impressed though her followers seemed like a pleasant crowd. From that encounter I wasn't made fully aware that at the heart of her teaching was the idea that Everyone is God though she kept alluding to some secret and 'birth right'. After getting to know some of her followers as a result of them happening to work in the market at the church, I came to know the central truth that was behind her sect and it was exactly as I believed. It made me feel good that some of her followers, who happily and openly believed in the same sort things I believed, were a part of my work environment.

Another new religious movement called The School of Economic Science happened to use the church one night for a concert of theirs. This was an organization that I had read a lot about and would often be included in various books about new religious movements, sects and cults. The organization is familiar to most Londoners through the large Tube advertisements advertising their 10 week philosophy courses, which were really a way of recruiting new members.

One night I was working at the church during a classical concert promoted by an organization called the Luca Trust, which had the stated aim of promoting leadership among young people. The concert was to be given by young people who were already involved with the Luca Trust. I recall that slightly before the concert the concert manager and I noticed that all the young people involved in setting things up and manning the box office and publicity tables seemed ever so slightly odd. Their demeanour and manner was unusual I thought. They seemed very disciplined and less spontaneous than your average teenager. Most events involving mainly young people at the church were ever so slightly more rowdy and just a bit more out of control than events made up of older people. However on this occasion things were the other way round. I didn't think much of it at first.

In the course of the evening I got talking to one of the main representatives of the Luca Trust, a young gentleman who actually worked quite near by as a business consultant. The conversation rambled all over the place but then at some point we got talking about meditation and our respective religious beliefs. It was then I discovered that my new friend was fully into the idea that Everyone is God. We talked a lot about Indian philosophy and Advaita Vedanta, which is the more formal term for these sorts of mystical beliefs in India. Eventually I would discovered that what was behind the Luca Trust was actually the School of Economic Science and that presumably most of the young people who were at this event were members themselves and probably through their parents.

I then went on to chat to some of the others involved with the event and was very happy and amazed that they had absolutely no difficulties with the idea that Everyone is God. Suddenly it felt great and inspiring to be working at this particular event and to be surrounded by so many like minded people. In retrospect and on reflection my guess is that one of the motivations behind this event relating to 'leadership in young people' is the same as that behind the London Underground Tube posters advertising their philosophy courses, i.e. a way of recruiting people to their ideas and cause. Something to which I'm not totally unsympathetic. This episode gave me a direct insight into how some Gnostic organizations go about promoting their truth.

Moving on, something of particular interest to me was that many of the traders in the church arts and crafts market were Muslim. More than that, there was an enormous diversity of all the different strains of Islam represented. Different sorts of Sunni from all over the world, i.e. Albania, Egypt, Algeria, Palestine, Pakistan etc. and some Shiites who came from India originally. In numerous discussions with these traders I was able to get an idea of some of the attitudes and beliefs which were held by them. There was an incredible diversity spanning the entire spectrum. I could see at first hand some of the enmity that existed between the Sunni and Shia. I seem to recall that was generally little or no interaction between some of the Sunni and the Shia traders. Also through numerous casual interactions I could get more of a sense of what a sample of typical Muslims actually thought about things, say relating to the world, how they saw Islam in relation to what was happening in present times. Some of these discussions would be debates and others involving more mutual agreement. This augmented my book study about Islam and which my social interactions would stimulate in the first place.

Working in the church was a very good generally for my ongoing study of religion. Sitting through hundreds and hundreds of separate little Bible readings in the course of the many services, morning prayers and ceremonies; really augmented my knowledge of the entire Bible.

Apart from Christian related activities there would be a lot of events held in the church which related to other religions as well. These sorts of events gave me a great opportunity to talk religion with actual practitioners of different creeds and so has greatly helped to enhance my outlook on things. Generally I would find that working at the church would give me a good context for meeting interesting religious people and contemplating religion.

During my time at the church I can recall quite a few interfaith type events which were held at the church. Some of these involved the launch of new organizations which would dedicate themselves to the cause of helping to reconcile all the religions of the world. This kind of thing particular resonated with me. They would usually involve a load of celebrities who were interested in religion and had signed up to be patrons of these organizations, often getting up to read passages from the scriptures of various religions. What a pleasure it was to be working on these kinds of events. I would have paid to attend these sorts of affairs, how amazing it was to be paid to be there and to be able to talk to the organizers and participants.

Along with the interfaith events involving all religion, there were also quite a few events that were in particular about the reconciling of Islam with Christianity and Judaism. These were great opportunities to reflect on the current situation, which was so often in the news. It was interesting to hear some ideas on how meaningful bridges may be constructed to help to promote the process of peace between these often contentious and belligerent factions.

On a completely different note, a variety of different Buddhist events also took place at the church, either on a regular or occasional basis. There were the regular Zen Buddhist meditations that occurred in the tower of the church. And for a long while on Saturday afternoons there were the mindfulness meditation sessions, which were inspired by the teachings of the Buddhist monk Thich Nhat Hanh.

I recall the leading lama of one of the four big Buddhist sects of Tibet came to the church to give a short talk and bless the London/UK devotees of the sect, who packed the church and queued up to greet their leader in person for a brief moment. The particular sect was apparently the one in charge of Tibet when Kubla Khan converted the Mongols to Tibetan Buddhism. Historically it was a rival for the now dominant sect of Tibet led by the world famous Dalai Lama, whose branch of Tibetan Buddhism is Tantric or Vajrayana diamond vehicle. So there was some feeling of a sense of history working that evening. At one point I spoke to the leader of this particular sect who came to church. He asked me where I was from, I said Hong Kong, and I could definitely sense his demeanour change to something ever so slightly less friendly and the flow of conversation became not as flowing. I guess he was seeing my humanity rather than my buddha nature. I also remember that in contrast to the process followed by the Dalai Lama's sect, where the next leader is a reincarnation of the existing leader; instead in the case of this particular Tibetan Buddhist sect then next leader was the son of the existing one. He was also there that evening and spent the time sitting and standing next to his father.

On another Tibetan Buddhist event at the church at which I also worked on involved the leader of a different sect. It was another colourful spectacle with a variety of Buddhist monks dressed in their saffron and red robes, but interestingly some of the monks were caucasian. The main event of the evening involved a long chanting session done by a dozen or so of the monks including their leader. It was quite hypnotic. At one point there was some terrible feedback on the sound system during the chanting which produced a deafening high pitched tone for a while. During the sound check while I was setting the up the mikes, one of the coordinators had kept insisting for the sound levels to be turned up and up but I warned there might be feedback. So things were set up a little louder than normal. The feedback problem took several seconds to fix, as I had to dash up to the front of the church to access the sound volume controls. I was quite impressed that the monks were completely unperturbed and chanted over the very loud squeal from the sound system.

Afterwards I checked out some of the stalls selling merchandise and leaflet tables that were set up as a part of the evenings event. I noticed for sale, a lot of new age looking strange contraptions which consisted of bits of welded metal rods with crystals of differing shapes and sizes attached to various places on these objects. They were advertised as having magical healing properties and offered the ability of psychic power projection. Also large sums of money were being charged for them and were a part of the sect's fund raising activities.

I picked up some of the promotional literature of the sect to read and discovered that the leader of the sect was none other than the Maitreya, i.e. the long awaited one of the Buddhist prophecies and next incarnate Buddha following the historical Guatama of Northern India around 2500 years ago. What an amazing honour it was to be so privileged to have worked on the evening when the church hosted the sect of none other than the Maitreya!

A major part of the church was the organization called Alternatives, who promoted new age talks held on most Monday nights in the main church area, throughout the year. I've already mentioned them earlier and described the basic set-up in some detail so to avoid repetition I'll recount here my later experiences which furthered my familiarity with the New Age at St James Piccadilly.

So I was already quite familiar with the Alternatives before I started working at the church. I knew quite a few of the people who had been involved with it in the past, some of whom I had a positive opinion of, but I'd already previously seen some quite negative aspects to the organization, some of the speakers they promoted and also the way they dealt with some people. Once I started working full time at the church then I was able to gain a lot more insight into what the organization was all about and learned a lot about how they operated, knowledge that would have been unobtainable otherwise.

All started well with the Alternatives organization, during my initial few months of working at the church. Though the management of Alternatives and I had some differences in the past we mutually decided to let bygones be bygones. Then something happened which started the process by which I came to clearly see what was really happening behind the scenes. One of the female volunteers, whom I was friendly with during my own time spent as an Alternatives volunteer, asked to meet with me after work. We met, had a chat and she told me that one of the directors of Alternatives was giving her a hard time. My feeling was that I was getting dragged into some dispute and my instinct was to not take sides.

Over time the situation between the by now ex-volunteer and the Alternatives organization deteriorated, lawyers got involved and a court case was pending. I met with the lady a few more times and even though I expressed my sympathy and found her side of the story totally credible because I had witnessed things not totally dissimilar to what she was complaining about. More specifically she complained of sexual discrimination and of one of the directors misusing his position of power and trust to behave in a sexually predatory way. Nonetheless I didn't think it was right for me to get involved on any one particular side versus the other, for a variety of reasons including reserving myself for a possible mediation role between the conflicting parties.

However something happened which allowed me to see far more clearly the lie of the land. One of the directors of Alternatives, who was also their chair of trustees and who also happened to sit on the board of trustees of the church, (i.e. the PCC or Parochial Church Council), over the course of a few conversations suggested to me that I should use whatever influence I had to dissuade the former volunteer from pursuing her complaint through the courts. He also expressed his concern that things might reach the media. He knew that the lady and I were friends and by then they were only communicating with her through their respective lawyers. He also made it clear to me than unless I cooperated with his wishes then I wouldn't make it past my initial 6 month probationary period of employment at the church and repeatedly emphasized the point that he had the power to influence this decision.

And so began the process by which the scales fell from my eyes. I started on the process by which I gradually came to see that the organization of love and light was a completely self-serving, greedy, and unethical money making enterprise wrapped in the living, breathing sheep skin of an active worshipping Christian community. Anyway, I made it past my first 6 months and my implicit contract of employment was renewed indefinitely, there was no reason why it should have been otherwise. During the rest of my time employed at the church, around 10 years, I would come to learn the truth about the New Age.

What I'd witnessed in the behaviour of the Alternatives director and trustee, was a clear conflict of interest. He was using his power as a member of the church board of trustees to try to gain an improper advantage for the Alternatives organization. What I subsequently learned was that he was regularly and repeatedly abusing his power especially in maintaining the subsidies and privileges they derived from the church. What was initially highly improper and unethical was later actually illegal, when laws in the UK were changed a couple of years later. This was when all churches were designated as and required to be registered charities. This is totally correct, as a large part of the churches income is derived from donations from members of the general public.

Concerning the actual talks Alternatives promoted, along with members of the public who wrote to church, I flagged up some of the questionable speakers whom Alternatives invited and the church hosted. These included the Australian new age guru, Jasmuheen who has at least four deaths directly attributed to her teachings. She promoted the idea of 'breatharianism' or rather her new age interpretation of it, and told her followers that they didn't have to eat, and could live off the air. She was actually caught eating in a TV expose, but some of her followers fully believed her and some of them ended up dead. By pointing out examples of speakers who were promoting harmful doctrines I was seen by some of the church management as a trouble maker.

One Monday evening when I was working the late shift at the church, Alternatives hosted the founder of the Theta healing group. I heard most of the talk from a speaker in the church offices, which had a feed in audio input from the main church sound system. The speaker promised to cure cancer and aids. A few months later I watched a BBC Newsnight expose of the Theta healing group, where in another talk at the London School of Economics, the same speaker had implied that her system could help people to regrow limbs. I flagged all this up to the church at the expense of being labelled again a trouble maker, but no action was taken. For a while afterwards the Theta healing group continued to use the church and it's rooms for workshops and talks. Eventually with the arrival of the new Rector, after an extended period with no head priest in charge, and my taking over room hire, appropriate actions were finally taken and at least the basement rooms which I managed were no longer used by them to promote their services and products.

During my time as a volunteer a new age guru called Andrew Cohen was mentioned in a group meeting of Alternatives directors and volunteers. He was a controversial figure who had early on in his career been denounced as a fraud even by his own mother. I learned that in the past he'd been a regular speaker at Alternatives but had been banned at some point. I also learned that somehow he'd been asked to speak again in the main church area by mistake. I wondered to myself, how could you ban a person from speaking then forget that this ban was in place, when it was exactly the same people in charge of Alternatives throughout the period in question.

A few years later while working at the church, Andrew Cohen was invited back yet again to speak in the main church area. Despite the fact that in the intervening years, after he'd been invited back to the church 'by mistake', the reports of mental and even physical abuse towards some of his followers had continued to pile up. Eventually his new religious organization became completely defunct when a prominent former follower confirmed all the negatives reports that had accumulated and came out with more revelations.

Another of the Alternatives speakers who caused a lot of controversy at the church was a speaker who claimed to be a psychic surgeon with the magical ability to cure all ills, using the power derived from channelling spirits. Even before his talk the church received many letters and emails of complaint from members of the public. I worked on the evening of his talk, and it was the usual stuff, i.e. miracle cures for the incurable ailments that probably afflicted many of the people in the audience. The church was very busy. I was told to look out for trouble as some concerned members of the public had written in to say that they'd be protesting during the event.

For a while I stood in the upstairs gallery area just to see everything was alright. I caught a part of the talk where the speaker described some 'scientific' experiment where a sick dog was drained of all its blood, and sea water was pumped into it arteries and veins instead. He then described how the dog was revived and jumped about happily like a new born puppy. I thought this was total nonsense and without thinking about it fully expected everyone else to do the same. But as I looked around and gauged the reaction of those immediate around me, I was surprised to discover that it seemed quite a few of the audience fully believed the literal truth and actuality of what the speaker had described, judging from their reactions and facial expressions.

One thing I learned over the years is that many of the people who become involved in the new age and subscribe to its ideas and therapies, are very gullible people and who have very poor critical faculties. But it is exactly these sorts of people the church should have been protecting. Instead of being lead to a place of relatively trust, i.e. the church, where whatever guards that they might have possessed, would have been lowered even further and then sold snake oil cures for their very real ailments. I pointed this out to some of the church management and I confronted one of the Alternatives directors about it, but yet less than a year later another psychic surgeon was invited to speak at the church by the Alternatives organization. I could probably write an entire book about the dubious and questionable gurus and speakers, promoted by Alternatives over the years, I've mentioned a few examples to give an indicator.

It would be wrong of me to over-generalize and give the impression that everyone involved in and anything relating to the new age, is false or fraudulent. I believe there is some good and genuine stuff out there, and of course a lot of it involves harmless cranks promoting eccentric beliefs that they genuinely and sincerely believe in. But what I'd encountered in the scene associated with Alternatives was so often false. I came away with the strong impression that mainly the new age was one great big marketing exercise and money making scam. Beneath the glossy packaging and the veneer of 'love and light', was primarily commercial and business interests.

Why all this was allowed to go on and the lack of oversight on the part of the church, as I've already described came about largely through the undue influence that Alternatives had on church affairs. The negligence on the part of the directors of Alternatives reflected that fact that some of them were playing the same New Age confidence trick themselves, that shouldn't have been promoted in a sacred space and place of active worship.

One of their directors promoted prosperity talks and workshops, that in a rather unsubtle and crude way alluded to the generation of wealth and money to anyone who bought into his ideas. The trouble was, he himself was actually relatively low income and hadn't actually generated much wealth or prosperity in his own life. Though he'd previously worked in the financial services sector and said he was a former banker, he wasn't really in a good position to tell others how to make money or gain the prosperity his promotional efforts alluded to. It seemed the poachers were appointed the game keepers. Most of the directors of Alternatives and also some of the Trustees were using the church to promote themselves, their own workshops and their businesses. Why should members of the public, donating to a church and registered charity, subsidize the promotion of outside business interests? Or the new age careers of the directors and trustees of Alternatives?

Over the years I discovered much of the new age is characterized by an almost total fixation on self and narcissism. Of course it's important to consider ourselves, and if we haven't got then we can't give. But what I discovered was that many new age gurus seemed to teach selfishness as a virtue. There was a constant emphasis on 'working on yourself' and not trying to change the world. That purely working on ourselves was the cure not just for our personal problems but also those of the world too.

It struck me that there was something of an imbalance in what the new age mainly taught. And a lot of this derived from the fact that primarily the new age was driven by commercial considerations and the requirement of having to make the customer happy. Once I met an aspiring young new age life coach who told me, he'd failed college, failed in a business, just come out prison and thought he'd try to become a life coach to teach others how they might succeed in life. This might seem ironic and even comical, but it was a pattern that I'd encounter again and again, even with the higher echelons of the new age scene, with some of the big name speakers and 'life coaches'. A lot of the new age gurus and life coach's were like paid sycophants who told people what they wanted to hear, inflating theirs egos for a short while and giving them a short rush in their workshops. But they were incapable of telling people what they needed to know, which might involve unpleasant truths, and therefore a fall in book sales and workshop enrollments.

This created the phenomenon of workshop junkies, constantly paying loads of money to go to new age workshops, but never finding the long term solutions because that wasn't what the new age was about. The commerciality of the new age was it's primary purpose but also its main weakness. Because its main purpose is to make money and make people feel good about themselves, it's never able to grapple to deal with the really difficult questions in life or provide unpalatable solutions, which may be exactly what is needed sometimes. The new age was there to sell products and enroll people onto the endless workshops.

I can best further explain these issues relating to the nature of the new age as I came to understand it, by giving an example of a group I worked with at the church which stood in total contrast to and was in many ways the diametrically opposite to it. Though this group also was involved in the process of people working on themselves, the methodology was quite different and less self centred.

One of the more worthwhile groups which the church hosted was Alcoholics Anonymous. At one point there were four AA meetings a week but most of the time there were the two weekly meetings, both held on the Thursday. And so I came to discover the Twelve Steps and Twelve Traditions of AA, and I came to learn about its spiritual dimension.

To those unfamiliar, a major aspect of the famous Twelve Steps and by the same token, one of the reasons why the AA formula for beating all sorts of addictions is so effective; involves the recognition of and the turning towards a higher power. The person going through the AA programme is left to decide whether he or she wants to call this God, the 'Force' or whatever. So for instance steps 2 and 3, talk about recognizing this greater power and turning towards it for help. Step 11 emphasized the importance of meditation and prayer, *'to improve our conscious contact with God as we understood Him, praying only for knowledge of His will for us and the power to carry that out'*. The AA understanding of prayer was exactly as how I understood it too. So apart from the fact that here was a set of teachings which visibly helped people who were in trouble, the spiritual aspects of it were totally in accord with my views of the 'higher power' and our relationship to it.

There was something very real and immediate about the AA meetings and the people who attended. Though AA was about people trying to beat the often very difficult problem of alcohol addiction, it was really a reflection of all of society and the purpose of spirituality in generally. So in a sense we are all addicted to the transient and fleeting material pleasures of worldly existence and this stops us from seeing a wider view of reality. In the same way an alcohol, gambling or drug addiction stops us from seeing the importance of all the other things life has to offer.

So if instead of alcohol addiction we substitute greed, selfishness, material fixation, power and status, then the purpose of AA is directly akin to one of the original purposes of religion in general which was to direct people towards the eternal and transcendent, i.e. the 'bigger picture' or God. Though of course, this original purpose may become corrupted, as it often seems to be and usually is unfortunately.

During my time at the church, working with AA, in helping sort out for them their rooms or in whatever way I could, was a total pleasure. Even if on one or two occasions this involved breaking up some fights and dealing with other sorts of trouble. I actually had a sort of affection for the AA groups and some of the people whom I dealt with regularly. Perhaps this was because it reminded me of my own struggles with addiction and drug abuse that troubled me so in the past, and I saw myself in the people who came to AA. Whatever the reasons, I thought the church hosting AA was one of the most important things it did.

The Meaning of Abraxas Fully Revealed

In late 2009 the full meaning of the Gnostic conception of God called Abraxas, in relation to my life, was made very clear to me in the most staggering set of coincidences. Years earlier in the Winter Solstice of 1998, I had my first encounter with Abraxas when I chanced upon a book in a library which just happened to be open on the page which contained a ancient depiction of Abraxas with my name WAI in bold letters directly under it. This had triggered a powerful and profound religious experience. Then 11 years later I finally read a book called 'Demain' by the Nobel Prize winning author Herman Hesse. I say finally because for years I had been encouraged by more than one friend to read it and I had become aware through my research that the book contained references to Abraxas. But not being a great reader of novels I'd put it off. Besides I didn't imagine that it could have any special relevance for me. I thought the novel would be just another exploration into the nature of Good and Evil with a few mentions of Abraxas being a concept of God which incorporated both the dark and the light.

However, when I read the book in the late November of 2009 I was stunned to discover that it seemed to be talking directly to me. It described to me the purpose of my life, what I had been doing with a lot of my adulthood thus far and what I was planning to do in the future. It seemed to me that my life story was a continuation and indeed consummation of the purpose and process that was happening in lives of the main characters of the book! A quick synopsis of the book would clarify what I came to understand.

The book Demian, which was published in 1919, is mainly set in Austria during the time slightly preceding World War I, though the story ends during the conflict and on its battlefields. It is about the coming of age of the main character Emil Sinclair who is befriended in school by a older pupil called Max Demian who introduces Sinclair to Abraxas and other ideas from esoteric religion. Demian and his mother, his father passed away, are well connected to the local spiritual and mystical crowd and their house is something of a venue where esotericists and various progressive types regularly congregate. These people as described by the author Hesse so reminded me of the kind of circles I would often find myself in and of a lot of my friends. i.e. people with an interest in spirituality, mysticism, eastern philosophy, meditation, also vegan and raw food diets. There was also in the book a strong political dimension and one related to social change and the creation of a new world order.

What particularly struck me was one of the characters that Emil Sinclair would encounter on his youthful spiritual odyssey, called 'Pistorius' who was a scholar, church organist but also somebody who had dreams of resurrecting the religion of Abraxas. That is really Gnosticism and the original truth behind all world religion. Several long passages in the book seemed to describe exactly the course that I had set my mind upon years earlier and that the Universe seemed to be guiding me towards. At the same time, the hopes and dreams of the character Pistorius were unrealized in the novel. He was an old man who had planned to return to the world the religion of Abraxas but was unable due to his fears and limitations. When I read the details of what he had hoped to do I was stunned to realise that this was exactly what I was trying to do with my life. Where he failed and was fearful to even attempt I would carry out to success and full fruition I felt. It encouraged me greatly that the mission I was attempting had also existed in the minds of others, that is in this case the author of the book Herman Hesse. The book seemed so perfectly tailored for me to read. The hand of providence had guided Hesse's writing of the book and guided me towards the vision of Abraxas that would in turn lead me to eventually reading Demian. It seemed most uncanny.

To quickly recap, in the time of my life, around 1996 to 1997 through fate and the consequence of a series of powerful mystical experiences, I had set out on the task of trying to communicate to the world the truth that everyone is God and that we are all one consciousness. I had come to dedicate practically all my time and efforts towards this end. In the Winter Solstice of 1998 I had serious doubts about this great task I had set out to accomplish. I was ready to give it all up and to set out on a less uncertain course in life.

So I went looking for a sign from the Universe to help me decide one way or the other. It was then that I chanced upon, in the most incredible of synchronicities, an open book in a public library with a depiction of Abraxas and my name written underneath, which triggered in me a powerful mystical experience. This reaffirmed my mission and gave to me a powerful symbol or token with which I could stay connected to the transcendent and mystical plane. And so my spiritual odyssey would continue together with the ultimate aim and purpose I had set myself. That is to communicate the idea that we are all God.

Almost 11 years later I would read the book Demian because it was highly recommended to me and also because I knew it had some references to Abraxas in it. I was shocked and stunned to discover that the book essentially told me what my life was about. The process and purpose of my life was exactly that of the main characters in the book, i.e. the bringing back into the world of the true religion of Abraxas i.e. Gnosticism, Sufism, Kabbalah, Tantra and Taoism etc. The three main characters Emil Sinclair, Max Demian and Pistorius I saw clearly reflected in my own life. Emil the seeker and student; Demian the agent and instigator; Pistorius the dreamer and visionary. But what neither of them could realize in the novel and in their fictional lives, I would make manifest in the real world and in my real life.

My life and my story was in a funny way a continuation of their lives and the story of the book. In a fictional way, Herman Hesse had captured in his novel a collection of sentiments and desires that existed around the time the novel was written and in which it is set. The purpose of my life was to fully realize those hopes and dreams in present times and in the world today. To resurrect the hidden esoteric religion represented by Abraxas. To restore the true religion and the common truth behind all the World's religions. And how might I do that?

For years I'd been on a quest to work out how the brain worked and to figure out what was the nature of mind. My work had made steady and sometimes rapid progress over a period of 25 years or so. In the course of my life journey I had several full blown mystical experiences where I became one with God or one with the Universe. They completely altered my view of things. And so I came to the conclusion that the nature of consciousness and the nature of God was really one and the same and that somehow we were all one consciousness, undivided and indivisible. I had discovered the God within, i.e. Christ within, Buddha within, 'Allah closer to you than your jugular vein', etc.

As work on my brain theory progressed I saw parallels between it and workings of the Universe, and also the process of life on earth and the process of society. I came to see the entire Universe as being reflected in the workings of the brain and mind. There was a self-similar or fractal pattern, a sort of cosmic template from which derived all the processes of Universe, the process of life and also the process of the brain and mind. So that this 'cosmic image' or 'image of God', was represented everywhere in the Universe and at all scales. At the scale of the entire Universe, right down to the level of society, brains, and even to the level of the functioning of our genes and DNA.

I discovered that the brain and mind acted as a sort of Rosetta Stone in which this cosmic template and image was completely manifest. So that through a complete understanding of brain and mind, it was also possible to derive a more complete understanding of the Universe. So that we may come to understand unknown and infinite mysteries of the Universe through an understanding of the known and finite brain.

And so I came to the realization that during my quest to understand the brain and mind, towards the original goal of creating artificial intelligence; I'd also uncovered a far larger and divine mystery. I discovered that consciousness was the manifestation of the one God and that in my brain and mind was being played out the process of God. In my mind and in my life I was manifesting the timeless mythic archetypes and the eternal cosmic battle between good and evil.

The ancient idea of the 'image of God', and the notion that, 'As above so below', became fully manifested in the brain theory. I realized I was able to fully articulate for the 21st century why it was that, *'As is the Human Body so is the Cosmic Body, As is the Human Mind, so is the Cosmic Mind, As is the Microcosm so is the Macrocosm and as is the Universe so is the Atom'.*

Furthermore, so many of the key metaphysical ideas behind the so called Esoteric or hidden religion, i.e. Gnosticism in Christianity, Kabbalah in Judaism, Sufism in Islam, Tantra and Advaita Vedanta in Hinduism, Vajrayana Buddhism and Taoism etc. were completely represented in and fully explained by the brain theory and its extrapolation to the workings of the Universe. For instance the recurring idea of the Cosmic Tree, the descriptions of the Universe coming into being through a process of progressive emanation and cyclical nature of being; were integral aspects of how the brain theory described the workings of the mind and by the same token the workings of the Universe.

Even with just the brain theory I knew I had made a major scientific breakthrough and would profoundly change the nature of the scientific worldview. But I also knew that in the long run it was the spiritual and divine knowledge I stumbled across, that was the far bigger prize. There had for a lot of my adult life been a strange sense that somehow life was being guided. So often it felt that the trajectory of my life was being influenced by a higher power. Eventually I came to understand my life had been set up in order that I should be given understanding of how the brain and mind worked, in order that I should be placed in a position of authority and influence to communicate metaphysical and spiritual truths. I thought I was the doer, but it was really the hand of providence that was doing. I thought I was the mover but all along it was really the Universe moving through me.

Once I had the brain theory to a sufficient level of development and extrapolated it completely to the Universe, then I made another momentous discovery. I found that I could then use this knowledge to explain exactly how it was that we could all be of one consciousness, undivided and indivisible. This happened in the most remarkable way. Because the answer had already been given to me in a vision I'd had years previously when I saw all the conscious entities in the Universe, each and everyone, from the beginning of the Universe to the end; strung out as beads on a single continuous string. I had seen the thread of life that passed through all of us. Years later I would be able to use the brain theory to completely explain the nature and arrangement of this thread. My mystic mind of visions and transcendent states of consciousness had come to completely converge with my scientific mind of neuroscience, physics, mathematical abstractions, and computer code.

The Future of Religion

So I came to believe that by explaining to the world the nature of brain, mind and consciousness, I would also be in the process and at the same time, explaining the nature of Life, the Universe and God. I would demonstrate to the world that the 'God in the gaps', i.e. the gaps science hasn't yet explained was where the true god of esoteric religion that became represented to me in the figure of Abraxas; was waiting to be discovered all along. The biggest mysteries of science involved brain, mind, consciousness, life and the Universe. I saw that what had formed in my mind over the years through the hand of fate was an understanding of these matters that could be communicated in a completely scientific way. At the same time this explanation was also the return of the key ideas behind the hidden or esoteric religion. The communication of the brain theory and its closely associated cosmological and metaphysical outlook was really the return of the Perennial Wisdom or the articulation of the Prisca Theologia (Original Theology) for the 21st century, in the language and conceptions of modernity.

I saw my work and my message as an apocalypse in the literal meaning of the Greek expression, i.e. an *'unveiling of the hidden thing'*. What was this hidden thing if not the hidden truth behind the hidden religion. The ancient Greeks also referred to experience of union with God as 'Apocalypse', i.e. a personal unveiling of the hidden thing. In understanding the process of brain and mind I was also able to derive an understanding of why it was that these mystical experiences had occurred in me and also how they might occur in others. So I came to understand that the purpose of my life was to deliver an historical apocalypse but also one which would start and facilitate the personal process of apocalypse in others.

I discovered a massive convergence of seemingly disparate notions. The 'gap' of the 'God in the gaps', the 'hidden' of the 'unveiling of the hidden thing' (i.e. apocalypse) and the hidden truth of the hidden esoteric religion, all pointed to the same thing. They were all talking about mind, brain, cosmology and consciousness; and this was exactly what I was going to be fully explaining to the world.

In the Demian novel, one of the main protagonists Pistorius had hoped to revive the religion of Abraxas, but he was too caught up with the ancient, old and preexisting. I knew that any world spiritual revelation couldn't rely on the existing religious institutions, the symbols of old and the teachings of past prophets and founders of religion. Instead it had to be grounded and have its base in the newest of the new, the cutting edge of science and the bleeding edge of high technology. But yet it had to completely acknowledge the old and ancient and make reference to it in any and every way possible. It was no good to ask people to have mere faith in this new revelation but it had to be solidly grounded in reason and fact. This would be provided by the Fractal Brain Theory and the completely scientific cosmology derived directly from it and which is the subject of a later chapter.

For years I had been Emil the student and Pistorius the dreamer. I would now seek to become Demian, and bring this apocalypse or revelation to the world and instigate the return of the hidden Esoteric Religion and Perennial Wisdom for the 21st century.

Chapter 10

The Fractal Brain Theory

Most of my adult life had been directed towards the goal of working out how the human brain worked and understanding the nature of mind. This continued right through the time I'd spent working at the church, where any spare moment I had and my days off would be spent in my studies and thoughts. I built on my earlier ideas but also would receive some breakthrough insights during this time. Things started to become crystal clear. All the pieces of the huge jigsaw puzzle of mind and brain came together in the creation of a Fractal Brain Theory that I came to believe would revolutionize the worlds of science and artificial intelligence.

In retrospect the funny church in London's Piccadilly was really the perfect context to have been working during the time when a lot of my ideas about the brain finally all came together, and a proper scientific theory of mind became more fully formed in my head. After all this was supposed to be Christopher Wren's favourite church and he'd designed quite a few. Why this is scientifically relevant I explain shortly. This particular church I found myself working in, was unusual for it's large clear glass windows. *'Nothing is more beautiful that light',* Wren was supposed to have said and so he designed a place to let in as much light as possible.

Wren the architect was also a Freemason in the true sense, before modern Freemasonry had even come into being. The stone workers and designers of Europe's churches and cathedrals were like the elite workers of their time, highly trained and highly intelligent. They were the ones who had the freedom of travel and also the sharpness of mind to gain knowledge of esoteric mysteries and truths behind religion which were hidden from most other folks at the time. For this reason and a variety of others, there has existed this association between on the one hand these masons and freemasonry, which came later; and on the other hand esoteric religion and gnosticism. Wren, a polymathic genius whose breadth and depth of knowledge, stretched far and wide, also had a keen interest in esoteric mysteries. He was also the founding member and leading light of the so called 'Invisible College', which was really a Freemason intellectual club which met regularly to discuss matters of science. Later this Invisible College evolved into London's Royal Society, which has been called the 'midwife of modern science'.

It would make me feel good to have my scientific thoughts relating to the brain theory and artificial intelligence; in the context that Wren had a hand in building, both literally and figuratively, i.e. the church and modern science respectively. Also the fact that Wren and the members of the original invisible college and so many of the founders of modern science shared my metaphysical and religious beliefs also encouraged me in my wider efforts to use my understanding of the brain in order to understand the nature of the Universe and God. To them the idea that 'As is the microcosm, so is the macrocosm', and also that, *'God may be understood from the things that have been made'*, would have been more than familiar to them.

So while it may have seemed that my investigations into the brain and mind were happening out of context, i.e. any academic or corporate research establishment; at the same time it felt like the perfect context for me to continue my quest. I came to the conclusion years later that it was this very being out of the 'normal' confined and highly specialized formal research context which allowed me to find answers which would have been next to impossible for more mainstream researchers to uncover. The reason for this was that science in the normal research context had become highly fragmented and compartmentalized, with each of the major categories of science further subdivided into myriad subcategories. Often this wasn't a problem and each of the sub compartments can proceed incrementally, perhaps with some interaction between the compartments. But when it came to trying to understand the brain and mind then this approach was no longer effective.

Science was divided but an undivided and indivisible truth was waiting to be found. When it came to understanding the complexity of the brain and the mysterious functioning of the mind, then here too the facts and separate pieces of the jigsaw puzzle were held in many different separated compartments, but obviously they all had to be brought together and understood as a single integrated whole. This is what mainstream researchers working in the fields of the mind sciences, neuroscience and artificial intelligence, had repeatedly failed to do. They couldn't, didn't or didn't have the inclination, to carry out the necessary task of bridging all the separate compartments needed to understand the brain and mind. It was very difficult to think out of the box when through the process of choosing to specialise in a particular field within one of the compartments of academia, a person has put themselves into a box.

In contrast I had made a conscious decision to exit the system early on because I felt, even in my late teens that, I wouldn't find the answers by going the traditional route. So I had charted a rather deviant course of self tutelage and independent research that had taken me on a strange journey that quite by chance would lead me to work at the strange church Christopher Wren built, who I considered as one of the original scientists who would have found the modern compartmentalized nature of science to be something alien. Like the patron saint of Wren's Royal Society, another polymath and esotericist called Francis Bacon, I would take 'all knowledge to be my province', and of course this included all knowledge relating to the brain and mind, which included neuroscience, cognitive science, psychology, genomics, informational and computational science, and also various relevant branches of mathematics.

The great scientist Isaac Newton was said to on occasions come to St James Piccadilly when he lived nearby in Leicester Square. Newton was described by the great economist John Maynard Keynes as the first scientist but also the last magician. By this he was alluding to Newton's keen interest in esoteric religion. He spent far more time thinking and writing about prophecies, Kabbalah (Jewish Mysticism), Alchemy and Hermeticism than he did about science. Many thinkers have put forward the view that his science really came from his religious and magical outlook, even prominent academics like Noam Chomsky for instance. Of course this sort of thing completely resonated with me. Quite by chance or perhaps through more synchronistic strange coincidence, in the years before I started working at the church, when I was unemployed for a while, I spent a lot of time working and reading in Westminster Reference Library which was built on the exact spot where Isaac Newton had lived.

London generally has a lot of history to it, this wasn't lost to me. Even though I existed completely outside of the modern scientific establishment, I always felt that what I was doing was a continuation of the process that had been set into motion by the likes of Bacon, Wren and Newton. And like them, but in a way quite unlike most modern scientists, for me there was no separation between science and the true esoteric or hidden religion. So in a strange way even though I respected a lot of modern scientists for all their wonderful theories and empirical findings I would use in my own work, at the same time I actually identified more with the original scientists of previous ages.

There were some other positive and very beneficial effects of having worked at the church for 10 years in relation to the development of the brain theory. One of these effects was that being in a stable situation encouraged doing the slow and steady hard work involved in developing a scientific theory. Whereas for much of my life my intellectual life had been a continuous series of boom bust cycles, where periods of intense creativity and advancement of the brain theory would be interrupted by periods of drug abuse, electric guitar musical interludes or depressions, when nothing much would get done.

Also as a result of doing a full time job for a long while, there was more money for buying all the very specialized books about the brain which were only otherwise found in the research libraries that I didn't have access to. These sorts of books containing overviews of the most cutting edge research, were often very expensive and several in my collection were priced well over £100. £50 or £60 was the typical sort of price though. Anyway, I managed to amass a sizable library of the necessary literature which was indispensable to my work. In addition it was very fortunate that over this same period, it became very easy to obtain electronic copies of the most important recent research papers over the internet which also helped me keep abreast of what was happening in academia and the corporate world. So even though I was outside of the normal research context I had pretty much the same access to knowledge as most of the people working in academia. But one advantage I had which they didn't enjoy, was that I was completely free to think my own thoughts, unaffected by the latest fashions, fads and trends; which were usually irrelevant distractions I'd often think to myself.

I had to pursue my studies and do my thinking whenever I could which was often on my feet, walking about and standing about, or perhaps on the train commuting to and from work. This forced me to evolve new ways of working where I had to hold things in memory and memorize a lot of things until I could sit down and write it all down in my notebooks. Over the years I became quite effective at working in this way, and it also helped me in my public speaking when you had to think on your feet. When I did get the chance to have a proper sit down to read and think, during my lunch breaks or sitting in a restaurant or cafe after work then because this time was so limited and precious it was used far more effectively than had it been otherwise.

It was most fortuitous that the largest bookstore in Europe, i.e. Waterstones of Piccadilly was located literally a few doors away from my workplace. I would spend most of my lunch breaks there and also any spare time I had before or after work. A lot of the time I would sit somewhere reading my notes and thinking, but a lot of my time was also spent reading text books about neuroscience cover to cover, in steady and concentrated instalments. So during a lunch break I might for just under an hour, load up in my mind and memorize as much as I could and then go back to work in the church on a memorial service, concert or one of the many other activities that would go on there; continuing the work in my head when I had a spare moment and later after work and at home. Most researchers would find this way of working impossible but over time it became completely natural to me.

An important and productive activity which helped the development of the fractal brain theory a lot was my periods of going for long running sessions jogging in North London's Hampstead heath, a large and expansive area of heath and woodland. One of the effects of going for these long runs is a super fluid state of mind which would kick in after a hour or so when the thoughts really flowed and a flood of new ideas would surge forwards. This effect would be synergized by sunshine, caffeine and chocolate, in the same way that I discovered mystic states could also be facilitated.

Several key insights were first obtained during one of these running sessions. For instance it was in the Summer of 2006 while jogging around Hampstead Heath, that I first saw in my mind's eye how it must be the case that all of the brain and mind should be encapsulatable into a single recursive function starting from a fertilized egg. With this great innovation, a multitude of ideas and concepts that I had formulated to try to understand the brain and mind became fused into a single unifying clarity. Even though after this flash of insight, it took years to work out all the intricacies and details of fully elaborating upon this idea, I knew it was correct because of the beauty and clarity I had experienced during my super fluid state of mind. It felt as if I had experienced a sort of mystical vision, though it wasn't of the same kind of intensity or otherworldliness of some other experiences I'd had. Nonetheless I had the strong feeling that a transcendent truth had been imprinted into my mind by the higher intelligence. Given this feeling of certainty, I was then highly motivated to add the flesh and bones to the basic insight, and this involved relating this flash of inspiration to mathematical concepts, ideas from computer science, and details from neuroscience and genomics. In this way my mystical intuition and inspired insight, was confirmed by my rational mind and became fully expressed mathematically and in relation to the latest scientific findings.

In around the Autumn of 2007 I thought I was ready to start communicating the brain theory that I'd been working on for so many years, since my late teens. In late November I did an experimental talk in front of a small audience of about 12 people just to gauge what the reaction would be. The talk was a flop, though my ideas were good, they were quite abstract and I hadn't found a good way of communicating them. Also I hadn't put in enough preparation and even though I had spent so much of my adult life studying the brain, this passion for neuroscience had slipped more into the back of my mind in the couple of years immediately prior to this time. So I hadn't spent a tremendous amount of time learning or thinking about actual neurophysiological processes or brain structures in the years leading up this talk. My knowledge of the neurosciences wasn't totally up to date though during this time I would occasionally read the odd neuroscience book or paper here and there; but not with any sort of regularity and nothing compared to my previous efforts in neuroscience study.

What I had been doing a lot of in the 10 years from 1997 to 2007 was thinking about and extending the abstract mathematical and computational constructs that I had formulated to encapsulate all the things I'd learned about the brain and mind up to that time. So I had been expanding upon and perfecting partial abstract theories about the brain which derived from the actual study of neuroscience that took up most of my life from 1986'ish to around 1996. The upshot of all this was that when I gave my brain talk in November 2007, I didn't come across as somebody who had a correct or convincing theory of the brain. My ideas existed in my imagination and in my extensive notes, but I couldn't communicate in the space of a few hours, what I thought was an awesome theory that explained how the brain works. So the talk didn't hit the spot, some of the audience were actually a little mocking. Though others were more sympathetic and understanding. The talk was to be about this great brain theory that I had been telling people I was working on, so people expectations were built up. However I failed to deliver the goods.

My brain theory which had taken up so much of adult life, existed mainly at that point visually and pictorially in my mind. All the brain and neuroscientific knowledge that I had learned was translated into this visual language and it was visually that the theory evolved in my head. My notebooks consisting of diagrams and sentences, but even the words only had their meaning when converted into their corresponding visual representation. This is why I couldn't communicate my brain theory easily and what I did manage to communicate didn't really impress people at all or else the significance of key points wasn't grasped and therefore not appreciated.

After this experience which was something of a failure, I was really fired up and totally motivated to do better. I would work hard to create the concepts and analogies that would allow me to communicate my theory. I would develop a language that would succinctly describe the visual ideas about how the brain worked that existed purely in my head, which would allow me to communicate my theory. So I went about systematically formulating clearer concepts for aiding the understanding of what I was trying to communicate, and thinking up better lines of explanation.

Also I began to systematically read all the latest neuroscience text books and anything else I could get my hands on and completely immersed myself in all the very latest research. I wanted to really get a better familiarization with all the latest research so that I would actually sound like an expert on the brain, which would be a prerequisite for people accepting that I had a definitive brain theory and which would give me people's attention so I could then explain it to them. This activity occupied my mind pretty much constantly to the exclusion of much else, for about a year and a half, tapering off a little there after. It was also during this time that I spent the small fortune on neuroscience books mentioned earlier. In particular there were a lot of new books about the prefrontal cortex which was where a lot of the cutting edge research was going on; and I read these avidly.

I really spent a lot of time reading all the latest neuroscience books I could get my hands on. I would also devour neuroscience text books. So afterwards I had a much better grip on what was known about the brain than I had previously had. Armed with all this new knowledge, I worked on formulating clear explanations of the abstract concepts behind the brain theory and systematically mapped the mathematical and computational constructs of the theory to all the new data on neuroanatomy and neurophysiology I was accumulating in my head.

An important milestone was reached in the Spring 2009, when I made my second public presentation of aspects of my brain theory to a small audience of people. This time the talk was a success. It went really smoothly and from the positive reaction of the people I derived a lot of encouragement. It was a real watershed happening. Something which had up to then existed almost purely in my head and in my notes had finally entered successfully into social space. This time I felt I'd hit the nail more on the head.

For years I had been saying to people that there was this amazing brain theory coming together in my head, now for the first time it had made its appearance to the outer world, to a room full of intelligent and discerning people. I had tried to attempt this previously but had failed. This time the reaction, instead of being one of disappointment and disbelief, was instead one of excitement and some acknowledgement. The talk was imperfect and the material was still a work in progress. But for the first time ever I was able to convey something of my Brain Theory in a way that seemed convincing and pertaining to how brains might actually work. At the very least, the material that I presented was far ahead of anything that was happening in academia and the big research institutes.

One of the members of the audience who attended this talk had recently finished a PhD in Artificial Intelligence and Robotics and was quite impressed. He very encouragingly told me that I seemed to have a familiarity with the brain that was better than his professors who were associated with London and Oxford University, some of whom were big names in neuroscience and whose books and papers I'd read over the years. I was a completely self taught guy who had obsessively studied the brain most of his adult life, but completely outside of academia and in isolation without any outside praise or encouragement. So when these occasional little morsels of positive feedback relating to my brain studies and theorizing occurred it meant a lot to me at that time. So even at this early stage of bringing the Brain Theory into social space, people could see the relevance and power of the theory.

After this initial success I did a few more Brain Theory talks later that Spring, refining my presentation and lines of explanation, also improving my diagrams and delivery. And from then on this process would be on going and the development of the brain theory would become accelerated by the public talks. In finding better ways to explain the brain theory to as wide an audience as possible then I found that I came to understand the theory better myself. I learned later on that this was called the Feynman technique, named after the legendary physicist Richard Feynman who described how he himself deeply grasped a concept by working through the process of figuring out how to explain it to a lay person without specialized knowledge. So in the same way, because many of the people who came to my public talks were non-technical, I had to break the theory down into the most basic and easily digestible concepts. In doing so I would be systemically breaking the theory down into its most basic building blocks and gain a much more detailed understanding of things for myself. Also I'd constantly look for analogies and metaphors which would aid in my explanations, and help me to communicate an idea in the shortest possible time and most easily graspable way. And in so doing I would come to discover symmetries or unifying patterns that might not have come to me otherwise.

In addition the public talks about the brain theory would focus my studies and book learning. It was highly motivating to regularly face a live audience, many of whom would be highly intelligent with technical backgrounds. So I had to really deliver the goods. I think that even though the theory developed mainly in isolation and outside of any formal research institution, this social dimension which came about through the public talks meant that, earlier than would have been the case, the brain theory was being oriented to being communicated to the wider world. This process of explicitly expressing the theory to other people in the form of words and diagrams, and getting things into a neat and presentable form helped toward the evolution of the brain theory and my ideas relating to artificial intelligence, immensely.

Around the same period of around 2007 to 2009 when I was very focused on the brain theory and learning about the latest neuroscientific research, I did a public speaking engagement at a yearly vegan raw food gathering called the Festival of Life. It was quite a large event with many stalls, shows and numerous other public speakers talking about all sorts of things. Because I spoke at this event every year and the same people kept returning year on year, I felt it necessary to generate new material for each of these talks, so I didn't repeat myself too much. Anyway I thought that in order to generate interest for my talk I decided to talk about what would happen in 2012. Many psychedelic, new age and various mystical people held the date 2012 to be very significant and believe that some awesome event would happen around that time and especially on the Winter Solstice of that year i.e. December 21st, which was considered the exact point at which the new great 26000 year cycle of time began.

Before planning on doing a talk on 2012, I hadn't actually shown all that much interest in the date as I thought the prophecies from the major religions of the world was where the real action was going on, not some prediction related to some obscure calendar used by the Mayans, who are a Meso-American civilization that existed around about 1000 years ago. But as I was doing all the research for the talk and reading up on the 2012 phenomenon and all the different speculations on what was going to happen I became fascinated and really got into it. I read that a lot of the speculations about what was going to be happening in 2012 revolved around things to do with consciousness, enlightenment and artificial intelligence. This was apart from all the lurid disaster scenarios that a lot of the commentators were describing.

Then I connected these speculations with the brain theory and artificial intelligence project that I had been working on all these years and which I felt at that point in time was really coming to fruition. I was feeling a real certainty at that stage that my theory and way of looking at things was correct. I thought that it might take a few years more to take the theory to a stage where I could publish and back up my theory with a whole load of software simulations. It thought this would occur in and around the year 2012. So if people were expecting some sort of revelation to do with consciousness and artificial intelligence, then with my brain theory, accompanying software and the work I had done trying to explain that the 'Mystery of Consciousness is the same as the Mystery of God'; I thought my work would perfectly fit the bill and deliver on people's expectations. So I reasoned to myself why don't I use 2012 as a deadline and coming out date. I had set myself a direct challenge.

I recalled the modern myth of the Dune Trilogy which is set on a desert planet, where the inhabitants of that world had a set of prophecies much like the 2012 thing. In the story the lead character who is from another world becomes stranded on this desert planet and in order to survive he deliberately uses the prophecies to gain the assistance of and not be killed by, the indigenous and warlike people who believed in these prophecies. He was aware that the prophesied one was predicted to come from another planet just as he was. So he cunningly adopted a name that sounded like, though not exactly the same as, that of the expected one predicted by the prophecies. As the story unfolds, through a series of twists and turns, the main character ends up fulfilling the prophecies anyway. I thought I could do this. If the 2012 crowd were expecting a big revelation, relating to artificial intelligence, consciousness and enlightenment then I could certainly deliver the first two criteria. The enlightenment thing wasn't something that I could promise to anybody. But at least I could explain to people what enlightenment is, that it actually exists and give people some pointers.

So 2012 became this great deadline for which I had to pull something out of the hat to do with the brain theory, just before or around this time. Looking back this really motivated me and stimulate a lot of work. I seemed to pull out even more stops and things shifted to an even higher gear. So I knew what I had to do. I had to continue my studies of the brain. I basically had to know the intricacies of the brain better than most neuroscientists and I also needed to evolve my explanations of the brain theory. From this somehow the brain theory would spring forth upon the world in 2012. All of this while doing a full time job and having a young family.

In the time leading up to the 21st December 2012 there was a real maelstrom of activity. The brain theory evolved really quickly and I gave a lot of public talks about it. I hadn't by then gotten into the process of sitting down and writing about the brain theory. The full time job and young family at home made this not as straight forward as it might be for most conventional researchers. It was far more straight forward to prepare for the public talks which I could do anyway in my head, walking about or perhaps standing on a train. So it might have seemed highly improbable that my brain theory would have been communicated to the wider world for 2012, if I wasn't producing much written output. However something incredibly fortuitous occurred, where once again the hand of providence would intervene in a chain of 'lucky' happenings.

In July 2011 I happened to be giving a political talk in a squatted building that was formerly a pub in North London. This in turn led to a series of talks in Bristol where in one of them, I met Dan the cameraman, who was from a small UK satellite television channel called PSTV or Paradigm Shift TV. It's another one of those funny coincidences that during my talk where I first met Dan and which he attended, I described how the brain theory would be the key that could spearhead the much anticipated great paradigm shift that a lot of the kinds of people who came to my talks were waiting for. To cut a long story short, after that several of my talks were filmed by various camera men from PSTV and these talks of mine were shown on UK satellite TV over the course of 2012.

I was still very much the voice in the wilderness, some guy working in a church doing talks in London and some other UK cities but suddenly I was able to reach a far larger audience than before. The positive feedback was encouraging and all sorts of people became introduced to my work. These filmed talks were also made accessible through internet video via Youtube and Vimeo etc. So this gave the talks further viewership. So from these very small beginnings the fractal brain theory started to be communicated out to the wider world. Like a small stone dropped into a pond the ripples started to spread out staring in 2012. It was as if some electronic messages in a bottle were cast out to the cyber-sea of the World Wide Web, slowing carried out by the currents of the internet, to reach whoever might be interested. Rather amazingly over a short period of time this lead to some very interesting and useful people coming to appreciate the brain theory. It also allowed me to connect with a lot of key people worldwide who shared in my beliefs and in my mission.

Around this time my most successful video was of a talk I did about the fractal brain theory in July 2012 and which started to be shown on UK Satellite TV a month or so later. From the feedback I received it made a strong and positive impression on a lot of key people and directly lead to a lot of other opportunities. A lot of people who watched it also shared it on social media so it really got around. I was still working full time at the church, and together with my young family I had very little time or resources to promote my message so it was rather fortuitous that the brain theory was able to promote itself. The sometimes gushing and generally positive reviews and feedback I received encouraged me greatly. Even the sometimes extremely negative feedback, especially relating to the cosmological and metaphysical outlook that was associated with the brain theory, would help me to sharpen my counter arguments and beef up my explanations.

A key opportunity which was brought about by my talks having been filmed and made available on the Internet, came about early in 2014. Stuart Hameroff who organized the famous consciousness conference in Tucson, Arizona USA, wrote to me out of the blue to say he liked my ideas and asked if I'd heard about his conference. Of course I replied and a few interesting emails flowed to and fro in a conversation thread. The next big consciousness conference was later that year in the Spring, but I didn't have the money to go and wouldn't have spent that kind cash to go to a science conference anyway especially with two small children. So with the distractions of a full time job and young family, the email thread went dead, pending some clever reply that I thought I was going to write, but never got round to.

Exactly a month later a multimillionaire cofounder of the Singularity University wrote to me out of the blue saying he'd seen my talk on the brain theory, and that he'd like to meet me and asked if I was coming to the consciousness conference. After I explained my financial situation in an amazing act of generosity he offered to cover all my expenses. So a few emails to various people later I was all set to go to my first ever science conference of any sort, and what a special meet up it would be. I'll talk more about the conference in the final chapter, which would fit in more with the roughly chronological order of this book, but I will expand here on a particular meeting I had at the conference, which is most relevant to the present chapter.

Especially in relation to the fractal brain theory, the most interesting consequences of being at the conference was that I had the chance to have some breakfast and a conversation with Christof Koch who is one of the worlds top neuroscientists. He was a long time collaborator of the late Francis Crick of DNA fame. Now he was the chief scientist at the Allen Neuroscience Institute which was funded by Paul Allen, Bill Gate's ex-business partner and cofounder of Microsoft. It was quite by chance that this meeting occurred. There was a video production company who were recording video interviews with the big names who were speaking at the conference and there were many. Most of those involved with this video production crew believed the same thing about consciousness that I did, i.e. that we are all one consciousness and that the mystery of consciousness and the mystery of God are one and the same. They were only really interest in the famous scientists and philosophers present but one of the crew heard me give a spontaneous speech about the God thing to an little informal crowd that had gathered around me.

So I was pleasantly surprised to be asked to give a half hour interview for them. I gave a quite a sparky performance, and I'd had a lot of experience public speaking so I came across pretty well. It was by sheer coincidence that Koch was waiting to be interviewed immediately after me and was standing by watching as I did my thing. He may have thought I was some up and coming academic researcher, not some self taught guy working in a church. Anyhow we had a good chat, I spoke briefly about my brain theory and gave him my card. The card was quite provocative, for it said that I was going to explain to the world the nature of brain and mind and revolutionize the worlds of neuroscience and artificial intelligence. Which was exactly his field.

The next morning Christof Koch came up to me in the breakfast lounge, where I was sitting doing my regular routine of drinking the free coffee, thinking and writing in my notes. He asked if he could join me. Of course I said yes and it was something of an honour. I'd read one of his books years ago while a student and he did some great work. After a bit of chit chat he went on to tell me a host of reasons why he thought my theory was wrong. And I explained to him why all his objections were flawed, incorrect or irrelevant. His final words to me were, 'so you think you have one algorithm to rule them all?', I replied in the affirmative; and he went off and that was that.

Many months later, at the end of 2014, I was reading a book called 'The Future of the Brain', which was a collection of essays by the world's leading neuroscientists each expressing where they thought their field was heading. I read with great interest the final chapter titled, 'Neuroscience in 2064', which was jointly authored by one of the editors of the book and Christof Koch. In this chapter, to explain what they thought the field would be like in 50 years time, they described a fictional story of someone who came back in time from 50 years in the future. This character of theirs from the future was a neuroscientist reporting what the state of our understanding of mind and brain would be by then. Their prognosis of the state of neuroscience even 50 years hence was pretty negative I thought to myself. They, Koch and coauthor thought we still wouldn't have figured out how the brain worked by then.

I thought I could do much better than their man from the future right now. What was especially interesting for me was when I read their man from the future saying in retrospect, *'engineers imagined that there would be one true brain algorithm to rule them all, [] that simply hasn't proven to be the case'*. This echoed exactly the phraseology Koch used at the end of our meeting. Koch couldn't see the possibility of a single unifying algorithm behind the functioning of the brain and mind, but that is exactly what the fractal brain theory described.

The reason why Koch and his coauthor believed there couldn't be a unifying algorithm was that they reasoned that because there is so much hardwiring and pre-specification by the human genome i.e. in the DNA, then this would necessarily create a variety of different sorts of algorithms which therefore could never be reduced to a overarching and unifying master algorithm that would 'rule them all'.

But the possibility which Koch and his coauthor hadn't considered was that this unifying algorithm would also encompass the functioning of the genome, and the process by which it specified the hardwiring of the various differentiated algorithms assumed to be existing in the brain's circuits. But this is exactly what the fractal brain theory described. For the fractal of the brain theory didn't end at the level of the neuron but continued down even to the level of the functioning of the DNA and genome working computationally. The one algorithm 'to rule them all', of the fractal brain theory, also described the algorithm which produced the hardwired specialized functions of the brain, and also the algorithm which in turn built upon and augmented these preconfigured functions. So that there was a single continuum and underlying symmetry of process as well as symmetry of description, that spanned the functioning of the genome in specifying the overall layout or 'rough draft' of the brain, right through to the process that changed the brain through learning, and also the processes which gave rise to our thoughts and behaviours.

The nature of the unifying algorithm, was far more powerful and encompassing than either Koch or coauthor had imagined, or that their fictional man from the future could relate.

The recurring theme throughout the book, 'The Future of Brain', which was jointly written by over 20 of the leading lights of the neuroscience world, was the need for the bringing together of ideas and the mountain of data and empirical findings about the brain and mind, which only existed in fragmented form. All the myriad fragments were contained in the separated specialized compartments of the different brain and mind sciences. The whole field was screaming out for some great unifying conception to come along. What I had in the Fractal Brain Theory was exactly what they needed i.e. an overarching unification of all the messy details of brain physiology and anatomy, but also a unifying of brain and mind. The brain theory was able to completely integrate the 'parts list of cognition' with the 'parts list of neurobiology' and the 'stuff of mind', with the 'stuff of meat', as it was quite poetically expressed in the book.

Furthermore the fractal brain theory also came to be able to include in the unified description the workings of genome in the process of ontogenesis and neurogenesis, i.e. the process by which our bodies and brains come into being starting from a fertilized egg. So the unifying of brain and mind, came to also completely incorporate the functioning of the genome, in a single all encompassing integrated description.

I had a major theoretical breakthrough at around the time I was reading the 'Future of the Brain' book around the end of 2014, though it had been in the making for the previous 8 years before that. In a funny way, reading Christof Koch's contribution to the book and the views of some of the neuroscience mega-stars on the significance of genomics in relation to the functioning of brain and mind, probably helped to motivate and catalyse the breakthrough. Many of the neuroscientists who contributed to the book were also speaking of the need to integrate the new findings from genomics into our understanding of brain and mind, though the suggestions made were quite tentative. Nonetheless what I read, really inspired me and fired up my engines of motivation and this helped me to produce the major theoretical breakthrough which occurred at this time.

I managed to completely extrapolate (or interpolate rather) the Fractal Brain Theory to the workings of the genome and the intracellular world of DNA, RNA, enzymes and proteins. So that the genome worked like a miniature fractal brain and the functioning of the genome in ontogenesis and neurogenesis, i.e. the production of our bodies and brains; is as the process of our brains in the production of our behaviours and thoughts. I discovered that there was one continuous symmetry of process from the unfolding of our bodies and brains from the fertilized egg, right through to the unfolding of our lives through our thoughts and actions, which all converge on the prime directive, which is the process of fertilizing eggs. This was something I'd suspected for a very long time but I had only managed to work out and fully elaborate the details of this idea during this time, stimulated in part by the 'Future of the Brain' book.

So I was able to express the idea and intuition I had for a long time, the single theory for mind, brain and genomics, in relation to the most current knowledge about the genome. It was a very exciting development, the unifying theory of brain, mind and AI, now also came to include genomics; so that a single unified solution spanned the lot. So the fractal brain theory had become a lot more fractal as I suspected would be the case. The seed for this huge integration came from my flash of insight that occurred to me, while jogging around Hampstead Heath eight years previously.

The Fractal Brain Theory had gone to a very abstract place and this went hand in hand with the process of explicitly formalizing and computer coding the brain theory. This is how the fractal brain theory converged with the world of genomics and DNA. As I read up on all the latest in genomics and watched the latest talks on Youtube by the leading researchers in the field, it had all seemed shockingly familiar, so that I was repeatedly getting these deja vu moments, even while learning new things that had only been discovered very recently by then. The details of genomic functioning I discovered were in so many cases identical to and perfectly corresponded with the abstractions I'd formulated over the years to explain brain and mind functioning. I saw a whole new level of the amazing and beautiful symmetry in nature.

For years I'd been trying to give the neurons of the fractal brain theory their own simple DNA, to enable the growth of a basic brain from an initial seed recursive atom or progenitor neuron. But then I would come to the conclusion that this DNA which is there to recursively create the Fractal Brain, itself works as a smaller fully fractal instance of a nested fractal brain contained in every 'neuron' of the larger fractal brain we're trying to generate! Also that this breakthrough in my conception of how the Fractal Brain Theory could be made to work also corresponded with what was known about real biological brains, neurons and genomes.

With this new breakthrough I knew that I had discovered something quite unexpected that would stun the world of neuroscience and science in general. It was a very specific claim and a quite amazing property of the brain theory that I could fully justify and explain very precisely and relatively succinctly; and which would be able to generate a lot of excitement in a relatively short space of time. I was going to provide the unification of brain, mind and genomics that so many of the world's leading neuroscientists were clamouring for and much anticipating. I knew that 'The Future of the Brain' was the Fractal Brain Theory.

The Science behind the Fractal Brain Theory

Behind the Fractal Brain Theory are three fundamental, very powerful and interrelated ideas; that are systematically applied towards the understanding of the brain and mind.

This in turn leads to three major critical breakthroughs which make up of the main body of the theory. The three fundamental ideas behind the fractal brain theory are Symmetry, Self Similarity and Recursivity. And the three major breakthroughs comprise firstly a single unifying language for describing all the myriad details and facets of the brain as well as the mind.

Our second breakthrough concept is a unifying structure deriving from our unifying language, which allows us to see how everything related to brain and mind comes together as a single integrated whole.

The third and most surprisingly theoretical breakthrough is the idea that all the various information processing of the brain and the many operations of the mind, can be conceptualized as a single underlying unifying process and captured in a single algorithm.

Taken together these properties of the fractal brain theory are set to revolutionize the worlds of theoretical systems neuroscience and artificial intelligence. And so we'll explain these concepts and breakthroughs more clearly and in more detail.

The Symmetry, Self-Similarity and Recursivity theory of Brain and Mind

This brain theory that is in the process of being revealed to world may also be given the longer title of, 'The Symmetry, Self-Similarity and Recursivity theory of Brain and Mind'. This is quite an effort to say, and so it is a useful and convenient shorthand to refer to the theory as the 'Fractal Brain Theory'. The word Fractal implies Symmetry, Self-Similarity and Recursivity so the title 'Fractal Brain Theory' is an entirely appropriate as well as useful shorthand. We'll go through each of these foundational concepts in turn in order to give a better idea of the significance and power of the Fractal Brain Theory.

Symmetry

Symmetry is such an amazingly powerful idea. In fact if the entire process of science had to be summed up in a single word, then a good candidate for this word would be 'symmetry'. Science can be said to be the process of discovering the patterns of nature and the Universe. But it is more than that, because science is also the process of discovering the patterns behind the patterns. That is, the meta-patterns and unifying patterns, which show us how all the seemingly separate patterns are really manifestations of the same underlying pattern.

And so we have the same problem in the brain, where we are confronted with a dizzying and myriad array of facts and findings with no obvious and apparent way of seeing any overarching pattern behind it all. So it makes perfect sense that the idea of symmetry should be applicable.

Indeed if symmetry is behind the very process of science itself, then why should the search for a scientific understanding of the brain be any other way? And so then the problem becomes, how to apply this powerful concept towards that goal and this is not at all obvious. The specific ways that the symmetries behind the law of physics are explored in science, don't translate in any sort of direct or intuitive way to the study of the brain.

The symmetry of mathematical equations or of regular geometric forms, seems far removed from the organic messiness and irregularities of biology and brain. And at first glance and superficial inspection, the brain seems so full of asymmetry and dissymmetry.

So one of the problems that the fractal brain theory solves and is how to interpret the brain and mind, using some of the most cutting edge findings in neuroscience and some bridging ideas from mathematics, in order to see clearly the underlying and unifying symmetries behind it all.

Physicist believe that there is an overarching 'supersymmetry' that unifies all the natural laws of the Universe, though this idea is still in the process of being fully worked out. By the same token, the Fractal Brain Theory is able show that likewise there is an overarching symmetry that is able to explain and account for all the diverse phenomena of brain and mind. With this underlying symmetry we are able to reduce all the vast complexities of the brain and mind into a very elegant and compact description. And so symmetry forms an important foundation of the brain theory.

Self-Similarity

The idea of Self Similarity is synonymous with idea of something being 'fractal', hence the name Fractal Brain Theory. An object that is self-similar or fractal contains smaller copies of its overall form within itself repeated and at many smaller scales. A useful way of looking at self-similarity is to think of it as nested symmetry, where a pattern repeatedly contains copies of itself within itself.

A much used example of self similarity is that of a tree, where the diverging pattern of branchings coming off the main trunk is repeated in a similar way in its branches and even in the veins of its leaves. So a tree can be described as self similar and fractal.

Fractal geometry which was discovered in the 1970s has been called the geometry of nature. Tradition geometry deals with straight lines, regular triangles, squares, circles and the like. Fractal geometry seems far better suited to describing complex natural forms such as mountains, clouds and snowflakes; as well as organic structures such as plants, animals, people and even entire cities.

It is even suggested by leading scientists that the entire universe may have fractal structuring. And so quite appropriately the Fractal Brain theory is the application of the idea of self-similarity in the context of understanding the natural phenomenon of brain and mind. It is an approach which has been suggested and tried before in the past few decades but which came up against hurdles which at the time seemed insurmountable. And on superficial inspection and with a limited understanding of the brain, then it is not at all apparent that the brain can be understood as being fractal.

But with the benefit of recent empirical findings from neuroscience and a novel way of interpreting the data, then the Fractal Brain Theory is able to show how indeed the brain and mind can be conceptualized as being perfectly fractal and completely self-similar. And this sets up a lot of the conceptual groundwork for the brain theory and gives the theory its organizing principle..

Recursivity

Recursivity really is a universal process and the process of life itself can be considered as recursive. The process by which life comes into being, starting from a fertilized egg, dividing into two, then recursively and repeatedly dividing into 4, 8, 16 and so on, to give rise to all the cells in your body, this is an example of a recursive process. And the process of sexual reproduction, and the diverging and converging lines of family trees, generation recursively following upon generation is another example of recursion.

Some thinkers even imagine the entire Universe and everything that happens in it as one big recursive process, so the idea of recursivity is pretty deep. Recursivity is a key concept that underlies computer science and the workings of all computers. The Fractal Brain theory shows that this phenomenon of recursivity is fundamental for understanding how the brain and mind works.

Three Theoretical breakthroughs: A unifying language, unifying structure & unifying process

The fractal brain theory is the systematically application of the fundamental principles of symmetry, self-similarity and recursivity towards the understanding of brain and mind. And this leads to three major scientific breakthroughs, which we'll elaborate in turn…

A Single Unifying Language

The first of our breakthrough concepts has been anticipated. It is a way of describing not just all the structures and processes of the physical substrate of the brain but also all the various emergent structures and processes of mind; using a single unifying language.

So for instance the 1996 publication, 'Fractals of Brain, Fractals of Mind: In search of a Symmetry Bond', described the existence of a 'secret symmetry', secret in the sense of being at that point undiscovered, which would allow us to conceptualize the brain and mind as a single continuum and describe it in the same language. This is the 'symmetry bond' referred to in the books title.

Professor of Psychology and commentator on all things AI, Gary Marcus, described recently in 2014 how useful it would be to gain a unified description of brain and mind, and how this could potentially revolutionize the field.

With the coming of the Fractal Brain Theory, the 'secret symmetry' is secret no more. We have now exactly this unifying language for describing all aspects of brain as well as mind. It is also a descriptive language which is supported by a vast array of empirical evidence, which suggests that it is not something ad hoc or arbitrary but rather one which reflects fundamental truths about how the brain and mind work.

Indeed one of the strengths of the fractal brain theory is that it does take into account and incorporates a vast array of empirical facts and findings from neuroscience and psychology. It uses the unifying language to describe in a common format, all this vast diversity of information. This leads to the second major breakthrough the brain theory enables..

A Single Unifying Structure

Intuitive we know that there must be some sort of unity and integrated structure behind the brain and mind. This is because we know that somehow, all the various myriad aspects of our brains and minds must work together in an unified and coordinated way to achieve our goals and objectives. We know from our experience and introspection that this must be the case, we have this personal sense of oneness and singular wholeness that gives us the impression of self and identity. But it has been very problematic for brain scientists and artificial intelligence researchers to work out how exactly this is the case physiologically and how this may be implemented.

Neuroscience exists as an ocean of facts and findings, with no obvious way to fit them all into a unified understanding. In 1979, Francis Crick of DNA fame, wrote that in relation to brain science, "what is conspicuously lacking is a broad framework of ideas in which to interpret these various concepts." 35 years later, this unifying theoretical framework still seems to be missing.

Neuroscientists Henry Markram's much publicized and very well funded billion euro brain simulation project can be seen as an attempt to integrate all the knowledge of neuroscience which exists into some sort of integrated whole. Here the aim is to merely to bring all the neuroscience together in order to program it into a big computer simulation, but without any theoretical underpinning behind it whatsoever.

A leading artificial intelligence researcher named Ben Geotzel is attempting to bring together a lot of existing partial solutions and previous attempts at AI, but is facing an 'integration bottleneck', without any clear way to make all the separate pieces fit and work together sensibly.

In contrast what the Fractal Brain Theory introduces is a very elegant way of arranging all the various aspects of brain and mind, and fitting them all together into a single top-down hierarchical classification structure. This partly derives from the having a single unifying language with which to describe everything. By having a common description for all the separate pieces of the puzzle, this is the prerequisite for fitting all the pieces together into a single structure.

Furthermore this unified classification structure also derives from what we know about hierarchical representations and relationships in the brain as suggested by the actual neurophysiological substrate and experimental findings.

This gives us a very powerfully integrated and all encompassing overview of brain organization and the emergent structures of the mind which are grounded in the neurophysiological substrate. It is an important step to fully understanding the brain and the creation of true artificial intelligence. After all, many of the biggest names in AI and theoretical neuroscience stress the importance of hierarchical representations and processes. What the fractal brain theory is able show is that the entirety of brain and mind may be conceptualized as a single tightly integrated and all encompassing hierarchical structure.

The single all encompassing structure of brain and mind in turn leads to the third, final and most dramatic breakthrough which the fractal brain theory delivers. Given our all encompassing unifying structure we may then ask, is it possible to define a single overarching process over that structure which captures all the separate processes happening within it. Or put another way, if we can represent the entire brain and mind as a single integrated data structure, then is it possible to specify a single algorithm over that data structure, which captures the functionality of all the partial algorithms of brain and mind? And the answer is yes.

A Single Unifying Process

This is the most surprising and perhaps even shocking property of the fractal brain theory. Because it shows that there exists a stunning simplicity behind the inscrutable and mysterious functioning of the brain and mind. The Fractal Brain theory shows how a single unifying recursive process is able to explain all the component sub-processes of brain and mind.

This has been anticipated to some extent by various researchers in the mind and brain sciences. For instance Eric Horvitz the head of AI research at Microsoft, has speculated that there may exist a 'deep theory' of mind but doesn't offer any idea of what this might look like. Steve Grand OBE who is a prominent British AI theorist and inventor, thinks there may exist a 'one sentence solution' behind how the brain works. And several prominent researchers such a Jeff Hawkins, Ray Kurzweil and Andrew Ng believe that there may exist a universal 'cortical algorithm' which captures the functionality of all the various different areas of cerebral cortex which together with the related underlying wiring comprises about 80% of the human brain.

So therefore it is already suggested by leading researchers that there may exist a single algorithm for explaining the workings of most of the brain. But the Fractal Brain Theory goes a lot further. Because what is behind the theory is a universal algorithm and unifying process that is able to span not just the functioning of the cerebral cortex but also that of all the other major auxiliary brain structures comprising the hippocampus, striatum, cerebellum, thalamus and emotion centres including the hypothalamus and amygdala. The Fractal Brain Theory is able to demonstrate how a single overarching process is able to account for and explain the purpose and functioning of all these main structures of the brain.

Significant for mainstream ideas about brain functioning is that the Fractal Brain Theory shows that cerebral cortex can't really be understood without considering the other 'auxiliary' brain structures.Therefore what we are talking about is a single algorithm behind the functioning of the entire brain, the emergent mind and intelligence itself.

Almost unbelievably the theory goes even further than this! For not only does the theory describe how all the functioning of the brain and mind can be captured by a single algorithm, but also that this overarching process extends to the process of how brains and bodies comes into being, i.e. neurogenesis and ontogenesis, and even describes the operation of the DNA genetic computer guiding this developmental process.

Astoundingly the fractal brain theory is able to show that there is a singular unified description and process behind the process by which life begins from a fertilized egg, to give rise to bodies, to give rise to brains, to give rise to minds and all the things that go on in our minds in our lifetimes, right back to the purposefully directed central goal of our lives which involves the process of fertilizing eggs. And so the cycle begins again.

This is a very bold, provocative and dramatic claim that the fractal brain theory makes. It may seem like a theoretical impossibility or some wild over-extension of thought and over interpretation of things, but it is also a reason why once these aspects of the theory are fully comprehended, then they become a powerful reason why the theory will quickly become accepted and gain adherents.

What at first seems fantastic might not seem so strange when we consider what is indisputable. It is a fact that everything that happens in our lives, everything that happens in our bodies and brains, every cell created, every protein manufactured and every random nerve firing that has ever occurred; and every thought and action that we've ever had or performed; All of this has emanated from a fertilized egg. Without this critical first event and tiny singularity in space and time, then everything that follows from it will not have happened.

The Fractal Brain Theory describes a common underlying symmetry of process which shows how all the separate emergent processes share a common underlying template and shows how we can use our unifying language to describe all the many separate processes including cell division (i.e. neurogenesis and ontogenesis), as well as the DNA operating as information processor; and along with this unified encoding of process we are also able to describe all the separate processes as recursive and so be able to link them all up into a single continuous recursive process.

Once we look at things in this way then this great overarching view of things might not seem so incredible but rather as something obvious. This great unifying algorithm and overarching recursive process is the central idea behind the fractal brain theory and the key to creating true artificial intelligence.

Recursive Self Modification: the secret behind intelligence

The process of cell division, and functioning of individual nerve cells seems far removed from the level of introspection, the complex thoughts that we have, and the intricate behaviours that we have to perform in our day to day lives. And so it may seem intuitively incongruous that there may exist a single algorithm and process that can span the entire gamut of everything that happens in our bodies and in our lives.

However there is a trick which enables the simplest of processes, i.e. cell division, to give rise to the most complex i.e. our intricate thoughts. This is recursive self modification. What the fractal brain theory describes is a recursive process that is able to generate hierarchical structures. These structures in turn manifest the same process but in an expanded and augmented form. The unifying recursive process then uses these augmented forms to further expand itself to create even more complex and evolved structures, which in turn generate more complex patterns of operation.

And so the initial seed process feeds back on itself in this recursive way, to generate our bodies, brains and all our mental representations, thoughts and behaviours. This is really the trick that makes the fractal brain theory tick, and the key to understanding the nature of intelligence.

The much discussed Technological Singularity also describes a recursive feedback process where one generation of artificial intelligence is quickly able to design the next augmented and improved next generation of AI, in a positive feedback cycle to create a so called 'intelligence explosion'.

A very interesting property of the fractal brain theory is that it describes this same process happening in the microcosm of the human brain and emergent mind. Likewise, intelligence is made up of a virtuous positive feedback cycle happening in our heads, but constrained by our biological limitations and finite life spans.

It will be seen as entirely appropriate, once this idea is fully accepted, that the key process that enables true intelligence, i.e. recursive self modification, is the trick behind creating artificial intelligence. Which in turn enables the trick of recursive self modification to happen on a grander scale to bring about the Technological Singularity.

Individual Artificial intelligences will then be clearly seen as a fractal microcosm of the macrocosmic Technological Singularity that it gives rise to.

The Special Significance of the Fractal Brain Theory

Our three major theoretical breakthroughs in systems neuroscience and AI, can be thought of as our three fundamental foundational concepts, i.e. symmetry, self-similarity and recursivity, taken to the maximum. Our single unifying language can be thought of as a single underlying Symmetry behind the entirety of all the diverse aspects of neuroscience and psychology. Likewise our single unifying structure can thought of as a single all encompassing self-similar fractal of brain and mind. And our single unifying process is the conceptualizing of all the separate component processes of brain and mind happening in all contexts and scales as being the expressions of a single seed recursive function.

These are the very powerful and profound properties of the fractal brain theory, which would suggest that the theory is something quite special and unique. When it is fully digested and accepted that it is possible to understand the brain and mind using the fundamental scientific and mathematical concepts of symmetry, self-similarity and recursivity, in this complete and comprehensive manner; then the fractal brain theory itself may come to be seen as something likewise fundamental.

Chapter 11

Science and Religion

There existed a great prize in the modern age, a seemingly impossible task that I knew the completion of which would have truly massive implications for the world at large and human affairs. As I progressed in my journey and my understanding of things evolved, together with the steady progression of my Fractal Brain Theory, I realized that I was in a position to realize and attain this great goal, which was the Unification of Science and Religion.

For many years I had been preparing myself for the role of revolutionizing the worlds of neuroscience and artificial intelligence. Later on I discovered that I would also be saying some very new and innovative things about the mysterious workings of the realm of DNA, RNA and genomics. The unifying theory of brain, mind and AI; also came to include genomics so that a single all reducing symmetry or pattern spanned the lot.

This had been the repeated pattern in the history of science, whereby time and again a host of seemingly separate phenomena were later shown to be different manifestations of the same underlying thing that could be captured by a unifying theory. So for instance the phenomena of electricity and magnetism became unified by the concept of electromagnetism; which then later incorporated the phenomenon of light to produce the even more encompassing theory of electromagnetism.

We can verify for ourselves this underlying symmetry and interchangeability between light, electricity and magnetism; when we consider how sunlight may be converted to electricity via solar panels, which may then power our electric cars via the action of electricity and the magnets in the car's electric motors. We could take this reasoning further, with hybrid cars, with the cars motion being converted back into electricity when the magnets in the dynamos of the brakes help to slow down the car; which then might be converted back to motion or light via the car's headlights. And so on.

Electromagnetism is one of the four fundamental forces of nature and scientists generally believe that all the other fundamental forces of the Universe i.e. gravity together with the strong and weak nuclear forces which help hold atoms together, will inevitably be unified together into a single theory 'to rule them all'. A lot of progress has already been made towards the realization of this assumption, so that electromagnetism and the two nuclear forces have already been unified. More generally scientists believe that there exists a single theory which would unify all the laws of the Universe, that is waiting to be found. This may be beyond the human mind to conceive and perhaps it would be something that only future artificial minds or human/machine hybrids would come to ultimately bring into being. In which case the critical step towards this goal is that a single human mind should first conceive artificial intelligence by working out how the human brain and mind worked. This had been my life goal and after a long quest which spanned the entire youthful period of my adulthood I came to believe that I was in possession of that understanding which would allow humankind to finally produce artificial intelligence.

But I also understood that there was another grand unification in science waiting to be realized, even though many scientists and philosophers thought this to be impossible. It was the unification of the sciences of what came to be called 'Complexity', which included the study of life and evolution, society, entire ecosystems, the whole mutually interacting biosphere, techno sphere and cultural sphere of planet earth; and even beyond. In fact this new science of Complexity which started to become very fashionable around the same time my personal quest for knowledge began in the later 1980s, would really encompass everything that went beyond what could be studied using traditional techniques of mathematical analysis. So even quite simple phenomena captured by simple equations that were 'chaotic' and showed 'complex' non-repeating behaviour were included in the science of complexity. I recall that over the years I would avidly devour any book that had 'complexity' in its title.

It was as if the more traditional scientific quest for the unified theory of everything, i.e. the bringing together into a single theory, of all the laws and forces of physics; was merely one aspect of things that failed to include that which was really interesting about the Universe, i.e. life, society, people and culture. So there was this whole other dimension to modern science which sought another even more profound unifying of human understanding. A complexity theorist called Melanie Mitchell who wrote a book which gave a good overview of her field, described how the science of complexity was *'waiting for its Carnot',* which meant they anticipated someone who might one day formulate the framework and theoretical constructs to bring together their much fragmented field. She described how they were really waiting for their Newton to come along. I saw years ago on a BBC documentary the prominent materialist philosopher John Searle, say that there will never be a Newton of the social sciences, which meant there could never be in his mind a great unifying of sociology, economics and anthropology together with a unifying theory of world history. How wrong I thought he was and how dismal were these philosophers who because they didn't have the power of mind to conceive something, therefore assumed that it would forever be inconceivable.

In my studies of brain and mind, I had for a long time seen parallels between what I learned about neurons and neurophysiology on the one hand and what I knew about society and the interactions of people on the other. In the course of things I also increasingly started to see deep parallels between the theoretical constructs I had constructed to understand the brain and mind; with the formulations that cosmologists had created to understand the Universe. So for most of the time that the creation of the fractal brain theory was happening in my head, in the back of my mind was also the idea that what was happening in the brain and the process of mind was also a perfect reflection of what was happening in society, the process of world history and also the process of the Universe. As my studies progressed and my knowledge of the world and the Universe increased then I was able to fully flesh out this basic idea.

So my intuition had turned out to be totally correct and in the course of time I was able to form a single integrated perspective of brain, mind, society, human history, life on earth and cosmic evolution; which explained how everything in the Universe was arranged as a single all encompassing fractal. Most importantly, that we could fully understand this cosmic fractal by understanding the brain and mind. I had discovered that there was something very special about what was happening in our heads and by the same token, in our lives. For the process of our lives, which was perfectly reflected in the representations or our brains and directly determined by the processes of our minds through our thoughts and expressed behaviours; existed as a reflection of the process of Universe. The human mind was as the cosmic mind and the microcosm was indeed a perfect reflection of the macrocosm.

This extrapolation of the fractal brain theory to the Universe was a recurring idea in science that kept resurfacing. Various prominent physicists over the years would describe the Universe as, *'a giant thought'*, *'embedded with platonic values'*, or with *'mind and intelligence woven* [into it]'. Papers started appearing in prestigious scientific journals such as Nature magazine, which is perhaps the most prestigious of them all, which described studies which pointed out parallels between the dynamics of the entire Universe with that of microcosmic networks, including the brain.

Also many contemporary currents that had become established in how the scientific mainstream came to understand the Universe would make it much easier to communicate in an accessible and compelling way, the perfect extrapolation of the Fractal Brain Theory to the workings of the Universe. For instance cosmologists came to see the Universe in informational and computational terms, which was exactly the nature and descriptive language of the brain theory.

And in the same way energy had been discretized into whole number compartments by quantum mechanics, the same happened to space and time which also came to be seen as griddy and quantized. This fitted hand in glove with the formalizations of the fractal brain theory.

Also the idea of an evolutionary Universe became widespread, evolution was proposed to be occurring everywhere in the Universe and from its beginning to its end. Scientists were even proposing that entire Universes came into being through a process akin to evolution and natural selection. At least one darwinist zealot was even proposing that the laws of logic themselves came about through an evolutionary process. This all fitted in nicely with the Fractal Brain Theory's incorporation of evolutionary processes at all levels, all contexts and all scales.

Then of course there emerged the idea of the fractal Universe which was supported by empirical evidence up to certain scales of many 100s of millions of light years and computer simulation studies, which suggested that over the course of time the entire Universe would come to have a fractal patterning.

And in the same way that cosmologists understood the Universe to emanate from the point of the Big Bang Singularity, so correspondingly the Fractal Brain Theory described in a single unified conception how our bodies and brains, together with our thoughts and behaviours all emanated from the singularity of the fertilized egg.

There was an extremely profound and dramatic consequence which resulted from this new understanding of the Universe and ourselves in relation to it, that I was preparing to communicate to the world. It had to do with the fact that all the representations of our brains and minds are geared towards specific purposes and are imbued with meaning. Therefore the extrapolation of the Fractal Brain Theory to the Universe would necessarily bring about an understanding of the Cosmos which was likewise one which saw the Universe as purposeful and meaningful. This would finally rectify one of the major fallacies of the current prevailing 'scientific' worldview, of a necessarily purposeless and meaningless Universe. I came to see it as my duty to correct this fundamental misunderstanding.

Recent developments in the world of mainstream science and cosmology would make this task much easier. Already a few prominent physicists such as Paul Davis, who was respected even by his more conventional peers, started advocating the notion that we could reintroduce notions such as purpose and meaning in our theories of the Universe.

Very recently the mathematically elegant idea called Time Symmetric Quantum Mechanics (TSQM) started to gain wider attention. This idea had been formulated many decades previously, but it was only recently that its creator started winning some prestigious scientific awards and the idea itself gained some empirical verification. This TSQM described a 'destiny' wave function which emanated from the future backwards in time to influence the more conventional quantum wave function evolving forwards in time. This fitted perfectly with an aspect of the brain theory which described how the constructs of our minds and representations of our brains, likewise would be created 'backwards' in time from rewards or aversions. So that through a process of backward chaining we would come to meaningfully attach behaviours, memories and ideas to those rewards and aversions, and from which our purposes were derived.

Another recent idea which is starting to become accepted and which had a lot of solid theoretical backing behind it, was the notion that the Big Bang, from which the Universe was supposed to originate, was really the 'Big Bounce'. This idea was closely accompanied with another idea which described how the pre big bang epoch, i.e. that which happened before the point of the Big Bang singularity, was an exact mirror image of the present Universe, however it was one where everything was time reversed. What this meant was that the Big Bang could be seen as the half way point, where the bounce and time reversal occurred. It could also mean that in our current time epoch we were bouncing back to a preordained conclusion, which was actually the true origin of the Universe; and not the big bang which was merely the point of reflection and time inversion.

Again what was implied was meaning and purpose. We could actually get an idea of what this preordained conclusion, ultimate purpose and meaning was; merely by extrapolating from what we knew about the process of life on Earth. If all life on Earth had originated from a common ancestor and was now increasingly coming together into a single integrated whole, the so called global village and one world order; then the simple extrapolation was that life would spread out to the entire Universe and that all life in the Cosmos would likewise become integrated into a single unified whole. Some philosophers and scientists have called this the 'Omega Point'.

This ultimate purpose of the Universe would be reflected in our own lives and the ultimate purposes we construct for ourselves. And the fractal brain theory would provide the necessary framework in which this cosmic purpose and personal purpose may be formalized and described. So there was a perfect merging of these innovative concepts from mainstream cosmology, i.e. time symmetric quantum mechanics and the time reversed pre-Big Bang epoch, with the aspect of the brain theory that dealt with purpose and meaning in our minds.

As we've already mentioned the fractal brain theory fully incorporated the idea of evolution in all its workings. This idea that evolution was happening in our brain and minds was already a compelling notion which had its adherents in mainstream thinking. It was identical to the idea of 'Memes', 'Genetic Algorithms' and 'Neural Darwinism'. If ideas and behaviours evolved in our minds then it was obvious that they serve our purpose and are meaningful to us. If we were fully able to extrapolate the fractal brain theory to the workings of the Universe, the process of society and the process of life on earth, in a convincing and compelling way; then by the same token we would also be showing in completely scientific terms how it is that the process of evolution and life itself was completely purposeful and meaningful. When this was coupled to the TSQM and Big Bounce ideas described earlier, then this would provide a very complete and new perspective on things. I saw very clearly how I might go about convincing the world, in completely scientific terms, that the process of human history, life on earth and cosmic evolution, was completely purposeful and meaningful.

I knew this was a huge undertaking and a real challenge ahead. I would need to get myself into a position in this world where I would be able to explain to the scientific establishment the true nature of the Universe in contradiction to the prevailing view, held by most of them. But this massive task would be made easier by the fact that the existing understanding of the Universe was really a mass of conflicting views, partial theories and open questions. Even though there existed dominant ideas, no one really had any certain or even good idea of what was the true nature of the Universe.

But I came to believe that there was a way in which clarity could emerge, whereby all the various disputes could be settled and the open questions answered. It would come about through the idea that instead of hoping that a final understanding of the Universe might come purely from the world of physics, another possibility was that it was possible to use the fractal brain theory as the basis and solid foundation on which a complete understanding of the Universe would finally emerge. I discovered that some of the various pieces of the jigsaw puzzle of cosmological understanding which the physicists had accumulated over the years, fitted together perfectly in such a way, such that this cosmological model itself was a perfect reflection of the Fractal Brain Theory in its description of the brain.

If the seed idea that the fractal brain theory might be extrapolatable to the Universe was like a skeletal framework, then these various ideas and theories about cosmology from the science of physics, provided the muscles, organs, sinews and skin, which was able to fully flesh out the basic idea. So that all these partial scientific theories which explained aspects of the Universe, all came together in a consistent and coherent way, to provide a full cosmological explanation. One that was fully in accord with the idea that the Universe was really a giant brain and functioned as a huge mind; which was what quite a few prominent physicists and cosmologists believed anyway.

When I was able to finally integrate the functioning of genomics into the fractal brain theory, then I realized that this gave me an even more powerful platform for introducing my new cosmology to the world. If I could first provide answers to two of the biggest scientific questions of the age, i.e. the mystery of brain and mind together with an explanation of genomic function in a single unifying theory then this would make it much easier to then explain to the world the nature of the Universe. I had to be taken seriously by the world, but more importantly I needed people to accept and believe the things I would be communicating. I had originally set out to discover how the brain worked and understand the process of mind, but along the course of the journey I would also come to uncover the mystery of genomic function, and I believed all of this would give me the necessary platform for also explaining to the world the nature of the Universe; which the fractal brain theory also effectively explained as well.

There was yet another very deep aspect to the fractal brain theory which related to the mathematical abstractions I'd reduced the entire theory to. The representation and computational atoms of the theory had a perfect correspondence to the atoms of mathematics and epistemology (The theory of knowledge or what it is to know). Over the course of a couple of decades I arrived at a very abstracted, compact and minimal condensing of the theory into a set of very simple primitives. From these theoretical atoms or quarks I could reconstitute the entire fractal brain theory, and by the same token all the complexities of neuroscience and cognition. The remarkable thing was that these most basic elements of the theory were also able to completely subsume and find correspondence with the basic elements of discrete mathematics, which is the more elemental level to which all mathematics and indeed all epistemology could be reduced.

Discrete mathematics includes subjects such as logic, set theory, boolean algebra and combinatorics. It was in one of the great intellectual achievements of the 20th century, Bertrand Russell and Alfred North Whitehead's book Principia Mathematica, that they showed how all of mathematics and logic could be reduced to set theory. In turn all the elements of set theory, logic and boolean algebra also have their correspondence with the basic atomic elements of the fractal brain theory. This will provide another compelling dimension for people to believe in the fundamental nature of the fractal brain theory which would help in wider goal of getting people to accept it as the foundation for understanding the nature of the Universe. Effectively what I had discovered was Liebniz's Monad. An underlying Atom from which all epistemology could be reduced and from which all human reasoning and thought processes could be derived.

We could also include probability theory and information theory as integral aspects of the fractal brain theory. Especially when we consider logic as a subset and limiting case of probability theory, and information theory as the assigning of probabilities over combinatorial possibilities. The basic elements of the brain theory in terms of binary trees and especially binary combinatorial spaces are exactly the language of information theory and computer science. There is a massive omission in information theory as it is currently understood and used by technologists and scientists. It has to do with the fact that information theory as formulated by Claude Shannon just after World War II, is completely devoid of the notion of meaning. Which runs counter to how we normally think of information. So in the same way, the fractal brain theory is able to produce a picture of the Universe that has the concept of meaning woven into it, by the same token an updated information theory which incorporates the idea of meaning, naturally and easily emerges from it.

The fractal brain theory wasn't just a theory of the brain and mind but also a whole conceptual framework which encompassed and unified all of the sciences of complexity i.e. genomics, sociology, anthropology, evolutionary theory and extended right through to cosmology. Together with logic and set theory, information theory and of course artificial intelligence.

So I came to believe that I was sitting on a huge scientific revelation that I thought could alter the course of history and the current trajectory of human affairs which was I thought not going any place good. In many ways I saw my work and what was coming together in my mind as the consummation of a process that had been set in motion by the likes of Bacon, Wren, Newton and Leibniz. I could go even further back and include Pythagoras, who is credited with coining the word 'philosophy' and Plato, whom Alfred North Whitehead described all western philosophy as being footnotes to his work. And like all of them I saw that my scientific investigations were really efforts into understand the nature of God.

The Mystery of Consciousness

I saw so many scientific and philosophic currents become integrated into the fractal brain theory. So apart from providing answers to the great mysteries of brain, genomics and cosmology, together with the integration of the fundamental elements of set theory, logic and epistemology; I also saw in my evolving understanding of brain, mind and consciousness the complete integration and elucidation of the central ideas of the hidden or esoteric religion. The emergence of the Fractal Brain Theory, once the perfect extrapolation of it to the Universe was complete, was also the stepping stone for understanding the biggest mystery of them all, i.e. the mystery of God. More specifically and perhaps of even greater consequence than a theory of the brain, a theory of genomics, the creation of artificial intelligence and the explanation of the nature of the Cosmos; was the emergence in my mind of an explanation of the

God within, or how we are all really one consciousness undivided and indivisible or put another way, how it was that everyone was God.

I discovered that I was in a position to finally explain in a reasonable way probably the most controversial and arguably the most influential idea in world history. It could even be thought of as the most controversial idea in the entire Universe, i.e. when any conscious entity in the Universe tells his or her fellow conscious entities, that they are the entire Universe and that all the conscious entities in the Universe are really the same conscious entity, i.e. the one God.

In a brief and highly condensed nutshell the explanation goes like this. First we start from the assumption of one consciousness, which is the only thing we've ever known and the only thing we can ever truly know. Following from Descartes, Kant and Berkeley, together with all the great Idealist philosophers and most founders of quantum mechanics; we can never have certain knowledge of the material or physical world, or so called objective reality. Therefore the trick then is to somehow account for this physical reality that seems pretty real and existent; and reconcile this account with our starting assumption of one consciousness. We also have to account for all the conscious entities that exist within the entire Universe from beginning to end with our one consciousness and starting assumption. We also hold that this one consciousness is undivided and indivisible in accord with recurring and universal metaphysical assertions made for the nature of God but also with respect to the relationship we have with other, that somehow we are all one consciousness; the recurring and universal idea in the hidden or esoteric traditions of all the world's religions and the ancient mysteries.

This is where a fractal theory of brain and mind which perfectly extrapolates to the Universe comes into play. For we know that we are conscious and that there exists a relationship of correlation between our consciousness and the physical substrate of brain. But because we are starting from Idealistic assumptions and not Materialistic one then we need not assume that consciousness is 'arising' from the brain.

Through the principle of Organizational Invariance we assume that people around us have the same sort of consciousness as us, because their brains and physical forms are much like ours. This is accepted by most ordinary folks, philosophers and scientists. We introduce a new and adapted concept which we'll call Scale Invariant Organizational Invariance, which we'll abbreviate to SIOI.

SIOI is simply the idea that if we consider that brains organized like our own would be associated with similar qualities of conscious experience as ourselves, then we may also reasonable assume that brains organized like ours but existing on a smaller or larger scale, would likewise be associated with conscious states not totally dissimilar to our own. If we now consider that the entire Universe as being fractally structured in exactly the same way that our fractal brains are, i.e. self similar and scale invariant at a multitude of scales;

then we may also assume that the various fractal levels of organization of the Universe, through the principle of SIOI or Scale Invariant Organization Invariance, will also be associated with conscious states similar to our own. From the level of the entire Universe, to the minds of life forms whose bodies span galaxies, to the minds of life forms whose bodies span entire planets, to human beings and a multitude of scales not mentioned; we may reasonably assume through the principle of SIOI and the assumption of the Universe as being like a giant fractal brain, that consciousness like our own would permeate the entire cosmos.

This view of being able to see all the conscious entities in the Universe from beginning to end and existing at all scales, as of the same kind of consciousness, i.e. like our own; is in turn the foundation for the next step which is to show how all the seemingly separated consciousnesses are really the same one undivided and indivisible consciousness. And how might we do that. The answer emerges from the account we must now give to explain the nature of physical existence and the appearance of a material Universe 'out there' that seems to have an existence of its own outside of our consciousness.

This involves the introduction of another idea which seems to be getting some recent attention and support from intellectual currents in modern thinking, but is perhaps one of most ancient and re-occurring explanations for the nature of the physical world. This is the notion that the physical world is not what it seems, i.e. it's illusory and that it is really made up of mathematics. So that the physical Universe and everything that exists within it, only exist in the same way that mathematical objects exist; that is they don't really exist in the way that we think they do. Modern developments in mathematics and science would come to make this counter intuitive and slightly baffling idea much easier to explain but we'll make a brief digression to describe something of the history of this idea.

It was Pythagoras (circa 500 BCE) who said that *'The Universe is a number',* and one of the later followers of his ideas Plato described the parable of the cave, which described the reality we normally experienced as being like mere shadows projected onto the back of the cave, and humans in their everyday experiences were stuck in this cave watching the projections, never getting the chance to perceive the truer and more vivid reality that lay outside the cave. Plato is also associated with his idea of the perfect 'forms', which were transcendent templates from which everything in reality was stamped and had their origin. Plato's ideas would be developed by the Neo-Platonists, who came up with the concept of the Logos which in a sense could be conceptualized as the master form which contained all the forms possible.

This concept of the Logos found its way into the Bible translated as 'the word', where in the beginning of the John Gospel it reads, *'In the beginning was word, the word was with God and the Word is God... through the word all things were made and without the word, nothing was made that has been made. "* The John Gospel is the most mystical and gnostic of all the books in the Bible and apparently the favourite of freemasonry. It is the only Gospel where Jesus actually claims to be God and the Son of the Father. In it he also alludes that *'you are all gods',* and that *'you are all sons of the most high'.* (chapter 10, verse36 & referencing Psalm 82.6 & 82.7).

Of course these aspects of the Bible are not taught in Sunday school so this interpretation might seem a bit incongruous at first. However within the context of the ancient greek mysteries, and the sort of things that the likes of Pythagoras, Plato and the Neo-Platonists would have believed, together with key tenets of Kabbalah or Jewish mysticism which has existed for thousands of years; then this more gnostic interpretation of the Gospels is not only plausible but quite obvious.

Important for present discussion is the relevance of these ancient lines of thought with respect to the idea of the existence of the Universe being mathematical. It can be argued that all these ideas are pointing towards and are trying to describe the same underlying notion of mathematical existence being the true nature of physical reality and the Universe or *'all things* [that] *were made'.* So we can trace a lineage of ideas from Pythagoras to those of the Plato (A Pythagorean), onto the Neo-Platonists, and right through to the Bible.

Later on in history Galileo would write that, *'The book of nature is written in language of mathematics',* Isaac Newton would declare that, *'God is a mathematician',* and the Nobel prize winning physicist Eugene Wigner would describe the, *'unreasonable effective of mathematics in the description of the physical world'.* Wigner was describing the remarkable way that abstract mathematical ideas pursued for their own intrinsic beauty without any practical considerations in mind, could nonetheless be perfectly applied without much modification to exactly describe the nature of universe and its physical laws. All the laws of physics are very neatly and succinctly described mathematically, so there seems to be a very tight relationship between physical reality and mathematics.

In more recent times some high profile mathematical physicists including Roger Penrose and Max Tegmark have popularized the ancient idea of platonic or mathematical existence, with Tegmark even quoting Pythagoras, and going as far as to reiterate the ancient suggestion that the 'Universe is a number' and existing only in the same way that mathematical objects exist. Funnily, at the present time of writing it has become very popular for materialist scientists and philosophers, to consider consciousness as a fifth state of matter, together with gas, liquid, solid and plasma. And the prestigious science magazine Nature published a paper which was proposing that the Universe might exist as a dodecahedron. So indeed there is nothing new under the sun and history does repeat itself. Along with Pythagorean and Platonic metaphysics and the cosmic dodecahedron, the quest for the 'quint-essence', had been resurrected for the 21st century. Perhaps next would come the revival of the Delphic Oracle and the Eleusinian Mysteries?

Indeed it would really be the revival of the central truth behind the ancient greek mysteries, also the mysteries of Mithras and Orpheus and the Jewish Kabbalah which will provide the final answer to the mystery of consciousness. This was the mystery of the 'all in the all' and god within, or put another way the idea that we are all one consciousness and everyone is God. So we return from our digression into the history of the idea of the Universe as mathematical object, to show how we can use this idea to show how all consciousness is one consciousness.

We fully subscribe to the Pythagorean, Platonic and Neo-Platonic view of things, that the Universe exists as a mathematical object, which we may call the Logos. It is a mathematical object that contains not just this Universe but all possible Universes. The physicist Paul Davis in his book, 'The Mind of God', described the possibility of a unified theory of physics that didn't just unify all the laws of physics, but also contained within it the exact initial conditions of the Universe, and from which the exact evolution of the entire Universe could be derived, in arbitrary even infinite detail, and from the beginning to the end of the Universe. This is actually another way of describing the Logos, or cosmic mathematical object of Pythagoras.

In order to facilitate the progression of our expanding account and explanation of the mystery of consciousness we'll now describe two recent developments coming from mathematics and computer science which make it more straightforward to explain how the notion of the Universe as mathematical object, can be used to show how we are all one consciousness. They are the discovery of a mathematical object called the Mandelbrot set and also the invention and commonplace adoption of the technology called virtual reality (VR).

The Mandelbrot set was discovered only as recently as the 1970s by Benoit Mandelbrot who is also the originator of fractal mathematics. The Mandelbrot set is a quite simple formula that contains within it a mathematical object that is infinitely complex and infinitely detailed. Most importantly the intricate patterning and detail of the Mandelbrot set is never repeating, so in a sense it really does contain a little universe of complexity. It is however also a fractal object so certain patterns within it are recurring at an infinite number of scales, though not in exactly the same way.

The mind blowing complexity of the Mandelbrot set, its infinite and exquisite patterns and its non random completely determined nature; make it a far better example of mathematical existence to use to argue the case that the Universe is also mathematical in nature. Before the advent of the Mandelbrot set all we had were mathematical objects such as perfect solids i.e. cubes or dodecahedrons, to use as obvious examples of mathematical existence. These objects seemed very far removed from the complexities of reality as we normally perceive it, i.e. the world around us. However the myriadly and infinitely complex Mandelbrot set gives us a far more compelling example of mathematical existence for arguing that the nature of physical reality is likewise a purely mathematical object.

Also the fractal Mandelbrot set of course fits hand in glove with the notion of a fractal universe, along with everything in it. Which in turn connects with the notion that this fractal universe is perfectly reflected in the working of our fractal brains, as described by the fractal brain theory. So in the same way that the Mandelbrot describes a fractal object, quite naturally we also propose that this equation of the Universe, which describes the entire Universe as a mathematical object, likewise describes the Universe as a fractal object. And though we don't know the details of this cosmic fractal formula, nonetheless given the assumption that the overall form and process of the Universe is reflected in our brains and the functioning of our minds, then through the brain theory we are able to obtain an overall picture of the structure and evolution of the Universe which is completely fractal.

We are now in a position to finally explain how all consciousness is one consciousness, and we do this by using our earlier idea of Scale Invariant Organizational Invariance (SIOI) and the technology of Virtual Reality as a metaphor. We have already establish how using the concept of SIOI and the fractal Universe that is as a cosmic brain, we may assume that all consciousness in the Universe is of the same kind of consciousness as ours, which is a necessary precursor and stepping stone for showing that we are the same one consciousness.

Now if we start from the assumption of one consciousness, i.e. our own and the only thing whose existence we may have any certainty of, then once we add the assumption that the physical Universe is mathematical and not really existing then we can no longer assume a multitude of separate consciousnesses out there in the physical Universe and the world around us, because it only exists in the mathematical sense. It is senseless to suppose actual existence, i.e. consciousness, from mathematical non-existence. But we still need to explain the relationship between that mathematical Universe that seems to be 'out there', and our own consciousness and our first person subjective experiences of that physical Universe including our physical bodies. This is where the metaphor of virtual reality comes into play. So we'll briefly describe the workings of virtual reality to better show why it is able to help us to understand the nature of consciousness.

Virtual reality is really based on mathematical formula and abstract data structures held in the memory of a computer, which allow the computer to render images onto a computer display or virtual reality headset the intricate details of the virtual world being explored by the user, either in some computer game, flight simulator or other VR immersive environment. So what we have are really mathematical objects which fully describe the virtual reality world and also completely describe the users interactions with it. But these mathematical objects only come to life and become perceived by the user when they are rendered onto the computer display or VR goggles, and this becomes the manifestation of the virtual world upon the 'real world' of the user.

The metaphor of virtual reality for explaining how we are all one consciousness then becomes more clear. If we suppose that the physical Universe exists only mathematically in the same way that the virtual world does, then it only becomes manifest when rendered into the subjective experience of consciousness. Because we are starting only with the assumption of one consciousness, then this Logos or mathematical object containing the Universe, only comes to life and is brought into actual existence when the forms and patterns within it, i.e. physical reality, are manifest as subjective experience of the physical Universe reflected in that one consciousness.

So the one consciousness acts as the virtual reality projection screen upon which the mathematical constructs of physical reality are projected. But these constructs are not projected or manifested as they are, in and of themselves, but rather they are projected as appearances in our first person subjective experience. This is exactly as the projection screen of Plato's cave. So our normal subjective states are projections of the cosmic mathematical object or Logos, and leaving the cave would be to see through the virtual reality illusion, and experience that we are the Logos and also the One Consciousness upon which all manifest and actual existence is projected. This state might be called Enlightenment, the Kingdom of Heaven, Satori or Nirvana. The ancient Greeks called it, 'Apocalypse' which literally translates as 'the unveiling of the hidden thing'. This would have been the understanding of the likes of Pythagoras and Plato.

But we still have something very important to explain. We have explained how given an illusory mathematical Universe, we can experience ourselves and our own consciousness as the one consciousness and God. What we also have to do is to explain our relationship to all the other conscious entities in the Universe, i.e. the people around us, everyone who has ever lived and who will ever live, and every conscious entity that will emerge in the Universe from its beginning to end. The answer to this question is also fractal, and is represented in the process of our lives.

The lifetime of a person is a succession of subjective states of consciousness, going from a sequence starting at birth, early life, adulthood, maturity and death. It is a single thread, where the days of our lives may be considered as individual pearls strung out on a long string. If we extrapolate this view of things to the wider context, then the solution to the puzzle of the one consciousness becomes very clear.

In the same way that the we are one consciousness and the same consciousness over the course of our lives as experienced one day at a time, so we are the same one consciousness experienced one life at a time. So in the same way as individual conscious entities, i.e. people, we sleep and awaken to a new day, so it is that as the one undivided and indivisible consciousness, i.e. God, we die and awaken to a new life.

When we look at things in this way, then in the same way that we did for the days of our lives, we may likewise sequence out all the separate conscious entities of the entire Universe from beginning to end, as pearls on a string; with a separate pearl for every individual conscious life form. Of course this would consist of a lot of pearls and it would be a very long string. Another way of describing this idea would be reincarnation or metempsychosis, which is a universal and recurring idea in all the esoteric and mystery traditions of the world; from Jewish Kabbalah, Sufism in Islam and Gnostic Christianity to Freemasonry, Taoism and Pagan Mystery Religion . Also of course Hinduism and Buddhism.

The idea of reincarnation and the idea of the one undivided and indivisible consciousness really go hand in hand. The metaphysical ideas under discussion are really this idea of reincarnation expressed in 21st century conceptions and supported by the Fractal Brain Theory and the cosmology outlook that is closely related to it. When we insert our Fractal Brain Theory and the idea of the Universe as a giant fractal brain into this way of looking at things, then it would be the case that every single pearl on this cosmic thread would have exactly the same fractal organization behind it. And when we also include the assumption of Scale Invariant Organizational Invariance, then every point over the entire thread spanning every single pearl in our cosmic thread, would be the manifestations of the one consciousness, experiencing the same kind of consciousness and qualities of subjective experience that we have.

So that at any point on the thread and in the life of any conscious entity, there may occur the state of consciousness of being one with God or being one with the Universe; which given our perspective on things, will be the true state of affairs. So the part in the all, i.e. any conscious entity within the Universe may experience itself as the all in the part, and this will correspond with the underlying but normally opaque truth about the nature of existence. We normally see ourselves as having our identities rooted in our physical bodies, existing within and gazing out upon a vast and impersonal Universe, but the true reality would be when we experience ourselves as the Universe reflecting upon itself, that is the Universe or God.

Even given what we've methodically explained so far, there still exists a huge chasm between this highly controversial idea of everyone being God and one consciousness on the one hand, and our everyday assumptions about ourselves and reality on the other. It seems totally incongruous and baffliing when throughout history people have made this claim of having been 'one with God' or 'one with the Universe'.

Given materialist or physicalist assumptions then it would seem a complete absurdity. How can a tiny speck, that we humans are, living in a vast, mind numbingly vast Universe, claim to be the Universe and God? If we hold materialistic assumptions then of course this 'solipsistic' view of things seems completely implausible.

However it's merely a matter of perspective, and changes of assumption allow us to see things that would forever be opaque to our imagination without this shift. The idea that it is possible to go East by going West seemed a complete absurdity, given the assumption of a flat Earth. Simply by introducing the notion of a spherical planet, then the absurdity becomes common fact. And given the idea that the Sun revolved around the Earth which was seen as the centre of things, then there were so many astronomical observations that just didn't make sense. With a simple change of assumptions, i.e. by assuming that the Earth revolves around the Sun instead of the earlier assumption, then everything became much clearer and many mysteries were satisfactorily resolved.

In the same way, once we start to question the highly questionable assumption of materialism or physicalism, then we can start to see other possibilities for explaining the nature of consciousness, especially the notion that we are all one consciousness.

It has long been argued that the position of Idealism, which holds that existence is fundamentally consciousness, is really the more consistent position. It starts from an assumption based on what we can know with certainty, i.e. consciousness and our first person subjective experience of things. *'I think therefore I am'*, Descartes famously wrote after coming to the conclusion that it was the only thing he could know with any certainty. So the proposition of materialism as the basis for understanding consciousness, i.e. trying to reduce what we know for certain i.e. our consciousness to physical matter and what we can never have certain knowledge of; is an enterprise that is flawed from the outset.

In modern times the assumption of Materialism has been further eroded by our explorations into the subatomic realm and the paradoxes of quantum mechanics. As we explored deeper the nature of matter then the notion of material existence seemed to vanish, first into empty space and then into a cloud of quantum probabilistic possibilities. The great physicist John Wheeler famously said that according to quantum mechanics, *'there's no out there, out there'*. So the assumption of materialism or physicalism has for a long time and increasingly so, been problematic.

This has helped paved the way for the return of Idealism. From the outset it is far more consistent to start from the assumption of consciousness. The problem with this approach in the past, of showing how Idealism might work in practice, suffered the problem that no one was able to take the proposition any further and explain how it might be the case. However with the advent of the Fractal Brain Theory, together with some of the modern ideas discussed earlier, e.g. the Mandelbrot Set and Virtual Reality; then it is possible in the 21st century to finally show how Idealism is the better way of looking at things.

Furthermore this idea that we are all one consciousness, apart from being a way of looking at things that has as its foundation in the simplest and most immediate of assumptions, i.e. the experience of our own one consciousness; is also actually the only provable thing there is on the only thing that is truly knowable. This is the experience of being God, being one with God or being one with the Universe. This most timeless and recurring of ideas is the secret of the prophets and founders of the world's major religions. It is also the truth at the heart of the hidden or esoteric religion and the ancient mysteries. What we have in the sorts of ideas and lines of explanation we have been exploring in this discussion, is the world changing consequence that finally we can explain this most controversial of ideas in a way that is completely reasonable, completely scientific and makes perfect sense. It also goes hand in hand with the Fractal Brain Theory, together with the fractal cosmology, the mathematical Universe and a host of other intellectual currents in modern science.

This explanation of the idea that we are all one consciousness or everyone is God, for the 21st century is really the resurrection of the hidden or esoteric religion for modern times. It is the return of the ever recurring perennial wisdom, and the modern expression of the 'prisca theologia' or primal and original theology. And the Fractal Brain Theory, taken together with its perfect extrapolation to the Universe contains all the rest of it, i.e. esoteric religion. Therefore finally the hidden religion will no longer be hidden and the truths contained within it will become fully manifested and articulated for the modern world. The core beliefs of Gnosticism, Freemasonry, Rosicrucianism, the Kabbalah of Judaism, the Batin or hidden meanings of the Sufi and Shiite sects of Islam, the Tantra and Advaita Vedanta of Hinduism, Vajrayana Buddhism of Tibet and Taoism of China, would become reaffirmed and fully rearticulated for contemporary times and the people of the present age.

I had originally sought to discover how the brain worked and to create artificial intelligence; but in the course of my life I stumbled upon a huge revelation. I saw a way of explaining to the world the mystical and spiritual core that is common to all world religion. I discovered that I could answer the two most important questions in all of philosophy which are epistemology and ontology, or the nature of knowledge and nature of existence respectively. The Fractal Brain Theory gave me the keys to the first, and the fractal cosmology derived from the brain theory gave me the keys to the second. A complete understanding of brain and mind is really the final word on the questions of epistemology, and the Fractal Brain Theory is the key to showing how the ground of all existence and the answer to the question of ontology, is the One Consciousness or God.

Furthermore, in working out the nature of brain and mind, and the mystery of genomic functioning, I knew that I had in my possession answers for and major insights to some of the biggest scientific questions of the age, encapsulated in a unified understanding. Together with the extrapolation of this fractal theory of mind, brain and genome to the Universe, then I realized that I could also provide answers to the biggest of cosmic mysteries.

Therefore in my understanding of mind, brain and consciousness, which were some of the biggest mysteries of the age, I saw the perfect intersection between the true heart of world religion on the one hand and all science and philosophy on the other. I had discovered how science and philosophy could be unified or rather reunified with religion.

Providence had brought about the circumstances and process by which the myriad separate aspects and building blocks of the great puzzle, became aligned and joined together in my mind that formed a complete and encompassing understanding of things. I discovered that all of humankind's diverged lines of inquiry, in theology, philosophy and science, really converged upon the same mystery. So that one answer contained all the answers and one key unlocked all the doors. In seeking to understand the brain I came to understand the nature of the Universe. In seeking to investigate the nature of consciousness I had come to understand the nature of God.

Since the time of Francis Bacon, Christopher Wren, Isaac Newton and Gottfried Wilhelm Leibniz, the knowledge of humankind had become greatly fragmented and divided in myriad separate and relatively isolated compartments. With the Fractal Brain Theory together with its closely associated cosmology and metaphysical outlook, I saw a way how these compartments could be brought together. I would take it upon myself to instigate the bringing together of the great divisions in science, and aim for the great prize of reconciling science with religion. I saw the unification of science with religion as a necessary step for the even greater prize of reconciling with each other the major religions of the world, which in turn was a crucial step in the huge and necessary goal of bringing together into a common understanding of things, all of humanity.

Chapter 12

The Problems of the World

One of the great benefits of working at the church was that it was a great place for me to be while I was studying and thinking about the problems of the world. Generally a church is a place where people brought their problems. Also many events such as presentations and conferences took place there which discussed and sought to understand the great problems of the World. Also relevant was the church's specific location right in the heart of London, which meant that just about every protest march and demonstration held there would go by outside along the street beside the Church.

When I started working at the church, St James Piccadilly, then this really opened my eyes more to the problems of this World, and powerfully shaped my political philosophy in so many different ways during my 10 years spent there. It gave me a variety of different perspectives on all the various problems and issues in the world that I might not otherwise have ever even considered.

A church is a place where people go when they are troubled, grieving and/or need someone to share their problems with. So simply by working in this sort of environment I was constantly encountering peoples personal woes, worries, serious disappointments and upsets. A lot of ordinary people came to the church to mourn, to reflect or because they were facing serious difficulties of one form or another.

Sometimes people just needed someone to talk to and share their burdens with. I'll have to admit that I'm not the best listener in the world when it comes to this sort of thing, but on many occasions I would be working in the church, get into conversation with some member of the public and before I knew it would get sucked into his or her concerns. I could sometimes get quite depressed by the things I was listening to and so would often like nothing more than to tactfully escape these situations. This was just a part of being in that sort of church environment for 10 years and almost implicit in the job description. I didn't sign up to be a counsellor or 'good samaritan' but you'd be put into that position from time to time. In hind sight it was probably a good thing, all the time spent listening to peoples woes and griefs.

I've already mentioned that a constant feature of the job was dealing with the homeless. When you got to know some of them better and the sort of problems they faced living on the streets then it was impossible not to feel sympathy. They described hard brutal lives of drug addiction, the constant threat of violence and sleeping on the streets with no future prospects and a complete sense of alienation from mainstream society. It would certainly put my own concerns and difficulties into perspective.

The problems of the world were constantly addressed in the prayers and intercessions made at all the various church services, where either one of the priests or a member of the church community would bring all the conflicts and strifes of the planet before God in pray and reflection. A small part of my job involved sometimes leading small prayer gatherings where at one point some improvisation is needed where I had to think up things to pray for. In a small but significant way over an extended period of time, participating in all these prayer and intercession sessions definitely orientates a person towards the concerns of the planet, the concerns of other people and the bigger issues.

I learned that this is the real purpose and effect of prayer, that is not to make requests to God and expect immediate and effective action from the divine; but rather that prayer really involves an internal psychological process whereby people gear themselves towards becoming more engaged in life and the issues of the World. What it really does is to align people to what they believed to be the will and purpose of God and so to alter their attitudes and behaviour accordingly. I learned in this way prayer can be very powerful.

Perhaps one of the most emotionally powerful prayer services held at the church was the yearly national 'Road Peace' service, which was a memorial service for people who'd died in traffic accidents on UK roads. It was all the more poignant because many of the deceased were young or people in their prime, and it was their families who came to mourn. This was in contrast to most memorial services or funerals held at the church where the deceased were very old along with the large majority of the congregation. So it was especially tragic that many of the lives being commemorated were those who had not yet really lived their lives.

There was another purpose to this service because there was a strong element of political activism that was an intrinsic part of it. It wasn't just about remembering and praying for the dead but also how we might be able to make the roads safer by increasing education in road safety or getting legislation passed to deter dangerous driving or enhance safety standards. So here is just one example of the sort of prayer that leads to action and a focusing of mind-sets towards constructive goals.

The effect this service had on me personally, was to stimulate in my mind thoughts about how my ideas relating to the brain and artificial intelligence might one day lead to technology that could make cars and the roads safer. So this prayer service wasn't about petitioning some almighty power above to improve road safety but rather to help us to become the agency that might contribute to this process through our thoughts and actions.

A completely different angle on the problems of the world came from an interesting feature of working at the church. This was due to its location in Piccadilly which is in central London. It happened to be situated on one of the main roads along which all the protest marches and demonstrations held in London, would course through. Though after the road system around Piccadilly was changed in the Summer of 2011, the usual route for these protest marches was likewise changed. But for a good 7 years during my time working at the church the usual route for the large demonstrations and protests would pass by the church every Saturday afternoon. The marches would start in Hyde Park, Speakers Corner, progressing from there to Westminster and the seat of Government. So for a long time a regular feature of working at the church would be to hear some loud commotion outside in the street and to see the sight of many thousands of people protesting and bringing attention to some issue.

Over the years just about every issue and problem of the world would seem to be represented by the activists and participants exercising their right to make peaceful protest and demonstration. Examples would be Environmental or Ecologically related protests, Anti-War demos, marches against the use of Torture, marches by various Independence groups and the protests of oppressed peoples, Anti-Zionist demos, pro-Israel marches, Religious groups asserting themselves, Women's rights, Human rights, Animal rights, Gay rights, Anti-corruption, Right Wing, Left Wing, any Wing and every issue seemed to be represented at one point or another; and which would march along Piccadilly right past the church.

On these occasions whenever I could, that is not tied up working on a wedding service or some other Saturday event; then I would always go outside into the street and see what was going on and what issue was being protested. It was good to see the people who made up the marches. It made the issues seem less abstract and gave it an immediately apparent human dimension to see the faces of some of the people who had taken up the cause. Sometimes I would have the opportunity to chat to some of the protesters but usually I was content just to watch things go by and absorb the atmosphere, reading the signs or perhaps a pamphlet or two, also listening to the chants and expressed sentiments of the protestors.

Looking back on things, I believe that my working and being at the church really opened my eyes to the problems of the World a lot more, and made them more immediate to me than they would otherwise have been from just reading about them in the news or books say. There was often a sense of being in a place where all the problems and concerns of the planet became washed up on the shores of St James Church, and I was like a beach comber constantly picking up a bottle containing a note here and there in order to have a read. Then throwing the bottle back out to sea sometimes quite affected by the message and sometimes not at all. But either way, consciously and sub-consciously, I can see in retrospect that my outlook was gradually and subtly transformed by these protest marches and demos. There again I suppose this was the intention of the protesters and those marching.

For many years there was a regular event at the church called the Global Development Forum which hosted discussions involving several panelists and attended by some quite sizable audiences. This event was run by an ex-Cambridge academic named Benny Dembitzer who was interested in the development of Third World countries but the events would sometimes also cover ecological and environmental issues. Benny seemed to be very good at getting some high profile politicians, journalists, activists and commentators to appear and give their views and participate in the discussions.

It was always interesting to stay around and watch the presentations and debates after I helped to set everything up and did the sound check on the microphones. It was interesting to see a lot of angles presented on Third World development issues including the input from the audience in questions and answers. Sometimes some of the members of the audience said more intelligent things than the panelists.

Eventually these very interesting discussions stopped taking place at the church because around 2008, the London School of Economics started to do something similar and in the same format, with the same kinds of people, but with free entry. So eventually Benny who charged an entrance fee for his event couldn't cover his expenses as the crowds dwindled and went to LSE instead. I worked on the last ever Global Development Forum discussion, when the attendance numbered less than a dozen or so people, and most them were probably with the invited guest speakers or members of the crew.

On the panel for this last ever event, there were a couple of Members of Parliament and a lady from the US State Department who had flown in especially for the nights proceedings, so it was a bit of a disaster. It just showed that it's a real challenge to get people to attend anything in London, where there is so much going on, and especially when there are competing events on offer which are charging less or are even being offered for free. Benny at the beginning of the event registering the dismal turn out, told his high profile panelists that he'd wish the ground would swallow him up, because attendance that evening was so bad. I can't even remember what the topic was that evening, so it probably wasn't very riveting and I suppose that's another reason why hardly anyone came. But some of the discussions were more memorable and even extremely thought provoking. Anyway, that was the end of one of more stimulating regular events held at the church.

The church also hosted a lot of specifically ecological and environmental events and conferences. Some of the priests and members of the church congregation were followers of the ideas of US Christian thinkers such as Thomas Berry and Matthew Fox, the so called Ecotheologians. I heard several sermons by Fox when he came over to talk about his Creation Theology. I could see that the synthesis of spirituality with ecological thinking was a powerful and compelling mix. It also seemed obvious in a way but it was good to hear these ideas spelled out.

I thought to myself at some point, was it even possible to have an outlook on the world that called itself spiritual, if it didn't take into account the environment and ecosystems on which humanity's existence and very survival was based?. In my own life I often found the most powerful spiritual connection to the divine came from nature.

I was also impressed by the openness of the Ecotheologians to other faiths, and also Native American spirituality. This resonated with my own interfaith ideas.

There wasn't much that was progressive about the Anglican Communion, but the creation spirituality movement within it was a notable exception. Interestingly Matthew Fox was expelled from the Catholic church and Dominican order, for the sort of views he held but was later accepted into the US Anglican church as a priest. Also his theological position on the nature of God, has been described as a type of Monism and more specifically Panentheism; which was not totally incompatible with my own beliefs. He also sought to communicate his Ecotheology through the use of multimedia, dance music and party like events; and even sought a reformation of Western Christianity, nailing 95 theses on the same door of the same church, that Martin Luther had used to kick start the Protestant Reformation. So here was an aging priest, by the time I'd heard of him, trying to push things forwards within the rigid confines of conventional organized religion. I found this inspiring. But it was his ideas on the synthesis of spirituality and ecology that had the most influence on me.

There was a completely different sort of ecologically oriented event which occurred in the church at the tail end of 2009. This was the memorial service of Edward Goldsmith who had founded the Ecologist magazine and was a leading light of the green and ecological movement. One attendee remarked, it was like the Ascot of the ecological world. The main spokespersons from all the leading ecologically oriented NGOs (Non-Government Organizations) and protest movements were there. A lot of famous and familiar faces associated with the world of ecological and environmental awareness came to celebrate a remarkable life.

For me, working that evening, it was a chance to soak up the atmosphere, be inspired by some of the fond recollections of friends and family of the deceased; but also to think about ecology and environment. Things were in such a bad state, with the continued and even accelerating destruction of the World's ecosystems, the ongoing mass extinction of species and of course the ever growing threat of climate change and its consequences. But as I stood there, at the front of the church looking after the sound system and generally keeping an eye on things, I looked at this great gathering of the ecologically aware crowd. I thought to myself how relatively impotent they were in face of the impending ecological disaster that was facing humankind. With all their connections, money and influence, was there really any great significant effect that any of these people could have on human affairs to alter the course of things.

There in the front row were the Goldsmith family, with their multimillions, including Zac Goldsmith who was then a member of parliament and Jemima Khan, the socialite; then there was somebody who appeared at every ecology related event, i.e. Jonathan Porritt the ex-leader of the Green party and Friends of the Earth; and I was told some lady who sat at the front had recently won the Nobel prize for her eco-campaigning. It was great that they were raising awareness of the issues, but what could these people, the high and mighty of the ecology movement, do to stop the ongoing destruction of the global biosphere and the imminent ecological catastrophe.

These were one of those times when during the course of my duties at the church I would be brought face to face with these sorts of disturbing thoughts and questions. It might also happen during some conference on some issue or perhaps when watching some protest march go by, reading the banners and absorbing the atmosphere. Steadily and surely these sorts of experiences would shape my worldview and outlook on things. They would often make me ask myself what I might possibly do one day to alter the course of things and influence such affairs.

I was a humble church verger, a sort of caretaker, contemplating the problems of the world but at the same time I also knew that I was already sitting on a powerful message relating to the true nature of religion, which also encompassed a unified theory of the brain and mind which I fully believed would allow me create artificial intelligence in the future. So I often considered how I might one day get into a position, whereby I would be able to influence the trajectory of human affairs, in a way that I knew was impossible for the important and influential people that I would encounter on my journey. I contemplated the powerlessness of the high profile people I'd deal with, while at the same time trying to figure out how I might one day obtain the potential and effectiveness they lacked in order to do all those things that everyone thought needed to be done, relating to the problems of the world.

So I would spend a lot of time thinking about how it may be possible to solve the problems of the World. If I could solve the problem of how the brain worked and the nature of mind, and also create true artificial intelligence, and articulate the unifying truth behind all world religion, then the task of trying to formulate effective solutions to the problems of the world, I thought within my abilities. And if the hand of Providence had guided and helped me in these major pursuits of my life, then why should it be any different for this other important set of goals. And so I never once thought or had any doubt that the idea of trying to figure out viable plans of action or specific solutions for saving the planet, was something that was out of my grasp.

Ever since I was a small child I had an awareness of the problems of the world. Throughout my life I had taken an interest in what was happening on the planet, obtaining information from as many information sources as possible. When I started pubic speaking, my talks were mainly about religion, spirituality, mythology and prophecies, taking a universalist approach and trying my best to cover views from all religions and spiritual traditions.

In particular I was trying to communicate the idea that the prophecies in all the world's religion's were talking about present times and the issues of the age. The picture that had formed in my mind and which I was trying to convey, saw the major issues of the world including the environmental, political, social, cultural and even technological ones; in terms of predictions contained in the prophecies of the world's major religions. Some of the most important predictions concerned the general conditions of the world and humanity, when the end times or the end of the age would occur.

There existed many quite specific descriptions made in the prophecies of the world's major religions, which seemed to me to describe some of the unique and unprecedented conditions of the planet today. This included the issue of the impending global ecological and environmental catastrophe; the unprecedented advancement of human knowledge and technology; the worldwide state of religion; and also the phenomenon of the rapidly converging global village or process of globalization. So within this prophetic framework, I fitted in all the myriad and specific problems and issues of the world.

I also came to equate the prophecies of world religion, to the recurring basic storyline found repeatedly in the myths of the world. They often included the backdrop of a society or people facing some calamity; the battle between opposing forces representing dark and light; and the hero quest for some prize which would save that society. I came to the conclusion that the prophecies of world religion were really projecting the basic mythic archetypes and basic storyline onto a future state of humanity and that they would be manifesting on a global scale.

And so my studies into the problems of the world were further motivated by the need to communicate my views about what was happening on the planet in terms of world mythology and the prophecies of the major religions, regularly to a live audience. This made me pay more attention to the things I read in the news or in books.

Therefore and relevant for present discussion, over the years partly as the result of working at the church and being exposed more directly to people who were seeking answers to the problems of the world or were protesting about them; and also because many of the people who came to my public talks were also inclined in this way; I increasingly and more systematically spent a greater proportion of my time thinking about how my message and mission would be able to impact the issues of the age, and the trajectory of human affairs. So over a period of over a decade I would more systematically and constantly think of ways in which the problems of the world might be solved. Also I would communicate these ideas in my public talks, so that my presentations would steadily have more and more emphasis on this sort of thing.

At first my little solutions, were quite simple and only partial. So for instance, I saw how the version of the prophecies I was communicating was more realistic and proactive. It encouraged people to create this *'New Heaven and New Earth'*, and take it upon themselves to realize the final happy outcome the prophecies through their participation and through their actions. This updated 'Providentialism' for the 21st century was a much needed tonic for the more passive and fantastic interpretations of the prophecies which were dominant, for instance in Fundamentalist Christianity; where people expected Jesus to appear in the sky to 'save' them and who would then deliver the New Heaven and New Earth ready made. Or another example would be in the New Age scene, where some people were passively waiting for the UFO mothership to land, or for everyone to be lifted to a 'higher vibrational frequency'; so escaping from the chaos and calamity ahead.

Also I saw that there was an interpretation of the spiritual path and also of the stereotypically mythic hero quest journey which would likewise encourage in people behaviours directed towards solving the problems of the planet. Perhaps making people into activists and advocates for the major issues, or even at the very least making people take a more active interest in things. This idea of the spiritual path and mystical journey as political and environmental activism went hand in hand with the interpretation of the prophecies and mythology I was promoting. But despite my wholehearted belief in truth and future potential of these ideas, I saw that on their own they were rather ineffectual and impotent.

Another partial solution and proposal that I came up with, related to the important problem of bringing together a divided humanity. I saw that the communicating of the common truth behind world religion would be a beneficial factor in potentially bringing people together and reconciling religious division. Also I thought the recurring idea in esoteric religion, that humanity was not merely of 'one flesh', but also of 'one soul', was another idea supporting the notion of cooperation between people. But once again there was a chasm between these well meaning sentiments and metaphysical assertions on the one hand, and the problem of bringing about real changes to the world and influencing of human affairs, on the other. There seemed an insurmountable or at the very least extremely difficult problem of putting these ideas into practical application given some of the realities of the actual world situation which would work against these quite simple proposals.

Later on I came to see that the solution to the problems of the world didn't consist of any one solution but rather had to be made up of a raft of myriad solutions. A sort of composite answer made up of many component solutions. I also saw that there was a necessary glue which would be needed to bind together all these separate solutions and which would make the composite, much more compelling, exciting and convincing. I realized that somehow all the solutions needed to be integrated within and be consistent with the overall new Worldview or Resynthesized Mazeway (Cognitive Map), which had been steadily evolving in my mind already for many years up to this point.

Many of the solutions were already out there, and many diverse groups and different people were the advocates and activists for these partial solutions, but what was needed was a bringing together of these diverse struggles. Because of the heavily fragmented nature of all these myriad movements, fragmented within each country and worldwide, each of them were pretty ineffectual and none of them could bring about the changes they desired to see. The nature of these movements may be called 'progressive', they often challenged the status quo and incumbent powers. Often they concerned issues of social justice, ecology and environment and also economic reform.

Building on this line of thinking, in around 2007 I had an insight which seemed to me profound then, but perhaps to some people it may seem obvious. This insight allowed me to see that the any lasting and far reaching solution to the problems of the world necessarily had to be a great composite of many solutions and the unifying of diverse struggles, championing a wide variety solutions addressing a wide variety specific problems. And this was because all the problems of the world were tightly, intricately and inextricably interconnected. So that any attempt to focus on one problem without addressing all the other problems to which it was interconnected, and which were also further interconnected between themselves; was doomed to failure and would lead to a generally ineffectual long term outcome.

Apart from the fact that all these disparate and divided progressive movements, couldn't influence political affairs, because they were fragmented; it was also the case that because of their circumscribed focus, each individual cause wasn't able to inspire sufficient numbers to join or attract the attention of a wide enough audience. And even if they could hypothetically get into a position to seriously influence things in relation to their specific cause, then because of the interlocking nature of the worlds problems, each partial solution on its own, even if implemented and temporarily effective, would be undone in the longer term.

I also saw that the more visible problems of the world, i.e. existing in realm of ecology, environment, politics, society and economy, which were themselves tightly interconnected within themselves and with each other; were in turn inextricably bound to and inseparable with the realm of ideas and idealogy. And here too there was tight interconnectedness of all the problems existing in these realms of thought and thinking. Ideas of the academy and the doctrines of the world, also existed in ecosystems of mutual interdependence and also mutual antagonism, just as is the case in nature and society.

So the unified solution had to not just bring together all the myriad solutions which already existed and also ones yet to be dreamed up, which would address the problems existing in the social, political, economic, ecological and environmental realms; but also integrate solutions to the problems in the realm of ideas and ideology. And this solution had to fit together all the diverse and myriad pieces of the jigsaw puzzle in a way that was consistent, compelling and also most importantly convincing. So that was the challenge which I saw as the necessary obstacle which needed to be overcome in order to be able finally formulate a long term and lasting solution to the problems of the world.

In the late Summer of 2007 while focusing heavily on preparing for a talk there came to me a flash of clarity where I came to see clearly laid out in my mind the nature of the problems of the world and their inter-relationships. Once I had this insight then it paved the way for me to see much more clearly, exactly what it would involve to solve the problems of the world and the next steps in the formulation of the overall solution. So I'll describe in outline what I saw and came to understand.

I saw all the problems of the world, as four dominos arranged in a row. Naturally seen in this way the solution to the problems of the world would be the toppling of these dominos. Continuing wth the metaphor I had the clear insight that it was possible to topple all of the dominos if somehow we could manage to topple the first one. If we could make the first domino fall, then domino 2, domino 3 and domino 4 would fall in succession. This would be the case because there was a causal link between what each of the successive dominos represented.

The first domino, number 1, represented the realm of pure ideas, and included science, theology, philosophy, mathematics, the social sciences or any mental pursuit happening in the academy or mind of any human being.

The next domino, number 2, represented the realm of the practical application of ideas and this was the realm of technology and ideology. Ideology in the sense that is defined usually along the lines of, '*a system of ideas and ideals, especially one which forms the basis of social organization, economic or political theory and policy'.* I also included in domino 2, all technology as we normally understand the term, i.e. machinery, computers, civil engineering etc. So from now on we'll refer to this normal definition of technology as more specifically 'Mechanical Technology'. In which case we will use the term 'Social Technology', to refer to things like political ideology, legislation, norms and social traditions. The idea of 'Social Technology' was invented by the political scientist Richard Nelson. We've adopted and adapted it as it is useful in our analysis. Therefore domino 2 represents the idea of technology in this new expanded and more general sense of being the implementation of pure ideas, towards the service of human purposes.

The first two dominos were distinct and what they represented couldn't be merged into a single domino because not all pure ideas became useful or practical. Also not all Mechanical Technology or ideas of social and economic organization or political control, i.e. Social Technology, necessarily derived from idealized abstractions. But there was a tight relationship between the two. Because of course ideas from science or economics could lead to either Mechanical Technology and Social Technology e.g. political policy. Vice versa Mechanical Technology that was developed perhaps serendipitously would help advance knowledge and the scientific understanding. And economic theories and even theological doctrines could be derived from and find their support in preexisting social norms and constructs.

So for instance scientific advance is supported by technological advance, i.e. the invention of the telescope; and ideas of equilibrium economics and ecosystems can be advocated in support of conservative politics and in support of the status quo, to facilitate the Social Technologies of political power and control. In the case of Theology, passages in the ancient Hindu holy text the Rig Veda, which state that lower castes were derived from the feet of the body of God and that the dominant Brahmin castes were derived from the Head; is just one example of how religion may be used to maintain existing power relationships. This sort of thing often occurs in all religions, sects and cults.

Next, came domino 3, which represented all the problems of the world in the social, political and economic realms. Here's is where the Social and Mechanical Technologies from domino 2, came to express themselves and become brought into effect. Here too there was tight interdependence between dominos 2 and 3. Of course Mechanical Technology impacted upon the world of economic activity. The entire industrial revolution came about through the advent of a series of mechanical technological innovations, including the steam engine, and this process is progressive and even accelerating in our own time. We are currently living in the Information Technology Revolution so the influence of Mechanical Technology on our lives and the modern world is very apparent. And of course Social Technologies in the form of political ideologies and economic doctrines obviously influence political economy and society.

But the opposite was also true. The politically and economically powerful could also influence the world of Social Technology, ideology and pure ideas, whereby certain ideas and ideologies could be promoted as being more true and become more entrenched in the academy and wider society, based not on empirical evidence, sound lines of argument or any good reason other than their usefulness in serving the purposes of those in power. The world of Commerce through lobbies and the funding of politicians is too often able to effectively control the formulation of the Social Technology of legislation and political policy, to its own advantage.

And in relation to Mechanical Technology, perhaps most obviously, the trajectory of politics and business will often dictate the direction of technological advance in the conventional sense, for instance in the case of research and design directed by the demands of the marketplace or the demands of war.

The last domino, number 4, represented the ecological and environmental problems of the world, and here the problems are manifested in the most concrete and visible way. This could be in the form of massive deforestation, decimated ecosystems, sea-level rises and climate change etc. The problems of domino 4, that is the ongoing and accumulating ecological and environmental catastrophe, is obviously being caused by the economic activity of the 7 billion or so and rising, people on the planet and the political policies or lack of, with respect to the world's environment and ecosystems. And vice versa and equally obviously, the effects of climate change do and will increasingly influence economics, most obviously for instance in the agricultural sectors. In the longer term there is probably not a single aspect of world society and political economy which won't be drastically impacted by the environmental and ecological changes that are already occurring but would be much more pronounced in the future.

So I saw this 4 step chain of bi-directional causality, depicted in my mind as four dominos which represented the problems of the world from the abstract realm of pure ideas; onto the realm of ideology or Social Technology and Mechanical Technology; to the realm of world society, politics and economics; and finally to the realm of the planetary ecosystem and global environment. So from the realm of the most abstract to that of the most manifest and concrete, I saw a chain of tight interconnectedness and interdependence. But most importantly it was also a chain of causality which went in both directions.

Seeing things in this way allowed me to better visualize the understanding I'd already reached concerning the total interconnectedness of the problems of the world. Seeing this chain of causality also allowed me to connect my thoughts relating to the problems of the world, with my earlier ideas about the importance of paradigms, mazeways, worldview or weltanschauung; and which we discussed in an earlier chapter. I saw very clearly that there was a perfect overlap between these notions on the one hand and on the other all of domino 1, i.e. the realm of pure ideas and also much of domino 2 especially relating to the Social Technologies of norms, values, ethics and legislation.

Therefore I had the first glimmers of how the tightly interconnected and interwoven Gordian Knot of the problems of the world, might start to be unravelled. If the problems of the world had at their root the ideas and ideologies which ruled this world, then the solution would necessarily involve a challenge to these incumbent ideas and ideologies, leading to their replacement by or assimilation into a set of more highly evolved ones.

I gained further insight into what this challenge to the existing ideas and ideologies might involve and the difficulties to be expected, by thinking further about the four dominos and considering the high level of interconnectedness between the problems existing within each realm, represented by the different dominos. So as well as the interconnections that existed between the different dominos, there also existed within each domain an even more complex and more intricate set of interconnections between all the myriad separate mini problems found within each realm.

So I will now go into a little more detail in order to explain some aspects of these interdependencies existing within each realm, because it will make it easier to understand the solution to all the problems of the world which came to steadily evolve in my mind. It will help us to better grasp what is the nature of the heart of all the problems. Of course it will necessarily only be a superficial exposition of this huge and weighty subject matter, i.e. the more intricate details of all the problems of the world. So we'll merely be skimming over things in order to provide merely a very selective overview and the briefest of summaries. We'll provide just enough detail to make our point.

In this explaining of the interconnectedness of the problems within each domain, we'll this time, instead go in reverse order starting from domino 4 and problems relating to environment and ecology, and then work our way back to domino 1 and problems in the realm of pure ideas.

It is obvious and an accepted fact that ecosystems are tightly interconnected, so that separate problems here will naturally have knock on effects. A simple and important example would be bees and pollination. If bees become extinct then so do a lot of the plant species and most of human agriculture. And also ecosystems affect the environment, so for instance it is now known that deforestation affects rainfall patterns and also the levels of carbon dioxide in the atmosphere, which in turn affect the climate in a variety of ways. Conversely changes in climate and levels of carbon dioxide will in turn affect ecosystems, changing patterns of vegetation and animal habitation. And increased carbon dioxide in the oceans increase acidity which destroy coral reefs and various animal species.

Moving down to domino 3, to illustrate the interconnectedness of the problems within the social, economic and political realms, we'll give just a few examples to illustrate a vast interconnected web of myriad and diverse issues.

There exists the problem of population growth and how to contain it. So the current 7 billion or so people on the planet today, already putting a lot of stress on planetary resources, is projected to grow to around 10 billion in the next 40 years. So a major problem is how to get people to have smaller families. It is known that access to improved health care and the alleviation of poverty leads to people having fewer children. When there is more certainty that the children you're going to have are going to survive then people generally are in a better position to choose to have fewer offspring. Also it is know that if women are allowed to decide on how many children to have, then they will generally make more sensible family planning decisions more often choosing to have fewer children.

So the major problem of population control is tightly bound to the problems of poverty, health care and female emancipation. To complicate things further, a growing population will make it harder to reduce poverty and improve health care, so in this instance the problems form a mutually reinforcing feedback loop.

And then all of these problems are in turn linked to political and economic problems, for instance war and economic underdevelopment. And in many places in the third world, the problem of female emancipation is unsolvable without tackling the problems of social tradition which are often dictated by religion; and which might also impede attempts at economic or political reforms. To more fully chart the interdependencies of the problems in the social, economic and political realm, might not just take a hefty sized book but rather a series of large volumes; but here I give just a few tiny example to give a flavour of things.

Moving to the next domino, number 2, and getting closer to what I came to understand as the heart of the problems of the world; are the interdependencies existing within the realm of social and mechanical technology and in particular the realm of political and economically related ideology. I discovered that there existed in the world today a set of tightly interconnected ideologies which were dominant and were a very significant factor in the cause of the problems of the world, and also an impediment to their solution.

Some of these ideologies included Neo-Liberalism which was an interpretation of capitalism which didn't recognize social responsibilities, and which suggested that free markets were the answer to all of societies problems and ills. The doctrine also called for the dismantling of regulatory frameworks and legislation designed to deal with some of the historical problems of free markets and in its extreme form also rejected any idea of government intervention in the running of the world's economies. Another name for this version of capitalism is Free Market Fundamentalism.

This ideology of Neo-Liberalism went hand in hand with the idea of absolute selfishness as a virtue, which was espoused by a 20th century 'thinker' called Ayn Rand and which was highly influential and was gaining increasing acceptance. A Library of Congress study, listed Rand's novel and manifesto for her ideas, 'Atlas Shrugged', as the second most influential book in the US after the Bible.

Added to this mix and was the idea of Selfish Genes Darwinism which was quite dominant in mainstream thought. It is a highly influential idea, which though existing as something theoretical and more in the realm of pure ideas and the academy. Nonetheless historically and in the present age, ideas from Evolutionary theory and Biology were and are readily translatable into the social and political realm as we shall more clearly see.

The selfish genes theory is easily transferable to the ideological realm, and applied to theories about society and politics in a form of sociobiology. Which means it is able to form a tight and mutually reinforcing nexus with our two earlier ideas of Neo-Liberalism and Ayn Rand's absolute selfishness as a virtue. This is another example of the interconnectedness of things, in this case in the realm of ideology or Social Technology.

The idea of selfish genes derived from the work of the evolutionary biologist George Price. He tried to explain altruism or the idea of helping others as really the underlying process of trying to help people who have genes similar to our own. So this 'kin selection' would actually help to promote our own genes and so from this viewpoint altruism was actually in a sense selfish. But the flip side of Price's work was that his mathematical formulations also explained the logic of genocide, i.e. killing those people whose genes are dissimilar to our own. i.e. other clans or other races.

Later on the chief advocate of the 'selfish genes' idea Richard Dawkins, while promoting what he saw as some sort of absolute truth, at the same time recognized what a horrible world it would be if people actually applied the theory of kin selection of selfish genes to how they lived their lives. He said he repeatedly claimed to be an 'anti-Darwinian', when it came to applying the idea of selfish genes to the organization of society and even said words to the effect that such a society would be, 'Thatcherite', i.e. a reference to Neo-Liberalism as implemented in the UK by Margaret Thatcher in 1980s, the equivalent in the US would be Reaganomics.

But the problem here is that ideas have a life of their own, and people did live their lives and organize themselves socially, economically and political, according to how they understood the world and what they held to be true. How could it be otherwise? So the idea of selfish genes really reinforced the ideas of Neo-Liberalism, and Ayn Rand's absolute selfishness as a virtue.

While there was some truth in the idea of selfish genes or kin selection, like all scientific theories they were really partial views on a highly complex phenomena, i.e. life. When these views were taken as absolute and total then this lead to fallacies. When these views influenced society and politics, which inevitably they did and increasingly will, then I saw that they would contribute significantly to the problems of the world, in particular to the problems of social inequality, economic injustice and the fragmentation of peoples, even genocide, if these ideas became more fully accepted without balancing views and an idea of the bigger picture.

There was a lineage of ideas from Darwin's original work in the 19th Century, to Victorian Social Darwinism, to Eugenics and what became later known as Racial Hygiene in Germany, which morphed into a doctrine called 'Theozoology' which influenced the young Hitler and which later became incorporated into Nazi ideology. The genocidal death squads of the Waffen SS didn't consider themselves as murderers but rather the agents of mother nature and the necessary protagonists in the evolutionary process of weeding out the inferior specimens, i.e. non-Aryans. How receptive they would have been to the later selfish genes doctrines and Price's mathematics of genocide. And would it be inconceivable that a future racist and genocidal ideology might find their support, inspiration and justification in the selfish genes or kin selection doctrine?

In present times we are living under the power of this incredibly tight and mutually reinforcing nexus of ideologies consisting of Neo-Liberalism, Ayn Rand's absolute selfishness as a virtue and also what can be called applied selfish genes Darwinism. And I saw these ideas as being particularly problematic especial in the areas of politics and economic activity but they also affected human society in general. They also contributed to the worsening of the environmental and ecological problems of this world, I believed.

It was so necessary to challenge these ideologies of selfishness which were so prominent in the current age. And this was no small challenge to take on the dominant ideologies of the world, which had the support of a very large number of people, including some of the most powerful factions in the world, together with massive financial backing. And the mutually reinforcing nature of these problematic doctrines, i.e. those of unmitigated self interest; made the task even more difficult.

But there was a way that the problem could be successfully attacked. And this had to do with an important foundation and even critical support that all these selfish ideologies required, and this had to do with the realm of pure ideas, i.e. our first domino, number 1. For ultimately all of these ideologies of selfishness, depended on intellectual foundations for their validity and very existence. They were justified by certain scientific theories (including the selfish genes doctrine), specific philosophical notions and also ideas from the social sciences.

This may be considered the real heart of the problem and the source from which the problematic selfish ideologies of the world have their justification and derive their strength. This is where I saw that a decisive victory could be won, and the place where these problematic ideologies could be attacked at their roots. In doing so, I saw a way that the first domino could be toppled, and which in turn would enable the process by which all the other dominos would likewise fall and the problems of the world in the social, political, economic, ecological and environmental realms could also be solved.

For years I had been working towards my life long quest of working out how the human brain worked and understanding the nature of mind. My work progressed to a point where I became certain I had found the correct answer and that this would impact dramatically on the world of science and also allow me to create true artificial intelligence in the process. What's more, I had also discovered that my fractal brain theory, could also answers the mysteries of genomics and also explain the nature the life, society and even the entire Universe. This was because I discovered that the fractal template of the brain, interpolated within into the sub-cellular domain of the DNA and genome; and also extrapolated without to society and the cosmos. And this in turn was the key to answering the biggest questions in philosophy and also enabled me to explain how it was that we are all one consciousness or God, which is the core truth behind the hidden or Esoteric Religion. Also I had discovered that the main central beliefs of the esoteric mysteries were completely embedded within and encapsulated by the fractal brain theory. So I had in my possession the means by which the ancient mysteries and the esoteric heart which can be found in all the world's major religions, may be revived for the 21st Century. We discussed all of this in earlier chapters.

This gave me a unifying picture of science, religion and philosophy which was derived from and encapsulated by the fractal brain theory. And once my ideas relating to the creation of artificial intelligence became mainstream and widely accepted then taken all together I came to believe that this would give me a platform from which I could successfully challenge the dominant ideas and theories of the world, that existed in the realm of pure ideas, i.e. in the academic institutions and religious schools, but also existing in the minds of people generally.

This was the great paradigm shift and *'revolution in mental conceptions'* that people were expecting, were hoping for, but nobody could quite articulate. I came to understand that I was in possession of a major revelation which would fit the bill, and give to a lot of progressive people what they were waiting for anyway. I would not just be delivering a set of abstract ideas relating to science, philosopher and theology but rather an entire worldview which would also encompass at least in outline form, history, politics, sociology and all the rest of it.

Concerning the interlocking nature of the problems in the realm of pure ideas, in the domains of science, philosophy, theology and social science; it was their tight interconnectedness which made it impossible for thinkers working in the fragmented and compartmentalized mainstream institutions to come up with the integrated solutions which Providence had set it up for me to find in my very unconventional intellectual journey that occurred almost complete outside of the formal academies. And it would be the extremely tightly interconnected nature of my unified solution to brain, mind, genomics, artificial intelligence, life, Universe, consciousness and God; which would help it to win adherents and successful replace some of the existing and dominant ideological, existential, scientific, theological, cosmological and metaphysical views of this world; especially the ones which were problematic. I came to see a massive and difficult task as something that was completely achievable.

While we've mainly been considering one set of problematic doctrines i.e. applied selfish genes, absolute selfishness as a virtue and Neo-Liberalism, and have been talking about our new paradigm challenging the foundations on which these ideologies are based, the paradigm shift we are talking about in the realm of pure ideas would also potentially challenge many of the other doctrines and ideologies of the world, including many political, tribalistic and religious fundamentalist ones.

What would come in their place was something I worked out later on and which is expanded upon in a later chapter about how I came to develop my Political Philosophy and the nature of it. It wasn't just about challenging and changing things but also importantly it was also about figuring out the exact nature of the better and more workable ideas, ideologies, norms and values which would replace some of the existing ones. This is described in a later chapter called and about Political Philosophy.

But there was yet still something else I needed to work out and explain to myself and to others. Even though I had this great revelation in the realm of pure ideas and possessed this new paradigm that I thought could alter the course of history, there was still the problem of translating what was in my head, in my notebooks and computers, into the wider world of mainstream society, academia, politics and commerce.

This would come later when I started to learn about reform and revolutionary social movements, and especially the deep relationship between on the one hand, the esoteric or hidden religion, mythology and prophecies; and on the other hand so many of the major revolutionary movements that had occurred throughout history and all over the world. I would also come to better understand the nature of politics and arrive at a better understanding of how my ideas and worldview would one day come to influence the political arena.

I also would later more fully understand the implications of my fractal brain theory when implemented as artificial intelligence and the impact this would have on the world's of commerce and economic activity; which itself would inevitably bring about profound political and societal changes. The new worldview which included the fractal brain theory, would lead to dramatic changes in the realm of ideas and ideology, but would be also impact more immediately in the form of technology, which in and of itself would be revolutionary. I came to believe that my work would be the key to the instigation of the so called 'Technological Singularity'. Taken together, these forces and potentials, which would derive from the new worldview would be the necessary intervention that would topple the first domino and go on to bring about the solution to the problems of the world.

The four dominos representing the interconnected problems of the world, spanning the abstract ideational and ideological realms, and onto the more concrete social, political, economic, ecological and environmental realms; was really a representation of the 'Zeitgeist' or spirit of the age. It really included the entire biosphere, cultural sphere and technological sphere. As such it contained all the issues and concerns, trends and currents of human affairs. This zeitgeist was like one huge problem to solve, but one that had the solution built into it. It was a gigantic multifaceted puzzle that was set up to be eventually and inevitably unravelled I believed. It was a matter of taking all the pieces together, understanding the nature of the Zeitgeist and then clearly articulating the solution. And this solution was an entire new paradigm and new worldview or weltanschauung, which would contain within it all the myriad component solutions, including the Fractal Brain Theory and the AI derived from it, as one integrated, consistent and coherent composite.

Out of this worldview would derive social and revolutionary movements which would instigate the necessary reforms this world so urgently required and put political will behind all the solutions to the problems of the world which already existed, but were either thwarted or remained latent. If the current dominant ideas and ideologies of the world were the 'thesis' then the new paradigm would be the anti-thesis from which the new 'synthesis' would be constructed, and which would itself be a composite of the existing order and the new paradigm.

The revolution that the new paradigm would instigate would be spearheaded by the newest of the new, inspired by ideas from the cutting edge of science in terms of its insights into brain, mind, genomics and cosmology; and would be pushed forwards by the bleeding edge of high technology in the form of the creation of artificial intelligence and the instigation of the Technological Singularity.

But at the same time it was necessary to acknowledge the positive aspects of tradition and give people an understanding of the new paradigm and worldview, in terms of previous ideas and ideologies. There had to be provided for people some sense of continuity which meant that though the new paradigm stood on its own foundations based on science and reason, but not relying on the outdated scientific paradigms or religious doctrines; it nonetheless needed to at least accommodate many of the aspects of the previous paradigms. While at the same time giving people a clear understanding of the bridge to the new and an upgrade path. And so the 'anti-thesis' or new paradigm would need to form an accommodation with the 'thesis' or existing ideas and ideologies of the world; and so form the new 'synthesis'. This synthesis would be the full articulation of the nature of the Zeitgeist, together with the resolution to the problems and issues contained within it. The synthesis emerged as the natural consequence of the application of the new worldview or weltanschauung to the problems of the world and the existing world order, and was simply its extension. I would gradually more fully work out the details and wider implications of this idea later on in my life.

So this is how I came to see the problems of the world and the nature of the overall solution which came in the form of the new worldview or, expressed in another way, the new global paradigm. In later chapters I describe how I came to better understand how it would be possible to bring this new global paradigm to life and make it effective in this world. And I also later describe how I discovered a way to resurrect, restore and reinvigorate in the world values and norms which might be called enlightened or progressive.

In my personal life I gained a new perspective and a new sense of urgency in relation to the problems of the world, in the June of 2009. This was when I got an entire month off work for paternity leave and had a lot more spare time than usual to think about things and life in general.

On the day of the Summer Solstice my first offspring arrived into the World, which was also appropriately, Father's Day. I had set myself the long term goal of creating Artificial Intelligence, but in the meantime, I had created a natural human intelligence in the form of my baby daughter Sylvia Electra. My first born came into the World while at the same time my brain theory was also emerging after a long gestation of over 20 years, when I was giving my first giving public talks about my Fractal Brain Theory which was still in development.

Seeing my baby daughter born was something of a spiritual experience, especially because the Solstices are often powerfully mystical times for me anyway. My partner and I had spent much of early June waiting for the birth which was a little late. I had an intuition in the back of my mind that the baby would emerge on the Solstice. It seemed so appropriate. When the birth happened which I witnessed, then apart from a new human life coming into the World there was set in motion a further personal transformation for my partner and I, for we became parents. We became responsible for the total care of this member of the next generation. The mission to communicate the wider message took on a new dimension.

There was now an added reason for striving to create a better world and contributing to helping to solve the problems of this World. For it is as if as parents we became more stake holders in this World through our children. In this World but not of this World while at the same time with a concern and responsibility for what happens in the World. The World which my baby daughter will inherit. Through the bond of love that a parent has for the offspring so comes a duty to preserve and the protect the future viability of a World that is able to sustain the happy, healthy and prosperous lives of its inhabitants. It felt as if after my daughter was born the mission suddenly seemed a lot more immediate and a lot less abstract. A new and powerful motivation awakened in me encouraging me, spurring me on, in my drive to succeed in what I was trying to do.

I was 39 years old when my first daughter Sylvia-Electra was born. I pondered what sort of World will Sylvia be living in around 40 years from now when she was my age? Suddenly all the things that I had been speaking about in my public talks about the problems of the World, took on an amplified immediacy and relevance. I always saw the tribulations and calamity that I expected in the years to come as the proper backdrop for what I had to do with my life. There is definitely a part of me, an adventurous spirit that appreciated living in interesting times. But the thought of the welfare of my daughter added another further perspective on things and gave me more of a sense of responsibility.

With the birth there came an amazing sense of the continuity and flow of life. I thought about the struggle and sacrifice that my mother and father made for my two brothers and myself. I thought about my father who was around 40 years old when I was born. At the time of the birth of Sylvia he was an old man of around 80 years of age. I thought into the future when I would perhaps be an old man of around 80 years and my daughter would be my age. What would the World be like then?

From an extrapolation of the current trajectory then it wouldn't be a very pleasant place at all. Would Sylvia's own children be facing starvation from the collapse of the Earth's ecosystems. Would she and her children be hiding from genocidal death squads with the collapse of society or the rise in power of new racist political ideologies? Will world society have degenerated into a new barbaric dark age of chaos and lawlessness, with the descendents of the elites of today living in closely guarded fortresses of luxury and opulence and everyone else fighting for survival and sustenance in the wildlands? Or would even all of this be a relatively optimistic prognosis? Will my daughter and her own children find themselves drinking from radioactive puddles in the aftermath of an all out nuclear war, the last remnants of a once multitudinous humanity about to face complete extinction, clearing the field for the cockroaches as the dinosaurs cleared the field for the mammals.

I gained a sense of the struggle and sacrifice that I would need to undertake for my offspring, future children and grandchildren. I found the transition into parenthood as something of an initiation, rite of passage and emergence into a new mode of being. The aim of trying to solve the problems of the world and helping to save the planet became not merely some sort of rarefied mythic and mystic quest; but also a very apparent parental duty.

Chapter 13

Revolutionary Movements

L ater on in life partly as a result of my public speaking activities and also partly influenced by working in a context where many political currents and people seemed to converge, intersect and meet, I sought to gain a better understanding of what is the nature politics and the political problems of the world. I gained insights into the subversive nature of spirituality against corrupt authority and the revolutionary nature of true religion. I discovered that the truth will set us free!

Even as a small child I took in an interest in Politics and Current affairs. After I began public speaking my interest in politics intensified and became more motivated. In trying to communicate the problems of the world and the political situation to people my understanding of things was broadened. Also a part of this process was the quest to try to discover solutions and the need I felt to articulate these ideas to others as they evolved, which in turn helped me to evolve them. Inevitably I had to consider the political problems of the world, for without solutions in this realm and the potential of all the other real solutions would mainly be severely mitigated and rather ineffectual. And so I went about on a more systematic study of the history, theory and nature of politics. I was able to arrive at some original insights when I interpreted what I learned from the perspective of the new world view or weltanschauung which had come into being in mind, earlier on in my life. I'll describe some of these new insights at the end of this chapter and also in the next one.

During this time of the formation of my political ideas, I was working in a church which was quite politicized, but also where people involved in politics of various persuasions, came for various services and events. This provided for me experiences and situations which stimulated my interest in political matters and provided the perfect backdrop for my political thoughts and learning. And so I'll describe some of these circumstances and formative experiences which helped shape and stimulate the evolution of my political thinking and outlook.

St James Piccadilly, was for various reasons quite a politically controversial church. I've mentioned in an earlier chapter, the interest that Margaret Thatcher took in the priest who ran the church in much of the 80s and 90s. She labelled him the *'Red vicar'* and *'A very dangerous man'*. After this intervention by the then prime minister, probably every Left leaning Anglican Christian living in the Greater London area would have probably developed an automatic affinity for the church, and many of them started to join the congregation. So swelling it's ranks during this period, from a dozen or so elderly pensioners to a vibrant crowd of several hundred.

The church of England has been called by one commentator, 'The Conservative party at pray', and there was and is some truth in this statement. However this certainly wasn't the case for St James Piccadilly which was quite strongly Left leaning, in the make-up of its congregation and also the priests. When I started working there, the strongly Left Wing aspect of the church had probably died down a little, but many of the people who came and worked there could be described as Left leaning and even socialistic. This has had a probably beneficial and balancing effect on me because throughout most of my life leading up to my working at the church, I've tended towards the Right or Centre Right on a lot of political issues; and some of my attitudes were even conservative in some ways.

This probably came about from some of the mentality I absorbed from my parents and also the fact that my views were derived mainly from what I had learned through the mainstream media especially television. Through much of my early adulthood, capitalism was the way, the truth and the life; and no nation shall come to proper social, scientific and technological progress except by way of capitalism. And after all I was partly made in Hong Kong, a place the quite visible success of which, most certainly came about through hard work, the risk taking entrepreneurial spirit and capitalism.

Capitalism is so ingrained in the Chinese culture. Some thinkers have even suggested that capitalism has been imprinted in the Chinese character and genetic make-up by way of historical social Darwinistic processes. I don't know if this is true but it's worth thinking about. Chinese civilization has been around for a long time and the process of commerce and the idea of money has long been an integral part of it.

From an early age Chinese children are taught about money. Gifts given to Chinese kids by their parents or relatives, generally came in the form of little red paper packets containing money, for instance during the new year celebrations or social visits. Also Chinese parents generally do their very best to teach their children from an early age to save money and to invest it. Though as a child this lesson was mainly lost on me. I tended to spend all the money that I was supposed to be saving and this horrified my Mother when she would eventually discover it.

My parents made their living running a small fast food business in the same building where I spent most of my childhood, and which was open 7 days a week and almost 364 days a year. My parents were self made people who through hard work, struggle and thrift made their way to prosperity. Our family in the UK was the experience of modern China in the microcosm. Capitalism was our way of life. So business and commerce was so ingrained in my make up and outlook early on in life. It was quite natural then that in my teens and young adulthood I spent a lot of time dreaming of becoming a tech entrepreneur and starting a business in my main areas of interest which was brains, artificial intelligence and computers. So this sort of thing would have reinforced some of my Right leaning attitudes.

To mitigate this state of affairs, I believe that what has happened is that in the course of things, my political leaning became more balanced by my becoming much more sympathetic to a variety of Left Wing sentiments that I was exposed to while working in the church.

Several of my fellow employees at the church and many of the members of the congregation could be described as socialist. At first I was slightly antagonist to many of their views but over many years of discussion and debate you begin to see the other side of things. One of a colleagues who an elderly gentleman and a long time socialist, came to work everyday with a copy of the Daily Star, a strongly left Wing newspaper. He'd been a student at the London School of Economics as a youth and all through his life had been a keen student of political affairs, so was a good person to have interesting discussions with. Somebody who gave a significant proportion of his pay packet to various charities and spent a lot of his time off work volunteering at his local Oxfam shop, he was someone who actually tried to live the Christian gospel as best he could. I didn't agree with all his views and we had some political rows from time to time, but nonetheless I actually found my work colleague quite inspiring.

A lot of causes or movements that are traditionally associated more with the Left, often held events and meetings at the church. For instance certain anti-war, nuclear disarmament, fair trade, trade union, civic action and peace groups will quite often use the main church area or some of the other spaces, for some sort of gathering. Some of these could be quite controversial such as a Pro-Palestinian grouping which was advocating the boycotting of Israeli exports and which was largely led by Left Wing Jewish people and in the church the most vocal supporters of the Palestinian cause were actually some members of the congregation who originally had a Jewish background.

On one occasion a full size and very realistic copy of a part of the Israeli concrete wall that was erected around the occupied territories of the West Bank, was constructed in the front courtyard of the church. It was huge! This replica wall was made by craftsman who built props for the theatre and film sets, and who paid great attention to detail. So a grey wall almost as high as the church itself was erected right in the heart of Piccadilly and stayed there for about a week or so. This wall in the courtyard was accompanied by exhibitions and stalls located within the church which tried to inform people about the political situation and some of the things the Palestinians were going through under the occupation. Spray cans and large felt tip pens were provided for the visitors and members of the public, so anyone could draw graffiti and write comments onto the wall, which made the replica even more realistic and just like the real thing. This protest event attracted a lot of people of all persuasions, especially Left-Wing activists, a variety of Muslims and British Zionists. The naturally generated howls of protest from the Israeli embassy. A lot of TV and media crews came along from all over the Muslim world, including Al Jezeera. Interestingly and predictably there was hardly a single mention anywhere in the British mainstream media.

My job during the time the 'wall' was in place, involved a lot of standing around making sure things didn't get out of hand. Of course I witnessed a lot of very heated debates between certain members of the public and some of the activists. On several occasions I thought that some of the discussions would degenerate into physical fights. Thankfully none of them did, and I say thankfully because I was the one who would have had to break them up.

The important thing for me was that in the course of my work at this time I was being literally being paid to listen to a variety of views, some extreme. As was usually the case I learned that things were never black and white, and both sides had valid concerns and points of contention. And of course you would hear some foolish nonsense. I heard views and ideas that I might have not otherwise encountered from both sides, i.e. those more sympathetic to the Palestinians and also the Zionists and supporters of Israel. I tried to put myself into their respective positions, and found that I would probably come to the same sort of conclusions that they did if I were in their shoes and had received the same conditioning in my life.

At various different points in my life I would have found myself perhaps a little antagonistic to some of the various positions. And over the years, my mind would change. I suppose over time, I learned there was no right or wrong. There was human nature, human self interest and the circumstances people found themselves in. The trick was to find a way to make everyone happy.

I should say that I found the sort of people involved with these sorts of Left Wing events were generally nice and agreeable. And they were more often than not intelligent and reasonable seeming. I would also generally find that the sort of people who took something of the opposite Right leaning point of view, people perhaps quite like myself in some ways, would have a harder less empathetic edge to them, certainly in comparison with some of the more Left Wing crowd. By coming into contact with different sorts of view points I would come to have a little more sympathy with these sorts of Left Wing issues, certainly much more than I would have had otherwise or by default. Listening to more Right Wing views, I could always relate to them in some ways, but at the same time reflect to myself that this is how I used to think.

Another way that the Left Wing association of St James is manifested, is in the patronage of some of the people who use the church or come to give speeches. For instance one of the leading lights of the Britain's Left Wing the late Tony Benn was something of a regular at the church often appearing to be the main speaker at some Anti-War protest or Nuclear disarmament event. I remember as a teenager when I had quite a more Right Wing perspective, how he used to irritate me slightly when I saw him on TV. With a little more maturity and knowledge of politics I came to respect Tony Benn as a man of principles and great integrity. I met him on several occasions chatting to him casually while setting up his microphones for him and doing the sound check. He had a tremendous personal warmth and seemed to show a real interest in me, asking me all about my background. Though he asked almost exactly the same questions everytime he spoke to me on those brief occasions, nonetheless I didn't hold it against him. After all he was quite old and probably met thousands of people in the course of his many duties and appearances. He was somebody it was impossible not to like and was quite charismatic too.

Another unusual political event of sorts with a very strong centre Left leaning occurred during the Summer of 2006. The Labour Party leader and Prime Minister at the time Tony Blair came to the church along with all of the major figures associated with 'New Labour' and most of his cabinet, in order to attend the wedding blessing of his press secretary and school friend Angie Hunter who had married the TV news anchor Adam Boulton. It was one of the most interesting days of working at the Church. Standing at the front of the church and looking around over the front few rows of pews it was a like a who's who of British Left Wing politics. Present leaders and prominent figures, together with those of the past.

I remember security was very tight with many police with large guns and MI5 personnel hovering about everywhere. In the days leading up to the event the police had come to check every light bulb and electrical fitting in the church. I don't think there any tiny space in the church and immediately surrounding area they didn't search. It was fascinating chatting to the police officers as they did their work, showing them around the place and opening up areas for them and unlocking doors as they requested. They even inspected the roof area to make sure there wasn't the possibility of some attack from a neighbouring building, but also scouting out good spots to place police snipers. I was most impressed by their thoroughness.

It was one of those events when I really saw how politics was something that I was being made keenly aware of and drawn towards as a result of my working in this unusual place. The actual day of the event was made all the more surreal by the fact that a large demonstration and protest march made against the Iraq War and also the Israeli invasion of Southern Lebanon in 2006; made its way past the church at exactly the same time as the ceremony was going on and the vows were being made.

The clamour outside was loud with the wedding guests inside the church were doing their best not to be distracted or at least to appear to be so. It was such a strange juxtaposition that I witnessed standing high up in gallery of the church where to my right wing I could see Tony Blair and all his closest associates; and to my Left Wing, out of the large windows I could see a large Anti-War demo. This was definitely a powerful formative moment. I thought what would have happened if all the protesters outside knew who were sitting literally metres, or an easy stone's throw away, from where they were marching. Also I knew that the Israeli ambassador was somewhere in attendance. I reflected on this as I watched a Middle Eastern contingent march past shouting loud slogans cued by one of the protesters who was using a hail speaker megaphone device. Here were two political currents that through fate were place side by side with each other. It was a good thing that they were not mutually aware of each others close proximity. There may have been a riot. During and in the days following I really thought a lot about the World and about Politics. Events like this could often make me do so, in this particular case more so than usual.

Onto something completely different, in 2010 a group called the London Citizens held a promotional event at the church. Later on the church would give the group its support, some members of the congregation got involved and the place would become a regular meeting place for them. This was a nationwide group that was a transplant of the grassroots activist groups which started in the USA in the 1990s, and which Barack Obama had been involved at some point in his political rise. They sought to organize people to protest local issues. So for instance in London, the local group which met at the church would protest and organize demos outside local supermarkets whom they thought were acting unethically, and also against the proliferation of local gambling establishments which were springing up in Westminster and which they thought were exploiting the local community. They seemed to have some financial backing because they could afford to keep on and pay the wages of some full-time young, intelligent and motivated activists, some of whom I met and who organized the promotional event. It was interesting to see what they were trying to do , i.e. organize people to become politically involved on a local grassroots level in what might be described as progressive causes.

The London citizens had bigger regional meetings, and some of the members of the church attended these. I suppose the wider purpose was to try to influence things on a more national and political level. I thought about what they were trying to achieve, what they were up against and also their limitations. It was worthwhile stuff but there didn't really seem to be an overall cohesive plan to it or clear end goal. This made me spend time thinking what that plan might be and what was missing from these sorts of efforts.

Some of the activists were driven by idealistic yearning and the desire for political change. One of the full time activists, an attractive young blonde in a dazzling blue summer dress, was perhaps over zealous and a little flirty in her promotion of the group and was keenly trying to get me to join them. I was playing hard to get. At one point in the conversation she said to me, 'aren't you interested in power?', in her attempts to get me involved with their activities. The senior activist was listening in, and I could see from her facial expression that she was thinking her team mate was trying the wrong approach.

But it was great to see such enthusiasm in these activists, and I was inspired myself by their idealism and interest in civic and political matters. It definitely stimulated my own interests and thoughts. It also helped to increase my growing yearning to get my own political ideas out there and which were gradually taking a more definite form. Starting from 2009 onwards I started systematically reading everything about political theory, history and practice, that I could get my hands on. And all along, this was with the view of using this new found knowledge towards the wider goal of helping me in the communicating of the side of my message which related to the problems of the world. I need to formulate and articulate the important political dimension that would be a necessary part of any solution that sought to be all encompassing. I was systematically learning about politics aways with the purpose in mind of trying to discover how politics could help or hinder in the solution to the problems of the world. My studies and thoughts would be much more highly motivated and a lot more inspired as a result.

In the Spring of 2011, one sunny Saturday afternoon, an event took place which triggered a whole cascade of happenings and which made me start making my first public talks devoted to politics. The annual TUC (Trade Union Congress) march took place and passed along Piccadilly outside the church. The TUC always hired one or two of the basement rooms in the church annex building, for the stewards and organizers to use so the church was in a way indirectly involved with the march and I would come down to chat to some of the people running the event.

It was always a big march involving many thousands of people, even 100s of thousands sometimes. On this particular occasion a large number of more

militant and anarchist elements got involved and there were many 'sit in' protests along the route, in big name shops like Fortnum and Masons or various
high street banks. All through the day there was a lot of trouble and stand offs
between some of the protesters and the police.

A mini-riot happened right outside the church gates when some of the
protesters had smashed into a bank across the street directly opposite to the
church. It was actually the bank I would use for my personal financial affairs,
so it great that it was so conveniently located near my work place. On this occasion the bank was the focus of some of the militant protesters. The bank had
closed its doors to prevent a sit in protest but the managed to force their way
in. And once they had broken in they had gone on to cover the place all over
with paint and graffiti, daubing anti-capitalist slogans everywhere.

There followed a tense standoff with the police who were in full riot gear,
supported by police horses. I was in charge of safe guarding the church, making sure the riot didn't spill into the courtyard, where there was an arts and
craft market, or the church itself. So I had to close the gates, at the same time
making sure that people who were not part of the protest but wanted to escape,
e.g. families with small children, could do so. So I had to man the gate to let
some people through and prevent any trouble as best I could.

Eventually the police charged and it was mayhem, the protesters dressed in
their own riot gear, i.e. motor cycle helmets and face masks to hide their identity, dispersed and many climbed over the church walls. One of the protesters
ran towards me, saw my walkie talkie, thought I was with the police and
immediately ran in the opposite direction presumably trying to avoid being
arrested by me, he was thinking in his mind.

After a while things calmed down a bit, but all through the rest of the
day there were constant scenes around Piccadilly of groups of police running
after or closely shadowing small splinter groups of protesters; the ever present sound of police helicopters hovering above; also everywhere the smell of
burning wood and plastic that had been set alight in the demos. As I was walking through the West end after work there were signs of protest everywhere,
broken windows, spray paint over various commercial outlets such as Star-
bucks and Macdonalds. It reminded me a little of the destruction that followed
the Poll tax riots of 1990 years back, while I was a student but it wasn't of the
same kind of extreme or scale. Nonetheless, it was another one of those days
at work which made me think about politics. I also remember thinking how I
needed to get my political message out there.

Later that same day, rather unusually, I went to a house warming party with
my partner and infant daughter who was around 2 at the time. I really didn't go
to many parties or even social events at this period in life. But I went because
it was nearby and was held by one of the organizers of the yearly vegan raw
food event I spoke regularly at every year. Anyway, I happened to see a friend
of mine there, Charlotte, whom I'd not seen in a while and told her about my

experiences earlier that day, and also that I was eager to start doing political talks. I had met Charlotte at one of the talks I had given at the vegan event a few years earlier so she respected what I did. Anyway she said she may have a good venue for me. She'd just moved into a squatted pub that was formerly known as the Devonshire Castle, in North London quite near to where I lived. After checking out the place a week or so later, it was perfect, and what an amazing stroke of luck I thought. Once again the hand of Providence was clearly at work it seemed to me.

And so in June 2011, I gave my first political presentation, it was titled, 'Revolutionary movements and how to start one'. The audience was very mixed, including some of the squatters, some political activist types, some students and various people from my mailing list. Anyhow it was well received and I used the place a few more times after that.

In the next talk at the squatted pub a month later, titled 'A new 21st Century Worldview (Weltanschauung)', which was also political and followed on in subject matter from the first, another very fortuitous thing happened. A friend of mine called Silvia attended, whom I'd not seen in a couple of years, and invited me to speak at a squatted technical college in Bristol where she now lived, which had become a community centre with the blessing and permission of local government. So Bristol council gave my friends all the keys and codes to the locks, and told them to use the place responsibly and to the benefit of the local community. What an enlightened policy I thought.

I wholeheartedly accepted the invitation and a couple of months later I made my way to Bristol and the Artspace college which was the name given to the former technical collage campus, now community centre run by my squatter friends.

When I arrived at the place I looked around and the whole scene had a real ghost town feel to it. It was a sizable college campus, with lots of the buildings and some warehouse spaces, but most of it was empty with only a fraction of the rooms being used, e.g. some of them as studios for local artists. Some of warehouse spaces were used as workshops for arts and craft projects and there was a large gas powered kiln for making pottery. One of the warehouse spaces hosted large scale metalwork projects and another was a push-bike workshop, etc. All over the place were religious murals of Hindu gods and Buddhist deities, and a myriad number of little Tibetan Buddhist pray flags, strung out on long ropes; were found in various places decorating the campus. Here and there the ground had been dug up to make little makeshift allotments where vegetables and crops were being grown. There was a slight feeling of being in the context of a 1970s post-apocalyptic movie. The whole place felt a little surreal to me, but at the same time it was most appropriate. I was the voice in the wilderness and this was like the social wilderness and something outside of mainstream society.

And so I gave the Revolutions talk again to a small audience of only a dozen or so. This was in September, shortly after the nationwide Summer riots that happened in the UK in 2011, and also when the expenses scandal involving the corrupt practices of many UK members of parliament was on people's minds, and faith in the political system was at an all time low. The talk made an impact on the people who attended, so that when I came back a month later to speak, this time about the Fractal Brain Theory, the audience had swelled to around 60 and more.

This time there was a man in the audience from a small satellite TV channel called Paradigm Shift TV or PSTV. Though it was mainly a talk about neuroscience and artificial intelligence, I gave a brief summary of the political material at the end. Most of the audience really liked the talk, but it was a mixed reaction because some of the people were put off by a talk that was mainly about the human brain and AI, suddenly switching to a quite hardcore political presentation. And some of the activist types who were expecting a more political presentation found the scientific and technological material uninteresting. Anyway, the main thing was that I got to meet Dan the cameraman from PSTV, who came to my next Bristol talk the following month in November, together with a whole load of people from the TV channel to check me out.

A few weeks after this, I gave a talk in London to factions of the Occupy Protest Movement which was at its peak around this time. They'd squatted an empty office building that was formerly used by UBS (Union Bank of Switzerland) and renamed it the 'Bank of Ideas'. Anyway, they were looking for speakers and new ideas for their movement. This was what was probably missing from the Occupy Movement that had some momentum at the end of 2011, i.e. an idea of exactly what it is they wanted and a game plan for how they might get there. One of the political activists who was living in the squatted North London pub, where I gave my first political talk, and was now involved with the Occupy movement, had told me about the place and suggested I do a talk there.

And so I arranged to do the Revolutions talk there one Sunday afternoon, along with a whole load of other presentations and workshops that were going on in the building the same day, which were mainly being given by Marxists and traditional socialists. I also arranged for my friend Dan from PSTV and another camera man who used to work for the BBC, to both come down to London from Bristol that day to video the talk as programming for their satellite TV channel. They were looking for radical paradigm shifting material, and that was certainly what I was doing. So things were all set for another political talk and what an adventure in public speaking it turned out to be.

The talk was scheduled for the early evening and I met Dan and friend, near the squatted bank building. We made our way to the building and went to inspect the room I was allocated for the talk. As we walked through the building, once again it felt like I had found myself on the film set of a post-Apocalyptic movie. There were many people all around who looked like extras from the movie Mad Max and others who looked like they came out of the play Les Miserables. Also there were a lot of student looking young people around and homeless people who had found a warm place to be.

There was also rubbish and graffiti everywhere, and also camping tents erected indoors and sleeping bags where people were living. The dogs running around added to the atmosphere of chaos. This wasn't a problem for me however. I actually found the environment quite stimulating, it felt like an adventure, a sort of journey into the underworld. My main concern at this point was that my two friends from PSTV had come with a lot of expensive video gear and I told them to guard against theft. I kept my bag containing laptop, video projector and accessories close by my side.

In one of those funny coincidences, I learned later on that my older Brother, who years earlier had worked for UBS, in their main London headquarters a few streets away, told me that he would from time to time be working in this very same building. Apparently it was where UBS dealt with large personal accounts. So this scene of post-apocalyptic chaos I found myself in, about to give a talk for factions of the partly anti-banking Occupy movement, was also where my Brother had worked for the banking sector, though of course conditions would have been a lot more tidy, clean and better maintained during his time there. Years ago I had read a book about the personality traits of older versus younger siblings, and the idea that antinomianism and subversive tendencies were usually traits of the last born, whereas more conservative attitudes were generally more associated with the first born. How correct that hypothesis seemed in this context. But back to the story...

After wandering around the building we finally found the allocated room where I was supposed to give the talk. It was a dank dark hole of a place with no lighting, broken windows, no electricity and some of the walls were literally falling apart. Parts of the floor was soaked with water from a leak somewhere and it smelled strongly of damp. It would be impossible to give any sort of presentation to any sort of audience in this place. People were already starting to arrive for my presentation and also saw the difficulty of the situation.

We needed to get another room, but all the possible spaces were being used by lectures and workshops giving by Marxist groups and the Socialist Workers Party, whom several people had told me, were trying to take over the Occupy movement and use it for their own ends. So within the Occupy movement there were political tensions and competing factions. On the one hand you had the idealistic young looking for new ideas, students, free spirited bohemian types and anarchists; and on the other hand you had members of the more traditional radical Left Wing factions who were better organized and more coordinated, and they seemed to be running much of the show. At points I was thinking that the situation I found myself in was a deliberate act of sabotage and that perhaps there were people organizing things here, who didn't want my talk to go ahead. Surely I thought anyone in their right mind could see that it would be impossible to do a talk here, but maybe that was the idea. Anyway I had to put these thoughts aside.

The situation seemed hopeless and going back to the guy at the front desk I found that he was very unhelpful and most unsympathetic. At one point I was going to say to the PSTV crew, words to the effect, 'Sorry guys, you've come all the way from Bristol but the talk isn't going to happen.'

But by an amazing stroke of luck a lady showed up who had caught the very tail end of one of my talks at the Vegan festival earlier that year, and who had almost attended a later talk a few weeks later but didn't and was determined to come to this one. Her name was Susanna and she was one of the druid priestesses who took part in all the Stonehenge Solstice and Equinox ceremonies, where clad in her ancient druidess garb accompanied by all the other druids, they would be making their ancient incantations and ritual celebrations to the motions of the life giving Sun.

It was quite by sheer coincidence that she knew well the head squatter, a free spirited anarchist called Pheonix, who initially opened the building and so was ultimately in charge of this Bank of Ideas. She had been his mentor when he was a youth, and they were mutually involved in some of the UK protests movements of the 1990s together; so she had some influence over the present situation.

Anyway my white witch druid friend did her magic and pulled some strings so that amazingly, after scouting out some potential other locations with her and her friend who was the guy ultimately in charge, we ended up with the best room in the building. This was the screening room, which was being used to show films but the projector had broken down, so it was available. And also fortunately I had brought my own video projector. Even though the talk was massively delayed and I spent a lot of effort to get the crowd who had come to see the talk to stay and wait, it would finally go ahead.

Dan and friend sprang into action setting up their multiple cameras on tripods and I got my act together. Taking some deep breaths to offset the effects of the adrenaline in my bloodstream. I did the talk and despite a load of interruptions which were edited out, we incredibly under the circumstances managed to get a good video capture of the entire talk.

At one point an old Marxist guy kept interrupting, but one of his much younger colleagues who came complete wearing a Che Guevara T-shirt told him to pipe-down because he wanted to hear what I had to say. That was most helpful. The title of the talk, 'Revolutionary Movements and How to Start One', was provocative in many ways. I think it attracted a group of traditional Marxists, not because they were looking to expand their knowledge and broaden their views, but rather were seeking to impose what they thought was a revolutionary perogative and put down any challenge to their supposed monopoly on these sorts of things. But I expressed the opinion during the course of the presentation including questions and answers, that I thought Marxism was largely irrelevant to the present situation and was mis-formulated right at the outset. However to be fair, I did also say that Marx had at least some good ideas. This didn't go down well with some of the old Marxists present whom I guessed were relics from the student protests and activism of the 1960s and 70s and were pretty much set in their ways. Another theme I reiterated was the decline and impotence of the Left, which also didn't go down well with some of the traditional Marxists and Socialists.

I expressed the idea that we had to go right back to the historical root of where progressive politics came from, and reformulate the expression of that source for the 21st century, instead of trying to revive the outdated doctrines. And my talk involved trying to explain the idea that the original source of many of the revolutionary movements throughout history all over the world, and the source of progressive politics itself; was the hidden esoteric religion together with the use of mythic or prophetic archetypes. I actually showed that this included Marxism and traditional socialism, tracing things back to the esoteric thinking of Hegel and ideas from the Bible. This seemed to fascinate at least some of the radical Left members of the audience, judging from their facial expressions and reactions. More generally it was the younger members of the audience who most strongly resonated with the things I was saying, which was appropriate because they were the ones who would be able to do the most with them.

One of things I learned about the Occupy movement and why it didn't really get anywhere was that there was a total lack of a plan and coordinating vision. The movement didn't know how to get what they wanted and didn't even have a clear idea of exactly what they wanted. The Marxists and socialist workers party people tried to impose their outdated ideas on the movement but the occupy crowd just weren't buying it. It was way past its sell by date and this was obvious to most people. Also the lack of any organization and centralized control within the movement meant it was impossible for it to formulate any sort of coordinated or long term action. It was hamstrung by the requirement to arrive at a complete consensus on group decisions; i.e. the need to pass the talking stick right around the circle so absolutely everyone had their say and nothing could be done which might offend anyone's sensibilities.

When a big meeting of the London Occupy movement did take place in order to formulate some plan of action to determine what the movement actually stood for, then the only thing that came out of it and the only thing that everyone could agree on was that offshore tax havens are a bad thing. Which may be true, but didn't allow the movement to form any sort of united stance relating to all the other issues and ills affecting the world and politics.

I learned that over time the Occupy Movement in London also became afflicted with some of the problems that beset wider society. There emerged dissent within the movement of power hierarchies forming and some factions having privileged access to exclusive areas of the squatted buildings, over other factions. This was often for very practical reasons, for example no access areas had to be created where expensive audio and video equipment could be stored against theft. But even this was seen as elitist and was made an issue.

In another development, due to trouble in the squats and also the tent cities, special security squads had to be formed; a sort of occupy movement police force which had to help sort out problems. This was exactly the sort of thing I had to do at the church, getting drunks and various trouble makers to behave, so I understood the necessity of what was happening in the Occupy movement, especially due to its being open to all comers, just like the church. This would have included, we've already mentioned drunks, but also some of the mentally deranged people who wander the streets of London whom I sometimes had to deal with. So the Occupy Movement in London became a little microcosm of wider society and some of the things that the movement was protesting about, i.e. power structures and the security apparatus, had to be implemented on a smaller scale within the movement; and which led to mini protests within the protest movement. It was educational for me.

 The video of this talk I did at the London Occupy Movement's Bank of Ideas, was also titled, 'Revolutionary movements and how to start one'. It was first shown on UK satellite TV a few months later and this gave me a huge boost. Suddenly my audience size jumped from around 60 people or so, to thousands. I was still at the lower rungs of a great big ladder to climb, but it definitely felt like progress. The talk had a further lease of life on youtube and internet video, and while the viewership was still in the thousands, this format enabled the political message to spread internationally. And so even with these small beginnings, I came to appreciate the power of video and media. So while I was doing a full time job and had a young family, together with the demands that created; nonetheless everyday people all over the world would hear my public speaking and my ideas would begin to slowly disseminate more widely.

A very beneficial upshot of the video capture of the revolutionary movements talks and its getting out there via the internet, was that it was seen by a lot of people worldwide who were involved in progressive and nascent revolutionary movements themselves, and a lot of them got in touch. This was great, because due to time limitations and a lack of inclination on my part, it wouldn't have been the other way round. Anyway this sort of feedback allowed me to get a better idea of what was out there, learn more about what was on people's minds and also about these new movements themselves, their positive and negative aspects, prospects and potential but also limitations. It would all help to shape my own message.

These sorts of experiences and the people I'd come into contact with, made me think a lot about what was the nature of the Left Wing, the meaning of progressive politics and also what was wrong with it. It was also important to understand how things went wrong and how things became the way they are today.

The terms Left and Right Wing, first emerged during the times immediately preceding the French revolution, where in the French house of parliament equivalent of the time, i.e. the 'Estates-General', the progressive factions representing equality, liberty, fraternity, meritocracy and the abolition of hereditary privilege; sat to the left of the French King and the conservative royalist forces representing tradition and the status quo sat to the right. And so we have the modern terms of Left Wing and Right Wing. However it seemed to be the case that in the present age, the power of the Left Wing and what it stood for, had all but vanished or was a shadow of its former self. From time to time you would read or hear about lamentations of the demise of progressive politics in the West, and even the fall of the power of politics itself as a counter balance to the power of money, hereditary privilege and basic self interest. This was an observation made by a variety of thinkers and commentators including prominent thinkers on the Left itself. So what was to be done?

It was another one of those strange coincidences in life, that for most of my later adult life and the period currently under discussion, I lived minutes away from Karl Marx's Mausaleum in Highgate cemetery. From time to time walking about in the local vicinity close to my home, I'd encounter a Chinese tourist asking me for drections to the location of Marx's tomb. I'd jokingly think to myself, another Chinese Communist party member looking to have a photograph of themselves standing by Karl Marx, to put on display in their office to boost their Marxist credentials.

It was an even stranger coincidence when, the leader of the UK Labour party and son of a leading Marxist academic, Ed Miliband showed up at my older daughter's birthday party around exactly the same time I was thinking a lot about the fall of the Left Wing and demise of progressive politics. By sheer coincidence, my daughter and his son were in the same nursery class together because we lived in the same catchment area. Anyway we'd hired a public space on the edge of Hampstead heath for the party and everyone in my daughter's class got an invite. The hired venue was a children's play centre called the 1 O'Clock club and which was a short walk from where the Milibands lived I later learned, and so they came along and I met Ed.

It was the end of June 2013 and he was very distracted by the politics of the Labour party, when at this time one of the major unions had withdrawn its financial support for Labour and for various reasons, so Ed was about to lose a significant proportion of the Labour party's funding. Other parents had told me it was 'hard work' to get a normal flowing conversation out of Ed Miliband at the best of times, but when I met him, his mind was obviously elsewhere. The impression I came away with was what a nice guy, a bit clumsy, and someone who'd make a good neighbour, not make too much noise or be any trouble; but future leader of the country?

Then again to be fair when all things were considered, was he much worse than any of the other leaders of the major UK political parties? On the Left, he was certainly a league above the leader of the Green Party at the time and the leader of Left leaning Liberal Democrats had made himself the discredited lapdog of the Right leaning Conservative party. But it was all so uninspiring. From this encounter the thoughts in my head around that time about the dismal state of the Left Wing and of progressive politics seemed to be made less abstract for me in my meeting the leader of the Left Wing Labour party and main bastion of progressive politics in the UK.

As we mentioned earlier, the idea of the Left Wing and the modern notion of progressive politics originally emerged out of the ferment of the French revolution in the 18th century. If some sort of revolution in human affairs was needed to rectify the social, political, economic, environmental and ecological ills of this world, then it certainly wasn't going to the come from the Left Wing as it existed today, and which was something of an impotent sham.

If the original Left Wing had opposed hereditary privilege then the phenomenon of the red princes and princesses, i.e. the sons and daughters of prominent Labour politicians given special access and fast track up the promotion ladder to become the next generation of Labour leaders; ironically seemed to be the expression of very hereditary privilege that the original Left Wing vehemently opposed. Wasn't this sort of nepotism more associated with the Right and forces of Conservatism. It seemed that Left Wing Labour politicians were just as corrupt and self serving as the rest, more interesting in serving themselves and their personal interests than the underprivileged classes. And I saw Miliband as like a Marxist princeling, son of a leading Marxist academic, living in a mansion of a house fit for a Russian oligarch, a career politician with no substantial real life experience of his own and little understanding of the lives of the majority of the people.

Any distinctions between the Left and Right were these days merely subtle and even cosmetic. But if revolutionary change and opposition to what was happening with the current problematic trajectory of human affairs wasn't going to come from the traditional and much diminished Left then from where would it emerge?

I would find the answer to this question by studying some of the most powerful and effective revolutionary movements that had occurred all over the world and over many centuries. This was coupled with my knowledge of the history of world religion and in particular what I knew about the beliefs at the heart of the hidden or Esoteric Religion.

For a long time I had already known about the antinomian and revolutionary nature of the original mission of the founders of religion, e.g. Jesus, Muhammad and Buddha. Jesus constantly challenged the status quo of his time and the religious establishment. The incident in the temple with the money changers was an antagonistic move towards the political powers in his day.

He was in effect attacking the system of taxation that existed at the time. The money changers exchanged special temple coins for an exactly specified amount of agricultural produce, i.e. grain or livestock, which was how the locals were taxed. The tax payee on obtaining his coin, by handing over his goods, would then take it up to the Sadducees or high priests of the temple, who would then tick off the man's name on the tax collection ledger and so his tax was paid. Taxation is the life blood of political power and the casting out of the money changers was the chopping at the very roots of political authority. Of course this sort of thing isn't taught at Sunday school.

Buddha directly challenged the caste system by proclaiming that everyone could become enlightened including women. His new egalitarian sect was open to all regardless of sex or caste. The upstart Buddha who came from a warrior caste caused a lot of upset to members of the dominant Brahmin priestly caste who hated him. He survived several assassination attempts and his death from eating wild mushrooms could plausibly have been the final assassination attempt that finally succeeded.

And likewise with Muhammad who challenged the dominant Meccan clans and on closer study of the history of Islam and his sayings, can be clearly seen to be promoting a progressive message of equality and tolerance, giving women property and divorce rights and eventually overthrowing the establishment of his time. He too survived several assassination attempts and spent his final years in chronic agony from stomach pains left from an assassin's poisoning of him.

If we include the old testament prophets railing against the corruption and injustice of those in political power then a very clear picture emerges. If strip away the corruption and innovations of religion added by political authorities, e.g. Roman emperors, Caliphs of Islam and Catholic Popes, and examine the truth and actual facts behind religion then we discover almost without exception the radical and revolutionary messages of the founders. We learn that true religion is truly subversive.

In my studies I then went on to systematically examine some of the most powerful revolutionary movements of the past Millennium, ranging from the Revolutions in America, France, Turkey and the English Civil War; to the Chinese Taiping and White Lotus Revolutions. And from Marxism and the rise of the Nazi Party to various revolutions that have occurred in Islam. I discovered two common factors which kept recurring in all of these political case studies. They were firstly, the so called Apocalypse or Prophetic Archetype, which I also knew to be found in modern myths such as Star wars, Dune, The Lord of the Rings and the Matrix. Secondly I kept discovering the influence of Esoteric Religion and Mystical Beliefs in the initial formation and also evolution of these movements, either directly or indirectly.

I would go to analyse and explain to myself and later to others in my public talks, why the incorporation of the Apocalypse Archetype and Esoteric Religion into the Revolutionary Movements I studied, were instrumental to their effectiveness.

I eventually came to the conclusion that this apocalyptic and esoteric factor was critical to why some of these revolutions were able to be successful in overthrowing the respective incumbent powers they challenged. In doing so I discovered a tried and tested revolutionary template or recipe for instigating dramatic changes in the social, political and economic realms. And I could clearly see the potential relevance of these ideas in relation to present times and I also sought to communicate this to others.

After some more thinking about the matter I saw clearly how I could formulate a modern reconstitution using this revolutionary template, incorporating contemporary issues and the problems of the world. Once I did this then I in turn incorporated this updated revolutionary message into my existing and steadily expanding worldview (weltanschauung) and evolving political philosophy. Which already included the means, via the Fractal Brain Theory and its closely cosmology and metaphysical outlook, to bring about the complete return of the hidden or Esoteric Religion along with the related prophetic and mythic archetypes for the 21st century.

In this way I came to understand that the full blown revival of the hidden Esoteric Religion and the return of the Perennial Wisdom to the world, would also quite naturally lead to the instigation of a global revolution which would include and inspire those often powerful factions and groups already existing within the various religions and various countries of the world, who already believed in the hidden religion and the imminent and full realization of the prophetic archetypes. All of this would come about through the communicating to the world of the all encompassing new worldview including its political message.

But there was still a major piece of the political jigsaw missing. Once we launched our paradigm shift and instigated a global revolution, what would be the values, norms and ideals that this worldwide social movement would stand for? How would it improve on the current global economic and political situation? How could this movement appeal and make sense to all the great divisions of humanity, all, races, all religions, all classes and all ages? And how would this movement succeed in solving the problems of the world?

I found these answers by continuing my investigations into the nature of politics, the purpose of politics, the study of human nature and also by thinking about where values and norms came from in the first place, particularly those values and norms which may be called spiritual, enlightened or progressive. Much of this happened during my time working at the strange church where so many political currents and the problems of the world seemed to find their nexus and intersection. This background to my life, so often usefully augmented my reflections and book studies. Also my publics talks and the people I would encounter through them further helped me to evolve my message by allowing me to absorb more viewpoints and ideas; but more importantly by reminding me that the ultimate aim of my studies and reflections was to address people's concerns and to somehow contribute to the solving of the problems of the world.

My personally experiences helped me greatly in the formulation of my political philosophy and political programme. We'll be discussing some more of these experiences and also outline of some of the conclusions I reached concerning the nature of politics and my political philosophy in the next chapter.

Chapter 14

Political Philosophy

Up to now I've been mainly been talking about the progressive, Left leaning and even revolutionary aspects of politics. I've also shared some experiences and personal encounters which helped form my views in relation to this side of things. So now I discuss some of the formative experiences of this period relating to the more Right leaning, conservative and capitalistic aspects of the political spectrum. Which would also shape my political outlook. My experiences provided for me a stimulating background context for me to develop my Political Philosophy and sharpen my understanding of the nature of political power.

It was by virtue of the decade spent working at the church that I would come into contact with and deal with members of the establishment, capitalist classes and various conservative party voting types. This was because of this particular church's location on the edge of Mayfair and also because despite its wild west aspects, it was still a high profile Central London church in Westminster. Because of this, the place would often be used for memorial services and the occasional funeral that involved members of the establishment, i.e. top civil servants, high ranking MI5 or MI6 officials (i.e. spies), captains of industry and various Mayfair or Whitehall establishment types. These people were the important cogs in the machinery of state and the top echelon bricks near the apex of the nation's pyramid of power. i.e. the establishment.

On these sorts of occasions the attendance would usually consist of a lot of Oxbridge & top public school people in their latter years together with some younger members of their families, who'd come to mourn, remember and pay their respects to the deceased. Also there would be weddings and baptisms involving more of the younger members of the establishment and privileged classes. So although we've talked a lot about the Left Wing and socialistic connections of the church where I worked, there was an equally significant more Right leaning aspect to the place and quite literally the Conservative party at pray as the expression goes.

St James Piccadilly was a place where the Right Wing Mayfair and White-hall establishment converged with the Socialist Left and Labour party. And where events relating to more Left leaning or even radical progressive causes, e.g. protest, trade union and social justice movements, were just as welcome and appropriate for the context, as where those which involved the establishment, moneyed classes and aristocracy.

If my already existing capitalistic and Right leaning views that I had absorbed in my youth mainly from my upbringing had been balanced out by hanging out with Left Wing people at the church, then I think my interactions with and simply repeatedly being in the same context as Right Wing or establishment people; would mellow my views and mitigate possibly more antagonistic feelings I might have developed along the way from my studies of politics and political power. I suppose the main lesson I took away was that we're all human and we're all in this together, whatever our class, race, religion or political leaning. This obvious platitude we may take for granted, but in my case at least, it helped me to be constantly reminded of this truth, in my dealings with a broad and diverse spectrum of people in my job at the church, including the privileged, rich and powerful.

There were several establishment type services which made an impression on me and made me think about politics, power relationships and life in general a lot. In the first few months of my working at the church in 2014, the place was hired for a Knights Hospitallers robing ceremony where members gathered from all over the country to basically be promoted in the order and given a new rank. There were a few members of the pre-reformed House of Lords present who were also high ranking Hospitallers. It was a treat to have been working on the event because I had already learned about the interesting history of the order in my studies and it was quite a visual spectacle to behold.

The place was busy with a couple of hundred people or so and everyone was dressed in black capes that went right down to the ankles and every cape had a big green star prominently on display to one side. And the higher the rank of the Hospitaller then the bigger the star. So the leading head hospitallers had a huge green star on their capes and the lowest ranking ones a smaller one, with various sizes in between according to status.

The ceremony consisted of people's names being read out and what rank they had been promoted to, who came up to accept the accolade and express obeisance to the high ranking Hospitaller. This was the human power and status hierarchy expressed in a very graphic and stylized form. It made me reflect on human society and my own views on this sort thing. I remembered purposely avoiding going to my own university graduation ceremony, it just wasn't my sort of thing, so I couldn't imagine myself wanting to be in their situation. I also didn't care about these sorts of rigid status hierarchies. One of the priests involved in the service, who was quite a maverick himself, quipped at some point that the Hospitallers were, 'a poor mans freemasonry'. But he was no snob quite the opposite, I thought he was just expressing his own reservations for this sort of strict hierarchy and pursuit of status game. At a later point I overheard another priest who was actually with the Hospitallers and came specially for the event, in conversation tell the priest I knew that he was also a Freemason along with his Hospitaller affiliations. What a complex mix it all was, I thought to myself.

It was a fascinating experience to get these sorts of perspectives on formal hierarchical status structures. Many years later, a new priest was put in charge of St James and was installed in what is called a 'collation' ceremony. This was attended by many priests all in their formal robes. You'll never see so many priests in the building at the same time and once again it was quite a spectacle. But the thing I remember most was when the new priest was making her vows, she had to promise to serve and be loyal to the monarch i.e. the Queen and all her forebears, i.e. any future King or Queen. It was in this moment that what was obvious to me and I knew already, became much more apparent. This church and the entire church of England, much that goes on in it and is allowed to go on, is all part of one huge power and status hierarchy and a central pillar of the establishment; but lessening in relative power year by year due to falling attendance of Church of England congregations.

So no matter how Left leaning or radical a priest wanted to be, perhaps through being inspired to live the gospel and follow the example of Jesus, at the end of the day they were constrained by the dictates and rules of the overarching power structure of the day. It was little experiences like this which made abstract concepts relating to power, hierarchy and status far more immediate and concrete for me, which helped me think about these sorts of things.

Sometimes there would be other services which would augment my political studies. I had been reading some John Pilger books and his writings about the Diego Garcia islands, the US military base and the problems the indigenous people there had faced. And then a little later I was working on the memorial service of the foreign office official who was in charge of the islands at the time. I remember hearing how the civil servant was a animal lover and had set up the world's largest nature reserve, hundreds of miles across, around the island preventing ships from coming near and violating the pristine wildlife in oceans surround Diego Garcia. Of course it was great that wildlife was being protected, but didn't this exclusion zone have more to do with the large US military base and the need for secrecy I thought.

On a separate occasion I worked on the memorial service of a recently deceased British army officer who had spent most of his life in Bahrain and had married a local. During and around this time I was watching a lot of documentaries made by the Left leaning BBC film maker Adam Curtis and a series of them called the 'Mayfair Set'. The series explored how the British army had made deep political, military and commercial connections with the Gulf states, beginning in the 1960s. And now here in this Mayfair church was the memorial service of one of the personnel who would have been in his lifetime directly involved in subject matter of the documentary. Watching the proceedings in the church, seeing the family, the native Bahrainian born widow and the new generation British Army officer son reflect on his father's life; it made me think about the human side of things. Once again my intellectual studies and abstract thoughts were given a personal perspective which helped in the formation of the views.

Another memorial service for a high ranking military man which stimulated a lot of reflection involved a general who apparently had a film made about him, because during WWII as a young army officer he'd single-handedly captured a German general in North Africa. What was most significant about this service was that in attendance were Lord and Lady Rothschild. The Rothschild banking family were believed by many conspiracy theorists to be the rulers of the world and the heads of world finance. I really don't really know the truth or otherwise of this idea but it made me think about what was believed about them. It was Henry Kissinger who said that, *'who controls the food supply controls countries, who controls the oil controls continents and who controls the money controls the world.'*

Now I should make it clear that I don't necessary always use the word 'conspiracy theorist' in a perjorative way. After all business, politics and life in general can be complex and humans will conspire. But I thought to myself, did one of the master controllers of the world really sit on those pews? Was I really in the presence of possibly the Cosmocrator head of the banking Archons of the entire planet? The Eye in the Pyramid? And after the service did Lord Rothchild go down to Chatham house, which was less that a minutes walk away from the church and also the putative UK headquarters of the world conspiracy according to the leading theorists; to touch base with his minions and plot the next moves in the great game of finance, geopolitics and world domination? All stimulating food for thought when one in the right frame of mind.

Some prominent conspiracy theorists believed that the Rothchilds had an 'esoteric agenda', and that they were motivated partly by their esoteric beliefs and adherence to mystery religion. If this was the case then I would hope that they'ed become avid followers of my ideas relating to Esoteric Religion and the Fractal Brain Theory which I believed encapsulated the central ideas behind the ancient mysteries.

Funnily there really did seem to be a strange connection with esoteric religion and banking, at least in the West and near East. I'd read that some of the earliest instances of international banking was associated with the gnostic Nizari sect of Islam, the so called Assassins. And then there were the Knights Templars, whom the Nizari influenced and were associated also with esoteric Christianity, and were for a time Europe's central bankers. And then there were the gnostic leaning Quaker sect, which produced from its membership, UK's Barclays and Lloyds bank. Perhaps the Rothchilds dabbled in a bit of Kabbalah or esoteric Freemasonry, which might perhaps make the banking meets esoteric religion connection a little more compelling and complete. Could it be some sort of cosmic set up, or was there a causal connection between esoteric religion and banking or vice versa. The mind boggled in the search for underlying pattern and higher meaning. Or perhaps it was all strange coincidence?

What was even funnier, was that some of the high profile conspiracy theorists also had an affinity with beliefs which were identical to those at the heart of the esoteric mysteries. The UK's lead spokesperson for exposing all things conspiratorial and relating to the coming one world tyranny, David Icke, himself spoke of his own mystical experiences of 'infinite consciousness'. Other conspiracy theorists would talk about mystical ideas of a transcendent oneness between all human beings. So how great it was I would think to myself that the esoteric mysteries might even one day reconcile conspiracy theorists with alleged conspirators and provide a common understanding. How neat that would be and what an achievement! I could even imagine a scenario where in the future all the conspiracy theorists and world conspirators got together in a state of mutual understanding and fellowship, to exchange notes and confirm which speculations were correct and which ones were off the mark. There again, maybe not.

I guess these sorts of personal experiences I had at the church, brought things down to earth; i.e. when one of the Rothchilds and alleged rulers of the world just showed up in ones workplace and sat on the same pews that perhaps some homeless guy might be sleeping on a short while later. Or perhaps where a member of the public might sit a while to pray, grieve or reflect on things.

Banking had become such an issue especially after the 2008 financial crisis and the bank bail outs together with the social discontent that emerged from it. The power of the central banks, e.g. the Bank of England and the US Federal Reserve, came more under the spotlight and it seemed people became more aware of their power and lack of transparency. I suppose it made people spend more time thinking about who really was in control of the world. And this also became an important part of my considerations. I don't know if I agreed with all the sorts of ideas circulating around, but it was necessary to be aware of them, and they helped to evolve my own views whether I agreed with them or not. Even if I disagreed with something then I needed to understand why that was the case and what the reasons were.

Relating to the issues of central banking and during around the same period that the Rothchilds came to church, I was invited to speak at the 2013 London Bitcoin Conference to talk about my fractal brain theory and its application to the creation of artificial intelligence. This gave me a chance to meet many people who saw this new form of decentralized electronic currency as a way of bypassing the power of the central banks, and so were involved with Bitcoin for mainly idealistic reasons. This was at the height of the Bitcoin craze when it was receiving a lot of media coverage, so the conference was very busy, with thousands of people coming along. The event was another adventure in public speaking and but also an interesting lesson in the problems with decentralized control. In the context of our discussion of politics and authority this is relevant so I'll spend a few paragraphs to expand on this occasion.

I arrived at the event excited to do my presentation. I discovered soon after arriving that the organization of the event was chaotic and no one person was mutually agreed to be in charge. So you had half a dozen people who we involved in the running things but no overall leader. I suppose this reflected the decentralized ethos of Bitcoin itself. This led to disastrous consequences. In one of the main speaking spaces where my talk was to be held, which was a cavernous club space with a big rock and roll style stage, one of the organizers was trying to have music played over the live talks and presentations of the speakers. This completely unreasonable idea came from the organizer because he had put a dozen or so stalls in the same space as the talks, so various Bitcoin start-ups had paid to use these stalls to promote their products and services. And so this organizer felt the operation of the stalls was being impeded by the attention of the people in the hall, being focused on the public speakers; and that the solution was to play music over the talks to divert peoples attention away from the speakers and onto the stalls.

I found the situation a bit of a farce. The suggestion was nonsensical and most of the other organizers also agreed that it was not a good idea. I was quite incredulous that someone was even making this suggestion let alone vigorous pushing for it. The organizer who was demanding for the music to be played over the public speakers, tried to order the sound engineer to follow his orders and because no one was officially in charge, the sound guy went by the instructions of the person whose name was on the invoices and contracts, and luckily this was the guy who hired me, who said no music while the talks were going on.

I had been brought in to talk at the conference purely on the strength of my Fractal Brain Theory presentations on YouTube and it seemed that there was some controversy around why I was given such a long time slot of over 1 hour when all the other Bitcoin speakers only had 30 minutes. The top speaker Richard Stallman, is arguably one of the most famous computer programmers in the world also perhaps its top hacker, and at one point I was actually given more time than he was, probably to the consternation of Stallman's fans among some of the other organizers, especially as I was quite unknown. So his time allocation was bumped up so we had equal time.

The event was running massively late, due probably at least in part to the lack of leadership and my talk was to be over an hour later than scheduled. This waiting time I luckily spent upstairs in the sound engineers area over looking the hall and stage and I chatted with the sound guy. I told him that I did exactly what he did but at the church, so this made for a little more male bonding which as we'll shortly see, paid dividends later on. And this is how I learned what was happening that day and the disorganization, from chatting to the sound guy.

I asked another organizer if everything was fine to go ahead with the hour plus talk despite things running so late and he said all OK. And so I started my talk about the fractal brain theory and artificial intelligence. Things were going well, I was standing on a big stage with a microphone talking to several hundred people and I could see that most of the audience were quite captivated.

But then after less than 30 minutes, the guy who was trying get music played over talks, signalled from the side of the stage for me to bring my talk to a close. I was just getting warmed up and the audience were keen so I was a bit annoyed and disheartened at first by this intervention. Anyway, I asked the audience if they wanted the talk to go on and it was a loud and resounding yes. And so I continued.

However the organizer guy kept trying to stop the talk and there were small elements of the audience who were antagonistic. The inexperienced organizer guy who was frantically gesturing for me to stop my talk probably made some of the audience think I was being greedy and over running my time allocation. But most of the crowd were with me as they resoundingly confirmed. But equally as important was the fact that I had the microphone and the sound guy was on my side, so the talk went on. Besides that I'd already received and accepted payment for my 1 hour plus presentation, so all things considered the show had to go on.

A whole bunch of people standing by the bar, probably some of the people who read about Bitcoin in the tabloids, who were only looking for a way to make a quick buck and were probably a bit drunk started booing loudly and yelling at me to get off. The people closer around the stage were shouting for me to go on. Anyway the years of public speaking, the time spent at speakers corner in London's Hyde park and the experience of dealing with difficult people at the church; all paid off and I was able to keep my cool, shrug off the distractions and continued with the talk. Battling through for the next 30 minutes, I managed to navigate the presentation to a successful conclusion and the enthusiastic applause of the vast majority of the audience.

It was one of those unforgettable public speaking experiences. Many people congratulated me afterwards and the drama surrounding the talk probably helped some members of the audience to bond closer to me and my message. I've rarely had such positive feedback for a public talk. Several people said words to the effect that they would be terrified to find themselves in that sort of situation, which increased their estimation of the talk a lot more. The whole experience was rock and roll bordering on punk rock.

The episode would also help to prepare me further for political talks which can often arouse strong passions. But the most important thing I learned, was the importance of having somebody who was in charge and proper management when it came to organizing these sorts of events. Sometimes the leaderless and decentralized way of doing things just didn't work and led to dysfunctional and difficult situations. This little adventure of mine into the world of Bitcoin was a like a microcosm of the wider world.

While I agreed a lot with some of the sentiments of the Bitcoiners and their concerns about central banking and traditional forms of organization; at the same time the other and opposite extreme was not without its own problems. This particularly talk apart from helping to evolve the my ability to communicate the artificial intelligence aspects of the brain theory to a more technical audience, also gave me a lesson in politics or the lack of.

If some of the politically motivated Bitcoin crowd believed that they could bypass the power of the central banks through the creation of an alternative Internet based distributed electronic currency, then another group which called itself the Zeitgeist movement, was trying to do away with the idea of money altogether. The movement came about from the efforts of a documentary maker called Peter Joseph who made a film called 'The Zeitgeist', which drew attention to the power of the central banks and covered exactly the same sort of banking conspiracies which a lot of 'theorists' implicated the Rothchilds in, all packaged together with sections about 9-11, the Iraq war and an alternative interpretation of religion.

The documentary synthesized a lot of ideas that were floating about in the 'cultic milieu' and internet counter culture at the time and gained quite a large audience. It was viewed by millions of people, and motivated by a sense of outrage or at least disquiet, aroused by the ideas they had come to accept as true; from this the Zeitgeist movement formed. So the movement essentially had its origins and founding on the basis of a documentary which collated a number of rather speculative ideas. I thought this meant that at the outset the movement was on shakey foundations if so many of the original ideas what stimulated its initial formation were questionable in the minds of most people.

To make things worse, like the Occupy movement, initially it was a movement without any answers or game plan. So Peter Joseph discovered the Venus project and the ideas of Jacques Fresco, in particular his idea of a 'resource based economy'. Joseph thought he had discovered something new and fresh that might be the answer to the ills of the world, but Fresco was really reiterating outdated and discredited ideas which were fashionable in the 1950s, that he would have absorbed as a young man. But most of the generally young followers of the Zeitgeist and Venus movements, wouldn't have been aware of this. These old ideas included the cybernetic society where science and technology will solve all societies ills and needs; with a command economy where artificial intelligence would play a central role making completely scientifically based decisions on the day to day running of society, but with some human oversight; where people would be allocated what they needed within the constraints of what was available and the worlds resources would be strictly controlled and accounted for thereby saving the world's environment and ecosystems. Therefore there would be no need for money, free markets or capitalism and all would be well.

I thought the 'resource based economy' would be a recipe for a disaster worse than the disaster it was trying to remedy. As did a lot of other people it seemed to me from the generally chatter and inability of the Zeitgeist movement to grow. I thought it was completely foolish to base a global social movement on such a flawed strategy. It should have been relegated to a minor tactic, as one of many, to be used perhaps in some tightly circumscribed and specific instances, not as a general all encompassing solution for organizing the entire World's political economy. It was a total non-starter and a dead duck being sold as the key to a better future for humanity.

The resource based economy would be problematic even in a simplified world, but once we took into account human imperfection, technological and scientific imperfection and the complexity of world society and people in it; then it didn't make sense at all. And to create this moneyless society, the movement needed people to give them loads of money. So money was useful in their worldview after all but then can't they imagine that money could be a more generally useful concept? It seemed a bit ironic. This created a schism between Joseph and Fresco, partly because it was Fresco who was pushing the money dimension and fundraising too strongly, so the movement split. After this it diminished and was never to regain its initial momentum which lasted a short while, but carried on walking wounded with a shrinking user base.

I did encounter from time to time Zeitgeist movement or Venus project activists either in my public talks or online, when they got into contact with me after watching my talk videos on the internet. So I connected with a load of Zeitgeist or Venus activists and at one point even agreed to do a talk for one of their London events, but pulled out after a disagreeable telephone exchange with one of the Zeitgeist management. A little commissar and apparatchik in the making I thought to myself. I generously volunteered my free time to do a public talk because a load Zeitgeist people expressed a lot of positive feedback for my work and I was asked to. I wasn't volunteering to submit to central control. If the Bitcoin crowd mainly rejected the idea of centralised control then here was quite the opposite. If the Bitcoiners needed a little more central control then the Zeitgeister needed less. It provided another little lesson for me. Here were two extremes, and it seemed to me that the real answer lay somewhere in between.

There was also something of an scientistic anti-spiritual element to at least the London based branch of the movement and this also turned me off. My views were corroborated by several current or ex zeitgeist/Venus movement dissidents who had similar experiences to my own and shared them with me.

What I learned was that despite the shortcomings of the movement, many of the people in it were switched on, well meaning, shared my sort of outlook and were in their own search for answers. I also realized that due to the heavy science and technology aspects of my own world view and political message, particularly relating to the Fractal Brain Theory and AI; in the future many of the current Zeitgeist and Venus following would naturally and inevitably gravitate towards what I was doing. I saw that these people I met in this context were on their own journey to understand what was happening in this world and yearned for a social movement that could be instrumental in putting into action their sentiments and wider wishes. And I was in the process of trying to come up with the sort of answers they were searching for. So once again, all these encounters positive and negative, were grist for the mill and contributed to the evolution of my worldview and political philosophy.

If some of my public speaking expeditions and connections made over the internet, gave me some insights into human nature and stimulated me to think about political matters, it was really my time back at the church which would constantly move my mind towards these sorts of matters. We've already discussed some of my encounters with the Left and Right Wing, the progressive and also conservative factions in society. But in the course of 10 years or so, there were so many countless little incidents or situations that stimulated my thoughts about politics and the current world situation.

It was little things, like Bill Clinton coming to do a book signing at the Waterstones bookstore a few doors away. The queue was unbelievable and must have included literally several thousand people hoping to be briefly in the presence of the charismatic former US president. Clinton popped into the church arts and craft market briefly at some point after the book signing event. He even bought something from one of the traders, a guy called African John, who was actually white but sold some great merchandise he'd personally bring over from Africa; he was thrilled to bits and it certainly made his day.

Years later Clinton's wife Hillary came to do a promotional event also at Waterstones and in my very last few days of working at the church. But this time her queue was negligible. It was so small I could probably have joined in during my lunch break and got her autograph! Not that the thought ever crossed my mind. I was content to stand a while and watch the spectacle as her motorcade rolled in with all the security men with the little plastic radio receiver ear pieces, just like in the movies. I thought to myself, this person who had come to spend a while in my favourite lunchbreak spot and book reading space, is perhaps going to be in a few years the most powerful person on earth. Little incidents like this stimulated my thoughts and augmented my studies.

When the former Russian spy Alexander Litvinenko was assassinated by being poisoned with radioactive polonium, it actually happened in Piccadilly at a hotel near the church. The same day he'd sat in the church cafe and also chatted with one of the traders in the church arts and crafts market, who was from Belourussia and sold all varieties of Russian dolls for the tourists. I remember before the incident I would from time to time joke to people without any serious suggestion, that I thought the Russian doll market stall was a sort of KGB'esque front, where little secret messages were handed over, hidden in the Russian dolls, and contained instructions to Russian intelligence operatives working in London. When one day, some men from Special Branch of the London Metropolitan Police came to the church with Geiger counters to trace the footsteps of Litvinenko and ask everyone for any useful recollections relating to their inquiries, then it felt like the church had become the location for a scene in some spy novel.

More generally the whole area, being right in the heart of London really felt like being at the centre and pulse of things. From a certain vantage point in Piccadilly you could see the houses of Parliament. Together with this all the centres of power and main institutions of state and monarchy were nearby. The Economist magazine, that propaganda mouth piece for Capitalism, but useful source of mostly reliable information which I started reading in my high school library had its headquarters and main offices right near the church. And just by walking down the street, perhaps on my way to do some banking for the church or buying supplies, you would see politicians, current and former. You would constantly see and sometimes meet people in the public spotlight.

So it was a great context to have been, if even to just be a fly on the wall watching proceedings and people from afar and reflecting on things. I believe that apart from learning about religion, human nature, doing a full time job, taking on diverse rolls, making my way in this world, paying the rent and feeding my family; Providence had also placed me in this context for an extended time period because it was the perfect place for me to develop my understanding of the problems of the world and to steadily evolve my political philosophy, absorbing and being influenced by the situations and experiences relating to politics that continually came my way. This was an invaluable addition to my book learning and other studies.

At the same time, around this period, when I was thinking a lot about the terrible shape of progressive politics and the Left, and the sad shape of politics in general; I was also considering the equally dire state of capitalism and all its attendant problems to do with inequality, social injustice and not least its effects on the environment and the World's eco-systems. And then there was the increasing power that money was exerting on politics, with too many politicians being bought and owned by private interests. After having been such a born capitalist from my family background, and perhaps even genetic make-up according to some social Darwinists; I also started to learn about what was wrong it capitalism, in practice and also in principle.

I learned about the need for the regulation of free markets and that many of the negative effects of the 2008 crash could have been prevented, if regulations that had been drawn up after the big Wall Street Crash of 1929, had been kept in place, i.e. the US Glass-Steagall Act of 1932, which Bill Clinton repealed in 1999. This act prevented peoples savings from being used for high risk speculative investments.

Even the godfather of Neo-Liberalism and the ideological source of Thatcherism and Reaganomics, Friedreich Von Hayek in his book 'The Road to Serfdom', spoke about the need to regulate against cartels and monopolies, which would undermine the proper functioning of free markets. Yet in recent times it was exactly this sort of anti-trust and anti-monopolies functioning of government which had been severely eroded, to give us the unfair and distorted form of capitalism that Von Hayek predicted. It wasn't just the Left that needed a complete shake up but also capitalism and its attendant doctrines. But this could never happen without a renaissance of progressive politics and a political awakening of the broad masses, but how would that happen?

I remember for a while in 2012 and 2013, I was systematically watching a lot of documentaries by the Left leaning BBC documentary maker Adam Curtis on YouTube. Over a period of a couple of decades had produced over 24 hours of information dense, well presented and wide ranging surveys of contemporary politics. He vividly described some of the major currents and ideas that had been significantly influencing human affairs over the entire modern period. I thought his work was significant, at the very least because it was seen by so many people but also because of the remarkable position he had been given to express his ideas to such a massive audience. I felt he'd really stepped up to the plate and delivered an insightful and informative body of work. And because so many people were familiar with his work and it was much discussed both by his supporters and critics; therefore this was another reason why I devoted the time to get a better idea of what he was trying to communicate.

So I'd comb through his documentaries, often pausing the video to back track and even took extensive notes. He asked exactly the same questions that were going on in my mind at this time, especially concerning what had gone wrong with progressive politics, capitalism and the process of politics itself. He produced what I thought were very stimulating and thought pro-voking analyses of contemporary politics and expressed well what he thought the problems were. Also I found myself in broad agreement with many of the views he presented. And even though he didn't have the answers, he did repeatedly make suggestions as to what the nature of the form of some of the answers might take and it was this aspect of his message that caught my attention the most. It seemed to me that the form of the possible answers he was trying to grasp and suggest to his audience; was exactly the nature of the answers to the problems of the world, including those in the political realm that I was trying to formulate. The ultimate answer I believed would come in the form of ideas, narratives and a new worldview or paradigm.

Curtis has said himself that he strongly believed in the power of ideas in the shaping of world affairs and that his documentaries traced the trajectories of the key ideas which had shaped the modern world, all told in story form. He was very good at highlighting the deleterious side of some of the most influential and dominant ideologies of recent times, i.e. Neoliberalism, mar-ket fundamentalism, also the idea of selfish genes and the perfectly rational agent as a model for human beings. He repeated expressed the need for some new vision or narrative that might revitalise the idea of progressive politics. Though he didn't know exactly what form this new 'story' or paradigm might take, he nonetheless often clearly articulated its necessity in counteraction against retrogressive tendencies happening in the world, and also how it might revitalise notions of a new way of doing things or a some sort of different po-litical order that would improve on the current ones.

At the same time he lamented the inability to form that new narrative, the weakening of political power in relation to financial power, the disillusion-ment many people had with traditional politics, also the decline of progressive ideals and the idea that we can change the world for the better through polit-ical movements. He was really articulating in his own way in the documen-tary video format, what many people were also expressing, i.e. the need for change, the need for some new paradigm, a new worldview or vision.

But what would this vision be and how might it solve the political prob-lems of the world. A lot of people were aware that this new narrative and envisioning of things was needed, but nobody was really able to articulate it or even work out where it might come from. Curtis, though he didn't have the answers, nonetheless through his wide ranging analyses was able to at least articulate a vague outline of the form the necessary solution or message might take and what it would need to achieve. This helped me to form my own ideas and at least frame them in a way that would be immediately accessible to a general audience and the sort of people who resonated with Curtis's ideas, which included large swathes of switched on people in the UK and London, who made up most of my audience at this time.

So what was my answer and analysis of the problem with politics. What new insights could I provide and how would this affect the current situation? After much study, thought and reflection, together with the influence of a wide and varied set of experiences in the form of personal encounters, circumstances and situations I found myself in over the years, some of which I've described in this book; also aided by my public talks and the requirement to articulate to others the state of my thinking; I was able to arrive at a certain level of clarity and formulate a powerful political philosophy which I came to believe could be very beneficial in shaping the future outcome of human affairs. So what was my big political idea and insight into the nature of political philosophy?

In our explanation of the political insight I came up with, it would useful if we asked firstly, what is politics? and secondly what is political philosophy? We could use the much quoted and straightforward definition of politics, attributed to political scientist Harold Laswell, which states that it's simply the process of, *'Who gets what, when and how'*. If this were the case and we simply defined political philosophy as thinking about politics, then an answer to the second question would be that political philosophy is when anybody thinks seriously about, 'How can I get what I want, when I want it and how I like it?'.

Of course there is certainly an important element of politics which involves power and status; thoughts of how to undermine our enemies and rivals; strategies to obtain or maintain possessions and services and the process of obtaining power and status in the first place. And so we have power struggles to define status hierarchies, power relationships and the structure of social organization; which in turn determine 'Who gets what, when and how'. What is true for individuals is also true for groups of people and entire nations or even larger groupings of people. And we could expand our simple definition of politics by also considering, 'Who gets who, when and how', in which case we would be taking into consideration the all important process of acquiring sexual partners and reproduction, the eternal struggle to love and be loved, and which also in turn is influenced by power and status or politics.

The point here is that ultimately politics is necessarily rooted in the decisions and behaviour of human beings, which is in turn rooted in basic human needs and preferences. So we can't think about politics without taking into account human nature. This is an obvious point, but we'll expand upon it in order to enable us to better explore the significance of our insight. So we next need to ask what is human nature?

If we want to understand human nature of behaviour then we could gain some understanding from psychology, neuroscience, and also genomics. We might find ideas from evolutionary psychology and evolutionary biology relevant to our understanding. After all on one level, we are animals and it is entirely reasonable that many of our hardwired behaviours and dispositions were selected for in the evolutionary process of natural selection. We can definitely see some parallels in human behaviour and that of animals. By the same token we can definitely see parallels between the politics within and between groups of Chimpanzee and Macaque Monkeys on the one hand and human politics on the other.

The former leader of the US House of Representatives, Newt Gingrich used to recommend that all his fellow Republicans read the book, 'Chimpanzee Politics', as a useful and presumably practically applicable study in power rivalry. The book describes how a younger chimp was able to skillfully climb the status hierarchy and become top dog. The book ended with an older rival who had been usurped eventually managing to form a coalition with another younger chimp to kill the upstart by ripping of his genitals. Human politics can get chimpanzee like sometimes but thankfully usually not to that extreme.

In another book about primate groups, 'Macachiavellian Intelligence', as the title suggests is a study into the complex and brutal power games among Macaque monkeys. The study describes the sort of thing you'd expect, fights and harassment to keep subordinates in line. It also vividly described the strict status hierarchies that exist within troops of macaques which could number up to 200 individuals. Where you were in this hierarchy determined who got what, who, when and how. This was most graphically illustrated by the description of a typical troops sleeping arrangement at night time when the entire troop would climb up into trees to sleep in safety. Here the pecking order and status hierarchy was made physically manifest with the highest ranking monkeys at the top of the tree and the lower ranking ones below and in strict order. Where the ones at the very bottom would be the ones most likely to be picked off by snakes, lions and other predators. In a way not totally dissimilar to human mortality in relation to social rank.

The idea of Sociobiology i.e. using our understanding of animal societies and biology to understand human society; may be taken too far but it can be useful and is sometimes compelling. Of course power and status hierarchies exist at all scales and levels of human society. These can manifest as class and caste division or even racial apartheid. Just like chimpanzee and macaque monkey hierarchies and power structures but on a bigger and wider scale.

However unlike the social hierarchies of our more primate cousins; the power relationships and status hierarchies existing within human societies may be maintained over many generations even extend over many centuries. So that the level of access and ability to get 'what, who, when and how', is passed on to successively generations, i.e. hereditary privilege. So we have the idea of hereditary dominant bloodlines and families. Also once we have hereditary privilege then we have all the things that people do to protect that privilege, and to maintain power and status over the generations. i.e. the need to maintain the status quo, tradition and conservatism. Or those royalist factions who would have sat to the Right Wing of the French King in the Estates Generales, interested in their own hereditary privilege as well as that of the monarch.

So without a doubt there is a 'self genes' and 'kin selection' factor in human behaviour and human politics. There does exist a natural tendency to have a stronger affinity for our offspring and our close relatives. In some or perhaps most people this affinity further extends to members of the same race over those of different races. There's an old Arab saying which goes, *'I against my brother, my brother and I against our cousin, my clan against the other clans and all of us against the foreigner'*. While this describes a state of affairs we might consider as not conducive to a properly functioning society, nonetheless elements of this saying are probably manifested in all human societies with varying matters of degree and extent. It may simply be an aspect of the process of Darwinian evolution and natural selection at work in human societies.

In an earlier chapter we already discussed the idea of selfish genes or kin selection but it's worth restating some things again here. We also earlier explored the related idea that the mathematics behind kin selection, or how being altruistic to your kin is evolutionarily advantageous; was also the mathematics of genocide. The corollary that came out of George Price's original work, which paved the way for Richard Dawkins to evangelize them, showed that it was also evolutionarily advantageous to kill those who are not as genetically similar to us as our closer kin. And once again there seems to be a lot correspondence with what we know.

Chimpanzees don't just murder one another as humans do, they also do genocide in a very systematic way that has been well documented by primatologists. A leader of one group of chimpanzees, which could consist of up to around 120 individuals living within its circumscribed territory, will rouse and agitate the other members. Then they all march off to a neighbouring territory and attack the group living there in a stereotypical pattern. First they kill the dominant male of that group, then all the rest of the rival group are systematically killed, including the baby chimps. After this extra living space is created and the territories of the genocidal group are extended. This is not totally dissimilar to the process of human genocide in order to gain living space (lebensraum) or other resources. Without a doubt there are certain aspects of nature which are red in tooth and claw as is the case for aspects of human nature. There does seem to be an element of 'survival of the fittest' and the 'stronger shall devour the weaker' in the natural world but also in human affairs. But is this the whole story and should it be the whole story? Does politics simply boil down to the man with the biggest stick getting 'who, what, when and how?'. If not then why not?

Richard Dawkins, the world's premiere militant atheist and most prominent evangelist for the selfish genes idea, himself likes to stress that he will repeatedly say that he is an, *'passionate anti-Darwinian'* when it comes to the notion of applying the selfish genes idea to the organizing of society and our lives. He states that it would be a *'very unpleasant world to live'*, and a

'*Thatcherite World*' in his own words. George Price himself was made so depressed by his own mathematics of Genocide, that this led him on a life where he tried to defy the logic of his own work, becoming a Fundamentalist Christian and giving away all his possessions to poor strangers and helping anyone and everyone who came his way, but eventually committing suicide in a state of destitution.

Though there is some accuracy in the selfish genes idea, it is also only one part of the story and one factor among other, mitigating and counter-balancing factors, when we apply it to understanding of society and politics. If selfish genes would cause a '*very unpleasant world to live*' then what we are interested in is what is the factor or factors which has made it otherwise, and make the world more pleasant and we might say more civilized, less selfish and less genocidal? While recognizing there is definitely this selfish genes and genocidal aspect to human affairs, politics and world history, there seems to be other aspects and influences at work, so what we need to do is to discover and explicitly articulate what these are. But we'll stay a little longer in the realm of evolutionary psychology and behavioural biology before we explain our little political insight, which will help to highlight its significance and potential.

If we've just talked about selfish genes then we should say something about schizotypal genes, defective genes and even 'evil genes', in relation to our political analysis.

There exists an idea that all of humanity exists on a schizotypal spectrum. Which means all the myriad, varied and complexly interacting genetic factors which can cause or predispose us to schizophrenia and insanity, can also into the right levels and combinations make us more effective and successful in life. Put another way, the factors which make us mad are also involved in what makes us human. There seems to be some correlation with high schizotypal genetic loading on the one hand; and creativity, high achievement and social rank on the other. However people high up on the schizotypal spectrum, without being full blown schizophrenic, also seem to have higher incidence of deviance, incarceration, lack of empathy and also sociopathic tendencies it has been suggested.

There is also another idea that sociopathic traits can actually be evolutionarily advantageous and that there may exist a constellation of genetic factors or 'sociopathic genes', which would predispose the people who had them to psychopathy. These psychopathic tendencies would then give the person who had them a competitive edge in reproducing his or her genes. Perhaps by allowing that person to be more devious and ruthless, thereby gaining more status and success, and access to mates. It has been observed and remarked more than once, that psychopathic and highly schizotypal tendencies seem to be more highly represented in the upper echelons of politics, commerce, academia and also religious institutions. So perhaps these traits do drive success in the real world and therefore allow the genes which encourage them, to also thrive and be more represented in populations than they would be otherwise.

If that wasn't problematic enough for our expanding view of biology meets politics, then we also have to consider our imperfect genes. Recent findings in the study of genomics or the science of DNA; tell us that on average there are about 60 different tiny changes in our DNA code or mutations that are not in our parents DNA. So that with each generation these small changes are cumulatively building up in our DNA. This data has been gathered from analysing the completely sequenced and decoded genetic information of many individuals, including many sets of data from parents and offspring. So that the differences or mutations that exist in the offspring but not any of the two parents can be isolated and statistically added up. Also the older the parent is when the child is born then the higher will be the numbers of mutations in the offspring on average. So this explains why older fathers are slightly more likely to produce autistic, schizophrenic or retarded children. Simply because there has been more time for deleterious mutations to accumulate in the sperm.

What this means is that with each generation there is an ongoing process of genetic degeneration going on with changes being made that will in a lot of instances affect us in subtle and perhaps not so subtle ways. At the same time there is a lot of redundancy in our chromosomes, so many changes might not have any effect at all. And very rarely there will be a mutation which will actually give us an advantage in life but generally this will not be the case.

So with each generation, out of the 60 or so mutations, there will be a handful which will impair the functioning of some gene or genetic regulatory mechanism. Because all the genes in our chromosomes come in pairs, one from our Mother and one from our Father; often the impaired gene function will be offset by a correctly functioning matching gene from our other parent. But sometimes this will not be the case and a malfunction will occur.

This is why inbreeding raises the probability of serious genetic illness or mental retardation, because there's greater change of the same defective genes being paired with no normal functioning gene to compensate. It is one of the reasons why it's a bad idea to marry a full sibling. It also why inbred communities, where cousin marrying is common, will have a higher incidence of physical deformation and mental problems. It also explains the seemingly higher level of genetic related issues in royal bloodlines which are highly inbred.

In the most extreme cases, genetic abnormalities may lead to premature death when some vital gene has been knocked out. Most times it will lead to some defect in the physical development or functioning of bodies and brains. These defects may be either subtle or otherwise. But generally the effect will be quite small and livable even if they're noticeable. But because these mutations are cumulative generation upon generation, we all inevitably have broken genes, where both genes from both our parents are broken so that function is impaired.

It is estimated that on average, everyone of us has around 20 broken malfunctioning genes. And as described earlier, inbreeding will promote the prevalence of specific broken genes within that gene pool. Sometimes these broken genes will manifest as serious genetic illness, but for everyone else on the planet, what this means is that we are all impaired, we are all imperfect and genetically degenerate to an extent. But very occasionally, with an occasional lucky through of the dice, our genes will degenerate in such a way whereby a specific chance mutation will actually give our offspring some new trait that will be advantageous. That will allow them to more successfully compete in the great game of life, and so propagate their genes, including the new mutant gene, further and wider.

Something that is particularly relevant to our political discussion is that over 70% of the genome is involved in dealing with the development or functioning of the brain and the regulation of our behaviour. So inevitably a larger proportion of the broken genes will be affecting our minds and our thoughts, again in some subtle and some not so subtle ways. This may manifest as myriad little mental quirks that might only be apparent to our introspection. It might manifest as eccentricities in our personality and behaviour. Or it may take the form of full blown mental illness and even insanity. So on top of our selfish genes, schizotypal genes and sociopathic genes, we are also riddled with defective genes, which will affect our mental make up in a myriad number of ways. Some of the mental effects of our broken genes may produce little foibles that we and others can work around, sometimes the changes might even be endearing. But in some cases they will be little mental defects that we wish we never had and which can be problematic for us and others. These little defects help to make up the diversity, character and colourfulness of the people we meet. They are part and parcel of human nature.

When we think about human nature we might start from basic homeostatic needs, for water, food, warmth and shelter. Then we have the requirement for sexual reproduction and security and status. But then we have to add all the other genetic baggage, already discussed, all the selfish, schizotypal, sociopathic and defective genes. And out of all this emerges society, social structure and politics. And if merely selfish genes will produce a 'very unpleasant world to live', then all the other genetic factors would obviously add further potential complications.

So all humanity is one great big mass of imperfection, defect, deviance and basic animal instincts. And somehow we have to all live together and make up functioning societies. Somehow these very uncivilized components need to form the emergent composite of civilization. How might it do that given the material we have to work with and the place we're starting from, i.e. human nature and its evolutionary, genetic and psychological dimension which will need to give rise to politics and social organization.

But we ask again rhetorically, is this the whole story? If not then what is the rest of the story or the other side of the story? And is this all there is to politics? Are we simply chimpanzee and macaque groupings manifest on a far larger, indeed, global scale. If this is not all there is to politics, then where does all the rest of politics and political philosophy come from, if not solely from human nature and our base instincts?

It was this line of thinking that over enabled me, over a period of 10 years or so, to arrive at a useful perspective and interesting insight. In my mind and reflections I called everything we have talked about so far, relating to human nature and our selfish genes etc. the 'default'. But then I realized that there was a counteracting factor which existed as a complementary opposite to this default. This extra input allowed us to offset and rise above our base instincts, along with our selfish, sociopathic, schizotypal and defective genes. It allowed us to entertain ideas of equality, meritocracy, liberty and universal brotherhood and sisterhood, over the default complements of class and caste division, nepotism and hereditary privilege, dominance and submission hierarchies along with tribalism and racism. It facilitated the idea of tolerance, benevolence and charity towards people who were not so genetically similar to ourselves.

This extra factor even gave us the very idea of progress itself and the notion that society was a magnum opus or 'great work' in progress towards a more just, fair, equal, properly functional and effective society; something that allowed us to move above and beyond chimpanzee and macaque monkey politics. What I discovered, for myself, was the very source of progressive politics and so called enlightenment values. It was the necessary foundation of civilization itself. So what was this X factor?

The special ingredient people were looking for was the truth that is found at the heart of all the world's religions and spiritual traditions. It is the Perennial Wisdom and Prisca Theologia or original theology. The hidden or Esoteric Religion that gave rise to the world's great faith traditions before they became corrupted by the same 'default' aspects of human nature, the same selfish, schizotypal and sometimes sociopathic aspects of our make up that so shaped politics and human affairs. And so I discovered that this Esoteric Religion really gave rise to all the rest of political philosophy, beyond the chimpanzee politics that humans also engaged in. It was the historical root of progressive and enlightened political thinking, i.e. notions of equality, liberty, fraternity, meritocracy and a just society. And the real source of what became the Left Wing of the French Estates Generales. It was the source of the original inspiration for so many revolutionary, reform and progressive social movements and political parties.

But I also learned that just like in case of religion, these progressive and enlightenment currents in political philosophy would also become corrupted by the same default of human nature, to arrive at the situation we had in the world today when the default of selfish, defective, schizotypal, sociopathic and even genocidal genes seemed so in the ascendence. So in order to revive the idea of progressive and enlightened politics, this would involve the revival for the 21st century of the hidden esoteric religion and its reinterpretation for modern times, in order to address the current social and political situation. In order to balance out the default and more basic aspects of human nature.

And so I'll now describe how I came to the conclusion that it was the hidden truth behind world religion, i.e. the esoteric mysteries, which was the key factor which instigated and allowed for the emergence of political thinking and political philosophy, above and beyond, 'who gets what, who, when and how', 'might is right', 'selfish genes', and the 'survival of the fittest'.

In an earlier chapter I've already described how I'd already made the connection between the esoteric source of religion on the one hand; and on the other hand, many of the most powerful revolutionary movements in history together with the antinomian, status quo challenging missions of the great prophets and various founders of religion including Jesus, Muhammad and the historical Buddha. It had already seemed to me, that true spirituality was truly subversive and challenged corrupt authority, inequality, injustice, social division and our base selfish instincts.

Later on as I came to learn more about the great works of political philosophy or progressive political interventions throughout history, together with the intellectual currents which give rise to them and enabled their coming into being; then I found again and again that at their source and origin was this same esoteric religion and hidden inner mysteries, which also gave rise to world religion and so many of the most significant revolutionary movements that have appeared in the past millennium.

Starting with Plato's Republic arguably one of the most influential political works of all time, we discover this esoteric influence. Plato's philosopher king was no modern day technocrat, but really an enlightened sage, who had left the cave of illusions, described by Plato's famous parable and which is included in the Republic as well as references to metempsychosis or reincarnation. So the esoteric references are quite explicit. Plato's philosopher king gains mystical enlightenment, coming back into the cave and default of human society and politics, to govern with ideals of meritocracy, civic responsibility, justice and higher notions of the 'good'. In contrast to ideas of virtue defined rhetorically in the Republic simply as 'helping our friends [and family] and hurting our enemies', which is actually a good summary of much of the politics and social interaction in macaque monkey troops.

This esoteric or spiritual dimension to the book Republic is acknowledged by modern day commentators, though its significance is vastly underestimated. Much of ancient greek thought is inseparable from the ancient greek mysteries. Luminaries such as Socrates and Plato the Pythagorean, whose thinking make up the ideas presented in Republic, would certainly have been initiates as was common at the time. Plato's parable of the cave and belief in Metempsychosis would reflect this involvement in the esoteric mysteries.

It is very reasonable to suppose that the same sorts of mystical experiences and mindsets which helped to give rise to the progressive and enlightened political ideas outlined in the Republic, are exactly those which gave rise to the same ideas which were promulgated by the prophets and founders of religion. The practices and beliefs of the ancient greek mysteries have a lot of intersection with and are in many instances identical with those found in the esoteric mysteries at the heart of all the world's religions.

Muhammad the founder Islam and its original mystic was not only a prophet and sufi but also a politician and effectively a political philosopher. We have such a distorted view of Islam these days, but on close inspection of the facts rather than a biased and superfical reading of things, there is no doubt that Muhammad's political mission was most certainly progressive. He gave women living in a very backward and misogynist society, property rights and divorce rights. Which was a big step forwards and certainly progress. Medina was the world's first city that had a written constitution spelling out and enshrining basic rights for its citizens. There was certainly a strong egalitarian aspect to his mission and which challenged to the existing class structures of his time. His message emerged in the context of war and a warlike society. Taking into account this historical context, then his message is unmistakably one of relative tolerance, equality, charity and compassion,

While there is the concept of Jihad which is equated these days with the taking up of arms and making war, it was originally stressed that this was the so called lesser Jihad. Jihad more generally translates as 'struggle' or 'effort'. So there was also the greater Jihad for social justice and the creation of a fair and equal society. Together with the most excellent Jihad which he stated as the perfection of character. Taken together we get a clear picture of a progressive political mission, promoting values that wouldn't have caused Plato too many objections.

We might also consider that Muhammad repeatedly emphasized the importance of knowledge and understanding. He said, *'Who ever leaves his house each day in search of knowledge is walking in the way of God'*, and that, *'The ink of a scholar is holier than the blood of a martyr'*. Then there was the importance of the idea of Ijtihad, which implies critical analysis and independent thinking. Are these not progressive and enlightenment values?

Of course, how religion begins is not necessarily the same as what it becomes. So progressive Muslims today, lament the closing of the gates of 'ijtihad' in the 10th century, a few centuries after Muhammad introduced it. And today the emphasis that the modern Muslim fundamentalists have of trying to go backward in time to an imagined idyllic past, and construct a retrogressive version of Islam, is really the total antithesis of what Muhammad's original progressive mission was all about. And which was really the beginnings of a work in progress, only partially completed; constrained and limited by the political realities of the time and practical considerations.

The main point for our political discussion is that we have another example here of esoteric religion in the form of Muhammad's sufi roots and his mystical experiences, giving rise to a political philosophy which can be called progressive and challenging the politics deriving from the default of human nature of our primitive and primate base instincts. This also offers hope that if we can fully resurrect the esoteric heart of Islam then we may be able to revive Muhammad's progressive mission for the 21st century. This future movement will probably be spearheaded by the young generally but perhaps also involve the existing sects and groupings in Islam today which have leanings towards the 'batin' or esoteric aspects of Muhammad's teachings, i.e some Sufi groups and some Shia sects.

Probably one of the main reasons, and there are a few, why Islam is in such a troubled state today, is because a relatively recent retrogressive, intolerant and warlike small Muslim sect from Saudi Arabia was given over 100 billion dollars over several decades to spread its creed all over the world. This sect is really the expression of the default and the manifestation of the baser aspects of human nature, that justifies itself with the language of religion and the guise of being the true Islam. Ironically their retrogressive interpretation of Islam as being the true state of affairs is so effectively supported by the militant atheists in their own fundamentalist zeal to find ways to discredit religion and God. If the progressive and original version of Islam was given the same amount of backing over the same time period, i.e. 100s of billions of dollars, then the general perception of Islam in the modern world, would be very different from what it is today. So here's the hope and the challenge.

We could do the same sort of analysis with Christianity, Judaism and Buddhism as we have done for Islam. Where we find at the source the same sort of progressive and enlightened thinking, and of course also later on the not so progressive manifestations of religious fundamentalisms in all these religions.

You sometimes hear about western civilization being partly grounded in Judeo-Christian values. If we look to the Old and New Testament and the actions of the prophets and Jesus as described in the Bible, then unmistakably these values were what may be called progressive. They challenged social injustice and the dictates of our base human instincts, our selfish and sociopathic genes. They spoke out against the abuse of power and corrupt authority, sometimes paying the ultimate price in the process. And they so often taught values of charity and helping the stranger, the orphan or foreigner, i.e. those genetically not as similar to us as our closer kin. They promoted equality and tolerance.

And we already mentioned in an earlier chapter but repeat that Buddha directly challenged the caste system, promoted equality and against convention said anyone including women could also become enlightened. We could talk a lot more about these religions, but suffice to say here that we do see a common pattern, and that is of the teachings of the founders of religion and the prophets, speaking directly in counteraction against the 'default' of the more negative aspects of human nature. The argument here is that it is these values and teachings of the mystics, prophets and founders of religion which provide that extra input into society and its politics, which is above and beyond and provide counteraction against the natural default of the more chimpanzee or monkey like politics. It is the X-factor that has provided the very foundation of civilization and the original source of the idea of progressive politics.

The militant atheist Richard Dawkins, who is hard pressed to acknowledge anything good coming out of religion, concedes that religion has played at least a minor role in the foundation of civilization and it's progressive and enlightened institutions. In a sense Dawkins' position is understandable. It is a challenge sometimes to see how a lot of modern religion, in the various forms of fundamentalism and institutions like the Catholic church, could have had or have in the future any positive input on the progressive and enlightened development of humankind. But here again the important distinction is between how religion begins and what it becomes. Which is the difference between the teachings of the prophets and founders of religion, versus the later misinterpretations, distortions and innovations of Roman emperors, Popes, Caliphs of Islam, also various later theologians and founders of new sects within the great faith traditions.

And what is an even more important and somewhat ironic, is the fact that religion is also corrupted by those same aspects of human nature, those same selfish, schizotypal and sociopathic genes which corrupt politics and human affairs. And the very same aspects of human nature that religion was supposed to regulate and attempt to rein in, in the first place.

So the selfish genes, which Dawkins says would create such a *'very unpleasant world to live'*, was appropriately exactly the same factor which was making religion so intolerable and 'unpleasant' for him. But what religion had become and the religion that Dawkins was rightly critical of, was very different from how these religions were when they began. Which especially is the case for early Islam, aspects of which Dawkins might find relatively enlightened and even agreeable to him.

His selfish genes were indeed making the world a very unpleasant place to live for a lot of people, and sometimes this manifested itself in the form of modern organized religion, in particular the fundamentalist variety. However it was a mistake to over generalize to all religion that exists in the world, how it existed in the past or how it might exist in the future. When we examine the facts we see that it was religion and the teachings of the prophets, mystics, saints and founders of religion, which again and again challenged the negative influence on human behaviour and society, of those very selfish genes that Dawkins knew would undermine civilized values and create such an unpleasant world. But he really over extrapolated and threw the baby out with the bath water, undermining that very factor would could counteract those selfish genes, and help prevent the very unpleasant world that he himself dreaded.

He was correct to point out the failings and evils of organized religion, and there were and are many. But in his sometimes fanatical zeal to dismiss all things relating to religion including its various esoteric aspects, which he was probably unaware of; in doing so he so vastly underestimated the beneficial contribution that the teachings of the prophets and founders of religion, had on human affairs and the progression of history. And this was despite all the later distortions and innovations, which were driven by the requirements of human nature, including the need for political control, taxation, conquest and maintaining power relationships. But even in corrupted religion, values of tolerance, equality, charity, selflessness and sacrifice could be found, but perhaps only in greatly diminished or de-emphasized form.

Religion was indeed problematic but as even the militant atheists conceded, it was not something that was going away anytime soon. It would seem totally incongruous to the militant atheists that the origin but also future revival of progressive and enlightenment values around the world, came from and would in the future be revitalized by religion, but in the form of an aspect of religion that they were either completely unaware of or dismissed out of hand, i.e. the hidden or Esoteric Religion, the Perennial Wisdom and ever recurring truth. And also that this was the way to fix the problems of religion and to return it to the original progressive and enlightened values of its founders.

If now we move on to examine the European Renaissance and Enlightenment, in order to understand the political thinking and ideas which emerged from these great movements, then again we find the heavy influence of the hidden Esoteric Religion, particular in the form of Rosicrucianism, Freemasonry and Hermeticism. And if we include the flood of progressive and revolutionary ideas that emerged once the Bible was translated from Latin into the common vernacular, then this can also be seen as an indirect expression of Esoteric Religion but via Exoteric Religion and its vehicle, i.e. the Bible. So we'll examine some of these currents in a little more detail.

There is no doubt there was a heavy input of Esoteric Religion during the time of the Renaissance. The Corpus Hermeticum which is a mystical text purported to be the distillation of the Egyptian mysteries, was common reading during this time and was an major influence on the leading thinkers. This text was first translated from Greek into Latin, by Marcilio Ficino who is considered one of the most influential Humanist philosophers of the Italian Renaissance and also helped to shape the future course of European philosophy. He was the first to translate most of the works of Plato, and in his life tried to form a synthesis between Plato's mystical philosophy and Christianity. With the backing of the Medici, who were the godfathers but more importantly the financiers of much of the Florentine Renaissance he founded a new Platonic Academy, which would come to play a large role in spreading and developing the ideas of the Renaissance.

It was Ficino who is credited with the original use of the term 'Prisca Theologia' which means primal or original theology. He equated this with the mystical ideas contained in the Corpus Hermeticum, also those of Plato and the Neoplatonists. Another luminary of the time and close associate of Ficino called Pico della Mirandolla also subscribed to the same ideas, as was common among the great intellectuals of this period and locale.

Most relevant for our political discussion, Pico della Mirandolla wrote the famous and hugely influential, 'Oration on the Dignity of Man', which has been called the 'Manifesto of the Renaissance'. It is considered a central text of the period and helped lay the ground work for much of later Humanist thinking. It would also provide the original basis for later Enlightenment ideas such as the inherent and inalienable rights of man. And which in turn would provide the corner stone for much Enlightenment political thinking which came later; and come to influence much moral, ethical and legal discussion as well.

The Humanism of Pico della Mirandolla derived from his esoteric outlook. His ideas relating to human dignity derived from the mystical idea that the human being contains the divine, and that the person and God are of the same identity. These beliefs go a little further that those spelled out in the catechism of the Catholic Church which states that the, *"dignity of the human person is rooted in his or her creation in the image and likeness of God."*. But the two lines of thinking are really varying degrees of expressing the same underlying truth, that ultimately there is an essential unity between who we are and God. This is the central and most important idea behind Esoteric Religion and the ancient mysteries. These are the real foundations of notions of human dignity and 'inalienable rights', on which progressive political thinking have their necessary foundations. They don't come from the idea of human beings as a collection of selfish genes and meat machines.

This heavy mystical dimension to the beginnings of the European Renaissance in Italy would be preserved in other later esoteric movements such as Rosicrucianism and Freemasonry. These two groups would play a significant role in the political evolution of Europe and later the world.

The Rosicrucian movement was brought into being by the appearance in Kassel Germany, in the early 17th century, of two documents called the Rosicrucian Manifestos. Both of them contained many references to Hermeticism, Kabbalah and also mystical Islam. A central belief of Rosicrucianism is of the Prisca Theologia described earlier. The esoteric and mystical heart of Rosicrucianism is not disputed, however the origin of the Manifestos is unknown and controversy surrounds their authorship.

Nonetheless, what is more certain is the impact of the ideas that these books contained, especially relating to politics and the search for knowledge. Many luminaries of this time have been associated with the Rosicrucian movement, for instance John Dee and also Francis Bacon who is often credited with being the originator of the scientific method. The Rosicrucians were a secret order and heresy laws were strict at the time, so direct evidence for Bacon's association is hard to come by. Nonetheless many of his ideas and writings are identical with those expressed by the Rosicrucian movement. The Rosicrucian Manifestos perhaps provide clues to their authorship, in the form of a series of initials, possibly representing some of the names of the originators of the documents. These include the initials F. B. which some people believe to represent Francis Bacon.

But what is of particular interest to us is what the movement stood for politically. These included the abolition of monarchy and the instituting of rule by a philosophic elite. Which is not too dissimilar from Plato's thinking which he expressed in his Republic. And there was to be a reform of knowledge including science, philosophy and ethics, an emphasis on serving the wellbeing of mankind, and also the process of a 'general reformation' of Europe. The movement promised a cultural and spiritual transformation of all European society. After the two Rosicrucian Manifestos were published and widely disseminated around the continent, they caused a sensation at a time of great political turmoil when people were in search for answers and a remedy for the predicament of the times.

Francis Bacon would closely echo the ideas of Rosicrucianism. He called for a 'Great Insaturation' which included the reform of both divine and human understanding. In Bacon's 'New Atlantis', he describes a sort of utopia ruled by Rosicrucians, who ruled through the appliance of spiritual and scientific understanding. Where the highest aims of its citizens was the pursuit of scientific knowledge and spiritual perfection. And being a polymathic genius, Bacon also saw the need to apply his understanding to politics and government, to create a more rational form of governance based on understanding and reason, over and above the irrationality and whims of men. Which relates to our earlier discussion about human nature, selfish genes and the default.

In many ways Bacon's ideas were a forerunner to the industrial revolution and the technological revolution that we're living through in present times. Out of his scientific method he foresaw and encouraged a, *"spring of a progeny of inventions, which shall overcome, to some extent, and subdue our needs and miseries"*.

Similar ideas of applying science for practical ends and to alleviate human suffering were also an important component of Rosicrucianism. One of their central aims was the discovery of the 'Panacea' or cure for all, which would bring relief and healing to all of humankind's physical ailments. It can be reasonably thought, that these ideas really helped pave the way for modern science and technology, including modern medicine. While we haven't yet discovered the Panacea, we have taken steps towards that direction, after the original groundwork was laid by the likes of Francis Bacon and the Rosicrucian movement.

These ideas were not just progressive, they were way ahead of their time, anticipating and also instigating a lot of developments that would occur later in the realms of science, technological but most importantly for the current discussion, in the realm of politics. These were important currents which paved the way for the European Enlightenment.

Spinoza, the so called 'God intoxicated philosopher', is also believed to have been heavily influenced by Rosicrucianism, which was by then a strong intellectual current, in his time and his locale. Many modern commentators see Spinoza as a key figure in the bringing about of the Enlightenment. But another movement would be perhaps even more influenced by Rosicrucianism, largely absorbing its beliefs and providing a further vehicle for their wider dissemination and also implementation, especially in the political realm. This movement was Freemasonry it was heavily influenced by Rosicrucianism and largely absorbed a great deal of it ideas and political goals. Freemasonry would play a prominent role in some of the later Revolutions that happened in France and also America.

It is the period during the French revolution which many modern scholars cite as the time when modern political philosophy began. From this intial epicentre there later emerged a flood of a wide variety of diverse and divergent political thinking. The two towering intellectual giants of political philosophy, writing during this initial period were in Germany Georg Wilhelm Friedrich Hegel and of course England's John Locke.

Hegel produced a very large body of work and was massively influential. Hegel the Idealist, was himself influenced by the Hermetic traditions and actually believed he was God or the Absolute as he referred to it. His work would later be distorted by the Materialist Karl Marx, a so called Left Hegelian and originally a follower of Hegel. So the influence of Hegel is not in doubt.

The great John Locke was equally influential particularly in the Anglo-Saxon world, and would base his political philosophy on the idea of people having a *'natural right to life, liberty and property'* and that the function of governments and therefore political power was really to protect those rights. This sentiment was echoed by the revolutionary Thomas Paine in his, 'Rights of Man'. It was these sorts of sentiments which really brought about the French and American Revolutions and influenced so much of later political thinking.

Relevant to our discussion is the intellectual context in which these ideas emerged, and which were put into place by the esoteric and spiritual ideas that were revived during the Renaissance. John Locke is believed to be a Freemason though this is disputed and Paine most certainly wasn't. But even so the ideas associated with Freemasonry, Rosicrucianism and Renaissance Esotericism so permeated the time of the early Enlightenment that it was hard not to be influenced by these sorts of intellectual currents, when so many of the associates of Locke and Paine, were confirmed Freemasons or strongly suspected of being so, i.e. George Washington, Benjamin Franklin, Voltaire etc.

So many of the leading thinkers and revolutionaries of this period all held the same sorts of religious beliefs which may be described as esoteric, one famous example would be Locke's friend and supporter Isaac Newton; or else if they didn't have a direct relationship with esoteric religion then they subscribed to the ideas which derived directly from it, via those of the Renaissance thinkers mentioned earlier, i.e. ideas about the dignity of man etc. These sorts of ideas which were derived from esoteric religion and the mystical thinking which so influenced the Renaissance, were really part of the Zeitgeist or spirit of the age; at the time of the early Enlightenment and period under discussion.

Of course later on in the course of things, there would be a heavy fragmentation and a diversifying of thinking when the influence of the original Renaissance input would be negligible or even reversed. An example would be the atheist Karl Marx's distorting of Hegel which we mentioned earlier and we could give dozens of other examples, e.g. all the various Materialist and Atheistic forms of Anarchism, Socialism, and Nihilism but for the sake of brevity we won't expand on this line of thinking.

The main point we're making is that when we examine the beginnings of the Renaissance and the Enlightenment, and the progressive and humanist political thinking that emerged during this period, then there is unmistakably this major influence coming from religion, and in particular the hidden or esoteric religion.

We have to ask ourselves if we take away this X-factor or this input from esoteric religion, would the ideas which gave rise to progressive politics and the emergence of the original Left-wing of the Estates Generales, ever have come into being and go on to become such a force in politics and European history. Without this input from esoteric Platonism, Neoplatonism, Hermeticism and the Prisca Theologia, would the very idea of inalienable rights, the very idea of human dignity and the very idea of progressive politics, have ever coming into being in the first place? Would the ideas of Equality, Liberty and Fraternity, also Meritocracy, have gained the importance that they did? And would we have ever gone beyond the original default politics of hereditary privilege, the divine right of kings to rule and might is right? Would we have gone beyond the chimpanzee and macaque monkey politics of our selfish, sociopathic, schizotypal and defective genes? I believe the answer is absolutely not, and that it is this critical input, this spiritual aspect, which has helped create and was the original source for the Enlightenment and Progressive values which so many people hold dear, but which have been so severely eroded in recent times. It is this input which has really enabled the emergence of civilization itself and it is this X-factor which prevents our selfish, sociopathic, schizotypal and defective genes from making the world an otherwise *'very unpleasant'* place to live.

To put it more bluntly, the idea of humans as mere meat machines and simply a collection of selfish genes does NOT imply the idea of human dignity and the idea of inalienable rights, quite the opposite. It rather implies the idea of the survival of the fittest and the stronger shall devour the weaker. It really implies the politics which boils down to *'helping my friends* [and relatives] *and hurting* [and killing] *my enemies* [or non relatives]', using and expanding on the passage from Plato's Republic.

It is the idea of humans being made in the Image of God and that the Divine is not just reflected in all of humanity but also somehow resides within us; which gave rise to and justifies ideas of human dignity and notion of inherent and inalienable rights. These are not just the historical facts as we've already outlined but also the more reasonable and logical explanation of things, whether we believe in God or not. And it these spiritual notions of what is a human being, which was the original foundation for Enlightened and Progressive political thinking.

So this is what I came to believe was the missing factor in the current age and which is the reason why the politics of selfishness and sociopathy is so in the ascendent today. It is because the original source and also the necessary justification for Progressive and Enlightenment values had been discarded and forgotten. This was the spiritual dimension and the hidden or Esoteric religion, which gave rise to Progressive politics and Enlightenment thinking in the first place.

So this was my political insight. Which was that we needed to restore for the 21st century the power of Progressive politics and the Enlightenment values which go hand in hand with it and which are necessary for its justification and its very reason for being. In order to do this I realized that it was necessary to instigate a Re-Renaissance and a Re-Enlightenment in order to revitalize Enlightenment values which would in turn resurrect the idea and power of Progressive politics. And because of what I had discovered about what was the original source and inspiration for the Renaissance, i.e. the rebirth of the ancient mysteries derived from the writings of Plato, the Neoplatonists and the ideas contained in the Corpus Hermeticum; then I realized that I had the key for bringing about this Re-Renaissance for the 21st Century.

Through the Fractal Brain Theory and it's closely associated cosmological and metaphysical outlook, which I believed encapsulated within it, the central ideas of the Ancient Mysteries and the hidden or Esoteric religion; I had in the my possession the means by which the Prisca Theologia and Perennial Wisdom could be resurrected and re-communicated to the people of the present age. Also thereby resurrecting the mystical philosophy of Plato, the Neoplatonists and the Corpus Hermeticum. Which would bring about this Re-Renaissance, Re-Enlightenment and the resurrection of Enlightenment thinking, values and norms. Which may be described as spiritually inspired. This in turn would be the necessary precondition for the resurrection of, but also very importantly the re-interpretation of what is, progressive politics for the 21st Century.

This wasn't going to be the return of traditional Left wing politics, Socialism and certainly not Marxism; but rather by going back to the source and learning from the mistakes of history, it would be a reformulation and re-expression of the implications of the Prisca Theologia or Esoteric Religion, in relation to the current social and political context and very importantly also with respect to the problems of the world.

This new understanding of what was and is the central truth behind political philosophy, above and beyond the default politics of basic human nature, will seek to completely reform and reconstitute existing political ideologies and institutions. It will challenge both the existing Left Wing and the Right Wing as they are understood and exist today. It would do this by directly addressing the corruptions that had accumulated over the years and restore the inherent virtues and positive aspects which were originally represented by these factions, but which had been made ineffective by our selfish, sociopathic, schizotypal and defective genes; to give us the present situation.

The new Worldview and new Global Paradigm therefore seeks to revive the Esoteric or Hidden Religion, which would spark the Re-Renaissance and Re-Enlightenment, which would bring about the anticipated Revolution in human affairs, and which would in turn resurrect Progressive Politics and reinvigorate the very process of Politics itself, to serve the interests of all humanity and to effectively tackle the Problems of the World.

Chapter 15

Deus Ex Machina

It seemed to me at times that I was living a random and chaotic life. But looking back on things I can clearly see now, plan and purpose to everything that has happened to me. If I had any doubts in my belief in the hand of providence, destiny and fate, then this wasn't the case after I'd followed for a while the synchronicity trail and explored further down into the rabbit hole. Things had been 'set up' to enable me to do things I wanted to do, i.e. work out how the brain worked and figure out how to create AI from this understanding. They had also be 'set up' to prepare me for what I had to do next.

2012 had been a very busy year, where I spent a lot of energy evolving the message and doing many public talks, all the while holding down a full time job. To add to the level of activity going on my second child arrived in September, another baby girl whom my partner and I named Marianne. The name was my partner's idea. When I looked up the meaning of the name on the Internet, and discovered that Marianne was like a goddess figure head for the French revolution, I liked the name immediately after that.

All through the year there was a definite sense that things relating to the message and the mission seemed to be progressing quickly despite everything that was happening. Also that year the satellite television channel PSTV was in full swing and some of my talks which had been filmed, were broadcast with some regularity. Apart from making me feel good, this exposure also introduced me to a much wider audience and to people who would never have known about what I was doing. Furthermore these talks would have another lease of life on internet video via websites such as YouTube and Vimeo. And so now my message had a far wider international reach and I was receiving a great deal more positive feedback from all over the place.

I had come to believe that something interesting and dramatic would happen on the date of the Winter Solstice 2012, which many of the kind of people who came to my public talks also anticipated. The Summer and Winter Solstices have often been in my life a special time when unusual and sometimes amazing things would happen. So I fully expected something unexpected to happen especially at this time. In the month or so leading up to December 2012 I was doing many public talks relating to the Fractal Brain Theory and the pace was quite exhausting. And this was on top of a full time job and new born baby. When the 21st of December finally rolled along, it was just another busy working day at the church.

It was a tight team at the church and the weeks leading to Christmas were so busy that we didn't have the option of taking holiday time during this period. There was a slight feeling of wishing I was in some exotic location on this special day. Maybe Stonehenge, or the temple ruins of Macha Picchu in Peru. But no, I was just in my usual work place. I can't even remember exactly what happened at the exact time of the Solstice. Probably rushing about, doing some task or dealing with some person. I often liked to keep track the exact time during a Winter or Summer Solstice when the Earth was at maximal tilt away from or towards the Sun. I liked to savour the exact moment when the direction of tilt would reverse and the days start to get longer, in the case of the Winter Solstice.

In the afternoon I had a little realization, it wasn't any sort of mystical experience or anything like that. Just a series of vivid thoughts. I realized that I didn't need to be in some special mystical location for the much awaited 2012 Winter Solstice, which many people who I knew, believed was the end of a great cycle of time spanning 26000 years. I was already working in the one of the most special and mystical places there could be, what with the location, together with the Blake and Wren connection, and a host of other factors. I realized the place where I was standing is my special 2012 location. The only reason why it wasn't exotic to me was because it was my day to day work place.

At this point, I hadn't made quite the splash on the world I'd hoped to make to coincide with this special date of 2012. In the back of my mind I was hoping that I could generate some sort of media event and get loads of publicity for the brain theory and the wider message, beyond the satellite TV broadcasts, but this didn't transpire.

Nonetheless I had a strong conviction that my little mission was on track. And if I fully believed I had this world changing message to deliver, which was fully the case; then the special 2012 Winter Solstice wasn't about some special place I needed to be, but rather whatever place I happened to be at on this date. And that place also happened to be a very special, St James Piccadilly, where I'd been working, at this point, over 8 years. I felt a little, the pulse and current of world history flowing through me.

The church and the time I spent there, had been like a sort of womb. But I felt I was starting to get diminishing returns on my time there and started feeling like it was time to move on. But it was not time to make the break yet. Providence would give me the signal when that should happen I believed. So I stayed on, continuing with my job and studies. Doing some public talks here and there. But I knew my time at the church was coming to an end.

In the Spring of 2014, through a series of fortuitous events, I was sponsored to attend the famous Towards a Science of Consciousness Conference in Tucson Arizona, USA. It was an opportunity to meet some of the superstars of neuroscience and science in general. So it was a very stimulating and interesting environment to be. So I'll spend a few paragraphs to describe some of the highlights for me, and also various significant happenings.

There was the neuroscientist Henry Markram, who was getting a lot of media attention after he was award a billion Euros to simulate the brain on supercomputers. His presentation was easily the best and most interesting for me. But while he presented a lot of interesting facts and figures, backed up by a load of impressive computer graphics, what was lacking was a theoretical framework for fitting it all together cohesively. I knew that this was exactly what I would be providing for the world of neuroscience in the future. In his talk he even suggested the fractal property of 'self similarity' in the brain, so I knew that when the time came he would be receptive to my ideas.

I managed to chat to Markram only briefly, shake hands and give him my card. It was a lucky chance meeting. A large crowd surrounded him after the talk and I couldn't be bothered to wait in line to say hello, so went to my hotel room for a bit. I think I wandered down to get some food or something and quite by chance he was leaving via a side exit and was only accompanied by an aide. Great I thought and rushed over to take advantage of the opportunity to say hello. He had flown from Switzerland to do his presentation and judging from the coffee stains on his shirt and crumpled look, he'd probably come straight off the plane. He did another seminar for a local university soon after his presentation at the conference and then flew straight back to Europe. What a busy billion Euro guy I thought. I felt quite inspired.

Later the same day I met Christof Koch, another top neuroscientist who collaborated with the late Francis Crick. The following morning we had a chat over a little breakfast and talked theoretical systems neural science. He didn't quite get the Fractal Brain Theory for now but he will in the future. He works for Paul Allen who is Bill Gates ex-business partner. Allen being from a computer programming background, will love the brain theory to bits, as will Bill I predict. I visualize the future and then I will create its happening. I talked more about this encounter in an earlier chapter which focused on the Fractal Brain Theory.

Meeting the mathematical physicist Roger Penrose was quite inspiring as I'd read quite a few of his books. It felt quite surreal and very stimulating sitting with Roger Penrose and his wife, plus some other scientists and having a chat about life, the universe and everything as you would in these sort of circumstances. When Penrose and crew arrived, I happened to be sitting with the main organizer lady who called everyone over to sit with us. This was a very fortunate meeting early on because she told me to upgrade my hotel room to the top floor exclusive level, that needs a key to operate the lift to get there. I went to the concierge desk and told them the organizer said for me to be at the top, and they complied after consulting with their management. This is where all the science and philosophic superstars of the conference stayed. I felt the universe conspiring to help me to get into a position to chat and meet with these people. Anyway, there was free breakfast, drinks and dinner up there, so it also saved me a lot of money too.

There were famous scientists and intellectuals all over the place! I felt like an imposter at times but I felt the Universe had put me there. I knew that the things I would be telling the world in general, were exactly the things they needed to hear. I didn't just hold my own in some of the intellectual jousts that occurred, even with some big names, but would win them generally. Public speaking experience with some quite wild crowds is good experience for this sort of thing. Also I'd be debating on my home turf, as people came out to challenge me and I'd heard all the criticisms before from the public talks and internet feedback.

I was quite emboldened by some of my encounters with what a lot of people would consider as some of the top minds in the world. Though they would rule the roost totally in their respective domains, when they come out to discuss some of the bigger questions like overall brain organization, mind, religion and consciousness, then their knowledge and thinking was actually quite weak I discovered. What I'd suspected for a long time had been amply confirmed.

I was very encouraged by the conference overall. When I did my presentation for the conference there were only perhaps 20 or 30 people in the crowd, as my talk was right at the end, people were tired, and I was a completely unknown speaker. But the talk summary attracted some key people and it went down really well. It certainly had an effect on the people in the room. Two people who attended my talk, came up to me at the end and said I should have been in the main plenary sessions with the big names. I told them that this is exactly what I thought. A journalist and someone who said he worked with

Hameroff the organizer, said they would personally vouch for me in future conferences. Another person who saw my talk would later invite me to speak at his medical university in Canada; which was my very first paid international talk and which gave me a major boost exactly when I needed it.

The last panel session of the conference discussed what progress had been made in the past 20 years and what lay in the future. The field had really moved sideways and but not made any progress. I read a while back about John Horgan the Scientific American writer reporting that all the journalists who had come 20 years ago to the very first Tucson Consciousness Conference, all concurred at the end that no one really knew what they were talking about with respect to what is the nature of consciousness. 20 years later not much had changed.

Susan Blakemore, a well known science writer and panelist, said something very interesting at this session which stuck in my mind. She speculated that it might take a 'neuroscientist to become enlightened or a zen master to learn all the neuroscience', for consciousness to be fully understood.

I was of the belief that it is the person who finally explains how the brain and mind works; and who also fully understands experientially and intellectual, the non-dual, transpersonal, we are all one consciousness thing, and who can explain a perfect extrapolation of a fractal brain theory to a fractal universe; who will be in a position to explain the true nature of consciousness, i.e. the mystery of consciousness and the mystery of GOD are one and the same.

Significantly the last day of the conference was exactly the 10th anniversary of my starting work at the church and which was the 26th April. So this was the day when, I told myself, I'd make a decision about my future.

And so I handed in my notice, the same day I returned to work back in London. My work agreement stated I needed to stay a certain time after handing in my notice, in order to transfer the large number of skills I'd acquired in my ten years, to other members of staff. So given this reasonable requirement, my very last day at work was to be appropriately the 4th of July or US Independence day.

My last couple of months at work in the church felt great. I was busy preparing for my new phase in life whenever I had spare time. So I was doing a lot of thinking, writing and computer programming.

My last day of at the church involved lots of saying goodbye to people and taking photographs with people I'd see most working days for the past 10 years. Was it emotional? Well yes, it felt great to be moving on!

There were a couple of very unusual synchronicities which happened that last day at church. As the place was closing up, I was in the courtyard chatting to the Muslim security guard Khan, who was from Pakistan, about the events in Iraq and Syria that were occurring at the time. I specifically said to him at some point in our conversation that I thought some of my ideas would in the future strongly appeal to the younger generation of Muslims and Jews who were living in that region.

Moments later a couple with their infant daughter who had earlier been in the church garden we're leaving and I said a friendly goodbye to them all. The man who I'd never seen before in my life replied farewell and also said that he hoped my research is going well. This surprised me very much and I asked him how he knew about my work. Apparently a friend of his called Rhona, whom I didn't know and couldn't place, saw me at a public talk and recommended me to him and that he was already subscribed to me on Youtube. I'd only had about a 1000 or so subscribers at the time. He gave me his card but I'd completely run out of mine after giving so many out during the previous few days.

Afterwards I said to the security guard words to the effect how great and amazing it was that the last member of the public that I would greet in my job also happened to know about and appreciate what I did. This was actually the very first and only time that this ever happened. Later on I inspected the guy's card and of all places he was based in Tel Aviv Israel.

More strange happenings as I drove home. After tying up loose ends I spent a while taking a whole load of photographs and walked about taking video footage of various places in and around the church with my smart phone. This was for when I'm feeling sentimental in the future, perhaps in my old age. It was late past 9:30pm, getting dark and starting to rain when I set off in my car. It had been a very hot day and the rain felt pleasant.

As I got out of central London and passed the busy intersection outside Camden tube station a few miles from my house and slowed at the light I saw a sight which stunned me. A slightly hunch backed, homeless looking person, wearing far too many layers of clothes for the warm weather, was waiting to cross the road. It was the schizophrenic bag lady who, in the early hours of the night before I started my very first day working at the church in the Spring of 2004, gave me an old book called 'Wai-Wai' which is my name written twice. In the strangest of coincidences in 2008 I found myself working at the memorial service of the deceased widow of the guy who wrote the book.

It now seemed to me most uncanny that on the day I finished my job of ten years I happen to encounter the homeless bag lady again. Though I'd seen her perhaps a couple of times in the intervening 10 years, from the window of a cafe and passing by on a bus, I'd not done so for a least 3 or 4 years.. As I reflected on the strange lady with the strange book, there was an amazing sense of closure and a strong sense that life really is scripted. I am as a sleep walker, treading a path that had already been laid down for me by Providence at the beginning of time. One chapter ended and another one began.

The Road Ahead

After finishing with full time employment I had a lot more time to devote to the mission. And things moved much more quickly and the evolution of ideas accelerated. There came a flood of new thoughts and insights. Importantly I now had time to write and produce my first book which is this book you're currently reading.

As I was nearing completion of the first print run of this book another synchronicity occurred. I was introduced to somebody by my Stone Henge druidess friend Susanna, whom we've already mentioned in an earlier chapter. I went to a party in February 2015 at venue called the Groucho Club in London's Soho and saw a guy who was involved in ecological and political issues and who wanted to meet me. Apparently he'd coined the term 'carbon neutral', had been involved with advising the government during the Blair years and even spoke at the UN in New York. The party consisted of an eclectic mix of bohemians and more businessmen and women looking types of people. My friend Susanna was there and also interestingly for me there was also in attenance a well known music producer whom I'd never met till then but I knew we shared several mutual connections, including my druidess friend who introduced us.

A month or so later I met up with the ecological guy in a cafe located on the edge of some woodland in North London's Muswell hill. The conversation was interesting but became especially so after we started talking about political and spiritual matters. At that time I was writing the political philosophy chapter of the first iteration of this book and in particular the parts about the Renaissance and Rosicrucianism. I was very interested to learn that my new friend was heavily into Rosicrucianism, and also books like the 'Corpus Hermeticum', Plato's Republic and Pico Della Mirandolla's 'Oration on the Dignity of Man'. It seemed quite synchronous because this was exactly what I was writing about around the time I met my Rosicrucian pal. The same day as our meeting in the woods I was typing away at exactly the same subject area that was then so stimulating our conversation.

A little further into the meeting, things got even more uncanny. My friend inviited me back to his place in order to show me a music project he was currently working on. We trekked across the wood to an area that was quite familiar to me. It was the area I'd lived some years ago. As we walked along I remarked that I'd lived on a particular side road years ago. My friend told me that was the road where we were going. As we walked down the street I pointed to the house I used to stay. I was quite shocked to learn that was exactly the house where we were heading to. Then we walked to the door I would walk out of at the start of each day years ago.

I was entering the house I'd lived 17 years previously and going to visit the flat directly above the flat where I stayed with my Texan friends, during the period described earlier in this book when my close friend had died. It was also the period when my mission to communicate spiritual, prophetic, political and metaphysical truths really began.

Many years later the mission had greatly progressed and here I was staring out of the window of my Rosicrucian friend's flat looking out on the same back garden I would stare out of years earlier, while contemplating various philosophical and religious questions. I was standing directly above the room where years ago I would explain my nascent ideas about the Universe and God to my kind and patient Texan friends.

It is completely random how we all came to be living in that house in the late 1990s, and how my new friend came to be living there years later. Also in the meantime, the house had changed hands in a pattern happening all over London, where an old lady owning a huge house passes away, the house gets completely refurbished and then rented out by a letting agency. So this coincidence seemed to me most synchronous. I could strongly feel the hand of Providence at work. London is a big city and there are a lot of flats to let. But it gets even stranger. My Rosicrucian pal was, at the time of that meeting, involved in a music project with the well known music producer we've mentioned earlier. 17 years ago at the time we were all living at that house, one of my Texan friends was actually working for this music producer's record label. Then I learn that years later the music producer is also a regular visitor at the same house and had actually been over for supper a few nights previously. It all seemed like fate.

About eight months later the synchronicity trail continued but involving a different context and another connection of mine. During a visit to an ex-neighbour place, whom I'd not seen in a few years, I discovered something quite remarkable within the context of this quest tale. I'd moved into a flat in the Spring of 2006, that was advertised in a newspaper. One of many hundreds of such notices for flats available to rent. Anyway I spent a productive 5 years living there and after I left I'd kept in touch with my neighbour who lived in the flat directly above mainly via the Internet. At the time of this recent visit the first print run of this book was out so I gave my ex-neighbour a copy as a present. I knew he had an interest in what I did so I thought he'd find many of the chapters most interesting. In the promotional notes on the back of the book I wrote that the book is 'A real life Dan Brown' novel and also I mentioned Freemasonry and Rosicrucianism as part of a list of matters relating to the book. Dan Brown is a best selling author of action novels does a great job of putting into wider circulation various spiritual and esoteric ideas which have been around for years, even for millenia or more. Some of the esoteric ideas he includes in his novels are legends or myths, sometimes they don't have the status above that of rumour. But a lot of his subject matter is historically accurate and some of the ideas relating to the ancient mysteries he communicates, reflect the actual beliefs of various spiritual and esoteric groups which exist and have existed over the ages. I sometimes feel as if my life is like a real life Dan Brown novel because the details of my journey and my overall goals have a lot of crossover and intersection with the sort of thing you seem to find in his books. But to continue with our tale, on this particular occasion in question, things became more Dan Brown novel than most days.

So I was visiting my ex-neighbour and we chatted a while catching up on recent happenings as you do. Later on in the conversation my ex-neighbour told me with words to the effect that he'd been keeping an eye on what I did over the years with a lot a interest and in particular the most esoteric aspects of the message. Then he said that there was something that he'd meaning to tell me for a while and that now was the right time. Anyway to get to the point, what he told me was that he was very involved with perhaps one of the most esoterically focused Freemason lodges in the country. It is unnecessary and inappropriate to go into too many details here. What's most relevant for our story is that I took this as a sign from the Cosmic Intelligence. I told my ex-neighbour that this was the most amazing of synchronicities and of course being of the same sort of spiritual orientation he didn't disagree at all.

So Speculative Freemasonry was alive and well, the movement hadn't lost its esoteric roots and core purpose, at least not completely. What an interesting and inspiring conversation I had with my friend, ranging from reincarnation, the Corpus Hermeticum book, Rosicrucianism, the spiritual meaning of the idea of the rebuilding of the Temple of Soloman; and a whole load of other esoteric matters.

I felt I had been given a sign. I'd had a difficult time in the months leading up to this meeting in my personal life so it was a needed reaffirmation of my path especially during this period. Once again I felt strongly the Hand of Providence at work in the setting up of this circumstance, which could not have been brought about by human agency. But this particularly synchronicity and inspiring signal from the higher power would in turn feed into a more significant mystical realization which would happen a month or so later at around the time of the Winter Solstice 2015.

But I first need to describe the wider context and surrounding circumstances which led up to the dramatic turn of events that occurred towards the end of 2015. The year or so leading up to that time were an extremely busy period. I had quit my full time job at the church and was now working full time on evolving and getting the message ready for communicating to a wider audience. So it was a period of intense study and thinking. I was also doing a load of public talks around this talk which helped motivate me and give me focus in the development of some new ideas. In August 2015 I chanced upon a book called 'Logic and the Art of Memory - The Quest for a Universal Language' by Paolo Rossi. I found it because I was spending a lot of time working on the mathematizing of the brain theory and so was searching for books about logic and set theory. When I read Rossi's book then I discovered that it wasn't about contemporary logic but rather the historical roots of logic and linguistics. It was really about the quest for a language in which all philosophic, religious and scientific ideas could be more perfectly and universally expressed. This process had continued over the millenia and occupied the minds of some of the greatest thinker in history.

The book was a revelation for me and I saw many parallels between some of the features and properties that this 'Universal Language' must have on the one hand, and on the other my own work especially the formal mathematical language I'd created for describing all the various aspects of the Fractal Brain Theory. For a long time I saw a deep parallel between Liebniz's Monad and the recursive atom to which the entire brain theory could be reduced to and from which it could be derived. Now I learned that Leibniz's idea of the Monad really existing in the wider context of the search for this Universal language as also did his formulation of the differential calculus. I also learned that many other great historical intellectual luminaries, were also heavily involved in this quest to try to discover and understand the nature of the Universal Language. Including Rene Descartes, Giordano Bruno, Francis Bacon, Comenius and the notable Rosicrucian Johann Valentin Andreae. So I saw a deeper continuaty between what I was doing and past endeavours once I'd read Paolo Rossi's book and taken extensive notes from it.

It was a few months later, short after meeting my Freemason ex-neighbour that my ongoing studies led me to a book by Umberto Eco called 'The Search for the Perfect Language'. This covered much the same ground as Rossi's book and Eco even acknowledges that his own book was in part inspired by Rossi's. But Eco's book covers more of the cultural and esoteric dimension of the Perfect or Universal Language; whereas Rossi's work is more of an academic, historic and epistemological work. So I was further illuminated by the new things I learned about the 'Perfect Language' at this time. If by reading Rossi's work I saw the deep parallels between the mathematization of Fractal Brain Theory and the Perfect Language, then Eco's work more fully expanded on the prophetic and mystical dimension of the Perfect Language; and here too I saw that the wider implications of the brain theory corresponded exactly with what Eco was describing.

In 'The Search for the Perfect Language', Umberto Eco talked a lot about the mythic and religious aspects of this historic quest. So historically it was believed that the 'Perfect Language' was the language spoken in the Garden of Eden and the common tongue of humanity before the schism of Babel. In the past philosophers believed that the recovery of this lost language would reveal the nature of truth, to theologians it would reveal the nature of divinity and to mystics it would be the key to hidden knowledge and power. What interested me in particular were several ideas that Eco related. They included the idea that the perfect language would finally be revealed together with all the secrets of the Kabbalah at the time of the coming of the Messiah; the idea that Universe itself was constructed from this perfect language; and also in one of the final chapters Eco talked about some modern parallels to this ancient quest and in particular the goal of creating artificial intelligence. As described in an earlier chapter of this quest book, I could inspire and motivate my work by seeing things in mythic and messianic terms. In another later chapter I described how I came to see how the Fractal Brain Theory could be perfectly extrapolated to the Universe and become a way of explaining it's overall nature. Of course the goal of creating artificial intelligence permeates this book. So if the idea of the Perfect and Universal Langauge had already inspired my work on the Fractal Brain Theory after reading Rossi, then Eco's book gave me a further inspirational boost.

It is important to note that before reading Eco's book and around the time I meet up with my Freemason ex-neighbour, I had made an important breakthrough in my work on the Fractal Brain Theory. All through 2015 I was putting a lot of time into working out the details of the idea that there exists a perfect corresponce between the genome, which contains all the DNA in every cell and the brain. So that genes are as neurons, gene regulatory networks are as neuronal networks and the genome is as a brain. I'd also managed to develop much further the idea, which had been in the back of my mind for years, that there should also exist a perfect correspondence between the main function of a genome, i.e. ontogenesis or the development of a body from a fertilized egg, on the one hand and on the other the main function of brains which is the production of thought and behaviour.

The more recent breakthrough related to the idea that the process of phylogenesis or evolution was happening in the brain. It came about after an intense burst of reading books about the latest findings in evolutionary theory and the molecular mechanisms by which evolutionary changes came about. Most of it was new to me and were things which had only been discovered by science in the last decade or so. Without going into too many details, in a nutshell my theoretical breakthrough was that I'd managed to incorporate all the new evolutionary knowledge, particularly from molecular biology, into my growing understanding of genomics and the ongoing extrapolation of the genome and its functioning to the Fractal Brain Theory. What I'd discovered is that there is a perfect correspondence between the process of evolution in shaping the process of ontogenesis and the process of learning and creativity in the shaping of our thoughts and behaviour. Of course this is not a new idea, the award winning Harvard computer scientist Leslie Valiant suggests that in the future there should be a unified theory of evolution and learning. Also there are the ideas of Genetic Algorithms in relation to AI, Neural Darwinism in theoretical neuroscience and Memes in the study of epistemology. But what I'd managed to do was incorporate all the latest evolutionary ideas into a complete synthesis of genomics and ontogenesis, and which in turn, at a certain level of abstraction, was fully unified with the Fractal Brain Theory. So it was a very exciting time for me intellectually at this point.

Shortly after this burst of creativity I spent a lot of time on the mathematization of the new ideas and looking at them in a more abstract sort of way. All of this work was necessary for translating ideas about brains, minds and genomes into computer code and artificial intelligence which an important part of the work. It was in this phase that I was reading Eco's book so that it resonated with me completely. I carried on progressing these lines of thought with much concentrated attention in the days and weeks leading up to the Winter Solstice of 2015.

Then there occurred a massive flow of ideas which really enabled me to complete the mathematizing of the Fractal Brain Theory. I managed finally to see how the entire theory, which now came to encompass also the workings and evolution of genomes, together with a way of creating true artificial intelligence, could be represented in the simplest possible way. This was in the language of discrete maths and formal axiomatic systems which is really the most fundamental level of mathematics.

If all physics reduced to mathematics then in turn all mathematics reduced to discrete maths which in turn reduced to formal axiomatic systems. In a discovery with much wider mathematical and scientific implications, I managed to compactify and data compress the entire brain, mind, genome and AI theory into the simplest possible formal axiomatic system. I'd already suspected for a long time that the most basic component of the brain theory, which I intuitively knew was the most atomic way expressing things, was equivalent to Leibniz's Monad or atom of epistemology. Now that I had this total convergence between the Fractal Brain Theory and the realm of formal axiomatic systems, then I realized that in effect I was in possession of the Perfect and Universal Language which I'd been reading about in the months leading up to this great discovery.

Historically this Perfect and Universal language was thought to be the necessary foundation for the unification, renewal and reformation of all knowledge. The Rosicrucian's believed that the discovery of the Perfect Language would lead to the re-establishment of the 'concordia mundi' or religious and spiritual unity of humankind. This idea was later adopted by various strands of Freemasonry. I saw the Perfect and Universal Language together with the Monad which was its most basic atomic element, as the necessary mathematical and epistemological underpinning of the entire worldview which had been forming in my mind during the course of my life, and which included the sum total of everything I knew to be true and which existed in my head. It was this new worldview or weltanschauung which would bring about the paradigm shift which I believe is the necessary condition for the re-establishment of the 'concordia mundi' for the 21st century.

With this final insight into the mathematization of the Fractal Brain Theory, which I equated with the Perfect and Universal Language; I was able to finally bring together all the pieces of the massive jigsaw puzzle that had been assembling in my mind for almost 30 years. My ideas about the brain, mind, science, philosophy, mathematics and AI, would come to completely mesh with my ideas about the problems of the world, society, politics, world history and cosmology. The components of my weltanschauung (worldview) and resynthesized mazeway (cognitive map), become much more integrated into a single tightly interlocking composite. Once I understood what I had done in the wider historical context and interpreted the entire new weltanschauung or worldview in terms of the Perfect and Universal Language then its wider implication was confirmed for me. And all of this is what I needed to now communicate to the world.

I also saw far more clearly how my life had been set up by the hand of Providence, to enable me to find all the correct pieces of the jigsaw in the first place. The synchronicity filled meetings I had with my Rosicrucian and Freemason friends acted as signposts which reaffirmed for me my path. And I saw how my life journey had set me up to interpret and integrate the pieces of this jigsaw puzzle in the way that I did, i.e. the experiences that I had, the people that I met and the circumstances that I found myself in. Looking back on things, I can see clearly how my life had been one big preparation for what I had to do next. And what was that?

I saw that the next stage was to put the ideas into operation and communicate them to others so that they might do the same. The ideas and the entire weltanschauung had to be brought to life in the form of social movements. Through my writings and public speaking I would introduce, steadily and methodically, the people of the world to this new weltanschauung or what might also be called the new paradigm. Out of it will initially emerge the beginning of the process by which the existing paradigms start to be reassessed, to be either abandoned, augmented or replaced. The impact of the Fractal Brain Theory and associated ideas relating to Genomics and DNA, which I believe is the correct answer and interpretation of things, will spearhead the introduction of the new paradigm. To be followed by the Fractal Brain Theory's closely associated cosmology and metaphysical outlook. And from there to the realms of politics, social organization, economics and religion.

It is a gigantic task that lies before us. But what may seem like some sort of romantic quixotic mission, I understood to be a very necessary undertaking. I came to believe that the future of humanity and the survival of the planet depended on its success.

A major reason in my mind why I believed in the inevitable success of the message and the power it had to change the world, was the technology which would emerge from the Fractal Brain Theory, which was central to the entire new weltanschauung. This technology is artificial intelligence, the holy grail of modern times, and the key factor that is necessary for bringing about the much anticipated and world transforming Technological Singularity.

The technological offshoot of the message by itself would change the course of history. When this was coupled with the rest of the new worldview, i.e. its philosophical, political, economic and spiritual aspects; then it was clear to me that in the message was to be found the means for changing the current trajectory of human affairs and setting the future course.

Early on in my life I had been heavily influenced by mythology both modern and ancient, in the form of the popular myths Star Wars and Odysseus. This was also to be an important factor in my later personal evolution, especially after I discovered the work of Joseph Campbell and started to more systematically apply my new understanding of myth to my own life. So I came to see the present world and my own life completely in terms of the mythic archetypes. Also in my life I had become intensely interested in the prophecies contained in so many of great faith traditions of this world. I believed that they were referring to world we live in today and that the prophecies are now. Furthermore I saw the deep parallels that existed between the world's myths and also the prophecies of religion. They were all really reiterating the story line. So the prophecies are really about the mythic archetypes being manifest eventually on a worldwide global scale. And this corresponded to my understanding to current affairs and the state of the world at present.

I saw my message as Apocalyptic in the true sense of the word, i.e. literally meaning the 'unveiling of the hidden thing'. The fractal brain theory and its closely associated fractal cosmology, I saw as a great scientific revelation but also a mystical and spiritual one. Through the communication of the wider implications and associations of the brain theory, I believed I was really re-articulating the esoteric or hidden religion for 21st century in the language and conceptions of modern times. I believed I was really bringing about the inevitable and eternally recurring return of the Perennial Wisdom; and reconstituting the Prisca Theologia or original theology for the present age.

In the process reviving the truth that was to be found in all the world's religions and great faith traditions, the Gnosticism of Christianity, Kabbalah of Judaism, Sufism of Islam, Tantra and Advaita Vedanta of Hinduism, Vajrayana Buddhism and Taoism. I was also effectively reviving the ancient Pagan mysteries and restoring the original meaning of the expression to 'Know thyself'.

As it was written in full on the entrance of the ancient temple of Delphi in Greece...

"My advice to you, whoever you may be.
Oh! You who desire to explore the mysteries of nature.
If you do not discover within yourself what you seek,
neither will you find it without.
If you ignore the excellencies of your own house,
how can you aspire to find excellencies elsewhere?
Within you is hidden the treasure of treasures.
Oh! Man, know thyself
and you will know the Universe and the Gods."

I wanted to remind the people of the world that, *'Limited in his nature, infinite in his desire, man is a fallen god who remembers heaven'*, and that, *'We're are gods in the chrysalis'.*

Quest - Wai H. Tsang

We are all striving to get back to the original state in our own way and fully realize ourselves, whether we knew it or not. To work our way through the dark forest and return to Eden. To reach those broad, sunlit uplands, individually and collectively. To try and realize our future personal perfect state of affairs that we held in our minds, i.e. our dreams and our hopes.

The Fractal Brain Theory and the understanding it gave me of what is the process of our lives and the nature of its purposes gave me insights into this how this process might be better and more effectively achieved. In relation to the existential, self-developmental and educational dimension the theory obviously had a lot of practical application. With the brain theory I wanted to show the people a better way to realize their full potential and a better way to get 'high'.

But furthermore and beyond that I would also restore the true meaning of Alchemy, the transformation of the lead of ordinary dull consciousness, into the gold of mystical illumination. To restore the meaning of gnosis and also explain how people might achieve it in the language of neuroscience and psychology in order to justify and assess the effects and effectiveness of all the paths of previous ages. The theory of brain and behaviour was also the theory of enlightenment, mystical illumination or the true holy grail of gnosis and realization of self knowledge. Therefore I came to see the Fractal Brain Theory as the Lapis or Philosophers Stone which would enable the understanding to bring about the alchemical transformation of consciousness. And from the microcosm of self onto the wider macrocosm of society and the world.

The world was as Camelot in disarray or as the messy state of affairs that greeted Odysseus on his return home. It was Middle Earth about to be overrun by orcs and trolls, the Matrix about to be taken over by the Agent Smith character or the Evil Empire Galactic coming to establish its permanent grip. The problems with the world in the realm of human societies, politics, economics, technology, environment and ecology but also in the realms of morality, ideology, ideas and science I saw very much in prophetic, mythic and apocalyptic terms.

All my life I had searched for the holy grails of the modern age. A final understanding of how the brain and mind worked; together with the knowledge of how to create artificial intelligence. The hand of Providence had guiding me in obtaining these I believed but along the way I had also obtained another sort of holy grail. The was the holy grail of mystical illumination and the original meaning intended for the allegory. It was this knowledge of mystical illumination or gnosis which I needed to return to Camelot in order to restore things and bring resolution to the problems of the world.

Then at some point I realized that unravelling the Gordian Knot of working out the nature of brain and mind, and the creation of the Fractal Brain Theory, was really the Sword in the Stone. It was the one task that everyone was aware of, which many of the greatest minds tried to solve, but none could achieve. The great and illustrious came to pull out the Sword in the Stone but nobody could. The person who would finally do it will be given the sanction and authority to give to the world a new worldview and bring about the much anticipated and very necessary global paradigm shift. The Fractal Brain Theory as the Sword in the Stone was the key and also the means for reorganizing human understanding, to unify science with religion and also for unlocking the greatest philosophical and cosmological mysteries. It would provide the foundation for the new worldview or weltanschauung which would in turn facilitate the formation of reform and revolutionary movements, together with the reformulation of enlightenment progressive political ideals and strategies for the 21st century. Which would then transform human societies and political affairs. But perhaps most importantly the Fractal Brain Theory and new weltanschauung would be the key for bringing about the coming together of humanity and reconciling of its great divisions.

When Odysseus, finally returned to his home there was special task that only he could perform which would prove who he was and his credentials. Only he could wield his special bow and hit the target through the series of obstacles. After he performed this special task then he could go about remedying the troubles of his household. The Fractal Brain Theory was the special task that once completed would allow the beginning of the agency which would start to solve the problems of the world and remedy the troubles of humanity.

If the Fractal Brain Theory was the Sword in the Stone and the exclusive task that only Odysseus could perform, then the technology that derived from it in the form of artificial intelligence, I also saw in relation to the mythic archetypes and the prophecies. Like the mythic Prometheus who gave the technology of fire to humankind, then the creation of AI was a similar kind of gift. And like the mythic Yellow Emperor of China, who would establish Chinese civilization, but also originate the technologies of paper making, silk weaving and rice cultivation; then AI would also form the technological foundation of a new world.

Artificial intelligence is the mother of all technologies. It is the technology that is able to create technology and the invention that is able to invent. This would lead to what technologists and futurists referred to as the Technological Singularity. A positive loop of rapidly accelerating technological progress that would lead to an 'intelligence explosion', that would propel human understanding and technological achievement to a whole different level. That would make everything that came before it seem primitive. A transformational phase shift in human affairs, so dramatic it would mark a new epoch in history. So it came to my mind that I would need to set up the institution which would facilitate the creation of artificial intelligence and instigate the advent of the Technological Singularity. I called this the Start-Up at the end of time. It would be the entity charged with implementing the Fractal Brain Theory as fractal artificial intelligence and creating the technological future of humanity.

These would include medical technologies of healing and health far beyond the capabilities of existing ones. These technologies would be as the Golden Fleece of healing and protection. It would be the long sought after Panacea of the Rosicrucians, finally made manifest for the benefit of all humanity. As for the Elixir of Immortality, we can at least create the medical technologies for prolonged life extension far beyond the 90 to 100 years or so of what is meant by a long life currently.

Also out of this Technological Singularity would emerge elusive energy technologies such as fusion power, which for so long have been known to be feasible, but yet seem always beyond the grasp of the human intellect. It is known that a few cubic kilometres of sea water from the Earth's oceans contained as much energy as all the oil, gas and coal which has ever existed on the planet. Given the 1.3 trillion cubic kilometres of sea water in the Earth's oceans then there was energy here which would allow humanity to transform the planet. It would transform the entire human condition for energy was the one factor upon which everything depended, all manufacturing, all economic activity and all sustenance. With this energy we will finally achieve material security and abundance for all humanity, 'They shall hunger no more, thirst no more, the sun shall not strike them nor any scorching heat'.

The wars fought over energy and scarce natural resources would cease, for from this fundamental abundance would derive all other resources in equal abundance. In the modern myth of Dune, people living on a desert planet called Arrakis fight over the scarce and limited resource of water. But in the underground depths of the planet are stored in reservoirs oceans of water waiting to be released. The prophecies of the desert people, the Fremen, predict the coming of a messianic agency which will enable the waters of life to finally be brought to the surface to rejuvenate and rehabilitate the entire planet. The Dune story was modern mythology with the mythic archetypes also directly expressed as prophetic archetypes. I saw these archetypes as directly applying to the situation of planet Earth in present times. I saw wars being fought over energy and material resources on Earth as like the struggle for water on the mythic planet Arrakis and I saw the advent of fusion power on Earth as like the massive reservoirs of water finally being released in the Dune myth. And this would help to make a thing of the past, one of the biggest causes of war I believed, to make it possible that there be no more war. And all humanity would live in peace.

This sort of access to energy will allow humanity to restore and heal the planet, to clean up the oceans, to sequester the CO_2, to regenerate the ecosystems and to clean up the toxic contaminations of the planet. If the gnosis would be the provision of a new heaven then the Technological Singularity would be the provision of new earth.

And then onto the rest of the solar system and the exploration of the stars. With this sort of energy at our disposal then it would be inevitable that we would come to colonize the rest of the solar system and terraform some of its planets and moons. Which in turn would allow us to access the energy of the entire solar system including the Sun, and this would in turn lead inevitably to the exploration of the stars and eventually the rest of the Universe. I saw this as the future course of humanity and the natural progression of things that the creation of artificial intelligence and the instigation of the technological singularity would help greatly to bring about in a relatively short space of time.

And the political and revolutionary dimension to the message I also saw in mythic, spiritual and prophetic terms. If we already had the start-up at the end of time, then to put the worldview and message into action there would need to emerge the social movement at the end of time which will restore to the world the progressive values of 'equality, liberty and fraternity', meritocracy, justice for all and the dignity of the human being. And these values would be properly rooted and have their foundation in ideas of the sacredness of the human life, that we're all made in the image of God and contain the divine within us. The source of these progressive ideals and norms in the first place and in history. The very idea of progress itself will be reaffirmed with the return of the ideas of the great work or Magnus Opus, that is the spiritual and material transformation of ourselves and all humanity. And this transformation would include the realms of politics, social organization and economics.

And where would this great transformation begin. Where will be the epicentre from which this revelation will emanate. It is and will be London and soon after quickly spread to the rest of the world. And what better place, the most cosmopolitan city in the world. Where people of all religions, races, languages, political leanings and persuasions were all gathered. The modern Meggido or Armageddon, that is a cultural, commercial, communications and logistical transport hub where the entire world met and crisscrossed. I saw London as the one place on earth where the great schism of Babel could start to be healed and the great divisions of humanity reconciled with one another. The perfect place to begin the process of the great bringing together of the complete spectrum and diversity of peoples in this world.

'A myth is a public dream and a dream is a private myth', wrote Campbell. This book is really about my private myth and personal dream. This biography is a story about what happens when somebody has lived their life overly influenced by the adventures of Luke Skywalker and Odysseus; together with the usually unforeseeable, often surprising, sometimes tragic and from time to time appalling consequences of this approach to life. But it's worth repeating, this is the power of myth and it is also the ultimate purpose of myth. I was influenced by these public dreams and these influences in turn became my private myth and personal journey. The next step is to translate this private myth into the realization of the public dream in relation to the situation of the world today. In order to take to a satisfactory conclusion the unfolding progression of current world affairs, which is the expression of the mythic and prophetic

archetypes already manifesting and unfolding on a global scale.

My story is really the story of the Fool and first card of the Tarot deck, in his foolish attempt to work out how the brain worked, create artificial intelligence and discover the World (the last card in the Tarot). Throwing his life to the Wheel of Fortune, sometimes living as a Hermit studying by the light of the Moon, but desiring to be as the Lovers. From time to time feeling like a Hanged Man, trying to find the Strength and Temperance to reach his destination. Working with the Hierophants assimilating some of their virtues and taking the guidance of the High Priestesses who came my way. I was striving towards the process of trying to gain Wisdom in order to make proper Judgement on things and decide what is Justice or not. I would later seek to construct a Chariot as the vehicle for communicating the things I learned. The whip of Abraxas would be my drive, the truth would be my shield and my sword. I would become as the Magician who needed to confront the Devil, within and without, to magically forestall the Death and destruction which was facing the World, by challenging the Tower of power which was leading the people to perdition. So that finally humanity may once again live in the light of the Sun, and realize its cosmic destiny in the Stars.

So what then is the Deus Ex Machina? The expression literally means God from the machine and originated in ancient Greece. It was the expression used to describe a plot device that would appear at the end of a Greek play, either a tragedy or comedy, which would resolve the plot and bring it to some happy conclusion or at least a satisfying ending. This plot device could be the late addition of a new character, an object or some extra ability gained by an existing character. And often it will be the case that the Deus Ex Machina will deal with an unsolvable problem or some bottle neck in the flow of the story, that can't be resolved with any existing element already in the story. So the Deus Ex Machina is like a sudden and abrupt intervention in the storyline that can't be predicted from the preceding events.

The play and the plot which concerns us here is the tragedy or comedy, depending on how you see it, of human affairs. The storyline is the progression of world history and the unsolvable impasse that's preventing the story from moving forwards are the problems of the world; in social, economic, political, environmental, ecological and ideational realms. So the Deus Ex Machina needs to be inserted in at this point and introduced into the unfolding story, so that the drama may reach a satisfying conclusion and happy ending. So in this context what then is the Deus Ex Machina?

The Deus Ex Machina isn't a person, for no one person can solve the problems of the world, *'Our days are but as grass and we flourish like the flower in the field'*. People come and go, but ideas remain, ideas spread and it is ideas which really change the world. Indeed, *'the pen is mightier than the sword'*, and *'You can resist an invading army but you can't resist an idea whose time has come'*. But here we're not talking about a single idea of even several dozen powerful ideas but really an entire worldview and new paradigm which, paraphrasing the great polymath Francis Bacon, will take all knowledge to be its province. The Deus Ex Machina is the sum total of all the myriad ideas and solutions which are encompassed in the new worldview and also which have their foundations in it. The Deus Ex Machina IS the new global paradigm.

'Where there is no vision the people perish', and '[the] *people are destroyed for a lack of knowledge'*. A lot of thinkers had been anticipating this new paradigm, new narrative, new weltanschauung, resynthesized mazeway (i.e. total cognitive map), 'philosophy of plurality', shift in consciousness or 'intellectual revolution'; but no one was able to quite articulate it. I learned about what it was that people were anticipating and were trying to articulate for themselves, and I used this knowledge to address their concerns and to shape my message so that the new worldview could be understood and its significant aspects more easily grasped. People were looking for answers just as I was, as I am everywoman and everyman and everybody is as I. So I directed my concentrated efforts and used the best of my abilities to construct this contribution to the joint work, which came out of my journey and is outlined in this book.

But what use and what good is the idea or worldview on its own. It only really comes into effect when it is lived, breathed and accepted into the hearts and minds of the people. When it is implemented in the form of the social technology of Politics, Legislation, Norms, Ethics and Morality; and the mechanistic technology of Artificial Intelligence and the Technological Singularity. And when it becomes the shared vision and common hope of all the people. When it can manifest itself fully and be fully expressed in the formation of social movements and the founding of the start-up at the end of the time.

This is the next stage of this odyssey and mythological adventure tale; the communicating to the people of this new worldview and the introducing to the world of the Deus Ex Machina.